INCIDENTS OF MY LIFE

Edmund Ruffin's Autobiographical Essays

VIRGINIA HISTORICAL SOCIETY
DOCUMENTS
Volume 17

Edmund Ruffin, December 1860. (*Cook Collection, Valentine Museum, Richmond, Va.*)

INCIDENTS OF MY LIFE

Edmund Ruffin's Autobiographical Essays

EDITED BY
David F. Allmendinger, Jr.

PUBLISHED FOR
THE VIRGINIA HISTORICAL SOCIETY
BY THE UNIVERSITY PRESS OF VIRGINIA
Charlottesville and London

Charlottesville and London
THE UNIVERSITY PRESS OF VIRGINIA
Copyright © 1990 by the Rector and Visitors
of the University of Virginia

First published 1990

Library of Congress Cataloging-in-Publication Data
Ruffin, Edmund, 1794–1865.
  Incidents of my life: Edmund Ruffin's autobiographical essays /
edited by David F. Allmendinger, Jr.
    p.   cm. — (Virginia Historical Society documents ; v. 17)
  Includes bibliographical references.
  ISBN 0-8139-1279-2
  1. Ruffin, Edmund, 1794–1865. 2. Statesmen—Virginia—Biography.
3. Slavery—Southern States—History—19th century. 4. Agricultural
ecology—Virginia—History—19th century. 5. Agricultural ecology—
Southern States—History—19th century. 6. Secession. 7. Southern
States—Politics and government—1775–1865. I. Allmendinger, David
F. II. Title. III. Series.
F230.R93A3   1990
975.5′03′092—dc20
[B]   89-77721
                                                                CIP

Printed in the United States of America

For
Corinna R. Gilliam
and
James S. Gilliam

Contents

Acknowledgments	xi
Introduction: A Farmer's Life in Antebellum Virginia	1
Incidents of My Life, Volume 2 (1851)	15
Incidents of My Life, Volume 3 (1853)	119
In Remembrance of Jane Dupuy (1855)	137
In Remembrance of Ella Ruffin (1855)	159

APPENDICES

1. Edwin [sic] Ruffin, of Virginia, Agriculturist (1851)	167
2. Statement of the Closing Scenes of the Life of Thomas Cocke (1840)	179
3. First Views Which Led to Marling in Prince George County (1839)	189
4. Queries to Ascertain the Action and Effects of Shell Marl (1840)	210
5. Statements of Marling and Crops (1852)	217
Abbreviations	220
Notes	221
Index	263

Illustrations and Maps

Edmund Ruffin, 1860 — *Frontispiece*
Map of Coggin's Point Farm, 1823 — *Following page 164*
Shellbanks, Prince George County
Marlbourne, Hanover County
Fields and main ditch at Marlbourne
Map of Marlbourne and its drainage
    system, 1845–55
Drainage ditch at Marlbourne
Lifetime membership certificate in the
    Virginia State Agricultural Society, 1854
Beechwood, Prince George County
Edmund Ruffin and family, 1851
Edmund Ruffin, from *De Bow's Review*
Ruins of Tarbay, Prince George County
Court House Field, Coggin's Point Farm

Acknowledgments

Many people have aided this project. Mary Denmead Ruffin, to whom I was introduced by my former student Drew Fennell Godden, helped me launch my first research on her ancestor. George Gilliam, Marion Ruffin Jones, Jane R. Grubb, and Tilghman Broaddus provided valuable assistance in preparing materials on Coggin's Point and Marlbourne farms. Ellen Strong, of the Earl Gregg Swem Library at the College of William and Mary, led me to valuable evidence concerning Ruffin's early farming and slaveholdings. John Ingram, curator in special collections of the library at the Colonial Williamsburg Foundation, gave generous assistance in gathering evidence on Ruffin's youth. Lyndon Hart of the Virginia State Library and Archives located evidence that made it possible to identify Ruffin's mother; Frank V. Emmerson, clerk of the Circuit Court of Surry County, and Jane Emmerson also helped in this work. The staffs of the Henry E. Huntington Library, the Southern Historical Collection at the University of North Carolina at Chapel Hill, and the Earl Gregg Swem Library of the College of William and Mary all offered their assistance and gave me permission to quote from materials in their collections. At the Virginia Historical Society I have many creditors, including Frances Pollard and Nelson D. Lankford. I owe special thanks to Sara B. Bearss, whose suggestions have improved this volume greatly; every editor should have such an editor. Kristine LaLonde, Michele Murray, and Anne Tyler Netick, interns and volunteers at the Society, checked the notes with close attention. I would like to thank, too, Jan E. Lewis, Jack Temple Kirby, and William K. Scarborough for their extremely helpful criticism and suggestions. And finally, Corinna R. Gilliam and James S. Gilliam have made research pleasant and possible by sharing their hospitality and their materials on family history. James Gilliam has guided me to all of Edmund Ruffin's homes, from Amelia County through Prince George to Hanover. There has never been a more generous colleague than he.

INCIDENTS OF MY LIFE

Edmund Ruffin's Autobiographical Essays

Introduction

A Farmer's Life in Antebellum Virginia

And should the incidents of my life, & results of my labors for agricultural improvement, be deemed worthy of being written for the public eye, he who may undertake the task may find some of the materials in this writing.

Edmund Ruffin, 1851

Edmund Ruffin had not yet become a legendary figure in 1851 when he began to write the history of his achievements. By that year, of course, he long had held a national reputation in "agricultural improvement." As a young man he discovered the killing acidity of soils in Tidewater Virginia and became the leading advocate of spreading fossil shells, or marl, to neutralize those soils. He was the author of *An Essay on Calcareous Manures* (1832)[1] and between 1833 and 1842 edited the distinguished *Farmers' Register*. Greater fame lay ahead, however, in events associated with the Civil War. Ruffin would throw himself into the movement for secession, would take part in the firing on Fort Sumter, and two months after the war ended would commit suicide.[2] When he began to compose his story in 1851, by contrast, the most striking incidents of his life all related to his career as a farmer and agricultural reformer. He cast his story as an account of achievements in the face of adversity.

How Ruffin Composed the "Incidents"

Originally Ruffin's "Incidents of my Life" filled three manuscript volumes, of which only volumes 2 and 3 have survived. These two holograph volumes came to the Virginia Historical Society in 1967 as part of a larger collection of Edmund Ruffin's papers donated by Mrs. Lawrence Tucker and Mrs. Braden Van Deventer. Ruffin completed the first two volumes of the "Incidents" in the latter half of 1851, filling 220 pages. Most of this composition he did at Marlbourne Farm in Hanover County, Virginia, apparently working at his small writing desk in the family library. He first became inspired to begin these memoirs when he was asked to provide a biographical sketch of himself for the October 1851 issue of *De Bow's Review*. Ruffin furnished his friend William Boulware, who prepared the sketch, published documents concerning his work and some notes about his private life.[3] "The hasty & concise notes then written for this purpose induced me to extend them into this much more full account, & was the sole origin & cause of the writing these sheets," Ruffin recalled.[4] By 21 January 1852 Ruffin's eldest son had read the initial two volumes of the "Incidents."[5]

The first of these two volumes, covering events between 1794 and 1823 in ninety-five pages, apparently disappeared after the Civil War.[6] In December 1853 Ruffin completed the much shorter third volume (containing thirty-seven manuscript pages), dealing with the intervening two years and adding some details from the 1840s. Finally in 1855 he filled the pages in the back of this third volume with two narratives about the deaths that summer of his daughters Jane and Ella. These narratives differ from the "Incidents" in form, but they amplify the earlier biographical volumes because they contain evidence on Ruffin's family life and his evolving dread of a particular kind of death.

The texts of the surviving volumes 2 and 3 reveal Ruffin's method in composing his life history. He did research for the "Incidents" exactly as he did for all of his writings, by consulting his manuscript farm journals and published works. He followed his life and career chronologically, having no design other than a progression through time. In sections dealing with the rejuvenation of Coggin's Point and Marlbourne farms, he adopted temporarily a topical outline. He edited the manuscript at least once, but with less care than he would have taken with a text intended for publication. He altered expression frequently, following his custom of adding synonyms, adjectives, and adverbs, as if hoping to refine his meaning, though usually gaining mere redundancy. Ruffin was fond of parenthetical remarks (as he himself confessed); these he inserted wherever possible. Straining for precision, he often wandered from his track. These wanderings created an artless story that revealed more than he knew.

Reclaiming the Missing Volume

Ruffin wrote the first two volumes of his "Incidents" when he was fifty-seven years old and still the proprietor of Marlbourne, his rejuvenated farm thirteen miles northeast of Richmond. He already had spent nearly forty years in agricultural reform. Between 1813 and 1835 he revived two farms in Prince George County, south of Richmond, demonstrating there the power of marl in restoring soil fertility. These projects alone made Ruffin the most acclaimed experimental farmer in Virginia. By the time he filled volume 1 and began the first page of volume 2 he had reached the year 1823 in his narrative and was in the middle of a discussion of low prices for corn, fluctuating markets, and the problems of profits and surplus production. Except for incidental recollections about the first reforms at Coggin's Point, in volume 2 he did not discuss his early life. With the disappearance of volume 1, his first twenty-nine years became a blank.

In the surviving volumes of the "Incidents," however, Ruffin left three clues that help fill that blank. These clues provide some evidence about the nature of the missing volume and point to other, surviving evidence about his youth and career before 1823. Three times in volume 2 he referred to material in the first volume, indicating that it had contained accounts of early farming practices and experiments. One of these references dealt with grazing, another with reclaiming a marsh at Coggin's Point.[7] The first volume must have had the same character as the second: this autobiography was a history of Ruffin's farm and his career as a farmer, a form of essay that became popular in agricultural periodicals of antebellum America. The nature of the work is suggested also by the fact that Edmund Ruffin, Jr., referred to his father's manuscript by the title "Incidents in the Life of a Farmer," which may have been the title Ruffin assigned to volume 1.[8]

Ruffin had abundant published evidence, apart from his manuscript letters and farm journals, to help him reconstruct the early history of Coggin's Point Farm. In 1839 he had published two autobiographical essays about this farm, of which the most revealing is "First Views Which Led to Marling in Prince George County."[9] This essay was nearly half as long as the missing first volume of the "Incidents," which probably covered similar events in a similar form.

Another clue about the contents of the missing volume 1 lies in Ruffin's suggestion in volume 3 that he had prepared hasty notes about his personal life for *De Bow's Review*.[10] Ruffin approved William Boulware's sketch before publication, indicating that he considered its chronology accurate. If he did include an account of his youth in the "Incidents," he probably derived it from these notes for Boulware. The chronology in that sketch derived immediately from Ruffin, and it, too, probably found its way into the missing volume 1.

A core of other evidence comparable to the missing volume exists in other documents published between 1839 and 1851. This material, as well as "First Views Which Led to Marling" and the sketch from *De Bow's*, printed in the five appendices, contains much of the missing biographical information and makes it possible for us to piece together a narrative of Ruffin's youth and earliest farming career in a form that his own missing account must have resembled.

The Pattern in Ruffin's "Incidents"

This man's youth passed in isolation, a condition that influenced his way of farming and the way he thought. Ruffin was born on 5 January 1794 at Evergreen Farm, a property in Prince George County of a thousand acres situated four miles upstream from Coggin's Point on the south bank of the James River.[11] He was the first child of George Ruffin (1765–1810), whose grandfather had left him Evergreen by inheritance in 1795.[12] Edmund Ruffin was his mother's only child. Apparently he had no memory of Jane Lucas Ruffin, who came from Surry County; she died sometime between May 1794 and August 1799, and her identity became obscure thereafter.[13] Her death removed Ruffin from his mother's few surviving kin and began the isolation that characterized his first sixteen years.

It is true that he was never completely alone in the world. George Ruffin remarried in 1799, to Rebecca Cocke (1771–1837) of Surry County.[14] Between 1800 and 1810 Ruffin's father and stepmother (whom he mentioned twice in the "Incidents") produced three surviving daughters and a son, Ruffin's half sisters and half brother.[15] Yet Ruffin was separated in age from these younger children; he went away to college before the youngest was born. In 1807 Ruffin's grandfather, a widower, died at Coggin's Point, and in 1810 his father died, completing his separation by death from the older generations of his family.[16] He then had no living grandparents and no aunts or uncles on his father's side of the family. Ruffin became an orphan at sixteen, supervised by two unrelated adults, his stepmother and his guardian, Thomas Cocke.

Solitude became a pattern in Ruffin's life even before his father died. At the College of William and Mary he made no circle of lifelong friends among his schoolmates.[17] Circumstances did not favor such collegiality, for Ruffin boarded and roomed outside the college and probably enrolled for only portions of 1809 and 1810.[18] When his father died in 1810, Ruffin left William and Mary and spent about two years at Evergreen, apparently at loose ends. Shortly after he finished militia duty in February 1813, a month after his nineteenth birthday, Ruffin obtained his inheritance, the 1,582 acres at Coggin's Point Farm.[19]

Ruffin had few connections with the people or the place he had inherited. He arrived at Coggin's Point as a single white man, a stranger to its group of about fifty slaves.[20] He had grown up at Evergreen. His grandfather, the former resident at Coggin's Point, had been gone six years, and Ruffin's father had not lived at Coggin's in nearly twenty years. In one of the two small frame houses that stood together in House Field he found his grandfather's papers, which he preserved for half a century as his only link to an earlier generation.[21] At the end of 1813 he married Susan Travis of Williamsburg, whom he must have met while attending college. Susan Travis herself was an orphan by 1813, her father having died also in 1810.[22] This fact, together with the couple's settling on the farm forty miles upriver from Williamsburg, meant that Ruffin was isolated, too, from any older kin in his wife's family.

One consequence of isolation lay in Ruffin's approach to farming, about which he knew almost nothing. There had been no time for him to learn about farming from his father or grandfather, and no uncles or male in-laws survived to instruct him. Ruffin had to teach himself. He could observe what neighbors did, but his chief instruction came from books. He depended on new theories in works about scientific agriculture by authors including John Taylor of Caroline and Sir Humphry Davy. Ruffin, too, became an experimenter. Because almost everything he did was new to him, it became important for him to keep written records, in part to refresh his memory about the routines of farming each year and in part to test his progress. Books, theories, and the keeping of records became instruments of success. They took the place of a father's instruction, a grandfather's memory. Their influence became apparent when he wrote about his management of wheat and corn and his experiments with marl, enclosing animals, crop rotation, and draining.

A second consequence of isolation appeared in the way he thought about the significance of the incidents of his life in farming and reform. Ruffin considered himself a self-made man who rose above his inherited status through hard work, ingenuity, familiarity with current scientific ideas, and ambition. The entire text of the "Incidents of my Life" became an elaboration on this central theme. Actions were judged starkly in terms of success in advancing himself and reform. Through his own hard work he had rejuvenated Coggin's Point Farm. Through his own ingenuity and research he had discovered the secret of marl. Through his own ambition he had doubled the value of his patrimony by 1827. Thenceforth, through shrewd investments in internal improvements and government bonds, his fortune would accumulate. Achievements also accumulated: writing the acclaimed *Essay on Calcareous Manures*, editing the *Farmers' Register*, conducting the first agricultural survey of the state of South Carolina, and then finally rejuvenating the fields at Marlbourne Farm. Ruffin's "Incidents of my Life" was intended to contain no hidden meaning that his readers might discern with surprise. His theme from the first pages of volume 2 through the end of volume 3, with all of its press clippings, centered upon his ambition and success.

By 1851 Ruffin had begun to consider retiring from farming. A widower for five years, he was now concerned about the next generation. All nine of his children who survived infancy still lived near him. Edmund, Jr. (1814–1875), had assumed control of Coggin's Point in 1839 (renaming it Beechwood). Agnes Ruffin Beckwith (1817–1865) had married a Petersburg doctor and lived with her husband on a small farm in Prince George County.[23] Julian Calx (1821–1864) owned a small farm called Ruthven in Prince George and was about to marry. Five unmarried daughters and one unmarried son remained as dependents: Rebecca (1823–1855), Elizabeth (1824–1860), Mildred (1827–1862), Jane (1829–1855), and finally the nineteen-year-old twins, Ella (1832–1855) and Charles (1832–1870).[24] For these nine children Ruffin intended to leave a record of his achievements.[25] Throughout volume 2 he adopted a defensive tone in confronting the collapse of the *Farmers' Register*, his controversial assault upon the banks, and his apparent failure to convince all farmers of the virtues of marl.[26] In volume 3, completed in December 1853, he shifted tone abruptly to a celebration of himself, supported by evidence in newspaper clippings. In both volumes he pursued his main purpose of writing a story about his successful career.

Ruffin appears never to have considered any interpretation of his life that might have placed him in the intellectual traditions that have come to be associated with the planter class in the antebellum South.[27] The "Incidents" was not the memoir of an aristocratic southerner secure in his social moorings, confident of his honor and power, steeped in the traditions of a precapitalist, patriarchal world. It offered neither an introspective history of Ruffin's beliefs nor recollections of significant, external political events. It did not idealize old times on the plantation. (Ruffin always referred to his properties as "farms," never as "plantations.") The "Incidents" did not even constitute a history of the Ruffin family. Ruffin probably did want to emulate his grandfather, who, through the manuscripts left in the house at Coggin's Point, had linked three generations. The surviving second volume, however, gives no hint that Ruffin produced an account of the family line or its estates, or that he included a genealogy in the manuscript. At this time he was not thinking of inheritance in genealogical terms.[28] Because he neither celebrated his Virginia family nor attempted original research concerning his ancestors, his children cannot have discovered much new evidence about their history in his narrative. The "Incidents" offered instead a moral record for his heirs, focusing on himself as the good example.

Farming and Agricultural Reform

Having fixed upon this interpretation of his life, Ruffin inevitably addressed his career as a farmer and agricultural reformer—the central subject of the manuscript—in terms of the difficulties he surmounted.[29] He treated farming as a series of experiments whose significance lay in whether they succeeded or failed in advancing reform. Ruffin had no interest in routine farming. He was fascinated by problems in applied science, such as the chemical reaction between shells and clay, the geological formations that created springs and swamps, and the movement of water through drains. He was intrigued, too, by the prospect of increasing production and profits.

It was in these terms of success and failure that he wrote about the marling and draining projects on his farms, projects that became feats of applied science. In these terms he discussed introducing clover, changing the shape of fields in order to plant crops in wide beds, trying new methods of seeding and harvesting. In these terms, too, he discussed his efforts to create a bureaucratic permanence for the state agricultural society. These accomplishments he viewed as single-handed triumphs over difficulties, an interpretation that grew from a sense that his personal history was a product of his own making.

In the course of his career Edmund Ruffin farmed three different properties, all of them in Tidewater Virginia. The first of these was Coggin's Point, the farm he was discussing when he began to write in volume 2 of the "Incidents." Ruffin owned this farm exclusively for twenty-six years, from 1813 until 1839, when he sold a half share to his son Edmund, Jr.[30] Gradually, by 1832, he expanded its improved acreage from 472 to 652 acres.[31] In spite of his interest in the farm, he lived at Coggin's Point only sixteen years. In 1831 he moved his family three miles south of the river to a newly purchased farm. This was Shellbanks, a property originally containing about 400 acres, which Ruffin enlarged to some 600 acres and proceeded to revive with marl.[32] At Shellbanks he founded the *Farmers' Register* and actually installed a press in one of its small buildings. He moved to Petersburg in 1835, taking the *Register* with him.[33] Finally, in 1843, after almost nine years away from the land, he bought Marlbourne, a farm of 977 acres, which he enlarged in 1849 to 1,600 acres. By the time he began his "Incidents," he had spent nearly eight years rejuvenating Marlbourne.[34]

Ruffin's farming at each of these places followed a pattern. Except for a brief experiment with cotton at Coggin's Point, Ruffin was primarily a grain farmer, growing wheat and corn for the market. The scale of his operations proceeded at a level he felt capable of managing by himself. Although he did own two large farms, he was never among the great Virginia landholders or slaveowners. He always felt the need to focus his attention on one farm. Instead of buying distant farms and becoming an absentee owner, Ruffin invested his profits first in personal loans and then in stocks and bonds. He did not greatly expand his own slaveholdings. The number of slaves held by Ruffin and his children did indeed rise, largely through acquisitions by Edmund Ruffin, Jr. The family held 145 slaves in 1840, 176 in 1850, and 216 in 1860. Ruffin's own holdings remained fairly constant, however: fifty-two in 1820, sixty-six in 1830, fifty-one in 1840 (including thirty-nine at Beechwood listed for his son), forty-one in 1850, and fifty in 1860.[35] He complained throughout the "Incidents" that he suffered a shortage of labor, caused by the demands of his large reclamation projects.

At each of his three farms Ruffin experimented with such new crops as clover and peas. He introduced new devices and methods, including an ingenious haycock and a six-field crop rotation, and bought more new farm machines than he realized.[36] Still, the thrust of Ruffin's farm reform was directed primarily at reclaiming soil fertility. This reclamation involved Ruffin in applying calcareous manures and in draining his fields, efforts that required vast amounts of animal and human labor. At Marlbourne between 1844 and 1850 Ruffin's slaves dug and spread 367,466 bushels of marl, which had to be transported from pit to field—a distance of half a mile to two miles—by mule cart hauling eight or more bushels per load. Each wagon traveled about twenty-five miles each day.[37] The Marlbourne slave force also altered the entire drainage system at that farm between 1844 and 1853. By 1850 Ruffin's slaves had constructed three miles of new covered drains, and by November 1853 they had excavated the main open ditch through the center of the farm to a depth of five to six feet throughout its length of about two miles.[38] In addition, they worked on small tributary ditches thousands of yards long. The results, displayed in the table of crop production that Ruffin included in the "Incidents," demonstrated the success of his reclamation. According to Ruffin's figures, corn production at Marlbourne doubled between 1845 and 1851, and total wheat production tripled. Though increases in yields per acre were not so dramatic as increases in the total crop, these too moved upward.

Unintentionally, Ruffin provided evidence in the "Incidents" about a social setting that determined his success and about two institutions that made it possible for agricultural reform to begin in the Tidewater. The pages of Ruffin's autobiographical writings reveal that the crucial institution of reform was the family. In Ruffin's career, the family provided the library and books in which he found essential ideas. The family supplied the apparatus and laboratory for chemical testing of soils. Through his family, Ruffin made the few critical friendships that constituted his intellectual circle and stimulated his ideas through debate.[39] The family supported and financed Ruffin's writing and publishing. The *Farmers' Register* actually began at Ruffin's home on Shellbanks Farm, and in Petersburg it became the most significant economic activity of the family.[40] Reform circled outward, not from the colleges or the state government, but from the family.

Reform depended also upon slavery, though Ruffin scarcely mentioned his slaves in the "Incidents." He wrote as if he himself had performed the labor of reconstructing his farms (he spread the marl, he dug the ditches, he seeded the clover), while in fact the entire rejuvenation rested on the labor of slaves. The only individual slave who entered the story was Jem Sykes, Ruffin's black foreman at Marlbourne.[41] Other, nameless people appeared as laborers cleaning mud from the main ditch at Marlbourne or herding livestock; these men and women, too, constructed drainage pipes and sowed clover according to Ruffin's demanding, precise specifications.[42] Issues concerning slavery did not arise in the "Incidents," except for one brief self-critical remark about Ruffin's shortcomings as a master in commanding laborers.[43] Ruffin intended in this document neither to defend slavery nor to convey instruction about controlling slaves; and because his account was not primarily introspective, it offered no evidence concerning his feelings about the mastery of slaves as a worthy ambition.[44] Slaves became merely assumed presences, essential laborers who made reform possible.

Despite his lists of achievements in reform, Ruffin betrayed all through volume 2 of the "Incidents" a frankness in assessing his career and vented anger at people he thought had neglected his work. A literal reader might interpret this frankness and anger as a confession of failure and as evidence for the hopelessness of reform in the slave South. Yet there is at least one other possible interpretation, involving Ruffin's personal history. Utterly committed to seeing himself as the determiner of his own rise in life, Ruffin really had no other way of judging his career than by harsh standards of success or failure. He sustained this attitude to the end of the "Incidents." When he began writing in the third volume in 1853, his emphasis fell heavily on the successful ventures of his life. Ruffin's frankness in assessing some early failures gave way to joy over the revival of his reputation, evidence for which he found in the newspaper clippings he assiduously pasted onto the pages of volume 3. In the end he insisted on this theme of success.[45]

Incidents Omitted

It was after Ruffin had finished his "Incidents" that he began to record in 1856 the astonishing incidents of his later life in a diary, one of the most dramatic documents of the Civil War period. The pages of Ruffin's diary are filled with accounts of events both public and private. In the diary, which was inspired in part by writing the "Incidents," Ruffin told of his participation at age sixty-seven in the first battle at Manassas, the Union occupation of Beechwood (formerly Coggin's Point) and Marlbourne, the escapes of the Ruffin slaves, and the decision of the Ruffins themselves to flee the path of war. He traced their efforts to elude the armies through exile at Redmoor Farm in Amelia County, thirty miles southwest of Richmond. He wrote about Julian's death in battle, his fears concerning the safety of his grandsons, the fall of Richmond, the passing of Confederate stragglers through Redmoor, the crowding in the house, and his eldest son's first efforts to begin farming again. He wrote until that final minute in June 1865 when he shot himself in the mouth.[46]

In contrast to his diary, Ruffin's "Incidents" revealed very little about events of personal, private, family life. The memoir disclosed little about his married life with Susan Travis Ruffin and their children. He omitted certain difficulties with his half sisters, his dependence upon Edmund, Jr., his special fondness for son Julian and daughter Jane, and his growing hostility toward youngest son Charles. In his "Incidents" he presented the public Ruffin, the Ruffin he wanted outsiders to see. Family matters he declined to explore, leaving them to be documented in the pages of his correspondence. In the "Incidents" he did deal quite openly with his feelings about his career, revealing that as early as 1829, at the age of thirty-five, he fell into a depression (the first in a series) that led him to regard farming with apathy.[47] Still, he was guarded. A stranger who knew this man only through the "Incidents" might well have assumed that Ruffin responded—down to the moment he took his life—merely to a series of triumphs and disappointments as a reformer in the Old South. Such an assumption would be misleading. Other evidence, dealing with events more personal than the draining of Marlbourne Farm, was available to Ruffin. He omitted that evidence.

He mentioned not at all the most traumatic event of his life before 1855, the suicide in 1840 of his guardian and best friend, Thomas Cocke. Ruffin's stunning autobiographical account of that suicide, "Statement of the closing scenes of the life of Thomas Cocke," lay in his papers when he covered that period of his life.[48] This was one of the two best narratives Ruffin ever composed, the other being his account of the hanging of John Brown.[49] He did not even mention Cocke's death in the "Incidents."

For that reason the significance of Thomas Cocke in the life of Edmund Ruffin has remained obscure, though Ruffin published numerous references to Cocke as his former guardian, friend, neighbor, and collaborator in experiments with marl. Between 1810 and 1840 Cocke was the most important older male in Ruffin's life. He became not only guardian but father figure as well. He was Ruffin's first convert to the notion that soil could be rejuvenated and actually created.[50] As Ruffin's account of their last conversations together made clear, it was Cocke who introduced Ruffin to the idea that the hour of one's death might be determined by one's will. When Ruffin himself committed suicide in 1865, he followed Cocke's procedures almost to the last detail.[51] This evolution of a notion about death remained private. Ruffin excluded it from his "Incidents," and he concealed it successfully from the world in 1865.[52]

When Ruffin's daughters Jane and Ella died in the summer of 1855,

Ruffin returned to the volumes containing his "Incidents" and added two memoirs of these young women, completing his writing in the third volume. (When his daughter Rebecca died in December, Ruffin simply wrote no more about death that year.) His memorial sketches revealed predictable attitudes of a prosperous nineteenth-century father toward his daughters, whose virtues of cheerful submission and selflessness he extolled unto his final paragraphs. The customary roles of men and women in the Ruffin family emerged clearly in his pages about caring for the sick. His narrative of Jane's deathbed scene captured individuals enacting familiar roles, with pious Julian leading prayers, Mildred playing hymns, and Jane herself urging her father and Charles—the only two members to resist evangelical religion—to meet her in Heaven. Here was a glimpse of Ruffin within the family.

He outlived all but three of his children. Having become the first Ruffin in three generations to witness the survival of more than one child into adulthood, he then suffered the loss of six grown children between 1855 and 1864. Jane and Ella were the first to die, beginning a wave of shocking losses to which Ruffin never adjusted. He took no comfort in thoughts of an afterlife; unlike his half sister Jane Ruffin Dupuy or his sons Edmund, Jr., and Julian, he could not believe in Heaven.[53] In this he was close to the thinking of Thomas Cocke, who saw death in terms of an endless cycle of returning to the earth. Ruffin's accounts of these deaths in 1855 reveal a development in his concept of death, a concept that would govern his own behavior ten years later.

Because he did not analyze either the symptoms or the course of disease for any of his daughters, the few clinical clues Ruffin left make it difficult to determine what took their lives. Jane and Rebecca must have contracted infections through childbirth, and Ella appears to have had congenital heart disease; all three may have been attacked by typhoid fever.[54] What horrified Ruffin was his daughters' awareness that death was approaching while they became helpless dependents. In his narrative of Ella's death he began to consider the ideal death as instantaneous and unexpected, without suffering or dependence. In this conception he had fallen under the influence of Thomas Cocke.

In this way, too, he interpreted events according to the scheme he had devised for explaining his career from early manhood, and he provided clues about the way he would die. Edmund Ruffin's suicide had its origins not in the spring of 1865 with the collapse of the Confederacy but in much earlier incidents. The text of his "Incidents of my Life" contains the earliest evidence that Ruffin had begun a way of reasoning that would lead logically to suicide. His dominant concern after finishing the "Incidents" involved his ability to care for himself, a standard he long since had defined as the key to success. Only a life in which he worked hard and maintained self-reliance would be worthwhile. This interpretation of past events gave a common theme both to Ruffin's life and to his death, just as it gave him a way of thinking about success and failure that was common among others in his culture both to the north and to the south of Virginia. It made Ruffin a representative man of antebellum America.

Editing the "Incidents"

This transcription of Ruffin's manuscript adheres to the policy of the Virginia Historical Society, with the view of producing a published document close in form to the original. It is a literal transcription of the "Incidents," incorporating no corrections or modernizations of spelling, grammar, or punctuation. Ruffin was a good speller, though he made an occasional mistake; his errors have been reproduced without comment. Often he lifted his pen between syllables of a single word, such as *newspaper*, and he displayed some inconsistency with such words. Except where Ruffin clearly intended to write two words, this edition combines syllables to conform to modern usage. Ruffin was not consistent in his handwritten abbreviations, particularly in referring to the names of states. This transcription preserves his inconsistencies as closely as possible in print. It is often impossible to differentiate between the letters *n* and *r* in Ruffin's hand; I have followed his printed works in determining some of these letters, as in *clean*, when it refers to ditches. Wherever possible I have cited Ruffin's diary in its published form, in the magnificent edition by William K. Scarborough. Citations to the manuscript diary refer to Ruffin's page numbers.

The entire manuscript of volumes 2 and 3 appears here, along with Ruffin's sketches of daughters Jane and Ella, including material by Elizabeth Ruffin Sayre that Ruffin copied in his own hand. Some minor instructions in Ruffin's writing, giving dates of clippings or directions to guide the eye of the reader, have been omitted. Printed materials, including newspaper clippings and published texts of Ruffin's articles, have not been reproduced, though these have been identified and dated in the notes wherever possible. Marginal insertions have been incorporated silently into the text wherever Ruffin clearly intended to include them as integral parts of the narrative. A few exceptions to this procedure, involving parenthetical material, are identified in the notes. Ruffin's own footnotes have been incorporated in the endnotes and are identified as his. Square brackets indicate indecipherable words or questionable readings, though these are few in number. In several places Ruffin left spaces for dates and figures but never filled in the information; such spaces are indicated by "[*blank*]." Superscriptions have been brought down to the line.

INCIDENTS OF MY LIFE

Volume 2 (1851)

Private.

Incidents of my Life
2

INCIDENTS OF MY LIFE

The price of corn for the crops of 1823, 4, & 5, had been very low. I could not during all that time, have obtained for either crop, as much as 40 cents the bushel, & the cost of freight to market. According to my rule for such circumstances, I did not sell my surplus corn, but put it up, without shucking, to be kept to the next year. The extent of corn tillage would then be reduced for the next year, by omitting some of the poorest land, which thus would have more than its regular share of rest & of improvement in consequence. But though not wishing to make more corn than for the use of the farm, when the market price was so low, more or less surplus was every year made, & kept on hand. Thus it happened that I had remaining some of the old corn of the crops of all the three years 1823, '4, & '5. This stock, put up in the shuck, nearly filled the three floors of a granary. During the time of making these crops, the price had once been as low as 25 cents the bushel with me, if I had made a sale. In other parts of lower Va, it was as low as 20 cents. I knew of the surplus of a large estate on York river, 5000 bushels, for one of these years, having been offered to a merchant in Williamsburg, for 20 cents. The offer was declined, for the whole quantity, but a part was bought at that price. Wheat also was very low for some years, & later than these; so that with all my increase of crops, my pecuniary income was still small, compared to the then production of the land. These low prices were the chief inducements to begin, & so long to continue cotton culture.

There was then no foreign demand for corn, & very little for our flour. The then stringent protective tariff (of 1824), & other commercial restrictions had cut off our former trade to Madeira & the British West Indies.[1] The refusal to buy commodities from foreign countries is equivalent to refusing to sell to them our own. For a people cannot possibly buy more than they can sell, so as to obtain the means for [buying?]. The annual product of Indian corn, the great crop of the U.S. was then necessarily consumed in this country; & generally within the year after its growth, as few persons were willing to keep a supply longer, whether for future consumption, or for sale. Indeed, so great is the usual damage to corn from weevils, & from rats, that the loss of keeping is very heavy, if in the usual mode of the corn being shucked, but yet remaining on the cob. This is best for ventilation; but gives free access to weevils & to rats. To guard against all th[e]se depredators, it is best to house the ears without taking off the covering shucks. But this is troublesome—requires much spare house-room—& prevents the shucks being used for provender in the winter after their growth, which was their indispensable on most farms.

The production of Indian corn is more abundant than of any other grain we make, but also more uncertain. The difference between a small, or even average & a large product, is very great. And when all that is made is consumed (or wasted) within the next year, leaving but little surplus to supply subsequent greater demand, it follows that the fluctuations of price will be also very great. Thus the price of corn has frequently vibrated, & within a few years, between 40 cents & $1 the bushel—& in 1817 it rose to $2 the bushel, & in or about 1824 fell as low as 20 cents.

After the succession of the years of low prices above [named?], in 1826 occurred a time of scarcity. My oldest corn was bought at 60 cents, for feeding horses, & the newer, at different &, still rising prices, until the latest sale, for corn of the crop of 1825, was $1, at my granary. Much the larger part however was sold lower, & below the market price for new corn. The oldest stock was somewhat damaged, both by being weevil-eaten, & by being a little musty. The later stocks were good. But still all old corn is suspected to be damaged, & cannot compete in price with newer. But my old stocks furnished [*blank*] bushels for sale. Afterwards the demand & prices in the interior of the country rose still higher. My journal for August 1826 has the following entry: "Heard [in Petersburg][2] of most distressing effects of drought in Mecklenburg, & to the south of that county. Whole fields of corn will produce nothing, or very little more. Corn is sending from Petersburg by Wagons to Warren, N.C., & is selling in Raleigh as high as $12 the barrel [$2.40 the bushel][3] The price in Petersburg is now $5 the bbl. & yet wheat is there only 85 cents, & 80 only would be given at my landing. In Baltimore, red wheat less than 85. The low water of the Appomattox, which does not furnish the mills enough to grind corn meal for their customers, has probably lowered the price of wheat a little. But even allowing 5 cents for that, & we still have the strange fact of 52 lbs of corn selling 10 cents higher than 60 lbs of wheat in Petersburg—& that difference increasing to 20 cents as the distance is increased from that place, which is now the point of *supply* for corn, & of *demand* for wheat—the first being therefore generally lower, & the second always higher, than in the country around. Most of us, of all classes, prefer corn bread for common use—& negroes still more, as they cannot leaven wheat flour. But still it is strange that custom & taste should cause *corn-buyers* to pay so much more than they could buy wheat for." My own wheat had been sold at 86 cents—& my latest sold corn, near the same time, at $1 the bushel.

It was not of choice, but under compulsion of circumstances, that I had retained so long my previous surplus stocks of corn, & finally obtained a good profit by the keeping. And so great was the loss by vermin of all kinds, & by some deterioration of the quality, that I had no desire to try the plan again, unless under the like necessity. Neither did I desire to make much corn for sale, as its tillage was was so injurious to my broken & washing land. Moreover, if sold to neighbors, & other country consumers, where the demand mostly existed, & sometimes the only tolerable prices, the sales were always for small quantities, & upon time; & such debts incurred for buying corn, were rarely paid when due, & often never paid. But I am satisfied that on large farms, where corn is the principal crop for sale, it would be a profitable plan to store corn, in the shuck, whenever at a very low price, say under 40 cents, to remain until a short crop should raise the price say to 70 cents or more. By proper precautions, all the vermin that my corn was exposed to, could be nearly avoided. The farmer so storing could scarcely fail to sell out, at nearly a doubled price, before his oldest corn would be 4 years old. The buyer would be much benefited if many sellers would pursue this course, as it would operate to prevent the extremes of both super abundance & scarcity. Prices would not be either so low or so high, as heretofore, when each entire crop of the whole country was consumed in the next succeeding year.

Low as prices were generally, the increase of my wheat crop to nearly thrice the former product, of corn largely, (notwithstanding the designed limitation of its production,) had very much increased my pecuniary income. All the proceeds not required for early or annual consumption, was vested in loans on safe security, & at legal interest. Although I was & am as much opposed to the law restraining the rate of interest on money as to any other absurd restriction on the freedom of trade, still I would never violate this legal prohibition, either directly or indirectly.[4] For it may be strictly obeyed in the letter, & violated to the extent of the utmost extortion in the spirit, & with active impunity from legal penalties.

It perhaps would have been my better policy, by aid of my profits & surplus income, to have increased my laboring force, & extended my farming operations. But it was not ventured at home; & I knew that to buy, stock, & cultivate other land, without my own continual attention, which of course could not be given, would be a losing business. Except to supply the necessary increase & improvement of farming stock & utensils, & at a somewhat later time, to buy some slaves, (mostly of my father's stock, as divided at his death,) I scarcely paid any money towards the improvement of my farm, or the increase of the farming capital.

The wheat crop of 1825 ought to have exceeded any one made before. The straw, & number of shocks, were full enough for 2000 bushels. But the actual product of grain was but 1452. The cause was great injury which my crop sustained from the rust.[5] But great as was my loss, it was small compared to most other persons. Scarcely any farmer suffered as little as myself, & very many lost nearly all. Some did not even reap any part of their crops, as the grain was so worthless that it would not repay the expenses of saving the crop. Scarcely any wheat made below the falls of the rivers was fit to make into tolerable flour. West of the Blue Ridge Mountains the crop was fine—& good wheat thence obtained sold as low as 75 cents in Alexandria. Of my whole measured crop of 1452 bushels, I could sell only 1085, (at 90 cents,) besides my seed reserved. The remainder was so injured by rust as to be unsalable. My Farm Journal (for Oct.) says of this remnant, "yet it is as good as the average of the crops of this & Surry county. The sale of the last crop, & the prospect of future prices, together with my unexpected success in cotton, incline me much to reduce the former crop & increase the latter."—"Many farmers on sandy lands, & some even on stiff soil, but distant from market, (in Amelia county,) have abandoned wheat for cotton, though they would have still contended with all the evils of their soils & market, if they had not lost both crop & seed by the last fatal season."—Under these general circumstances, in making even as little wheat as I did, I was unusually successful; & my greater success, & less damage from rust, was owing to the power of marled land[6] to hasten the maturing of the wheat, & so to resist that disease.

Again in 1826, & also for several successive years thereafter (at least 5 in all,) the wheat crops were bad from different causes. But one cause peculiar to mine, which I did not then know of the operation, was the long continuance of my fields without any trampling or grazing of stock, except on small portions. The soil had in consequence become too loose & "puffy" for wheat (& also for clover,) & the long rest of 2½ (& sometimes 3) years in four, without grazing, had permitted the land to become full of bad weeds for wheat, & of destructive insects. The latter plague preyed upon the growing crop—& the former lessened the product & greatly injured the quality of the grain. With all these successive bad years for wheat—the peculiar cause of injury to my corn crops—& also my having withdrawn all my best land from bearing wheat to be put annually under cotton, it is no wonder that in the next term of three years (1825, '6, & '7,) my average crop of wheat was but 1402 bushels, & the average to the acre only 8.

Of the next crop (sown from Oct 1 to Nov. 2, 1827,) I find the following notes, written soon after. "The whole sowing is too thin; but this evil is nothing when compared to the thinning generally, & entire destruction in many places, by the grasshoppers. My neighbor, T. Cocke,[7] viewed my fields with me on the 29th, & agreed with me in opinion that their ravages had then lessened the probable product by several hundred bushels. Yet this is in what I thought the most favorable seasons for avoiding them; as the extreme dryness of the earth prevented any grain sprouting until after the rain of the 9th of Oct. That circumstance, added to my increased care, & to the fruits of my costly experience gained in losing so much of the three last crops from various causes, induced me to believe that I should at last make a crop of wheat equal to the capacity of the land. Already I am disappointed; & am almost inclined to abandon wheat as a principal crop. At all events, while the price keeps so low, (75 cents this year, after Aug. 1st,) I will not sow more than 100 acres, which I can prepare well & in time, so as to sow all between the 10th & 20th of Octr. in which short time only it seems safe to sow."—This crop made (1828) only 936 bushels, on 153 acres, & but little more than 6 bushels average to the acre.

But for these notes, made at the times referred to, & also with due allowance made for the effect of cotton culture on the farm, the mere reports of the wheat crops would indicate an actual diminution of the previously obtained improvement & fertility. And sundry later crops, made during a long time of my having another residence, & different & entirely engrossing engagements, & giving no personal supervision to my farming, did not generally or frequently exhibit better evidences of much greater productive power in the land. Nevertheless it existed, though kept generally dormant by various causes. And when, at a still later time, & under a better rotation, & better direction, the products rose rapidly to amounts exceeding not only all my recent expectations, but even my earlier & most sanguine hopes. These statements will be presented hereafter.

At the close of 1827, my farm journal has the following note: "All my crops this year have been bad, from neglect & mismanagement, as well as unfavorable seasons. For cotton it has been the worst season known since it has been raised here as a crop. The corn has fallen very short of previous expectation. The whole crop is estimated at 1665 bushels. The price is under 40 cents. Never were farmers' profits lower. Yet in this time of general distress, of numerous & unexpected bankruptcies among farmers, I have reason to be thankful for my comparative prosperity. I make out to live on less than my income—do not owe a dollar—& have more than doubled the amount of my patrimony."—

In 1829 was made my fifth very bad crop of wheat in succession. It now seemed to me that success with that, formerly my main & all-important crop, was not to be looked for in the future. I came to the conclusion that the climate had changed so as to be unfit for the remunerating production of wheat. During these five years there had been different causes of disaster & loss in different years including some acts of very bad farming; but rust was the great & most general cause of the failure of production. But with all my information of the particular sources of loss, which were noted in my farm journal, it is still to me a mystery why the results should have been so bad, & so long continued. Latterly, wheat culture on the same farm, & in that neighborhood generally has been eminently successful, very far exceeding the most sanguine anticipations of early times. In the failures referred to, if I had stood alone, I might have ascribed them to satisfactory causes, in my own peculiar management. I was even disposed to infer that my fallowing had been destructive of fertility—& that even marling had proved injurious. But the latter suspicion was put at rest by the still manifest inferiority of spots on my own farm left without marl—& also of neighboring farms not marled. For example: The Evergreen farm, in the possession of my mother-in-law,[8] had not yet been marled. Formerly, the wheat crops there had been larger than mine. In 1828, when my crop (as above stated,) was only 936 bushels, that of Evergreen, from 120 bushels of seed sown (& certainly from more than 120 acres of land,) made only 292 bushels.

These long continued failures of my wheat crop, & also the regular low prices—the generally still worse prices & worse market for corn—& the now latter[9] low prices for cotton, added to the then manifest injury of cotton culture to my land—all seemed to make me despond. Without the encouragement of hope, & the prospect of success, I was incapable of making proper efforts—& soon ceased to make them. This last & worst result was still more owing to another cause—my change of residence.[10] And though that change was at first but to a few miles distance, it seemed, in addition to the other causes above referred to produce a general & finally almost total withdrawal of my personal attention from my farming—& of course, as long a general course of bad farming & small returns, even though fertilization might be (as it was) continuing to be increased, & the powers of the land capable of highly rewarding better attention & management.

Wheat had been deemed at first my main & almost only sale crop. The corn, formerly, was not enough to leave much surplus over the consumption of the farm; & even when much more might have been produced, I did not plant full crops (according to the then rotation,) for two reasons; 1st, the general low range of prices, which allowed no profit, & scarcely any market—& 2ndly, even if prices had been high enough, corn-tillage was very hurtful, when spread over the whole of each field, & necessarily including so much broken & washing land. Cotton, had at first, while selling at 12 to 14 cents, proved much better. But the price had gradually declined to 9 & 8 cents—while the tillage had proved more injurious to my farm, & more opposed to, its improvement, than that of any other crop.

In[11] 1828, I moved my family during the sickly season, & in the next summer permanently, to Shellbanks, a poor & healthy place which I had bought in the neighborhood. I had for some years designed building & removing to some other part of my farm. But the uncertainty of the healthiness of any untried locality, had delayed the execution of the very costly & also hazardous experiment, until I bought this place, which was known to be healthy, & of which the house was only 3 miles distant from the middle of my farm. I determined then (after a trial of two summers,) to repair & add to the buildings, & make this place the permanent residence of my family. I supposed the distance from my business to be but a small disadvantage, compared to the hazard of again finding a sickly home in building on a new & untried site, on my farm. The three miles of distance I could gallop over in half an hour, so as not to be much longer absent from my work, than if at my former residence. Yet these three miles & this half hour served, in addition to the other causes, to separate me almost entirely from my business. The operations of the farm had ceased to be enough interesting or attractive to engage my continued attention. I had endeavored to employ capable & trustworthy overseers—& they had proved unworthy of the trust. But while my confidence in each successive agent continued, it operated the more to make me indulge myself in withholding my personal attention. Every little obstacle of weather, of indisposition, & of aversion to effort, or attraction of amusement, was soon sufficient to induce me to decline my ride of half an hour to see my work. I had always been a creature of habit—& now I was permitting my former habit of attention to change to the reverse. At last, my farming business became actually distasteful to me. I rarely saw the operations—unless when my presence was necessarily required, & then the forced attendance was so much the more irksome & disagreeable. Three different overseers were in succession discharged, during their times of engagement, & as soon as their offences were known, for cruel or other abusive treatment of some of the slaves. And in my absence, it seemed hopeless, in employing any overseer, to avoid one of the extremes of either abuse of the slaves, or such entire relaxation of all proper discipline, that the presence of such a superintendent was worse than there being none.

It was one of the results of this state of feeling, & of my increasing negligence, that with 1828, I ceased keeping a journal regularly—& though the effort was renewed from time to time afterwards, it was not persevered in, until a much later time, when my farming labors were resumed in a different locality, & continued with with all the excitement felt & more than the benefit derived in former years. The want of written notes of crops, except in some few & accidentally preserved memoranda, prevents my knowing the amounts of most of the crops, between 1829 to 1835. But they were mostly inferior. Still some were large enough to furnish evidence that the land had not lost any of the highest fertility before furnished by marling—though the production was rarely equal to the apparent capacity of the fields. In 1835, my residence was removed to a distance,[12] & my personal attention entirely withdrawn from my farming; while its immediate direction was placed on a different & better as well as more uniform management than before. With this year, 1835, (though ahead of my narrative in other matters,) I will bring down my table of crops, so far as the amounts are known. As the first six years of my farming labors were first of sanguine hope & then complete disappointment—& the next six of rapid improvement & success—so the following brought results which showed improvement not advancing, if not actually of retrograde progress.

Table of crops from 1825 to 1835 inclusive. (from Essay on Calcareous Manures.)[13]

I will here pause, to fall back to bring up other occurrences which have been passed over.

The removal to Shellbanks for health, first for the sickly season only, & afterwards as a designed permanent residence, was not so much called for at that time, as in years before. My own health, since leaving home in the summer, had been nearly restored. But a single trial showed me (by the occurrence of a severe bilious fever) that these annual absences could not be safely omitted. My wife's health, for some years had greatly improved, & generally & for months together she was entirely well for the time. Her health did not suffer at all as mine did from the exposure to malaria—or marsh miasma. Our children, though generally suffering more or less in each autumn, had suffered less latterly than in former time. But I had designed for years before to change our location, & to build elsewhere on my farm—& the design had been postponed, first & early by want of funds, & afterwards by the great hazard of selecting & building upon what might still prove to be an unhealthy site. To avoid this very great risk, I chose the other very bad alternative, of residing off of the farm. But whatever I lost in other respects, we gained in the inestimable blessing of health. Thenceforward, bilious diseases almost ceased among my children; & my own previous temporary good health became permanent.[14]

But to prevent mistake, or seeming contradiction to what I have written since on the sickliness of our climate, it is proper here to state that the Coggin's farm had become much more healthy of late years, as exhibited in the health of my negroes much more than in my own family. The former greater sickliness was no doubt in part caused by the reclaiming & cultivating of the tide marsh. This though sunk very low, & no longer used except for grazing, had not been abandoned again to the tides, until after my removal.[15] My own family being within the peninsula, & with this seed-bed of miasma lying south of our dwelling, had all the worst effects. Most of my negroes (except house servants) had been removed to healthier localities, & out of the worst exposure to the marsh miasma, brought by southerly winds. But allowing everything due to the effect of marsh exposure, & its effects, & also to removal from it, it seemed that a more powerful & beneficial effect on health had been caused by the general marling of the farm. This opinion was strengthened by observations made on many other farms, & subsequently of the country generally.

My example in marling had been slowly followed by most of my neighbors, & had spread extensively through lower Virginia long before the time of my latest remarks.[16] But so slowly & hesitatingly had nearly all proceeded, even after no longer incredulous of the benefit, that when my previous products had been doubled, very few others had as yet added one-tenth to theirs—& the far greater number, who had equal or greater facilities, had not begun to apply marl. If all others had reasoned as to the enduring effects, & therefore great profits, as I did, even the prospect of such improvement, in advance of all effort, ought to have raised the prices of lands—as is the case now. But then, few persons had been taught to draw the distinction between fleeting & long abiding or permanent manures.[17] And even when a dressing of marl was admitted (on some soils) to be better for early production than an equal amount of stable manure, it was not thence deduced that the marled land producing a certain amount of crop was worth more than the dunged land bringing as much. Yet the first was as durable as the second was transient. Thus, with as yet such small extent of improvement, & such small surplus of net profit, over the first expenses incurred,—it was not strange that the general farming condition of this region should have continued to grow worse, for years after my use of marl had shown its great value, & even after my crops had been more than doubled. The general & long continued low prices of wheat & most other crops, & the general want of money, the very general indebtedness to banks or other creditors of all the improvident & speculating farmers, had produced a general state of depression—& of ruin in many particular cases. When for a short time, a general scarcity of corn made its price very high, it was not a profit, but a general & heavy loss to the farming community. For in such cases, the great demand for corn was in the country, & very few farmers in the same region had much surplus to sell. A few, like myself, in 1826, by having accidentally an old stock on hand, might profit greatly by such an occurrence. But there were ten buyers of corn among farmers where there was one corn-seller; & much more corn was demanded for the consumption of our region generally than all its stocks could supply.

About the time of my buying the land which was afterwards called Shellbanks, these causes had reduced the agricultural prosperity to its lowest ebb; & it was some years after that time before the steadily increasing agricultural improvement of our lands, & the general confidence in the permanency of the improvement, together with better prices for our increased crops, began to give a general & great impulse to agricultural prosperity in eastern Virginia.

The circumstances of the sale of the land in question will seem to indicate the then general condition of prices & profits of lands, & of the funds & the debts of the owners. The tract was held & sold at the estimated quantity of 450 acres, though it was afterwards ascertained to be not more than 400. It was hilly, & much washed & impoverished by the usual bad culture of [the country?].[18] All of the land was then quite poor, except a [*illeg.*] [*illeg.*] around the dwelling—& some 25 acres of low land, which was [*illeg.*] impoverished by bad culture, & worthless for want of drainage. There was plenty of good marl, of which none had been used. This land was sold at public auction, to the highest bidder for cash, & commanded only $650. Even at that low price, no farming on clear profit could have been made on the purchase, if the cultivation of the land were to be continued as had been general [*illeg.*] [*illeg.*] not only on this farm, but on most other land in [*illeg.*] Va. One of the main causes which brought the former proprietor[19] to ruin, was his having, 10 years before, bought 100 acres of the same, (& the poorest part,) at $9 the acre. This then high price was produced by the great *appreciation* of property, (as it was erroneously supposed & called,) induced by the enormous emissions of paper currency by non-specie paying banks, & the subsequent reaction & after *depreciation* of market value of the same property. As great fluctuations of market value occurred to most other lands of lower Va. within these times; & of all the thousands who bought lands at the high prices, & were compelled to sell at the low, all were ruined. Neither were such low prices confined to forced sales for cash. An adjoining tract to that which I bought, of rather more than 200 acres, which had been bought at $2300 during the time of bank-paper prices, had been long lying idle, & in market without any chance for a purchaser. My other purchase made the acquisition of this adjoining land desirable to me; & I bought it, at private sale, & half the price on credit at $2.30 the acre.[20] This piece, though poor, was generally level, & was worth more for its quality upon improvement & cultivation, than the other land, though the other had buildings which had cost some $1000 for the original erection.

Having then surplus labor beyond the demands for the ordinary cultivation of Coggins, I used it, at leisure times, for the marling of Shellbanks. Some cultivation of the best land was done the next year, by a tenant,[21] & nearly the whole of the before arable land had been both marled & cultivated by me before 1835. Still no regular farming force was established there. The work was done by the Coggins force. These & other labors of improvement helped to occupy my attention after the change of my residence & the withdrawal of my personal & regular attention from my principal farming operations. None of the crops made at Shellbanks are included in the tables or other statements of my crops which statements are for the Coggins farm only.

In 1821 I had written & addressed to the Agricultural Society of Prince George, my then extended experience & views of the theory of fertility. This essay "On Soils [*blank*]"[22] was published in the American Farmer (vol III.) by order of the Delegation of the United Agricultural Societies of Virginia. This was the earliest *printing* of my views though, as before stated an earlier & shorter communication of the same theory & general views had been made in 1818.[23] The essay attracted much notice, & had much effect in extending information of the beneficial effects of marl, & inducing distant farmers to commence marling or liming. This piece was the foundation of the "Essay on Calcareous Manures," which was afterwards published in book form, in 1832. Enlarged as was then the work, & embracing much of new but incidental matter, the theory set forth, & the substance, were not at all changed, in that or any of the still more enlarged later editions.[24]

The first edition (as it has perhaps improperly been called, because the first in substantive or book form of publication,) had been prepared for the press in 1826, & would then have been published then, but for discouraging circumstances.

My nearest neighbor & most valued friend, Thomas Cocke was nearly 20 years my senior. Yet this difference of age, & our former respective relations as Guardian & ward, had not prevented the growth & continuance of intimate & warm friendship between us. My friend was a man of uncommon mental power, pure principles, great liberality, & kindness which he carried to the extent of imprudence. He was the last remaining individual of the preceding generation. In his youth he had lived almost a recluse, with scarcely any associations but his books. After some subsequent years of social intercourse with his elder neighbors, their deaths had again left him almost alone. During his early & middle life he had never had a companion of equal mind & similar literary tastes—& his partiality for me was in some degree owing to my making some approach to that position. Before our intimacy, he had conversed but little with men, & very rarely with any but very inferior minds. His information, his views, & even his ordinary language, were all derived from books, & very little from conversation. Though he never wrote a line for publication in his life, he could have written well. His clear understanding & perception, & still more the entire sincerity of his friendly criticism, had aided me much when consulting him in regard to my earlier writings on agriculture or political subjects.[25] He had taken great interest in my efforts, & was highly gratified with what he deemed my success in my earlier writings. Especially he valued my theoretical views of the causes of & means for producing fertility; & though a slow convert to my doctrine, he became in time, an enthusiastic disciple, both in theory & practice. He was privy to my every thought on this, as on most other subjects; & of course, knew, from our frequent & full conversations, every view that I entertained, before all were laid before him, arranged in writing, for his opinion & friendly censure. I read to him the whole essay. Whatever might have been the cause, he formed an unfavorable opinion of its manner & style; & as little previous reputation as I possessed, he feared that I would put it to hazard, if assuming to appear before the public as the author of a *book*. I had been before afraid to take so bold a step; & the still more extended fears of my friend were sufficient to discourage me from the designed publication. The manuscript was put away in a drawer, & remained there for nearly six years, when other feelings & new views prompted & induced the publication. A legible copy was then made, as the printing was to be done in Philadelphia; & except verbal corrections, I believe no change was made in this copy from the manuscript prepared in 1826, & which still remains among my papers.[26]

The fears of my friend Cocke were removed upon his reading the book in print—which he readily admitted to appear much superior to the same work in writing. My own fears, on other grounds, were also removed by the results. The work was very favorably received by the public. Its arguments & facts were deemed conclusive; & if any important objection was ever made to either its matter or manner, no report of the censure came to my knowledge. Still, I was dissatisfied with my readers & applauders because they were too easily convinced. Few carefully followed, or strictly scrutinized the train of argument, or disputed any of the steps. They were content to receive the results as fully proved truths.

This edition was but a small one, (750 copies as reported by the Philadelphia publisher.) The publication was at the joint risk & for the joint profit of the author & publisher. But though all the copies were soon sold, there was no profit left. This was to me then of no importance, as I sought only the publication of the work, & its extensive circulation, & had had no expectation of any pecuniary remuneration.

This publication was one of the fruits of my then idle time. Another was my learning French, in which language I read many volumes—& though never acquiring a correct or grammatical knowledge, I was enabled to readily catch the purport, & to translate with sufficient accuracy as to the author's meaning. Thus I was enabled to read such few French agricultural writers as I could meet with; & for such, my practical knowledge as a farmer, made me a more accurate translator than would have been an accomplished French & English scholar, who had no knowledge of farming. Even with the aid of such knowledge, I found so many provincial terms, & words not in the best dictionaries, or, if there, not defined with sufficient particularity, that agriculture was the most difficult subject I every attempted to translate. This study of French, undertaken without any object, was afterwards of great use to me; & it enabled me to translate for publication many agricultural or scientific articles from French authors.[27]

The success of my publication of the 'Essay on Calcareous Manures', was the cause of my soon after attempting a still more arduous undertaking, of similar character. This was the commencement of a new agricultural journal. I issued a prospectus of the plan & proposals for subscribers to the work, in the winter of 18[*blank*]—[*blank*]; & so many names were soon offered, as to induce me to assume the risk of the publication.[28] In a few months after announcing the scheme, the first monthly number of the "Farmers' Register" was issued, & the publication was continued under my sole charge, for ten years. With this publication was begun a new & distinct era of my life—a long & exclusive dedication of my time & my labors to the public service, in the promotion of agricultural improvement. For general agricultural & public interests, these labors were eminently beneficial. To my own private & pecuniary interests, this undertaking a new, & so engrossing & expensive a business, was in the end very detrimental. At this time, of such complete change of my position & mode of life, of such entire abandonment, for a long time, of all attention to my own farming business, it will be convenient to suspend the onward course of my narration, & to close what may have been left unfinished of remarks on my previous practical operations. The results of any new opinions or practices of mine, whether the action was right or wrong, if of any importance, will be remarked upon, under the different heads to which the subjects will belong.

Non-grazing of arable fields, or the "enclosing system.[29] This was the only part of Taylor's general system[30] to which I have adhered—& which, with proper limitations, I continue to value, as one of the most important means for improvement of poor lands, after their having been drained & marled, or limed.[31] Without draining, if that is needed, no land can be improved, or cultivated to much profit. Without calcareous manures, no acid soil can be enriched. And even if neither of these wants had existed, or if they had been supplied, no poor farm, from its own crops only, can be furnished with enough of putrescent manure,[32] without permitting nature to furnish vegetable matter to the fields, in their own growth of clover, or weeds, when clover cannot grow. This aid even, produced scarcely a perceptible benefit on acid soils, without the addition of calcareous manures. But with this aid, & with enough rest to the poor land, Nature will give to it more putrescent manure, in its own vegetable cover of weeds, and far better if of clover, than double the limited supplies of prepared manures, from the cattle pens & stables, littered with all the coarse offal of the crops. My exclusion of grazing stock had not been complete. At first, for some years, I had no separate enclosure, as a standing pasture, & of course the few cattle necessary for scant family supplies of milk & butter, & the few oxen for labor, were herded on the fields then at rest. These were at most, from 25 to 30 cattle. I kept no sheep—& my hogs were outside of my enclosure, on some forest highland, & with access to all my unenclosed marsh. Under such management, I do not think that I ever derived any returns from hogs that more than compensated for the corn they consumed, in their daily feeding, & their last fattening for slaughter.

The cattle when in the fields were kept on the parts which were richest, or foulest with grass, & on hill-sides & other waste land, useful for grazing, but unfit for tillage. The Point field,[33] for some [*blank*] years was enclosed separately, & each half fallowed alternately for wheat every other year, & all grazed in the interval of time from the removal of one crop of wheat, & the sowing of another. But this rotation (of 1, wheat on fallow, & 2, rest, & partly grazed,) without any tillage or cleansing crop, for [*blank*] years, permitted the land to become so foul with root-weeds & grasses, that the wheat crops were worse & worse, until the course was abandoned in [*blank*].[34]

All this grazing extended over little other than the richest or foulest parts of the farm. The great body of poorer arable land was scarcely grazed or trodden at all, for many years. The ill effects of this, in making the soil too open for wheat & clover, & filling the land with bad weeds, & with destructive insects, have been stated.[35] I have since inferred, & latterly have acted in conformity, that all light & dry land ought to be grazed, & trampled, for some one part at least of every course of crops. But that it should not be extended farther than deemed beneficial to the crops—& still to leave to rot on the land much the larger portion of the growth of grass or weeds, produced during the times of rest for the fields.

Live-stock. No profit was ever sought or found in my grazing or keeping of live-stock. No more were kept than necessary for table, & not enough for full supplies for the family, in meat as well as milk & butter. The whole business of my hog raising & fattening was deemed profitless. The whole stock management was so bad indeed, that it is entirely useless to bring it forward, except to confess the errors, & to show that no farming profit was derived from this source. No sheep were kept, after the early selling of my flock, because no separate enclosures were to be maintained. Also I was under the erroneous opinion that sheep required extensive range of pasture, & were more destructive of vegetable growth & therefore more opposed to the improvement of land, than any other live-stock, compared to their returns. Latterly I have learned that all these opinions, which I received upon common belief & report, were mistaken; & that directly the reverse propositions are much nearer the truth.

Working beasts. Oxen have never been of much use or value to me. Our hot summers unfit them for their usual irregular labor at that time. Their rough & hard fare in winter & spring keeps them poor & weak. Without better treatment & better management than I have ever been able to have for oxen, they are of little value for labor. Their only value to me, was that costing little in maintenance, so that the little work they did was almost so much clear gain.

For the plough, & for nearly all my marling & regular hauling labor, horses were used at first, & afterwards mules.

Corn tillage. After so greatly injuring all my land of rolling or hilly surface, by ploughing in ridges—& not only by straight ridges, but also by horizontal & with graduated & very gentle slope—I abandoned all.[36] Thereforward, on all my high land, the ploughing was flush, on on a level surface, & generally as steep as the depth of soil allowed. Whenever the surface was steep enough to be in much danger of being washed, the rows for planting were laid off crossing the slope, & around the hill-sides in something like horizontal direction. But it was not designed to obstruct the course of the flowing rain water—nor to prevent its passing downward by the shortest & most inclined passage. The plan was to permit the most unobstructed passage for the surplus rain-water, but never, if to be avoided, in the same direction with the ploughing. The tillage was as level as possible. Cultivators, & trowel ploughs without mould-boards were only used so that no raised furrow-slice was made.[37] Weeding, but no hilling, was done by the hand-hoes. While the land remained clean enough, the cultivators worked well—& did all the ploughing, except one deep & close running of trowel ploughs, just before wheat-harvest. But the growth of wire grass & blue-grass, & green-sward,[38] the effects of marling, afterwards compelled me to give up the attempt to use cultivators; & before the abandonment, I had had very bad & difficult tillage for some years previous. But whether by cultivators or other ploughs, the principle of my tillage has remained the same—the object being to preserve a level surface, and deep & clean tilth.

The numerous insects fostered by my non-grazing system, & also the field rats, were very destructive to the planted seed, as to the young plants of corn. Thus it was difficult to obtain a "stand," & the crop was always more or less shortened on that account. With this exception, my crops of corn were of good growth & production. And even when my wheat & clover were almost regular failures, the corn would give evidence that the fertility of the land had certainly kept increasing.

Owing to the arable land of the farm being so much intersected by narrow valleys & ravines, wet bottoms, & bordered externally by forest, & by marshes covered with swamp trees, there is an uncommon extent of harbor for vermin—birds, squirrels, & rackoons—which depredate very much on every crop of corn. Near the tree-covered marshes, the whole growth of corn was destroyed regularly by squirrels & racoons—& even ripening wheat was greatly injured.

Wheat & fallow. In my early farming, the universal practice of my neighborhood was to make wheat only after corn, (tobacco culture being lately ceased,) & fallowing was known only by report. I was anxious to introduce wheat on fallow; because, according to the only usual practice, the quantity of wheat culture & products were dependent upon the extent of the preceding corn-culture. And as the latter was so injurious to my washy land, I wished to limit its extent, as well as to increase that of wheat culture. Still I was long afraid of fallow as a supposed exhausting process. I had been strongly impressed with Taylor's doctrine, that all exposure of a naked & ploughed surface of soil to evaporation, was inducing a waste of its fertilizing parts; & hence inferred, that ploughing grass land in August, & exposing the new surface to the hot sun, even if giving an additional better crop of wheat, must serve to impoverish the land by the action of the sun & air, as well as by the support of the crop. Hence, my fallowing at first, & for years, was mostly done in September, & sometimes even in Octr., to avoid the supposed greater exhaustion of the land, if beginning early in August, though this latter course made the best crop.

I had done very little fallowing before the land had been marled. The first considerable fallowing, of marled land, brought much better wheat than I had ever obtained before. This increase, which was the combined effect of marling & fallowing, I ascribed almost entirely to the improvement of fertility by marling. And when, after beginning cotton culture, I ceased to fallow extensively, both for want of labor & land for that purpose, & my wheat crops were greatly reduced below previous products, I did not ascribe the diminution to its proper & sole cause, but feared that some of my earlier fertilization had been lost. The only regular annual fallow was of half (about 42 to 44 acres) of the Point field, alternately with grass (or weeds) every other year. This, as before stated, became so foul, that the products diminished, until that particular course was abandoned.

The four-shift rotation (of Taylor), put fully into operation by 1824, & persevered in until 1839, when strictly adhered to, did not allow any land for summer fallow. But, in the latter portion of that time, a variable proportion of each field, in its first year of rest—either the richest or the foulest part of the field, was fallowed for wheat, & so yielded three grain crops in the four years, according to the Shirley & Westover four-shift rotation,[39] instead of two grain crops only, as upon Taylor's milder course.

One important cause of my latter ill-success in fallow wheat was the inefficiency of the two-mule ploughs used. These were quite too small, & the teams too weak, for the then improved & better covered land, & especially for summer ploughing. In consequence, there was bad ploughing, & bad seeding, & short returns. These mule ploughs were first introduced in 1826; & summer fallowing, with four-mule ploughs was not begun until some 7 years later. Even with the then better ploughing, the foulness of the land, & its loose "puffy" texture, & the general absence of clover, all still operated to prevent such production of wheat as the soil could have brought under reversed conditions. It was not until still later (in 1839) that the introduction of the five-shift rotation, & other improvements of corrected practice, served soon after to bring up the wheat crops to their proper rate.

Long before, all my early fears of impoverishment of soil by its exposure to the sun & evaporation, had yielded to better reasoning, & to experience. In a naturally poor soil, artificially enriched by putrescent matters, I do not doubt that every turning of the soil, & exposing a new surface, to the hot sun, serves to destroy more or less of its previous stock of fertilizing principles. But this waste is not the result of evaporation, but of increased decomposition; the products of decomposition may be so lost, because the soil had not the power to combine with & so retain these products. But in a well constituted soil, whether natural or artificial, having enough calcareous matter to combine with & secure the putrescent, or the early products of decomposition, I now believe that the fertilizing parts will be so held secure, whether the soil be ploughed or not. And if losing nothing, the fallowed soil must gain—not only by the reduction of its heavy cover of vegetable matter to a condition fit to feed the wheat—but also by the access of air to all the parts of the loosened soil, & consequent benefit conveyed to & fixed in the soil, in the chemical ingredients of both the air & the water so introduced. It is now understood that oxygen is thus given out by enclosed air to the soil. *It may be* that some of the nitrogen also is left & fixed.[40]

Manure. My bad practices & ill success with prepared putrescent manures have been mentioned incidentally & generally, so that not much more need be added on that hand. The then general practice of the country was also mine at the very first. This was to give no more of litter to cattle, than enough to hold the animal matter by absorption. Few persons, before being instructed by Arator, had any idea that the vegetable matter itself was a valuable manure, independent of all the intermixed animal matter—& none believed that cornstalks, or anything other than wheatstraw, was worth collecting for litter or using as manure, provided enough had been furnished to absorb the animal excrements. To keep for the cattle a dry & comfortable bed was indeed thought another benefit. But so rarely was enough dry littering furnished for this or any purpose, & so wet was the mass of litter & manure in the winter pens, that many persons maintained that to put cattle on litter, & in pens with bush-sheltered sides, was decidedly injurious to the health of the cattle—& that they had fared better upon the still older plan, of naked & temporary pens, in winter, without sheltering, as most farmers now pen cattle through summer. And doubtless these persons were right, in this objection to the then usage of bedding cattle on thoroughly wet & miry litter, with but partial shelter from wind & rain. But they should have ascribed the ill effects to the defects of the plan, & not to the plan properly carried out. I can well remember intelligent persons who had returned to naked & moveable winter pens for their cattle, under the opinion that they were more healthy than any littered & sheltered pens.

The manure so made in the former best common practice, with as little of the supposed adulteration of cornstalks or other poor vegetable matter as possible (other than the very small crop of wheat-straw,) was left ex[posed?] until in July or August, when near the time to scrape the yard & dry it, for treading wheat. The manure was then very rotten & black, & rich—but usually only 2 or 3 & very rarely 4 inches thick. It was carried off on hand-barrows & heaped. Of course, heating & renewed & violent fermentation would follow, & a waste of perhaps half the bulk & value, before the manure was carried out the next spring, & ploughed under, for tobacco—or, in after times, for corn. Of course the quantity was not so great as to cost much labor in the application.

I found on my farm such a pen of manure in progress.[41] But the next winter I began upon Taylor's advice to bring in all the cornstalks, & to carry out all the manure before having rotted. Still I did not then deem it possible to omit all heaping & even a partial fermentation. Therefore this great labor was executed, & a very partial & imperfect heating & rotting obtained, before carrying out the manure the same spring, & ploughing it under for corn, on poor land. The results, in benefit fell far short of the cost—& in a few years this plan was abandoned. Finding so little benefit to the crop, & such inconvenience in the tillage upon these heavy applications, I resorted to carrying out the manure from the yard, (to avoid the labor & waste of fermenting heaps,) & ploughing it under, to there lie until the land was put under wheat the next autumn, or corn the year after. This was the most costly & absurd of all my uses of manure. According to my present views, the fermentation proceeded much faster & to less benefit, for the manure being ploughed under, instead of lying spread on the grassy surface.

Afterwards the manure was sometimes heaped early, & remained until rotted, or was left to lie in the pen to rot. In the latter case, by having abundant littering, & a thick coat of manure, the waste was not deemed very great; & at any rate, the manure so prepared was rich, & always beneficial, & very manageable in application.

While these changes were making, & disappointments experienced, my first benefits from marl had been obtained. This caused manure-making to be much neglected for years, & until all the heaviest labors of marling had been finished. Then, directed by my theoretical views, I returned to collecting materials for & making & applying on marled land putrescent manure with my former zeal, & with general good success, & undoubted profit. For a year or two I followed a practice then common on the Rappahannock lands, of applying the manure, in any state)[42] on the surface of corn land, & after the crop was planted. I did not find the effects so great as when the manure had been earlier ploughed under. But still the difference was not supposed to be greater than the difference of labor of the two modes of application.

It was much later, about 1834, I think, that I began to apply any manure, in the unaltered state, as a top-dressing on clover. This practice I have preferred to all others, & have continued to this time. The reasons on which this peculiar practice was founded have been fully set forth in an essay which I published in 184[*blank*];[43] & they would occupy too much space to be repeated here, if ever so concisely. I have continued to deem this application a great economy of labor & of manure.

I have, since adopting this mode, added much to my materials for manure, by raking leaves in forest land. These were sometimes applied immediately on the grass land, as top-dressing, & sometimes as litter for cattle pens. These supplies from the poor forest land, where, if left, they would have been useless, & would have decomposed in waste, poor as they may be, are so much of clear benefit to the arable land, if the soil is so constituted as to fix the manure. But not so, if any such supplies, of corn stalks, or high stubble, or wheat stubble, or weeds, were already diffused over arable land needing them as manure. To collect & cart such materials to the barn yard, convert them to manure by mixture in the pens, & then to haul out & spread the same on either the same or other land, is a clear loss of the double cartage, the collecting & spreading & also of the adding four-fifths to the dry weight, in water. A certain amount of vegetable matter is necessary to mix with & absorb the animal excretions in stables & cattle pens. But when there is enough for that purpose, it is waste of labor to add more. Even all the stacked straw not required for this mechanical operation of absorption, nor for the food, or the abundantly comfortable littering of animals, had better be carted dry to the land, & spread, than to pass through the cattle pen to the same ultimate destination—. As 20 [lbs][44] of dry straw, by merely being made wet, will weigh 100 lbs; & 80 lbs of every 100 lbs of manure, from a yard in the winter or spring, is nothing but water, & adds no enriching value whatever to the land.

Draining.[45] Except in the embanked marsh, of which failure enough has been said,[46] there was very little arable land on my farm that required draining—& for that, the ordinary means, of open ditches, were mostly unsuitable. There were three small pieces of land & flat alluvial ground extending to lower tide marsh. These few acres were used as meadows of coarse grass, & a few more acres adjoining were high enough for grain crops. These parts required central (or side) open ditches to carry the streams, & take off the rain floods. But even for the springs bursting out at the foot of the hills bordering on these flats, & in most other cases of springs or oozes at the bases of hills, or elsewhere, open ditches were of very little use. The hilliness of the farm caused the surplus water of heavy rains to pour down in temporary torrents, so as somewhere to fill up & completely choke with mud or sand any spring or side-ditch crossed by these rain-floods. After numerous failures from this cause, I learned by such experience that covered drains only would serve the purpose required, as they only could keep open under this continual exposure to crossing torrents of rain water, & the mud & sand brought down from the higher ground.[47]

The principle or theory of covered draining was obvious & simple enough. All that was required was to make the ditch in the proper place to intercept all the spring water, & to lead it off, & to construct a pipe or open passage for the water at the bottom of the ditch, & fill all above with earth, as before the digging. But the great difficulties, & causes of general subsequent failure, were in my not knowing the extent of the various dangers to the permanency of such constructions, & therefore not sufficiently guarding against them. When beginning such attempts, & even to the last of these early operations, I had never seen a covered drain, made under other direction, nor but one individual who had ever made a similar attempt—& who probably did no better than myself, in his limited operations. Of course I could have no light either from experience, or from proper instruction. The little information on this subject then accessible to me in European books, was too concise & general to convey any useful directions. And even if the volumes on draining, which I have more lately seen, had then been before me, they would not have warned me of most of the errors which proved destructive to all my early labors of this kind. Even if provided with the material, stones, then almost exclusively used in Europe, for covered drains, I should only have reached the same failures at a vast deal more cost of labor. I have not yet met in books with any directions for constructing covered drains, which, if followed ever so carefully by a novice, would not have led to complete failure. It is still a mystery to me, how the continued operation of covered drains is preserved, in Europe, with no more safeguards than seem to be afforded.

I began this work in about 1822. The places which mostly required such drains, were lines along the bases of hill-sides, where meeting the margins of low & flat alluvial land. These lowgrounds, were, at first my reclaimed marsh, then still under tillage—& the other alluvial ground, above mentioned, which were but a little higher than the highest tides. Indeed all these pieces had originally been tide marsh—& had been raised in the course of time by the earth washed down & left by rain-floods. As tide marshes are almost perfectly level, my side ditches, cut alongside, & just high enough to take in the oozing springs, had very little descent (or "fall") in their courses.—For want of a sufficiently low outlet, the depth of the digging was generally too little—in some parts less than two feet. Whether the returned & covering earth was removed or not, & whether left even with the surface or raised to allow for settling, it was almost impossible, with such shallow covering, to prevent rain-water entering at the surface, & running down in a stream to the pipe. This would be done generally by the searching water of some rain-torrent—which would continue to enlarge the entrance so made, & wash down sand, until choking the pipe of the covered drain entirely. Thus, a drain of some hundreds of yards in length would be utterly ruined in a few hours. There were still other certain causes of failure. From a mistaken notion of saving labor, in many cases old open ditches, deepened, were used as the channels of the new covered drains. These old ditches were usually not high enough above the line of the oozing springs—& moreover, they were more difficult to cover, & consequently much more exposed to the access of surface water than ditches dug entirely new. The nearness of the water in my covered drains to the surface invited the cray-fish to bore down to it, & construct their houses—& their holes offered open & easy entrance to the surface rain water, even if it had been otherwise excluded. Added to all these errors, I used for making the conduits much seasoned wood, which would have soon rotted, & so spoiled the drain, if its operation had not before been destroyed by other causes. Each of these errors would have been enough to cause the failure of any covered drain. It is then not to be wondered at, that of all that I made in two years, amounting to some thousands of yards, scarcely one operated properly for three years, & most of them failed in a few months. I had at first estimated very highly the value of my improvements thus made; but after laboring so long in vain, I was compelled to abandon all such attempts, & to return again to open ditches, objectionable as they were. Yet at a later time, & by exercising more judgment & care in the location & construction, I have been eminently successful in covered draining, on a different farm; & on the Coggins farm, my son & successor has succeeded in such constructions, on ground even more difficult than had been the subjects of my attempts & failures.[48]

The first covered drain I ever made was near to a hill much encumbered with rolled stones. These, & others from the river beach were used to make the conduit, on the English plan. The labor of carting the stones was very heavy, & the drain was soon choked, for its want of sufficient depth, & also of sufficient fall.

At a later time, I used materials which I still prefer to all others, as being cheaper to prepare, admitting of more rapid laying down, & making a more perfect pipe than any others except the recently invented tile-pipes. This plan was to use two green pine sapling poles, laid parallel in the bottom of the ditch, & 2 to 4 inches apart, & these covered by rived pine boards, 10 to 12 inches in length, laid transversely crossing the poles. This is the best construction which I have latterly practiced. As small pine poles were scarce on Coggins, because there had been no exhausted land recently "turned out," (which land is soon thickly covered by young pines,) I had to use split pieces of larger trees instead.

For[49] pieces of low ground, above mentioned, I adopted a novel plan of open ditches, which was found very convenient & useful. These lands, above the height of highest tides, had abundant fall. As is the general usage in regard to narrow low grounds, the stream had been led off in a side-ditch, at the junction of the high & low land. This line, as usual in such cases, was very crooked, and therefore opposing many obstructions to the passage of the water, when swollen by heavy rains. A still greater cause of obstructions was that both sides of the ditch, being left untilled, soon became a thicket of shrubs & briers, which would over-hang & meet across the ditch. With every rain-flood the obstructed stream would overflow its bank, & the water in its designed bed being thereby made sluggish, it could not sweep out the sand which was brought in from the hills. Of course, these crooked & obstructed side-ditches were rapidly filled, & the more completely towards the upper end; & the cleaning[50] out of this barren sand was made an injurious addition & covering to the rich alluvial bordering land, which was there abundantly high.

My first improvement was to change the passage of the stream to a new ditch in the middle of the bottom, meandering with the general course of the bottom, but still much straighter than had been the route at the side. The land was tilled, & the margins kept clean to the edges of my new ditch & its stream. With this advantages of straighter course, & clean margins, the ditch could vent much more water, would be rarely overflowed, & by its continued & rapid current, would sweep the sand received from above to my sufficiently low place of deposit. For the sand at the bottom of a stream of ordinary fall is continually moving around as may be seen by any observer; & will so mve on, for any distance, so long as the fall remains, & the outlet is unobstructed. But as my streams, & the ditches conveying them, reached lower land subject to the tide, of course no more descent than to tide water could be obtained. Then the sand brought down continually by the stream, & from its highest source, would settle when reaching the tide level. The accumulation, if suffered to remain, would soon make an obstruction to the sand which would then stop higher & higher up the ditch; & if the cleaning out were long neglected, would choke the ditch to its upper end, & much more at its upper than its lower end. To prevent all these evils, & to put the sand to good use, instead of its encumbering & spoiling good land above, I made the lower extremity of the ditch wide & deep for the purpose of receiving the sand. Further, to postpone the necessity of cleaning out the sand, & also to facilitate the operation, two or three parallel ditches about 10 yards apart, & connected both above & below, were made about 100 yards long, through the ground too low for tillage. These parallel "receiving ditches", say 5 or 6 feet wide & dug 4 feet deep at first, would receive all the sand for a long time; & until they were full, no sand would remain stationary in the stream above. At some convenient time, the accumulation of sand would be shovelled out of these receiving ditches—the stream being kept in the one most open, until the others were cleaned. The coming down of the sand is unavoidable. But by this plan, it is put out where serviceable in raising the low land, instead of above where it is a nuissance. A few such cleanings out of these parallel receiving ditches, in the course of some years, will supply earth enough to raise the interval of marsh high enough for safe tillage. When the margins & intervals are thus raised as high as desirable, other like parallel receiving ditches are to be opened, & the older ones, as well as their margins, made arable land. This is indeed making land by a slow & laborious process. But it is in fact a benefit gained without cost—inasmuch as equal or more labor would have to be performed, in the ordinary way of clearing out ditches, & that to the injury instead of the benefit of the land.

Ploughing in ridges (for surface drainage) was not required on but little of my high land, & would have been injurious, to nearly all, by inducing greater washing. Therefore in all except the early practice, the first ploughing or "breaking up" of land, had been flush. The "lands" marked off by the first furrow were as large as convenient, & of any irregular shape that best suited the land, or guarded against washing. Where there was any slight natural depression, into & along which surplus rain water would flow, but which had too little descent to be in danger of being washed, the middle of this depression was made the middle of a broad ploughing "land", & the furrow-slices turned outward, so that the closing open water-furrow was made in the central line of the depression. This mode of ploughing was repeated, whenever the land was again "broken up" by a flush ploughing, or so often as necessary for the purpose designed. This deepened central furrow made a good & sufficient rain-ditch, to drain the depression which would otherwise have suffered by wetness; & while it was deeper & better than a small ditch made by the spade, it presented no obstruction to tillage, or the crossing of ploughing or of carting. This simple & yet very beneficial mode of aiding draining by the ordinary ploughing was especially useful on the highest table land of my farm, which I found under forest-growth & very poor, & which had been cleared, marled, & brought under cultivation. This land was mostly of sandy subsoil, & required level tillage. Though of general level surface, there were lines of shallow depressions, which were covered by standing rain-water all winter & spring, but were dry in summer & autumn. These shallow, but in some cases long & extensive ponds, were separated from each other by slightly higher ground. When the land was first cleared, & still full of the stumps & roots of trees & ploughing very difficult & imperfect, it was necessary to dig small ditches through these slight eminences, & so connect the lowest parts of the ponds with each other, & draw off all the water to & discharge it at the lower end. As there was nothing but rain-water, a ditch of 18 inches deep, where deepest, served for this & any such purpose. When, at subsequent cultivations, ploughing by the mould-board ploughs was practicable, the furrow-slices were turned outward from the central line of these former ponds, & the small ditch which had been cut along that line. Two or three such operations served to almost obliterate the ditch (to the eye) while the draining effect was much improved. While the tillage thereafter was no more obstructed than if no ponds or ditch had ever existed, the draining was as efficient as it could have been made.

Now simple as is this plan, the direct reverse course was generally, & still is, very often pursued on almost all other farms. Where a rain-ditch is required to take off such shallow temporary ponds, or to dry a depression subject to rain water only, the general practice, in ploughing, is to turn the furrow-slices towards instead of from such small ditches. Thus their margins are raised instead of being lowered; & this, with the banks being also raised by cleaning out the ditch, makes it deeper, in relation to its banks & margins, while it is often permitted to become absolutely shallower than at first, & less & less effective for drainage with every ploughing of the field, & every raising of the banks; and also more in the way of tillage operations, as the banks become higher, & the ditch deeper in relation to the banks.

From the former statements of my erroneous views of the operation of open side ditches, & my absurd construction of them, (for the reclaimed marsh,) & my later failures in nearly all the first labors in covered draining, it might well be inferred that I was extremely ignorant of draining. Nevertheless, twenty years ago I was far better informed on this subject, than my neighbors. And however much has since been increased the general light on this subject, there still exists a very general & great degree of ignorance, even when improvement by drainage is most required. My own general views in 1833, & my then recent practice on the Shellbanks low-grounds, were set forth in an anonymous communication to the Farmers' Register, in Nos 7 & 12, of the first volume.[51] Among many correct rules there presented, there were some strong examples of remaining ignorance & error. Among these, were these two: 1st the permitting any angle, no matter how obtuse, to be made in a ditch carrying a stream subject to be increased greatly in volume & rapidity by rain-floods; & 2nd the permitting any covered drains to be of as little depth as 30 inches, if possible to have more.

General direction & overseers. While ready to claim for my theoretical agricultural opinions, & my general plans founded thereupon, full as much of merit as others would accord to them, I have always, & truly, disclaimed all pretensions to being a good & judicious observer, a good manager of business, a good economist—&, that which requires these & many other things, a good practical farmer. That my success has been great is owing to the general plan being good, which would permit much to be lost in improper details, & yet leave large profits. Many other farmers, who possess most of the requisites which I am deficient in, have yet done much worse than myself, because their general plans & theories were bad. Projectors & schemers are rarely good operatives; & therefore it is not a subject either for surprise or lamentation that I did not possess both the talents of planning & executing. But I am well convinced that if my general plans for improvement had been as zealously pursued by a farmer having equal facilities, & also the good judgment, good management, & the other qualities which I wanted, he could have effected in the same length of time, twice as much improvement, & accumulated twice as much profit & wealth, as I have done. In the general, & for any department, I never have been a man of business. I am very deficient in order & method. As a farmer, especial deficiencies are that I have no genius for, and little knowledge of machinery & its proper working—even of ploughs & of gearing. I have a bad eye for observation in all things that are not my peculiar & preferred subjects of attention & study. I am no judge of horses, or other live stock, & take no pleasure in their care & management. I cannot exercise that uniform & inflexible demeanor which is necessary for the proper & easy government & discipline of subordinates, & especially of slaves; & so little observation do I possess, that laborers may decieve me, & slight or neglect their work, before my eyes—& they would soon [learn?] to know that I would not see one half the things which the most ignorant among them would not fail to notice. Knowing as I do these defects, it is not so much a matter of wonder that I should have done ill, as that I have not done worse than has been the case.

My being first (of choice) without an overseer, which began at the end of my second year, was not continued more than two or three more years. Afterwards, though always wishing to have such aid, I was several times without, for considerable times. It is the only business known to me in which good abilities & services cannot be obtained by paying for them liberally. In this the increase of wages often operates to lessen the value of the services. I made every effort—& never objected to paying good wages for expected good service. Yet I never had any other than very faulty overseers during all the long time of my life that has been under review.

When I had removed my residence from the country, & had withdrawn almost entirely all[52] my personal attention from my farming, I was especially anxious to engage a safe & trust-worthy overseer, even if not one of the best managers & crop-makers. By means of some of his communications to the first volume of the Farmers' Register I had made my first acquaintance with Andrew Nicol,[53] a Scotchman, who had then not been very long in America. He had been employed as an overseer in Virginia, upon very humble wages, & with still less confidence. He had been unjustly & humbly thrown out of this poor service, & was almost friendless, & in very necessitous circumstances. While still personally a stranger, he had applied to me by letter, asking my aid to get him into service—& I had made the attempt in vain. At last, notwithstanding the obvious objections of his being a stranger to our farming, & unacquainted with the government of slaves & also fearing that his health would suffer on my farm, (so different in climate from his former residence in Scotland—) I offered him the service, which he eagerly accepted. Though accustomed to a life of agricultural labor, he was a man of some education, & much more subsequent reading—& well acquainted with the agriculture of his own country. I did not expect very great administrative talent & superior direction of my farm. But I found attention, intelligence, fidelity to & regard for my interests—& moreover gratitude to myself. I had offered as wages $250 a year, which was a high rate—& subsequently, without his asking any increase & after the like engagement had been made for another year, I increased his wages to $300. Of course his family was supplied with house, food, servant, &c. as is the general usage of our country.

Mr. Nicol took good care of my affairs, & endeavored to carry into effect my plans as well as the means permitted. In fact the means were very scanty—& had been designedly kept so for years before. For I had found that no matter how much force of teams & hands was furnished, to my previous overseers, there was little or nothing done beyond the regular & necessary work for making a crop. But the most important value of my new overseer, & especially in my situation, was that he treated my slaves with kindness as well as justice, & they were well cared for in health & in sickness.

Mr. Nicol remained four years in my service, & in that of my son, (who succeeded me as part owner & sole director of the Coggins farm) & then, after being engaged for another year, an offer was made to Mr. Nicol, through me, so much to his advantage, that we consented that he should accept it, & yielded, for his benefit, our claim to his engaged service. The new situation was that of steward on the Sandy Point estate, the most valuable & extensive farm in Virginia, the property of Robert B. Bolling.[54] Mr. Nicol has continued in that service to this time (1851;) & while his own prior acquaintance with farming of high order, has had there a much better field for useful display than in my more limited & rude operations, I trust that still he was much the better qualified to act well in this new service because of having before been in mine. When our connexion was separated, we parted with feelings of mutual respect & regard.[55]

I would have preferred to be merely the editor of the agricultural periodical designed—leaving to some experienced publisher to be the proprietor, & to attend to the printing, publishing, & all the business & financial matters. But this could not be done in the then low condition of the publishing business in Virginia. No man of business, & no other than myself, was willing to incur the hazards of failure in the novel attempt. Of course I was obliged to be proprietor & publisher, as well as editor. Still I supposed that I could have the printing done, & well done, by contract. There was no want of printers, who were ready to undertake the work; & I could have had as many proposals as there were printing establishments for book or job work. But there was a greater & an insuperable difficulty, in obtaining the execution of the service in due time, & proper manner. I closed with the offer of Thomas W. White,[56] of Richmond, who was a good practical printer, & executed good work; & from whose office there did not issue any news paper or other periodical, until mine was undertaken. Of course I felt sure of the punctual issue, which is of vital importance to every periodical publication. But I soon found that my work merely served to employ hands upon the intervals of other smaller, transient, & therefore more profitable jobs. It followed that the issue of the monthly numbers was never in proper time—nor could I estimate upon any time. I had expected to select or prepare at home the matter for each number, & to transmit it early enough to the printer—& merely to have to be in Richmond two or three days, at most, just before closing & issuing each successive number. But when going for this purpose, I rarely was able to effect my object, even if staying there a week, in idleness. Before the close of the first year, these inconveniencies had become intolerable—& there were others not more tolerable. My next resource was to undertake the printing also. I engaged a competent master printer in Baltimore, & bought all the necessary printing apparatus & materials.[57] A printing office was arranged in a house at Shellbanks; & for two years, the printing was there executed, & the numbers mailed at the neighboring post office.[58]

There was now no difficulty in regard to the punctual issue—nor to the sound execution of the work. But no other work could be obtained for the establishment, which was necessarily on a larger scale of operations than my own work could furnish employment for. There was also much difficulty in securing hands, & especially to supply sudden vacancies, owing to the preference of such persons for the amusements of a town life.

There were other circumstances which operated more & more strongly as time passed to induce the change of my residence to a town. From the beginning of the demand, to the preceding year, I had been very fortunate in providing for the instruction of my children, at home, under a private tutor, who was a good scholar & an excellent teacher.[59] But my eldest son had already completed his course at home, & also at the University of Va, & my second son was about to enter college.[60] There remained as pupils only some of my daughters; & for these my friend & tutor advised me to procure, in preference to himself, a female teacher. This course was adopted. A female teacher was obtained, from the then only source of supply, New-England.[61] The female was employed upon recommendations—high enough of course. I found the female very deficient in the most ordinary scholarship, & as much so in lady-like manners; & after enduring her for six weeks, & finding things worse & worse, I paid her 6 months wages & discharged her. Being resolved never to import another teacher from the north, & none being available from any other source, I was the further urged to seek a new residence, convenient to good schools. This reason, concurring with the wants of my printing & publishing business, induced me to move with my family, to Petersburg, in the spring of 183[blank].[62] This step, as subsequent results showed, was the most injudicious that I could have taken for my own interest, & produced more loss & evil than any mere business act that I ever performed.

The ten years during which I conducted the "Farmers' Register," perhaps made up that portion of my life which was of most benefit to public interests, & also to my own reputation. Nevertheless, it brought to me so many causes of difficulty, disappointment & vexation—so many & heavy pecuniary losses—& withal so many subjects for self-condemnation, (in my injudicious conduct in business matters, & the mismanagement of my private affairs,) that it is more disagreeable for me to recur to & reflect upon this than any other time of my life. I shall therefore get through the memoranda of this time as quickly as possible. For the main subject, & nearly all the brighter lights of this time, & some of the shadows also, the ten volumes of the Farmers' Register serve as ample materials. The work itself tells of my early success, of my useful services to the improvement of agriculture, & of high appreciation of these services by very many of my countrymen. It is not of these, but of other incidental matters to which I must refer.

From some time before the commencement of this publication, & while residing at Shellbanks, my personal supervision & immediate direction of my farming at Coggins as was before stated, had almost ceased. The business therefore was ill managed, & altogether had become disagreeable to me. My new business of agricultural writer & publisher was now seen as engrossing & delightful as had formerly been my farming labors. When my residence was changed to town, I did not expect again to return to to the country, or to my earlier business. Hence I became desirous of selling all my landed estate & nearly all other property, because it would necessarily, without my presence & direction, yield little profit, & no pleasure. Investments in public stocks then offered high interest, & such income would be attained without trouble or care, and (as then believed) without risk. I should have effected this desired change of my property, but for the difficulty of finding a purchaser at fair price for my larger farm—& that I would not sell my slaves to any other person than to the purchaser of the farm, who would keep them together, & by which arrangement my negroes would not suffer in their change of ownership. condition.[63] This extensive sale could not be effected. But the very wish for it increased my separation from & aversion to my country business, & prevented all effort to increase the stock, & enlarge & improve the operations of the farm. During the interval between my leaving the country, in 1835, & the direction of the Coggins farm being assumed by my oldest son in 1839, I did not spend in all my visits, as much as 20 hours on the premises. At each visit I gave but a few hours to my farm, & the remainder of the time to my old friend Thomas Cocke, who lived at Tarbay, close adjoining.

It had been my purpose to give my sons good educations, & to fit them for working men, in such profession or business as they might prefer. I was entirely opposed to following the *universal* practice in Virginia, of every gentleman's son, who cannot inherit a sufficient patrimonial estate, (& many who do,) studying for either the profession of law or medicine. With these views, my oldest son, immediately after closing his course, & taking the degree of A.M. at the University of Va, had commenced the business of civil engineering, on the Richmond & Fredericksburg Railway, then just commenced. When this work was completed, he continued to serve, upon & throughout the construction of the Greensville & next the Raleigh & Gaston Railways.[64] During this time, the railway mania, as a prominent part of the general speculating madness, was at its height.[65] Subscriptions both from private individuals & from the state government could be had to execute every new railway scheme. Before the completion of the Raleigh & Gaston road the banks had all suspended payment, railway shares had ceased to pay dividends, & the bubbles of speculation had bursted everywhere. No more public works were begun, & some, in progress, were abandoned.[66] But few engineers could obtain employment. My son had risen to the next to the highest grade, that of Principal Assistant Engineer, and in that capacity had completed the northern half of the Raleigh & Gaston railway, which was begun & partly constructed by other direction. When this was done, he had no longer an engagement, nor the prospect of obtaining one, when there were at least ten unemployed engineers for every demand for one for service. He therefore determined to change his pursuits to farming. Some time previously he had married Mary C. Smith,[67] a young lady to whom he had been attached from the very early youth of both. By this marriage, in addition to many other & far greater acquisitions & sources of happiness, my son obtained considerable property, & very much more than I could expect to give to him as a sharer of my own property. If governed merely by regard to his pecuniary interest, he would at once have abandoned his previous employment, & devoted all his attention to the property of which he was now in possession. But he was fond of his profession, & ambitious to reach its highest grade. He had therefore persevered in the pursuit, not only to the sacrifice of greater interests elsewhere, but when family expenses & inconveniences in that situation were nearly as much in amount as his salary.

After vain attempts made by my son through some months to find for sale some suitable farm, the position of things brought back to my mind my before abandoned design of selling my land. This possession was preferred by my son, & also by his wife, to whose choice the decision was entirely submitted. The Coggins farm, & all its stock &c. except the slaves, were appraised by gentlemen the most competent to judge, & at their valuation, one half of the property was bought by my son. He brought to the farm slaves deemed of equal working value to mine, & under his entire direction & control, the farming operations were conducted, first on partnership, & subsequently at a rent for the land of one-fourth of the grain products, until in 1848, when the remainder of the land was sold to him. The place for his new dwelling had been selected principally with a view to health—near the river bank, & fully a mile from the old mansion.[68] In this most important respect, our hopes have been more than fulfilled in the healthiness of the locality. But in addition, the natural scenery was of rare beauty, & of great capability of being improved by art. The natural features have been preserved as much as possible, & still present the main attractions to the eye—though an excellent & handsome mansion has since been erected, & its yard & garden &c well improved with taste & care.[69]

This half of my farm was sold for $10,800; & at a later time (1848,) the other half at the same price. The payments were made at the convenience & choice of the purchaser. The first sale & entire transference of control of the farm, relieved me of what had become a grievous burden. My son began farming entirely inexperienced, & with everything to learn. He had indeed the recourse to my advice as to general matters; but with the expressed understanding that he was freely to reject it, unless approved by himself, & also that compliance was quite convenient. But the disadvantages of a new beginner were removed in a short time, & in a few years he was a better operative farmer than I had ever been—though still something in my mode of rough & slovenly & careless management of details.

I had removed to a town residence & town associations at the unfortunate time when the great expansion of paper banking, had begun to greatly depreciate the currency (without that effect being then known,) to enhance prices, & profits of almost everything[70]—& to stimulate speculation, & to reward the first & cunning operators, at the expense of the more tardy & ignorant followers, who made later investments & bore nearly all the final losses. I belonged to the latter class.

As I had never had enough enterprise to extend my farming capital & operations by incurring debt, nor even (to much extent) by using for that purpose my own subsequent accumulations of profits—and being entirely opposed to settling distant farms, I had had no employment for my money except in loans, or bond & security.[71] As I would take no more than legal interest, & required no payment of principal (unless at long notice, if need for it should occur,) there was no lack of applicants for loans, in the past great scarcity of money, & also the subsequent increased demand for purposes of speculation. My loans being deemed favors, were made in preference to such of my personal friends, or intimate acquaintance, as needed & applied for them. The expressed conditions were that the interest should be annually & punctually paid. I could not have acted more unwisely. Borrowers of money upon long time are of course pressed by other debts—& the dues last paid, whether of annual interest, or of principal when required, will be those of *friends*, & not of strangers. Of course my interest was paid regularly in but few cases, if indeed in any—and my requirements thereof, slow & few as they were, always gave offence to creditors[72] who were friends—whereas the demands on the very hour when due, from a stranger creditor, & even if a usurer & extortioner, would have been deemed all right. My business as a money lender, for a few years, was upon much more than my own score. My step-mother had requested me to relieve her of the duties of legal guardian to her three younger children, then minors, by assuming them myself.[73] This had placed in my hands very much more money than my own, which I had to lend, & for which it was still more necessary (being so required by law,) that I should have the interest punctually paid. When assuming this trust, I found some large existing debts insufficiently secured; & for these as well as for others of like suspicious responsibility, in after time, I was bound to require additional security—& in default of either sufficient security, or payments of interest without intolerable delay, I was compelled in a few cases to compel payment of the principal, & of course by resort to law. In no other case, either as guardian or for myself during these times, did I ever require, the payment of the principal of a bond, earlier than the convenience of the debtor directed. Yet, with all this course of moderation & of indulgence on my part, I lost something of the regard, if not incurring actual hostile feeling, from most of those debtors who had been my friends. And I do not think that there were any but two exceptions, in regard to long standing loans in such cases. Of course, I had become heartily tired of lending money—& still was at much loss to know what else to do with my capital in money.

But my removal to town soon relieved me of this difficulty—& also, in time, of much more of my capital than I then had surplus. Under the stimulus of a greatly expanded paper currency, all sorts of joint stocks of incorporated companies were created, for constructing railways, cotton factories, & working gold mines or other mineral treasures. Nearly all that had gone into operation were paying large annual dividends, (& very often out of the capital stock,) & of some not yet in operation, the stock was largely above par value. As an example—when books for subscriptions to the Greensville Railway were opened, the whole sum required was subscribed in an hour, & some 30 or 40 per cent. over. In a few months, & long before the completion of the road, this stock sold at 15 per cent. above par, on the investment to be paid. No wonder that I congratulated myself upon being a subscriber for & holder of this stock for 10,000$. Behold, I had cleared $1500 thereupon in a few months, & before half my subscription had been called for. Yet this road did not pay a cent of dividend until some 15 years after its completion, & its being in full use.

In this & other like investments, I was made to suffer the consequences of the then great abuses of the banking system, & the general misconduct of the banks of this country.[74] And I who had been, & still was, strongly opposed to the system, & who would never have any concern with banks, (other than something to deposit money in them,) was as blind to the present condition of things, as were nearly all other persons, including the wise & the prudent no less than the foolish. To the latter class, in matters of business & finance, I certainly belonged, notwithstanding all my success in accumulation, both before & subsequent to these times, from other sources, & by other action. Whatever may have been my powers of mind in certain directions, (now, alas! woefully impaired by age in all—) I was always very deficient in observation of details, & of things which would be noticed by even ignorant & dull minds. I was greatly wanting in judgment—the most useful of all the different mental powers—& this is much the same thing as being wanting in common-sense, as understood in common parlance. Especially was I ignorant of men—& was subject always to be deluded by my credulity & trust in their professions, of which the falsehood, or improbability would have been suspected by, if not evident to other persons. When I now look back, & think of the many times in which I have given implicit faith to the unsupported assertions of strangers, & in consequence, have committed my interest to the charge of their capacity & integrity—& that nearly all such acts of trust were misplaced—I am astonished that my losses, in such respects, many as they were, should not have been ten-times more in amount. Probably I was saved from utter ruin from this foolish & misplaced confidence in persons, not correctly or fully known, by two safe-guards. One of these was, my fixed rule of not incurring debts—& the other of not standing as security for the debts of other persons. This last rule was easily impressed on me by the advice & the statements of my grandfather,[75] who was equally confiding & more yielding than myself—& who lost large sums by being security for other persons. My making no debts for myself rendered it easy for me to avoid being security for those of other persons. My having adopted this avoidance as a general rule of conduct, served as a sufficient excuse to all persons applying for such aid—& soon relieved me from them, & the pain of refusing. I have indeed varied from the strictness of this rule in a few cases—for friends for whom I was willing, if necessary, to lose the sums involved—& by which some losses were sustained, & which attempts to aid I do not regret for myself, but only that they were of no use to the parties designed to be thus served.

So long as I had lived secluded on my farm, these defects of my mind had not been much brought into operation. I had but few business transactions with men, in buying, selling, or bargaining—& these in values generally understood by all. I had nothing to sell, but my annual surplus grain—& for that, had merely to know the then market prices. My purchases, for articles of family & farm use & consumption, were more numerous & more difficult; but still in them no very great errors could well be made. But in my new business & residence, my incapacity was tasked daily, & in every matter of business—& in almost every trial I was made a loser.

Having determined some time before to make no more new loans to individuals, it was necessary to fix upon some other modes of investment. My confidence in railway or other joint-stock companies was of slow growth. And before I would venture to hold any such stock, I had become the creditor of the Petersburg & Roanoke R.R. Co.[76] for several thousand dollars of their bonds. These bonds were convertible to stock, at the pleasure of the holder; & the annual dividends had for some time been as high as 10 per cent. before I ventured to exchange my 6 per cent. bonds of the company, for its (then) 10 per cent. stock. When I did so convert the bonds, the price of the stock was about 14 per cent. above par value—at which advance I bought as much more stock as made in all 50 shares of $5000, at $100 the original subscription price per share. Further investments in this favorite stock were only prevented by my preferring to subscribe for new lines, which were supposed would be as profitable—& all these were expected to yield regularly 15 per cent. per annum. In this delusion I was led by the advice of those best-informed persons, in whose opinions I confided—& some of whom doubtless believed what they said. But they bought railway shares to speculate upon—& I for permanent investments. Indeed, I never bought any stocks, or other more tangible property upon speculation—but to hold for the income expected. I have already adverted to my investment in the Greensville R.R. Still worse, I subscribed $10,000 to the Raleigh & Gaston R.R., & subsequently bought some 20 shares more—which road was bankrupt from the beginning—never paid a cent of dividend—& finally was mortgaged & sold for its debts. When prices of these stocks began to fall rapidly, & prospects were very gloomy, I went to consult with my former advisers as to what they designed to do with their shares, & to know what sacrifice I ought to meet in disposing of mine. But I found that most of my advising friends had sold out their interests long before. For a long time, these three investments were all profitless—& I at that time supposed my whole outlay (some $27,000,) in these three railways a total loss. But this was the case only with the R. & G. The other two have lately been paying 6 to 7 per cent. annual dividends; though still the [price?] of the stock is greatly below par, showing the [amount?] of public confidence in the stability of the present profits.

These were my largest but not my only stock investments. I bought shares in existing cotton factories, at a premium, & in unused water-power at enormous appreciation for prospective factories which have never been (& never will be) commenced. All these, I either sold subsequently at loss—or have retained the right, because unsalable, to what is totally worthless.

And these were not all the supposed profitable investments which my town residence induced. I bought at different times, when prices were sinking, three tenements, all great bargains, as then supposed. But they sunk still lower—& finally, after deriving little or nothing as rent, for 3 to 9 years' possession, these tenements were all successively sold for much less than they had cost me at first purchase.[77]

Still there were other & more losing investments, or other [*illeg.*] of money. But enough has been said on this subject.

I have brought together in one view on this subject, the occurrences of ten to fifteen years. However numerous & great were my losses, of this kind, they had all been paid for before being incurred. And my income from my farm, my still remaining monied capital, & especially from the publication of the Farmers' Register from the earlier time of its existence, enabled me to bear these losses as they successively & gradually occurred. But before the close of my publication business, that also was to become a source of loss.

The subscriptions to the Farmers' Register amounted to more than 1000, at $5 each, before the first volume was completed.[78] The number of copies printed (or for which I paid for printing) was 1500 to 2000 for the first 3 vols. The copies not issued immediately to existing subscribers, were kept, in several numbers, or in sheets. And whether from carelessness in the printers, or deficiency of sheets in the quires of paper, it was found subsequently that the copies of particular numbers fell very far short of the estimate. A single short number or sheet, of course was equivalent to reducing all others to the same short measure. So my first serious loss was the losing some 100 to 300 copies of one or all the first three volumes—for which I had fully paid.

The later gradual demand for the work from the beginning in time absorbed all the remaining copies of vol. 1, (perhaps 1400 altogether saved.) When these were all exhausted, & still more were demanded by new subscribers, I bought back from subscribers as many copies as I could obtain of vol. 1, first at $5, & finally at $6, to furnish to buyers at $5, to complete their sets, ordered from the beginning. And when no more could be re-purchased, I at last printed another edition, of 500 copies, of nine out of the twelve Nos. of vol 1. But after incurring this expense, there was but little more demand for sets from the beginning of the work; so this expense was another considerable loss.

The low-priced agricultural papers were then being established throughout the northern states, & this seemed to diminish my subscription list. The "Cultivator" of Albany, in its original smallest size, had been issued at 25 cents a year.[79] The publisher was enabled to do this, & with profit, because the N.Y. State Agricultural Society, in advance, authorized the publication & generated the sale of 20,000 copies. The low price, & the influence of the numerous members of this rich & public-spirited society, induced enough demand for this large edition—& the demand continued, while the price of the paper (as enlarged) was increased to $1. Still, though much smaller than the F.R. it was much cheaper in proportion to size. Besides the very far greater circulation of this & other northern papers, which alone would have made lower prices more remunerative than in my case, there were other elements of cheapness in the lower cost of northern printing, & engraving.

Most foolishly I attempted to compete with these cheaper publications. I could not at once put down the price of the F.R. to one half. But I thought to induce my subscribers, & others, to enable me to do so ultimately, by holding out inducements to them to procure other subscribers. Thus, without lowering the price for single copies, I offered in the proposals for vol 4 & thereafter, to supply two copies to an old subscriber & a new name sent at the same time, for the price of a single copy. To meet the very large demand that I expected, I increased the regular impression from 2000 to 4000 copies—& persisted in this for some 4 years. All worked wrong. Not many of my old subscribers availed themselves of the reduction offered them—& yet many were discontented because others embraced them. They reasoned thus: "If the work can be furnished to some persons for half-price, it might be to all—& all paid beyond that amount is extortion."

Thus my list did not much increase, while I was printing to supply thrice the actual number. I still estimated my profits by the amount due. But much the larger portion of the debts in arrears were never paid; & of the portion collected, much of the amount fell to the share of the collectors. All my expenses & difficulties were increased by my ignorance of the business I was carrying on—& the net receipts as much diminished for the same reason.

Not satisfied with my losses & difficulties caused by conducting one publication, at different times I planned several others. Of these, all either were abortive attempts from the beginning, or so far as executed were at my entire cost & loss.

The political state of the country for some years succeeding the stoppage of all bank payments in 1837, & the consequent financial difficulties, appeared to me very favorable for the enunciating & establishing sound political principles.[80] The old state-rights doctrines had long become mere idle words—& both the then existing great political parties were as destitute of principle as was possible. This was during the presidency of Van Buren. I projected a monthly magazine & review, which, while free from all adherence to either of the existing political parties, would maintain the original state-rights doctrines, & the principles of the old republican party. Any one of the least judgment could have foretold the utter failure of such a scheme. For the publication, in exposing political abuses & corruption, would necessarily oppose both the great parties, embracing nearly every citizen, & there was no party organization, & but a few isolated individuals from whom my scheme could derive aid & support. My only promised & afterwards actual co-laborers, as writers, were indeed two able men—Judge Abel Upshur,[81] & Professor Beverly Tucker.[82] Professor Thomas R. Dew,[83] also allowed me to expect the aid of his forceful pen, but did not contribute any thing in the short existence of the "Southern Magazine".[84] I issued a prospectus, which will be here copied, & will show the principles & objects of the designed periodical.[85] In advance of any subscription, the first monthly number, was printed & sent abroad as a specimen. With this issue, it was intended to suspend the publication until it had received sufficient promise of support from subscribers to venture to proceed. But my anxiety to put before the public an able review, by Judge Upshur, of the then pending difficulties between the governments of Virginia & New York in reference to the kidnapping of slaves,[86] induced me to issue a second number of the magazine. This, in printing, amounted to one sixth of a whole year's expense; & still more, as a considerable stock of paper suited for the work & also a new font of type, had been bought for this purpose. I did not obtain the names of 200 subscribers—& the scheme was necessarily abandoned, with the total loss of all the costs. For in issuing proposals, subscribers had been notified & requested not to send any payment, until the regular continuance of the work should be begun, & made known. In some few cases, notwithstanding this prohibition, subscribers had remitted a year's payment. In all such cases, their money was either returned, or if distance made such return hazardous & costly, an equivalent was supplied of my other established publication. Thus, no one lost anything by the failure of the Southern Magazine, except myself.

For the only two numbers of this work, I wrote the greater portion of the original matter. My pieces were "Revolution in Disguise[87]—a review of Condy Raguet's[88] work on "Currency & Banking"—a review of the "Bland Papers"[89] an article on the condition of Liberia, & the causes of failure of the colonization scheme—"Bubbleton" (an allegorical exposition of the then existing evils of fraudulent banking,)—& all the short editorial notices of other inserted articles.

Another minor periodical, the "Bank Reformer" I issued, for its designed limit of six months, & circulated 3000 copies of each monthly number, & also a concluding supplement. As this circulation was expected to be almost entirely gratuitous, & at my own cost, I was at least not disappointed in that being the result. But the causes of this procedure are of earlier dates, to which I will now return.

In 1837 the full-blown bubble of paper currency bursted. All the banks in the U.S. suspended specie payments. The market value of the bills of the Virginia banks at once fell 10 per cent. below their normal value. Universal commercial & pecuniary difficulties overspread all classes of people—& the public treasuries in still greater degree. The legislature of Va was immediately called, & as designed by the call, that body legalized the suspension of payments by the banks, by repealing the before existing very stringent penalties for any failure to pay. Moreover, the collection of debts in any other currency than the depreciated bank bills was by legislation made impossible; so that, in effect, this depreciated currency, & to any extent of depreciation, was made a legal tender.⁹⁰ Thus, (as had been done before,) these enactments were flagrant violations of constitutional rights in two respects, viz: the making bank paper a legal tender, in effect, & of course the only currency—& in impairing the obligations of prior contracts between individuals. For when a debtor was enabled, by law, to pay a previously existing debt of $100 with bank paper nominally promising to pay $100, but in fact worth but $90, the creditor had one-tenth of his due confiscated by the government,—& that not for benefit of the treasury, nor even of the debtor, but for the banks, which by their fraudulent course had involved all creditors in this general calamity.

At first, to those like myself not initiated in the practical operations of banks, (however much I had studied & had opposed the principles of the American banking system,) this suspension of the banks of Va was deemed an unavoidable result, & to be of transient duration. In this belief, I felt disposed to excuse the delinquency, & to submit without complaint to my share of the evil effects on the community. Any solvent bank, so situated, by merely suspending further issues of paper currency (as new loans,) could have resumed payments in a few months. But this, the only honest course, would have cut off not only the before excessive but also the most moderate profits of the banks. Moreover, it would have left unsupplied the craving borrowing class, for the benefit of which all our banks have been established. Further—not only did this class of borrowers constitute directly an important proportion of the legislative bodies, but indirectly influenced the action of the remainder. And in Va, where the commonwealth is in partnership with the banks, the treasury would have greatly suffered if the banks were not sustained in their profits, & of course in their fraudulent denial of payments to all creditors. The banks not only did not draw in their circulation, but actually increased its previous expansion—which they could now do safely, having no fear of being compelled to redeem their bills.⁹¹ Instead of a suspension of payments for a short & necessary time, the legislative farce was repeated for five successive years of remitting all bank penalties, & extending the remission to the commencement of the next session—when, instead of the always promised resumption of payments, another act of remission & indulgence to further suspension would be passed.

After seeing that this was the settled policy of the banks & the government—& that the whole community submitted, almost without a murmur to this enormous system of fraud & pillage, unexampled for the deliberation & perseverance with which it was prosecuted, I determined to resist, if I stood alone. And, in Virginia at least, I did stand alone in my open denunciations of, & struggle against, this iniquity. There were very few persons connected with the newspaper press, or residents of towns, or in any way concerned in traffic, who were not, directly or indirectly under the influence & control of the banks. Even if not then debtors to banks, all such persons thought they might need loans—& their chance for obtaining them would be utterly destroyed by any expression of disapprobation of the conduct of the banking powers.

In my original prospectus of the Farmers Register, (& which had been republished repeatedly in after years,) one of the classes of subjects promised to be embraced was "The discus[sion][92] of such subjects of political economy as are connected with the preservation & support of the interests of agriculture."[93] Subjects of this class had in many cases been discussed. But not one question had arisen of such momentous bearing on the interests of the agricultural community as that of the existence & continuance, without limit of either time or amount, of this irresponsible issue of irredeemable paper currency—& that paper moreover constituting the only currency of the whole country. Yet when I attempted to defend the interests of agriculturists & the public from this worst of evils, my course was denounced by not only the people of towns but also many of the country, as violently as if my conduct had been that of their plunderers, instead of one striving to protect them from being plundered.

The immediate occasion of my commencing this discussion in the Farmers' Register, was an article in another agricultural paper, the American Farmer, by the editor John S. Skinner,[94] who then was & thereafter continued the zealous advocate of the great benefits of the paper money banking system—(for none other has ever existed in this country.) In this article he correctly mentioned that the discussion of the currency question belonged properly to agricultural papers—while he distinctly showed his opinion in favor of the system of paper currency. I copied all the material portion of this article in the Farmers' Register, & added the following editorial comment:

"We entirely concur [p. 157. vol 9] is so much wanting. ED. F. R."[95]

After this beginning, there followed various articles of my writing, in which the evil principles of the banking system of this country were displayed, as well as the beneficial operation of the proper banking system of discount & deposite. Other pieces exposed the particular iniquities of the recent & present action of the then non-paying banks of Virginia especially. As might have been expected, & to which I had no objection, these articles excited the most rancorous hostility of the principal actors in bank operations & frauds permitted by law—& of their principal tools. But to all my numerous charges brought, in general terms in the Farmers' Register, & with more particular & pointed application in the Bank Reformer, & during all the time of about a year through which most of these publications of mine appeared—to all my denunciations & exposures of the general & particular frauds of the system, & the implication of numerous individuals of high standing, who as bank directors participated in these legalized frauds, not one of my charges was ever met in print, or any issue thereupon brought fairly before the public view. But while the actors in these iniquities, & their tools, (among whom the editors of newspapers were the most efficient,)[96] thus studiously shunned all open discussion of my arguments & charges, they used every weapon of falsehood, calumny, & of denunciation, to do me injury. For strenuously defending the plundered interests of agriculture, & speaking undeniable truths in their defence, I was assailed & calumniated by all the crew of plunderers, & had no one to sustain me among all those whom I sought to defend. Even personal violence was resorted to, & attempted in manner the most cowardly & assassin-like, & infamous (if justly judged—) & yet all the whole procedure seemed to be at least tacitly excused by the community of Petersburg, & openly applauded by many of the least scrupulous. Indeed, if I had been a bank director, & as such had participated in the most enormous acts of plunder of the duped & cheated agricultural & general interest, I should not have incurred from the plundered class a tythe of the odium which I did by trying to defend them from plunderers. All my admitted services to agriculture were deemed by many farmers, who had most valued these services, as insufficient to atone for my opposition to their supposed interest in upholding the banks, in all their acts of wrong-doing.[97]

The laws which were annually thus enacted, (indeed at three several times in each of most of the annual sessions of the legislature,) to allow the continued suspension of payments by the banks, were not literally what they were termed.[98] The legislature did not fully authorize this flagrant wrong—but it did what was equivalent in effect. The legal obligation on the banks to pay their debts of every kind, & of course for their bills in circulation & checks drawn on them for deposites, remained untouched on the statute. But all the stringent & summarily available penalties for non-compliance which before existed were repealed, or their operation suspended. Before, the banks were subject to summary judgments, by mere notice in court, & very heavy interest &

damages to their wronged & suing creditors, besides forfeiture of all their chartered privileges, if convicted of the offence of refusing to pay their bills on application. However efficient in operation was the suspension law to guard the banks from performing their obligations, the offenders were still liable to the ordinary censure of law, as in the case of all other debtors. Thus, the holder of a bank bill might sue for his debt in the courts, & obtain judgment & levy execution. But there would have been so many difficulties in the way, because of the entire novelty of the attempted process, & the ambiguity of the bank laws in this respect—there were so many legal quibbles which would be used to evade or delay trial—& the banks were so well defended by able counsel—it was so essential to their interest to foil every creditor who insisted on payment—that a suit at law against a bank for debt, would have been certainly defeated by trick & delay. Thus it was in the power of the bank to throw more loss, in delay of payment & in legal costs, on even a finally successful suing creditor, than he would have sustained by being cheated of even double the depreciation of the bills to be sued on.[99] Of course, there was not a single case of any creditor suing a bank, because of the refusal to pay its bills.

These difficulties & impossible obstructions were so obvious, that I did not attempt this course, though willing to incur some loss to enforce such claims, & to punish the offender even if suffering more myself. But success at any cost was hopeless. Still there was summary process remaining for debts under $10, which could be sued for (by warrant as it is called,) before any single magistrate, without any form, & nothing being required except to prove the debt, & that the debtor shall have notice to defend. I had secured some $5 bills of two of the banks in Petersburg. On two of these bills, one against each bank, I brought a warrant every week. It was then the usage for a magistrate of the town to sit one certain day in every week to try warrants. My first suit of this kind, & all the succeeding, were regularly & at length argued by counsel on both sides. My claim was simply for the payment of a $5 bill of the bank on its face professing to be payable on demand—& which payment had been demanded & refused. The suspension of payments had become a party question to this extent; the whigs unanimously sustained the suspension, & all the inequities of the banks. Nearly all the democrats, (making the regular majority in the legislature & in the state,) opposed these offences strongly *in words*; but there were always enough of the party to vote with the whigs in all bank questions to serve to sustain every abuse practiced by the banks. As these renegades from the principles claimed for the democratic party never lost their political position, or influence, by thus siding with the banks, I held the whole party responsible, and, as a party, deemed it no better than the whigs in regard to the bank question. It seemed to me impossible that any magistrate, whatever might be his party, or political bias, could have decided against my claim. Yet, at three or more different days of trial every whig magistrate did so decide & upon different ground each time, each of inconceivable absurdity. The course was this. If the sitting magistrate was a whig, he gave judgment against me of course. If it happened that a democrat was sitting, a whig magistrate was sent for, & who quickly obeyed the call made for the bank, & by his decision neutralized that of the other magistrate who was in my favor. Thus the contest had continued, weekly, & four or five different whig magistrates had all decided against my usual claims. But though no one of these bank tools refused to perform the required duty, still it was a disagreeable & dirty business, & no one was willing to so forswear himself twice, until every one of his fellows had taken his turn once. Thus it seemed that I should exhaust all the whig majority of the magistrates without having one to sit twice, or their even permitting a democrat to decide once. But at last, it happening that one of the latter was the sitting magistrate—a plain & honest man, in an humble but independent position, & with whom I had no acquaintance. No whig could be found ready to come (as before,) & defeat the first magistrate's expected verdict—& by this accident, for the first time a judgment was given in my favor. As soon as this was done, all opposition ceased—& my remaining $5 bills were thereafter paid when presented, & I had no more opportunity for executing the law. If the decision of this one magistrate, in opposition to all the preceding, had been illegal, or erroneous for any reason, certainly it would have been easy enough for learned counsel to expose the error; & such exposure would have strengthened the cause of the bank much more than it would have been weakened by the erroneous decision. But not only was no such exposure attempted, but not a word was uttered in opposition to this decision.

Before this decision, my defeats had been matters of triumph for every bank man, & of ridicule cast on my efforts. When the one late decision of a plain & illiterate but upright magistrate had served to overthrow all the legal quibbles & defences of the banks, & to stand as undoubtedly correct, it might have been expected that any persons who had participated in the prior unjust decisions against me, would have said something in their justification, if still deeming themselves right—

or of regret, & apology to me, if convinced of their having done me injustice. But not a word, on either score, was uttered by any individual, nor by any one of the newspaper editors who had rejoiced to publish far & wide my defeated efforts.

The prior decisions against me had involved another absurdity. The bank bill standing as a mere evidence of debt, being decided against, was necessarily rendered invalid. Like a fraudulent or illegal account, against which final judgment had been given, it should (by law & usage) have remained in the constable's hands, as a mere voucher of the judgment, & in no case to be returned to the plaintiff as his property. So that by these judgments, if duly carried out, I ought to have been deprived of my bank bills, just as if they had been proved counterfeits. But this deduction, however legitimate, was too monstrous; & after some weeks delay, & the later judgment in my favor, all the other bills were returned to me, I believe by the mere motion & sense of right of the constable.[100]

The infamous manner in which the bank tools exhibited their hostility to me, made me more resolved to persevere in my course. A more extended field was required for my action than the pages of the Farmers' Register offered, & therefore I established the Bank Reformer, to be issued monthly, and as before stated, 3000 copies were circulated gratuitously at my own expense.[101] This publication was devoted exclusively to exposures of the evils & frauds of the banks, & the banking system.

The hostility excited against me was used to injure & cripple the circulation of the Farmers' Register—& with much effect.[102] This action, & its result, I had early foreseen, & had fully appreciated the force of the malignant influence. But it did not in the least lessen my efforts in the contest.

These occurrences took place during the issue of the 9th volume of the Farmers' Register. At its end, my publication business was almost profitless; but as so extended a business could not be closed at once, I determined to do so at the end of the 10th volume, & of another year.[103] This intention was much earlier announced—and at the time designated, carried into effect. I then retired from that bond of connexion with the public in Virginia—disappointed & mortified—soured with the injustice & ingratitude of my countrymen, & with a determination never to renew a connexion with the public in any form.

I omitted a previous occurrence. A year before this time, the legislature of Va had instituted a Board of Agriculture, though upon a most parsimonious & totally inefficient plan.[104] I was appointed by the governor one of the 8 members which constituted this board—& also was made its secretary, by the votes of the members. The Board did very little—except to plan operations which not one but myself ever attempted to perform. A number of reports were made to the Board, of which reports I wrote about one half the whole number & amount of matter. These reports were published first in the Farmers' Register—& subsequently collected in a legislative document, published the next session.[105]

I was soon heartily tired of belonging to this inefficient body—& which could not be much better, upon the niggardly existing organization. But I had no good excuse for withdrawing my services, until one was furnished in my being appointed by the government of South Carolina to conduct an agricultural survey of that state.[106] I then resigned my place on the Board of Agriculture.

This to me highly honorable appointment by the government of S. Ca. was made in December 1842, just at the close of my publication of the Farmers Register, & when my arrangements for that close, so far as depended on my own action, had just been completed. Before commencing with my new service, I will concisely state the closing scenes of the old.

To enable me to carry on the publication of the F.R. it had been necessary to establish an excellent printing office, fitted to do much more work than merely my own publication. Some few original works were printed for their authors, & in good style.[107] But so little of other printing than my own was offered that the establishment was more costly throughout than to have paid a fair price for my printing, if it could have been so obtained. Why it could not, has been before stated.

When closing my business, I had an office well furnished in type, presses, & all printing materials, & 4 capable apprentices, indentured to me & who had been taught in my office.[108] Their remaining times of service I had no right to transfer, & so they were all lost to me. The printing materials I sold, & rented the office to my head printer, Laurens Wallazz,[109] who had engaged to print the F.R. to be continued by Thomas S. Pleasants.[110] The latter failed soon in this & other engagements; & by his breach of contract with Mr. Wallazz, caused to the latter a ruinous loss. Under these circumstances, I released Mr. Wallazz from his obligations to me both as tenant of the office, & buyer of the printing establishment. There was no other chance for sale of such property, in a little town like Petersburg, & by an absent proprietor like myself. The house remained closed, & tenantless, for some length of time, & finally I gave away the contents.[111]

When closing my publication, there remained due to me for subscriptions about $8000. Of this amount, I received from collecting agents something more than $500—& less than $50 paid to me voluntarily by subscribers in after time. Whether the large remainder was entirely or mostly withheld by the indebted subscribers, or that part, whether small or large, was paid to sub-collectors & not accounted for to their principal—or was even collected & retained after they had been discharged from this employment, (which might well have been the case, & I kept entirely ignorant of the facts—) I have no means of ascertaining. But in whatever means it occurred, I have never received $600 of the $8000 thus due to me.[112]

Nearly 1000 subscribers remained on the list, when I transferred it. Mr. Pleasants was an excellent agricultural writer, & had acquired my entire confidence as a man of truth & honor. I knew he was careless & dilatory in business matters, & slow in his payments. But I deemed him a man without guile, & of the purest integrity. I had trusted him, in our previous transactions, for advances made for him on various scores, & of which I never kept any account, & of which dues to me, not a cent has since been paid. In transferring to him the possession & prospective profits of the F.R. by our contract he was to pay me $500 a year, & have the privilege of buying the property in the publication at $3000 if he should so choose at a later time. He was to pay Mr. Wallazz for the printing, & thus would have it done more economically than I had. The subscription list, & the condition of the publication, independent of better prospects of the new editor, offered a safe return, after paying all expenses. But in fact, not one article of expense was paid for during the whole duration of the continued publication, (which was only 3 months—) & the poor printer, after being ruined, only at a much later time, obtained payment for printing but one of the three numbers for which payment was due to him. The paper-maker got nothing. And these were the only two expenses of printing to pay for by Mr. Pleasants under this new arrangement.

The printer was to have been paid for each monthly No. as soon as it was issued. When three had been printed, & not a cent had been paid him for either, he wrote to me (then in S. Ca.) for advice as to what he should do. He was acquainted with the terms of the contract between P. & myself; & therefore knew that if the publication was stopped its possible future value would be all lost to me. This loss he was very unwilling to cause—& he had reason to believe that if he discontinued the printing, no other printer could be engaged, as no one would serve without being paid. I was thunderstruck by the communication. But promptly advised W. not to regard my interest in the matter, but to stop at once the further waste of his own labor & expenses in printing, which were his all. He did cease to print the work—& therefore without a word of apology or even of notice to the subscribers, the publication itself ceased & was never renewed. How much money had been paid by subscribers to Mr. Pleasants before this cessation, I have no means of knowing—as he printed no monthly lists of such payments, as had been my uniform usage. But I infer, from their former usage, that a large portion of the subscribers had remitted their dues for the year in advance, & very early in the year. I know also that some others were remitted after the publication had stopped, & were neither returned nor acknowledged. Further—some who owed arrears to me, improperly & very foolishly sent them to Pleasants, (or at least so they stated.) Of these alleged payments, inquiry was made of P. by letter of my agent, twice over, & no answer was returned. It happened that for the $500 rent to be paid me for the first year's use of the F.R. as a new matter of business, I had obtained P.'s bond & security. This was subsequently paid to me by his security. But all the previous dues to me, making several hundred dollars more, I have never received payment, nor asked for it. Of all my erroneous opinions formed of men, none has equalled that which I had found & long entertained for Mr. Pleasants.

During the time of supposed universal prosperity, just before the banks suspending payment, & the accompanying prostration of values & of profits, I had made a rough estimate of the then value of my property, & made it to be near or quite $100,000. This was before any of the considerable losses before referred to had taken place, or at least were known to me. These & other actual losses, at different times, as afterwards supposed, amounted to more than $30,000. In this estimate all my investments in the Greensville Railway $10,000 was included—though that, after being dead capital for 15 years, began to pay dividends, & of course was not a final & total loss. And I did not include in that estimate the later heavy losses of subscription dues, my printing establishment, & other matters connected. But if counting the losses in railway shares by the correct & [*illeg.*] estimates of later times, & adding thereto all other known & considerable losses in investments of capital & failure of debtors, my general loss in these respects was not less than

$30,000. If the loss in the printing establishment &c. value of my publication, & debts from subscribers (or collecting agents) were added, they would greatly swell the amount. But I do not include them in this estimate of loss; but put them as more than absorbing all the otherwise clear profit that would have been derived from the Farmers' Register, with its actual patronage or support, & if properly managed in its business matters.

If I had succeeded in purchasing a suitable farm, which I had been for two years trying in vain to effect, I could not have accepted the honorable charge offered to me in S.C.[113] But being, of necessity, without present employment, & entirely disinclined to remain a resident of Petersburg, where I with my family still occupied a house of my own, I was free to undertake the service. Accordingly, I so wrote to Gov. Hammond,[114] but limited my acceptance & time of service to one year only. The appointment had been made for two years—& the appropriation for the salary ($2000 a year) also. In a few weeks after receiving notice of my appointment, I was in Charleston, & forthwith commenced the duties of my office. As my labors were of course vagrant, & on routes & in places which were the most uncertain & irregular, absence from my family was a necessary incident to the service. My wife & younger children, (the three older being then settled in their respective houses,) continued to reside in our house in Petersburg. Between the beginning & end of my year's service in S.C. I made but three short visits to my family.

It is unnecessary to state here any particulars of my procedure in S.C. The Report which I made to the legislature at the end of the year states fully the general results.[115] I also kept a very minute private journal for about the first half year, & for nearly all the time spent in the lower country.[116] I may presume to claim that no person employed by any government, for discretionary duties, ever labored more constantly & assiduously than I did. I did not spend a day without more or less labor, & generally with full labor for all the day, during all my service in S.C. until my health sunk under the exposure to swamp miasma, & I was obliged to resort to rest in the upper mountain region. After this, I was attacked much more severely, & also very strangely by a different disease—and had not recovered when I resigned my office at the end of the year, & returned home. The last few weeks of my field duties were well & faithfully performed for me by my second son, Julian, who left his farm & business to give me that assistance.[117] The results of his investigations, on localities which I could not before visit, I submitted to the Governor of S.C in a supplementary report, written after our return to Virginia.

I had entered upon the duties of the agricultural survey of S.C. with sanguine & high-wrought expectations of being able to induce the use of the beds of marl—which I knew, from very slight previous information, to be rich & very extensive—& which my personal investigations showed to be very far exceeding all that had been known to any residents in both respects. I hoped thus to enrich the state, & thereby to exalt my own reputation. But I have been greatly disappointed in the issue; & am compelled to believe that the results have not yet amounted in value to the state to one-thousandth part as much as I had expected, or as would have been, if my instructions had been only followed by even one person in the hundred of all those to whom they were suited to greatly benefit.

My labors & great & imprudent exposure in S.C. had not only seriously damaged my health for the latter half of the time of service, but, as was feared, had permanently impaired my always feeble constitution. I had not been well during the last five months of the year—& I returned home still sick, & under medical regimen. But my health soon was gradually improving; & in the engrossment of new & interesting labors which followed my speedy change of residence to Hanover county, I neglected my regimen, & forgot my sickness, even before the symptoms had entirely abated.

While I was in S.C. & not long before my expected return to Virginia, I received notice of a public expression of the high estimation of my former countymen, of Prince George, of the benefits of my early labors to themselves & to the agriculture of Va, & an invitation to attend a public dinner, & to accept other testimonials of respect. The correspondence, & report of the consequent proceedings will be copied here. In accepting the invitation, I fixed upon an early day after my expected return to my home. The scene for the entertainment was at Garysville, near to my former [*illeg.*] residences at Coggins & Shellbanks, & in the midst of the large neighborhood over which the improvement by marling had been commenced & extended over, from my example & instructions.

I knew that I should be expected to make a dinner speech; as I had no experience in that way, & no habit of public speaking of any kind, I prepared in writing, in advance of the occasion, the remarks which will be here copied; & when called for, endeavored, by recollection, to express the same in substance, though not at all in the same words. The printing was from my writing. I designed to improve the occasion to present in strong but entirely truthful expressions, the actual benefits which had been produced by the introduction & use of marl in that county, where its extended use had been earliest, & the most beneficial. The facts which I stated were uttered in the presence of the children or other successors of my earliest followers & co-laborers in this mode of improvement, & each one of whom knew, either by general report, or personally, the facts in all the matters referred to as having occurred in that county. In the presence & hearing of so many witnesses, who could have detected any inaccuracy or exaggeration of statement, no speaker, in my circumstances, even if disposed to misstate or exaggerate facts, would have dared so to depart from the strict limits of truth. Therefore, though I was the utterer of the testimony, & not a disinterested witness, all my auditors, in effect, were confirmers of all that I there said. In this view, the proceedings were not merely deserving of notice as complimentary to me for important services, of peculiar character, to my country, but much more in presenting full & unquestionable testimony of the mode & results of a great improvement—social, moral, & political, as well as agricultural. Yet, except in a new paper in Petersburg, of extremely limited circulation,[118] these proceedings were not published, nor even adverted to, by any paper in Virginia—nor elsewhere, except in the Charleston Mercury, of S.C.[119] The two principal papers of Virginia, the Enquirer & the Whig, had been especially requested by the meeting to publish the proceedings—without the slightest notice being paid to the request. If any such complimentary dinner had been given to any political personage, though noted only for the unscrupulous promoting of his own private interests, or his altogether selfish ambition— or to any worthless vagabond of military life—some foreign traveller of no account at home—or even if a presentation of plate had been made to a very ordinary stage-player, (as has since been done by some of the *elite* of Richmond society,)—any of these proceedings would have been republished in every paper in Virginia, none of which noticed the only such honors ever offered to me. I confess that I was deeply mortified by this general neglect, which however was but in accordance with the general slighting & ungrateful conduct which I had long experienced from the public in my native state. And this circumstance strengthened my previous determination to withdraw into the most perfect seclusion, consistent with the full extent of social intercourse, with neighbors &

friends, & with all who sought to become my friends. But further service to the public, & all intercourse with the public, I designed carefully to avoid.[120]

For more than two years before I gave up the direction of the Farmers' Register, I had been anxious to change my residence & pursuits, & especially desirous to return to the country, & to my former business of farming. I preferred to return to the vicinity of the scene of my former labors. But I had excluded myself from both of my former possessions. I had sold Shellbanks, for $10 an acre, when I thought never to need it again.[121] I now proposed to buy it back, and offered a larger price—but was asked $16. I had sold the undivided half of Coggins farm to my oldest son, who I hoped would ultimately run the whole, by later purchase. Hoping that it would remain his property, & undivided, much longer than it could be in my hands, I had no desire to dispossess him, even if I had retained the right. Various farms for sale were visited in the course of three years, without my being able to find one to which there were not strong objections—& not one was for sale in my old neighborhood. When I closed my publishing business at the end of 1842, I was still without any home except my house in Petersburg, a place which I heartily disliked & despised & was determined to leave as soon as I could make another settlement. And until such settlement should be made, of which there was then no immediate prospect, I should be without regular business. It was this position of my affairs which induced me to accept the appointment just then offered me of Agricultural Surveyor of South Carolina; though I limited my acceptance & service to one year only. While engaged in this service my efforts to purchase a farm were not suspended. In October, 1843, my son, Edmund, by my authority, bought for me the farm in Hanover county, on the Pamunkey river, which I have since occupied.[122] With my residence and labors on this farm was begun another variation of my life, & a new era, & a new course of action, which will probably also be my last of active life.

As I had announced, when first accepting the appointment, I resigned my office at the close of 1843, & hastened to Virginia to transfer my moveable property & my family to my new house. The winter was excessively wet, & stormy, & nearly all my goods were moved by land carriage in the worst condition of roads I ever knew—my furniture &c from Petersburg, & my farming implements &c &c. from Coggins. The teams of both my sons, together with my own, required more than half the month of January to complete the transportation—& were all nearly broken down by the excessive labor & worse abuse undergone. My own mules had two weeks more to rest & recruit before they were fit to recommence any regular labor. With my family, I left Petersburg with the last of our moveables, & reached our new home on Jan. 18th 1844.

The removal to a new residence is at all times a wretched business for a family fixed comfortably before. All these difficulties of house & table affairs, & discomforts of all kinds, I pass over, to remark on the condition of the land, & the first difficulties of my farming.

This farm to which I gave the name of Marlbourne, contained 977 acres of land, of which about 735 was of the low & nearly level land termed "second low-ground," & about 242 was of the high & poor table land, & the long hill-side connecting this highest land with the low. The high land was nearly all sandy & very poor naturally, & of which only some 20 acres around the mansion & the Winter Hill in West Field, had been cleared & made arable. The remainder, though in forest, was mostly of land formerly worn out, & now under pines of second growth, & the wood of very little use for fencing timber or fuel.

The low ground, like all the great extent of the wide Pamunkey flats, was of ancient alluvial or drift formation—or of soil & underlying beds which had been transported by & deposited from the waters of some enormous ancient flood, rushing from the direction of the upper country towards the present sea coast. The bottom, through which the narrow Pamunkey meanders is from 3 to 5 miles wide, for more than 20 miles below the falls of the river. All this great body of land had similar general character—but with great & frequent variations of soil, & of value. All had in past times been greatly abused & as much worn out as the owners could effect. Of latter years, some farmers had used their peculiarly valuable eocene marl,[123] & had thereby greatly improved their lands. Scarcely any of this improvement had been made on my land; & in all other respects its condition was very low. The last proprietor was a wretched farmer & manager of his business.[124] The condition of the farm & its fitness for production had been getting worse & worse for years before its sale. When it was advertised for sale, I consulted the neighbors of my acquaintance as to its value & probable price. The gentlemen thought it would not sell for more than $10 the acre, & was worth no more. Another, who thought more highly of its value than any other person, (& who also was accustomed to appreciate lands highly,) thought the land was worth $15. No one supposed that the price could be higher than $15; & when the bidding reached that mark, the proprietor privately expressed his great gratification thereat to the trustee. Nor would the land have sold for more, but for my competition, & my son's knowing my anxiety to make a purchase. I had written from S. Ca. to authorize him to buy the land at $16, which limit he exceeded, & bought at $17 the acre. As subsequent results showed, his bidding this higher sum was for me a most fortunate thing. Nevertheless all of us thought at the time that a price above the value had been paid.

Indeed so wretchedly out of order was the farm, that it could not be known what was the capacity of the land for production. Most of the dry land, both sandy & clayey was reduced very low by exhausting tillage— & the stiff & untractable clay, (of which the large proportion & frequent occurrence is a serious abatement to the value of the farm,) by want of drainage, & being often ploughed when wet, presented the appearance of naked galls, or as if the soil had been washed off, leaving naked & bare the yellowish clay subsoil. There was some still very rich land; but it was the lowest, & wettest, (the bottoms of former ponds, filled by the deposition of rich black clay—) & they only remained rich because they had not been enough drained to be worn out by tillage. Many of the spots of this "wet land," which I found afterwards to be of a rich black clay soil several feet deep, appeared before & was so deemed by me, to be as poor as it was wet, judging merely from the kinds of aquatic grasses there seen.

Owing to the general level & low surface, & the very small rate of descent in any direction, & also the extreme stiffness of most of the lowest land, much draining was required; & numerous ditches had been formerly dug, but nearly every one was left too shallow, & had been still more filled up during the neglect of years. So imperfectly did the ditches act, & so wet was the ditched ground everywhere, that it was impossible to judge by the eye what manner of draining was required. It would then have been a saving of more than $1000 worth of labor & of crop subsequently lost, if I had had levels run & marked over all the wet grounds. But not suspecting the need of this, I inferred that the old ditches had been laid off in the proper routes; & where the ground was wet, & yet had choked ditches passing through, I did not doubt that the sure & proper remedy was to clean out & deepen these same ditches. And so I went to work, & proceeded as fast as the weather & other demands of the farm permitted. During the cold weather, when laborers could not stand in mud & water, all that could be done was to take out the mud with broad hoes, the laborers standing on the dry margins of the ditches, but as nearly all hands could do something at this work, & there was a vast quantity to be done, nearly all the ditches were thus more or less imperfectly cleaned out before the spring. Then men were put to deepening & completing the ditches with spades & shovels. And then I learned, by the level of the water, the remarkably small measure of descent. In several cases of stretches of ditches of half a mile in length, or more, the water had no fall; & in some cases could be discharged from either end towards the other. The highest spot of my lowest land was indeed the summit level of that kind of land for lines of a mile in length on my own farm, & for two or three other farms both on the east & the west of mine. By a little deepening of the main ditch,[125] (which was done some 8 years later,) the greater part of all the streams of my land could be directed & discharged in opposite courses, & into the river at two different outlets, which are three miles or more apart.

In consequence of this want of fall, ditches had been cut in improper courses; & after cleaning out & deepening such to great extent, while confiding in them as having been judiciously laid off, I subsequently filled many such, & substituted them by more judicious labors. Thus, for some years, because of my want of enough knowledge of the new features of my land, I had to undo, at much expense of labor, much of the work before done by myself, as well as by my predecessors. These difficulties & the consequent blunders were the greater with me, because the surface & character of this land being so entirely different from all the subjects of my former labors & observation. Previously, I had cultivated very hilly lands, on which the passage of all streams of rainwater had too much descent. Here there was almost no descent. The demands for & modes of drainage in the two different situations were as different as these natural features.

In addition to the improper locations of many ditches, & their being then useless by neglect of cleaning, the banks were (as is the general practice still,) left on one or both, sides so as to shut out the entrance of water, & to increase the obstruction to tillage & the loss of land, caused by every ditch which teams cannot step over. Where these old banks (increased by my own labors) were not afterwards used to fill up the ditch, I had to work, at leisure times, for years, to throw back these raised margins of ditches, & in many cases to take them to greater distances by scrapers & carts. Thus, wherever I knew that a stream-ditch[126] was to remain open, & permanent in its course, my object & care were to lower & slope its margins down to the water's edge, in the course of time. This great labor, in the eighth year of my occupancy, is still in progress, & not as yet near completed.[127]

The cultivation of the farm had been until of later years upon the three-shift rotation. But latterly, it seemed that there had been no certain or regular course or plan of cropping, except to till the land that would cost the least labor. Thus, some parts had been much overcropped, or not allowed to rest for years. Other parts had been rented to neighbors, & to yield extra crops, to be cultivated. Other land which had been left idle so long as to get in foul condition, requiring much labor to be prepared for tillage, for that reason had been allowed to continue idle still longer. Such was the condition of the field which is next to the Spring Garden farm,[128] & which in the present division is called the North Shift. This, with somewhat different interior boundaries, & size, I chose for the first corn crop. Some 15 acres of the most exhausted parts had been at rest so long as to be set in broom grass, & young pines about 6 feet high. These parts I omitted. The ploughing of the remainder was begun late in winter, with two-mule ploughs, & while the still poor & weak mules were overtasked by the required labor, the work was badly executed. The previous grubbing of bushes, & cutting of briers in advance of the ploughing, had occupied all the weaker hands not engaged in cleaning ditches. The first team-work done, (except hauling wood for fuel,) was in marling—for which a pit had to be uncovered, & every other preparation made.

There was some poor miocene marl, accessible with much difficulty, in two deep valleys penetrating the high table land, from which a little had been dug & applied by former proprietors. But, in addition to its poverty, it was difficult to work. The valuable eocene marl found on the neighboring river lands "thinned out" to only 1½ feet thick at the lower out line of my river land, & was covered by so much overlying earth as not to be worth digging. Thus this farm was supposed destitute of marl, for any useful purpose. This, when I first viewed the land, presented an insuperable obstacle to my buying it. But on so stating it, Mr. Carter Braxton,[129] the trustee, & also the proprietor of the adjoining farm, Newcastle, which had marl in inexhaustible quantity, & exposed to view in many places, voluntarily offered to me the use of his marl, should I make the purchase, without limitation or condition annexed. The friendly feeling which was at least one of the motives prompting this voluntary offer, I properly appreciate—& I felt no difficulty in accepting it, because, however great the value would be to me, the gift cost nothing to the proprietor. His supply was inexhaustible; & his marl had not then become, nor has it since, a commodity that could be sold: nor can it ever be in the locality remote from navigation, where I worked.

My overseer, (who had acted some years before on Coggins farm, &

had there learned to work marl,)[130] had opened a small pit over the thin marl on my own land, before my arrival. The little so exposed was dug out, but no more was uncovered there. On Jan. 20th I began to uncover marl on Mr. Braxton's land, at an old digging of his; & on the 29th, enough of the uncovering having been completed, & a road made, I began to haul the marl. As both the late time & the distance to my field for corn forbade marling for that crop, the first marl was applied, in very thin dressing, on land the preceding year in corn, & designed to be now put under oats—& by aid of the marling, thus to get some land fit to bear clover as soon as possible. There had been no wheat sown—& I therefore aimed to have a large field sown in oats. There was no clover on the farm—& there was but very slight evidence, furnished by some plants still remaining, that some had formerly been sown on a few acres of rich low ground.

Considering that marling was the only reliable ground for improvement, I designed to lose no opportunity for pushing that operation. The wetness & softness of the ground in winter was the great obstacle. Soon a severe freeze made & kept the earth as hard as stone, & enabled me for the time to haul marl to great advantage. I was getting it on my land at the rate of 3 acres a day, at about 200 bushels, when ice had become full thick to be stored for use. But though I had both an ice-house & a good & convenient pond to furnish ice, I could not give up the marling while this temporary facility was offered, for the luxury of ice—& so lost the supply for that year.

I had devoted 2 mules out of my then whole number of 8, to the labor of marling always when weather permitted. But the other teams were also to aid this work, when not required otherwise.

All the working force I had of mules & hands, had been brought from Coggins. The only 4 oxen, had been bought here. As there was no long provender for animals, & not even litter, except what I bought, it would have been much too expensive to keep any stock except the necessary draught animals. Therefore my half of the stocks of cattle & sheep were not brought from Coggins farm until in June, when the grass of the pasture field was enough advanced for their support. Of course but little manure could be made this winter. Some leaves had been raked in the woods, & hauled in for litter, & for top dressing of land for oats.

The ploughing the field for corn was not begun until Feb. 12th. 130 acres were sown in oats, by March 23rd; of which I had previously marled 68 acres. 120 acres were sown in clover.

My corn crop yielded better than I had expected. Still, the whole returns that year from crops were small. The whole crop of corn, on 156 acres (by estimate) amounted to 2830 bushels; & the oats on 130 acres, to 2000 bushels, both quantities fixed by rough measurements & estimates. The surplus corn, which only was sold of this year's crops, did not quite pay the actual expenses, exclusive of interest on capital employed. But while the apparent loss was thus more than the whole interest, there was real gain in improved capital, & capacity for future production, in nearly 68,000 bushels of marl having been applied during the year 1844.

In the novel circumstances of my land, & my want of sufficient acquaintance with them for years after beginning the cultivation, I necessarily committed many errors, & sustained much consequent loss of labor, & of products. I tried to be informed, & was in many respects directed, by the experience of my neighbors. But while thus benefitted in some things, in others I was more misled by erroneous opinions, than if I had followed entirely my own imperfect views, & reasoning in advance of all experience.

It had been long a popular opinion, which I have heard expressed by intelligent men, upon common understanding, [report,][131] that "The Pamunkey lands were very good for corn & oats, but were not fit for wheat." My good friend & neighbor, & early disciple in marling, Gen. Corbin Braxton,[132] had led the way in this neighborhood in improving by the use of marl; & he & others had found very great benefit to wheat, produced by this manure. Still, even among these best & most successful cultivators & recent improvers, the opinion remained that, for some unknown cause, the Pamunkey lands could never equal those of like apparent soil & fertility on James river, in producing wheat. It was also understood, & seemed to be true that, as a general rule, wheat of the Pamunkey land did not yield as much grain, as would an apparent equal growth on James river. In discussing these points with some of my neighbors, in the early time of my residence, one of my remarks in opposition, drew forth the question whether I supposed it possible that the Pamunkey lands could be brought to equal those on James river in producing wheat—& my answer in the affirmative, & even claiming a superiority for the Pamunkey lands, was heard with incredulous surprise. My grounds, as stated, were that though none of the Pamunkey lands were of as fine wheat soil as the best on the lower James river, yet the average quality for all was better, & the superior advantages of the eocene marl, & the better clover growth thereby produced, would serve to make up the deficiency—or at least bring the average product of the

Pamunkey farms to be equal to the average of those on James river. It is now but seven years since the conversation—& already nearly all my marling neighbors have by this time reached a production of wheat double as much as their largest previous crops (though before on marled land—) & in most cases double as much as they had then expected ever to reach.

The causes of the then & previous low production of wheat in this neighborhood, & on the Pamunkey lands generally, were to be found in a combination of insufficient draining of the lower & wetter lands— insufficient marling, wherever marling had been done at all—together with the disadvantage of much of the soil being too sandy to suit the production of wheat. The deficiency of marling was the most operative of these causes, & has since been generally removed. The dressings before had been generally too light, even if of calcareous marl. But in fact, the green-sand earth,[133] lying below the calcareous marl, & containing less than 5 per cent. of carbonate of lime, had been used without discrimination, & in as great quantity, as the marl, & no difference of value had been suspected as existing between the two layers. Professor W. B. Rogers,[134] when making his geological survey, in his erroneous views & representations of the value of green-sand, had possessed [impressed][135] the leading marlers here with the opinion that the green-sand was much the most valuable ingredient of these peculiar marls. Almost every digging was through different layers of marl some richer & some poorer in carbonate of lime, & the lower bed containing from 2 to 5 per cent only—but all supplied with green-sand in considerable proportions. Every such digging had taken parts of all these layers. The bed where I began my excavations, as worked formerly by Mr. Braxton, had at top but from 3 to 5 feet of the best calcareous marl, of 38 to 40 per cent—next a much poorer layer of 1 or 2 feet—& below, the green-sand earth of only 2½ per cent. of carbonate of lime. Of all these, some 8 to 10 feet had been used, irregularly mixed, or separate, as might happen in the digging & loading, & in the use for years, no difference of effect or of manuring value had been observed, looked for, or suspected to exist, between these very different earths. This was surprising & unaccountable to me, when first ascertained as the prevailing opinion, in an examination of the lands & marl beds made in 1840. Nor is any explanation since more satisfactory than what I will state as my later inferences, deduced from later observations of the general practices before marling. Both this marl, & the green-sand bed below, certainly contain sulphate of lime.—This ingredient is probably the main cause of this marl being so peculiarly favorable to clover—& in this effect, the green-sand earth, for a few years, is very little inferior to the upper marl. Also, I have since believed that this marl, & probably the lower bed, have some other manuring ingredient, in very small quantity, but showing good effects especially on wheat; & this I suppose to be phosphate of lime. If this supposition is correct, the sulphate & phosphate of lime, with a very little carbonate, might especially on clover, & wheat following the clover, produce good effects for some years. And before this temporary action had ceased, another application of the like earths, or some other treatment, might serve to continue to hide the difference in both energy & durability, of the different manuring earths. After my labors were in progress, it was still maintained by some extensive marlers, in argument, as well as in their practice, that the green-sand earth was as good as the marl.—But nevertheless, the use of the former soon ceased; & latterly no farmer has used any of the green-sand bed, unless his farm furnished that only. There have since been some of the latter cases—in which the calcareous ingredient was very small, & yet satisfactory benefits found, on the first growth of clover, & on the subsequent crops. I do not pretend to fix the value on the kind of the manuring ingredients, (except the gypsum;) but the carbonate of lime alone is certainly too little to make the whole mass worth using for that, the usual main value of marl; & I predict that the other & greater (& probably over-rated) effects will cease after a few more crops.

But while at work at my first diggings, even I had to use of this green-sand bed, to which I attached so little value. But, except for some experiments with the lower & least calcareous earth, my then use was mostly confined to upper part of that bed, which is largely intermixed with the more calcareous bed lying above. If all this intermixture had been rejected, I should have had but 3 feet depth of marl to work, & for that to remove from 6 to 8 feet thickness of overlying earth, sand, hard gravel, & wet & very adhesive clay. After working out all the marl here uncovered, in June of that year, I moved to another spot about 300 yards to the east, where, in the bottom of a small ravine, the marl was visible. Here the marl was 7 feet thick, & varied between 5 at the western & 8 at the eastern extremity, of all the extensive diggings which I subsequently made at this place.

As soon as the oats were sown, I proceeded to marl on the nearest land for corn, until the ploughing overtook me—when some 20 acres of it had been covered. Then the marling was moved to the land next to be prepared for [any?] crop, which was low (or "black") land designed to be put under fallow wheat the same autumn. This is the mode of application the least beneficial at first. The ploughing under the marl deeply, & there being no subsequent stirring, except the very superficial harrowing during seeding, leaves the marl mostly unmixed with the soil, & therefore useless. Still, as I did not doubt, after the first year, my ability to keep my marling in advance of my cultivation, I thought it better to give even this small chance to the land for the first wheat, though not one-tenth of the marl might act, until when subsequently brought up to the surface again, by the next deep ploughing. No certain effect was seen on the first crop. Indeed, this marl, on the neutral soil of the Pamunkey low grounds, rarely showed much effect, & generally little or none, on the next grain crops, & was not of much effect until on the next growth of clover.[136]

As but little of my land in corn was then worth putting under wheat, it was very important that there should be a good fallow sowing. As there was no clover to plough under, & no regular succession of recent previous culture, I had to continue the irregular course of late years pursued. The richer parts of the low land now in West field & Middle field were designed for this purpose. But a drought kept this stiff & obdurate soil so hard that the ploughing of it could not even be begun until late in September [*blank*], & part had to be entirely omitted, being still unploughed when too late to continue sowing. The remainder was ploughed during October, with great labor, & yet very imperfectly, by 4-mule ploughs. Previously, when kept so late by the drought from preparing this land, & fearing that it could not be done, I had ploughed some other higher & sandy land, as a substitute. This made the surface for my first wheat culture still more irregular than had been designed. At last, however, I had (or estimated) 134 acres (of both fallow & corn-land) sown in wheat, under great disadvantages, but embracing as much as could be prepared of the richest low ground.

With the spring of 1845, I began the making of covered drains. The many failures which I had made more than 20 years before, & the knowledge I had gained of the causes of those failures, enabled me now to resume the work with much useful experience & renewed confidence. But I was still in the dark as to some other of the necessary requisites for success; & besides, the circumstances of soil, levels, & water, were very different from such as had existed on the high & hilly land of Coggins farm.

It would be tedious, & scarcely intelligible if I were to describe my operations in covered draining at length & in the order they occurred;

& as different & erroneous views of the evils to be removed, & the supposed proper remedies, made my rule & course of procedure to vary at different times, & with different degrees of effect. It will be better, at some later time, to arrange the whole, & present these operations in a digested & connected shape.[137] For the present, I will merely state concisely the worst evils which required covered draining, & the results.

It would be inferred from what has been already said of the condition of the farm, that all the previous drainage had been very defective. No covered draining had ever been thought of—(& none had been attempted in all this neighborhood—) & the many open ditches had been in every case too shallow, & many of them improperly located. The main ditch, which received & discharged all the streams through the eastern end of the low ground, had been made at first, as it appeared, by merely opening & deepening the natural bed of the stream. From the lower extremity, it was crooked, & where highest, near to the Sulphur Cove, & where a new & straighter course had been dug, it had been improperly placed. Still, though knowing that these defects could not be borne, & that this old course would have to be abandoned when a better could be made, I was compelled to deepen all this old main channel, & as much as the level of the place of discharge, & the difficulty of digging under the current of the bold running stream permitted. Thus, besides cleaning out the deposited mud, & earth fallen in from the sides, I gained about 8 inches more than the original depth, & of course so much a lower discharge for all the open ditches emptying into the main one. Into this I had to discharge the first covered drains made. This main ditch also for all its lower course, & greater extent, was near to the northern side of the belt of lowest ground, whereas all the oozing springs came from the southern side, & mostly showed at the foot of the long knoll of higher sandy ground which stretched across the whole farm. Below & eastward of the barn, the low ground is narrowest—& there only, the low ground soil in part is sandy, like the adjacent somewhat higher ground. In this sandy part the low ground was wet, without showing any standing or flowing water. Some neighboring springs & mere oozings had been taken off by side & cross open ditches. But notwithstanding sundry cross ditches, which conveyed no water except the surplus of heavy rains, the spot mentioned had continued too wet for cultivation. It was not more than three-quarters of an acre. But being in the midst of good arable land, it would have been very inconvenient to leave it out of cultivation. So its cultivation as well as its drainage had been regularly attempted, as it seemed for a long time—but both had been entirely in vain. I found the place wet, & covered by a thicket of briers & bushes. The main difficulty at first was that no water showed, nor could any even be found entering from that side into the main ditch. And in the old side-ditch above, where the land was dry enough for tillage, so little water showed even in winter, that I waited for & expected it to dry up in the spring, & supposed a ditch there must be unnecessary. But when digging as low as the discharge into the mainstream admitted, I found that the greater depth reached spring water in abundance, & as far as I extended the deepening, in the old side ditch, as well as through the still wet land. But though thus draining & collecting much water, it was evident that all was not got. My deepest digging in or along the border of the sandy knoll, was in a loose gravel, yielding water everywhere. As the want of more descent forbade digging deeper into this gravel, of course the still lower supply of water was not cut off, & *might* still pass under & across the bottom of the deepest digging. In endeavoring to obtain as much depth as possible, the bottom of the new ditch was left with too little fall for its safe and continued operation, & the danger of failure was increased by the sides of the ditch at bottom being of loose sand & sandy gravel, from which the veins of water entered. But as these defects could not then be avoided, the drains were covered; & they seemed to drain the land well at first, & for some years. But because of these defects, & as might have been expected, these drains were afterwards partially choked, & other cross drains had to be made (& covered,) which being at a lower level, & giving more fall, again dried the land.

The failure of these first operations, even if it had occurred earlier, & more completely, would not have caused surprise. For I was aware at first of the existence of several capital defects, in the want of sufficient depth, of sufficient fall, & of the digging not reaching the bottom of the porous & water-glutted sandy gravel. My clover sowing, on oats, in 1844, upon which so much of my prospective improvement depended, was a general failure, owing to the summer drought killing the young plants.

The effect of the spring's marling was barely visible on the oats, & starting on the little clover that there lived. Where clover had been sown without marl, scarcely any plants survived the drought. On the corn land marled (late in spring,) the effect was quite evident at the junction with the corn not marled. But the effect was very small compared to the as early effects which I had always found elsewhere, when operating upon acid & naturally poor soils.

My cattle & sheep, had been brought from Coggins in June; & still earlier a few hogs, to begin to breed a stock. With the obtaining litter in my oat straw (used in feeding mules & horses) & of corn stalks, the making of manure was begun regularly, in November.

The novelty of this first operation attracted much observation of some of my neighbors—& I could easily infer from remarks made that my work, even if entirely successful & permanent, was deemed a waste of labor, as the cost was more than the estimated value of so small a piece of land. But, in such a situation, it would have been profitable to pay even double the improved value of the spot, in fitting it for cultivation, rather than undergo the inconvenience of leaving it out of cultivation, & obstructing all the close adjoining tillage & diminishing its products, by the shade & vermin of the thicket. This was one of the very many cases in which it is much cheaper to make a certain improvement, than it would be to omit it.

[This operations & remarks at full in Farm Journal, Jan. 1845][138]

There were two other jobs of covered draining executed this spring, (1845) both of which were attended with new difficulties on account of new & peculiar features of the strata. One was to reclaim a boggy basin in the now West Field, (next to road from House to Barn, & near foot of hill,) for which open ditches had formerly been attempted in vain, & which had long been given up to a growth of alder shrubs & China briers. A ditch was cut surrounding it on the three sides next the hill, & as deep as the outlet & the small descent permitted. This was in the under-stratum of ferruginous clay[139] which is all along the base of the hills. The peculiar obstacles which this bed opposes to draining will be hereafter described. It is enough here to say that the covered drain did not completely dry all the surrounded land; but approached that end nearly enough to make the whole very productive arable land. Another system of drains was on the sloping ground rising from the black low land since called the Sulphur Cove, to the close adjacent tract of Talley's, then owned by Pate.[140] There were also peculiar difficulties of strata here, increased by my ignorance of them. But the main difficulty, removed long after, was that some of the sources of springs were in my neighbors land, & without including them, the scheme of drainage could not be entirely effective. Still all the wet land was made arable & productive, except a few small spots, where the injurious supply of waters had been cut off.

As imperfect as had been my under-draining so far, I was then much better satisfied with the effects than with my surface draining for rain-water only, which is usually the easiest & most simple affair. The great difficulty of this was caused by the great & irregular variations of different soils & slightly different levels of surface—basins of impervious clay being intermixed with higher knolls of sandy soil, & sometimes of poor clay rising like islands (as doubtless they had been originally,) in the midst of the larger pieces of low black land. My then views will appear from some remarks entered in my farm journal, March 14th, 1845.[141]— "The under drainage of this land I think I understand, & can easily effect. But the surface draining is much more difficult & is as yet very deficient. It is true that nothing more is needed for the purpose than to let the rain water pass off into the stream-ditches, with as little delay & obstruction as possible. And this may be done tolerably well by grips[142] across the beds[143] & under-furrows,[144] wherever there is a depression that otherwise would retain standing water. But under the usual existing conditions of all such places, of an impervious sub-soil—beds crossing numerous shallow depressions—[the want of fall in the routes for grips—][145] & the ditches universally heretofore having banks on each side, serving to *dam off* the water which the ditches were designed to drain off—the carrying the above simple rule into practice is very laborious, & never-ending labor, & therefore has not been fully performed by me. It would require a thorough opening & renewing of all the numerous grips required in each field under tillage, & of the adjoining parts of water-furrows leading into the grips, after every separate ploughing & harrowing process, of preparation or tillage. I have neglected this—& was the more willing to do so because designing to adopt a different & better plan for shaping & draining the surface—by sloping down & removing the ditch margins, & thus permitting the water-furrows to empty everywhere over them, & by giving new directions to the beds, where required. These changes, (& perhaps with the aid of a general deep coultering[146] of the subsoil where it is impervious to water,) will serve to make the soil dry enough. But this will be a work of years, & can only be effected gradually. And in the meantime I fear that the great evil of the farm will be the want of surface draining. The field last year in corn [North Field][147] & lately marled & under oats, is especially suffering by neglect, though it is not the least affected by springs, or under-ground water.*[148] About 20 acres of the wettest spots remain unmarled, having been too wet for hauling upon. It being now too late to prepare for oats & clover, the now extending of the marling over the omitted parts will be useless for the present year."—These early views of difficulties were correct—but not entirely so the supposed modes of removing them. Much indeed has since been done, & with good effects & great profit, in surface draining by surface operations. But after nearly 8 years practice, I have formed the (as yet speculative) opinion that under drains with aid of vertical borings, & downward discharges of the water, will be the only effectual mode of surface drainage for these basin-shaped depressions of impervious soil & subsoil.

My plan of conducting my marl-digging was this year arranged, as it continued until the close of my operations at that place. As the whole procedure is fully stated in another paper, it would be superflous to report it here.[149] I will merely mention that this last manner of working was very much cheaper & more effective than that adopted (from necessity,) at first; & yet this had been a very great improvement on the former practice of the proprietor of this marl, & of his neighbors generally. Mr. Braxton soon after opened a pit for his own working on the opposite side of the ravine, & situated still better than mine. And though his imitation of my mode of procedure was very deficient, still his marling was done at not more than half the cost of labor which he had regularly expended formerly.

My corn crop this year was on East Field. It was cultivated (like the previous one) partly on the usual plan of this part of the country, with single-horse mould-board ploughs. But I had not at first liked the plan much, & this was my last conformity with the neighborhood usage, except on some of the lowest land, most like to suffer by wet. There, for some years later, I still used 11 feet beds, with two corn-rows on each, & mould-board ploughs for the water-furrow balks.[150] The general practice was narrow beds, 5 or 5½ feet, for each corn-row. The summer was very dry & the corn crop suffered severely with drought, & its product was much reduced. All the field had been marled (at 350 bushels or more) but very little effect therefrom could be seen on the corn. The crop of oats was also much shortened by the drought.

The drought was again very injurious to the new-sown clover—(& even on oats, & on wheat following last year's corn—) & the clover of 2nd year was so dwarfed as to be not worth mowing. No abundant rain fell until the beginning of August. The plentiful rains then, & the unusually bare surface of the land (owing to the drought,) made the fallowing for wheat very easy & rapid. Two-mule ploughs still were competent to do this ploughing on all the higher & not very stiff land. A four-horse plough worked on the more stubborn soil.

Though[151] much injury was expected to the wheat, from the drought before & up to the maturing, the crop was good in quantity, & remarkably heavy. Mine weighed 63½ lbs at the mill in Richmond where sold.

Before the reaping of my wheat, it had attracted much attention from some of my neighbors, for its good promise—& the moreso because my general slovenly management, & especially in preparing for & covering wheat, as reported, had produced expectations of the returns falling short. Some of my neighbors dined with me when the wheat was in head, & walked to look at the crop. After various comments, & general approbation of its appearance one of the company, (one of the best practical & marling farmers of the neighborhood, & who had estimated the value of my farm very low,) said to me, "Well! I believe your crop *is* the best of the neighborhood. But you will not make such another for seven years." "Why so?" I asked. "Because you have so much of your richest land under this crop." "That is true," I said, "there is certainly an overproportion of the best land. To make a crop at all, I had to take land wherever it could be got; & aimed to get in the best. Nevertheless, I shall not ask for the half of seven years, to make as good a crop as this." The total amount of this crop was 1977 bushels. The very next succeeding was 2432; & of all since to this time, no later crop has failed to largely exceed that quantity.

The levelling & removing of old & new ditch banks & margins, of open ditches designed to be permanent, the deepening of stream ditches, & other draining operations not of indispensable & immediate necessity, were continued at leisure times, every year. And much as has been done, much of such labors still remain to be done. All these labors, like my continued & regular marling operations, important as they were, need not be more particularly mentioned than has been done.

In the first year of my farming here I had begun a practice which since has been been my regular course. This was the cutting down the stalks of corn, & putting them in shocks, to secure the fodder, instead of pulling off the lower leaves & cutting off the top of the corn, as was then (& nearly still) the universal practice of the country. As I have in another paper described my practice at length, & stated my views of the superior advantages, no more need be said here on the subject, except that this procedure has continued regularly on my farm, & with undiminished approval.[152]

The borders of the Pamunkey long had the bad reputation of being very unhealthy—& much more so than on most other of the tide-water lands of lower Virginia. Few of the river farms were deemed safely habitable in autumn, by their proprietors. My own present residence also in former times been very sickly. But in all later time, it had been deemed healthy, & remarkably so in comparison to all other river farms. The change for the better had doubtless been produced by the extension of draining; which imperfect as it had been, had served at least to remove many shallow ponds of stagnant water which before had been always diminishing by evaporation alone during summer, & so leaving naked the former bottoms of rich black mud. These worst sources of miasma had been long ago partially removed. But enough remained in imperfectly drained ground. It was with much apprehension that I encountered the still remaining dangers. But my own family & my overseer's,[153] as well as my negroes, passed through the first autumn with but very few cases of sickness (for any malarious locality,) & since that year, every one has been still more healthy. The members of my own family all remained at home during the sickly season, except some visits of my children to my other children in Prince George.[154] At any rate enough of us remained at home through all the sickly season to give the situation a fair trial. Of these, three were my youngest children, then at school at healthy localities, & who were at home only through August & September. I kept carefully a sick list, for 5 months of that year, from July 10th to Decr. 10th.[155] The whole number of residents was 53. Of these my own family made 8, the overseer's 4, & 41 were my slaves. The cases of sickness were 17, of which no one lasted longer than 5 days. The whole number of days of indisposition (keeping the subjects from their work or usual employments,) amounted to 57. One white person only had any sickness. This was the overseer, who had a bad cough with bilious symptoms. Every case of sickness among the negroes, was of ague & fever, except two—& all very mild. That season was deemed unusually healthy for all the neighborhood, & of course I supposed that my family fared better than would be the case generally. But since that time, sickness among my slaves has been still less; & ague & fever the only form of malarious disease experienced, has scarcely appeared of latter years.[156]

The health of my own family had long been good. My own health, so long & always bad, had been restored & had continued good since our removal to Shellbanks—with the exception of the dangerous illness contracted by exposure in the low country of South Carolina. I had come to Pamunkey under the remains of that attack, & under regimen for its cure. But in the engrossing & interesting labors then required, I neglected & soon forgot my regimen, & under every exposure, soon recovered my health.

My wife[157] still longer than myself had been restored to & had continued to enjoy the blessing of almost perfect health. As her previous & most grievous sufferings from disease had not been produced by the former sickly residence which had caused my ill health, she had recovered long before our removal. But after enjoying this happiness for some 16 years, she had now to undergo the long & painful infliction of disease from new sources, leading to her death. In the spring of 1845 she had been affected by a slight pain in one of her wrists, which, though gradually increasing, scarcely attracted her serious attention for some time. Her physicians deemed it at first a rheumatic affection. The disease extended, until resulting in great pain, & a privation of almost all use of her limbs, & growing prostration of every bodily power. This state of increasing suffering was closed by death, on the 21st of February 1846.

My daughters assumed the charge of the household duties left vacant by their mother's death; & their careful & affectionate attention has since served to aid my labors, & my happiness, as much as the existing circumstances permitted.[158] To their affectionate & also judicious conduct, I have since owed even my ability to continue to pursue my accustomed labors. If continued application to some interesting & engrossing occupation were not to me a positive source of happiness, it would be as requisite to avoid my sinking into a positive state of wretchedness, even though there were no other cause except mere idleness. But the aid to happiness found in the most successful & productive employment would be nothing if not founded on other grounds of domestic happiness & family affections. In these latter respects, & in all family relations, though not without [*illeg.*] & heavy afflictions, I have been eminently blessed—& still more so in the conduct of my affectionate & beloved children.

The winter, spring & summer of 1846 were remarkable for the quantity of rain. The cultivation of my corn was much obstructed thereby— & in some ground the most exposed to wetness, the tillage was very insufficient, because of the continued wetness of the land, & the production small in proportion. Still, the crop being on my best field, (the present West Field, with adjacent rich low-ground of Middle Field,) it brought a much later crop than I had made before. It was estimated at 35 bushels average to the acre. All the field had previously been well marled, except a few acres inaccessible at the time of marling. Since the first years crops, the marling had been kept in advance of the tillage of each field.

The wetness of the summer extended through half of the time for wheat harvest, & the crop was lessened in its actual product, by the rains during its growth, & also by the loss in harvest. If the continued rains had lasted one day longer, I believe that nearly all the wheat would have sprouted, & been lost. That so much was saved was a remarkable blessing. The circumstances of the harvest, with all its dangers, & the relief, appear in my farm journal.[159] This crop (as mentioned incidentally before) made 2432 bushels.

The extreme wetness of the season, so injurious to the grown crops, was excellent for grass. The extremely thin remains of the clover sowing of last year seemed to be wonderfully thickened, as well as very luxuriant. On 40 acres only had it stood even moderately thick. On this last part, I obtained a very fine crop, & mowed, for green feeding & hay, as much as my force could manage. I also permitted several of my neighbors to cut & cure hay upon shares. But this I will never do again. I do not choose, for so small a remuneration, that so much fertilizing material shall be carried off the farm. And besides, owing to the bad management, the share of hay left for me was not of half its proper value.

My method of curing clover hay in skewered cocks had been practiced by me to small extent before. But this fine crop gave me the first opportunity for its extensive exercise. This, more than any other of the new practices I introduced, seemed to be approved by my neighbors; & I believe that all of them who make clover hay now, follow this plan. (See full account in an article on "Clover culture", published in American Farmer in 1851.)[160]

The wetness of this season continued through the latter part of August & early part of September, & had bad effects on my harvest of cornfodder. This was the only year in which any injury to fodder or to corn was experienced, in consequence of cutting down & shocking the green corn. This damage was caused by carelessness, & the then absence of all fears of danger; & might have been, as it has been since, entirely avoided by proper caution & care. (See account of the general practice, & of the particular fodder harvest of that year, in Am. Farmer, for 1851.)[161]

The covered draining done & attempted in the spring of 1846 was all in West Field (preparing for corn,) & had not been so successful as heretofore. For the slope of hillside, in the ferruginous clay under stratum, the injurious oozing water could not be all brought together. And in the very loose sand which forms the subsoil of some of the oozy slopes of Winter Hill, so much caving was caused by the then water-glutted state of the sand, that the digging could not be sunk to the still lower clay. Some of this failing work was resumed in the autumn, when there was least water supplied, & was then successfully completed. All the covered drains, completed, in West Field, in 1846, amounted to 1558 yards.

What I had seen in South Carolina of the growth of field peas (Indian or native) among corn, both planted & broad-cast, had induced me to try both here. Every year some had been planted—& this year, also broad-cast sowing was extended to more than 20 acres. This was mostly among corn—but about 8 acres as a separate fallow crop, to precede wheat. The good growth of both (of course on marled land,) was very encouraging—& still more the supposed benefit shown on the wheat which followed. With this extent of experience & success, I now resolved to adopt pea-fallow, & green manuring by that crop, as a part of my rotation. I had before, though cultivating very irregularly, designed the crops, & ultimately regular shifts of the land, to come under the five-shift rotation, then in use with a few only of the most improving farmers. This rotation is 1. corn, 2. wheat, 3. clover (fallowed to precede) 4. wheat, 5. Pasture. I now proposed to divide my arable land into 6 fields, & give another year entirely to broad-cast peas, as a green-manuring & fallow crop, to come in between the crop of corn & the next succeeding wheat; or otherwise, to sow the peas among the corn, & to give two years to clover. This scheme could be reached only gradually. And it was not until in 1848 that I began the regular & full operation by having a whole shift under broadcast peas, as a distinct crop, to be ploughed under for wheat. (See first plan of p. 254 of Farm Journal, 1847.)[162]

In 1847 South Field was to be put under corn, after all the other land had borne that crop. It had been marled in 1846, except a portion inaccessible in winter, & which was also covered before the next spring was over. The cultivation of this field had been postponed to the last for two reasons: Having a separate enclosing fence, it served as the most convenient grazing land. And it required more extensive & difficult draining than any other field, which was another reason for delaying the undertaking. With the preparation of this field, the last remaining division fence was removed.[163] Thenceforward, my hogs were confined to a pen, & my cattle & sheep herded on their grazing land. The inconvenience of this course, & the damage from stock trespassing on crops, by neglect of the boys kept to herd them, are both great evils; But not so great as the cost of maintaining division fences, especially with my scarcity of fencing timber & labor.

The covered drains made in the south-western slope of South Field, in the spring of 1847, amounted to 1982 yards; which served in part to substitute, & in part to supersede 2479 yards of open ditches before existing, & of which none could have been otherwise dispensed with, although not one was deep enough, or could be kept deep enough to drain effectually. The plan & the difficulties of this drainage were described at length, & with illustrative diagrams in Farm Journal for 1847, beginning at page 244.[164] All these drains were for this year effectual. But for a cause not feared before, some parts ceased to be sufficient in the next winter & spring. This cause was that the pipe, either left too small at first, or (more likely) become so by partial sinking of the woodwork into the too soft earth at bottom, was too small to discharge all the water supplied when the earth was glutted with rain-water. Seeing the consequent surcharging of the surface soil with the water thus obstructed, I thought the passages below were completely choked, & so much of the covered drain spoiled. But as the dryer season came on, this surcharge disappeared, & the pipe again was competent to discharge all the water from the higher source. Remedies have since been applied, & others still are required for other like defects, by cutting new & larger drains & deeper out-lets, & intersecting the older drains at the obstructed places. But whatever have been the failures, on the whole, both the operation & the durability of my covered drains have exceeded my first expectations. With the previous numerous open ditches, all of them obstructing tillage, this richest part of the field would have been scarcely worth cultivating, even if well drained; & it certainly was worthless, the ditches being of very partial draining effect.

For much the larger portion of the field, surface draining by water-furrows, cross-grips, & rain ditches were sufficient.[165] This field & the River Field (north of public road) were in corn, making the quantity of 175 acres, & producing 4500 bushels, an average of nearly 26 bushels. This excess of land in corn that year was required for two reasons: 1. the land had not been under any tillage crop before since my occupancy, & needed tillage for cleansing: 2. as the whole of South field (124 acres) was not to be put in wheat, but to be left for pea fallow the next year, more corn-land was required for that time, to precede wheat, & to prevent that crop for 1848 being cut too short.

In 1848 my new rotation was put in full operation, by South Field being all sowed in peas. The season was so favorable, that it served to deceive me as to the hazards of this culture. The growth was superb.

The wheat also of 1848 had the benefit of a very favorable season, & produced what I then thought a wonderful crop—altogether incredible it would have been, if predicted before being measured. The crop made on 256 acres, was 5127 bushels, or 20 bushels average to the acre.

The health of one of my daughters, Mildred, required her going to the Springs in the mountain region in 1848, & she could not go without my being her companion. Accordingly I left home with her & another daughter, Jane, for companionship & the pleasure of both, the beginning of August, & did not return until the last of September. This absence would have been a serious disadvantage to my farming operations, & care of the farm, at any time. But with 1847 I had begun the system since pursued, of dispensing with the services of an overseer—except the giving charge to my most trust-worthy negro, Jem. Sykes,[166] so far as his condition permitted. To his care was left the entire charge of the farm & its operations for the time of my absence, except for short visits of my son Julian, made at intervals of two weeks, merely to see how things stood, & to give general orders to Jem to serve until his next visit. Julian had kindly offered to leave his own farm (in Prince George,) & to give his whole time to the direction of my business, during my absence. But I knew that he would make a great sacrifice in so doing, & therefore I would not accept more than the lesser service above-mentioned. But his transient visits though very useful for general direction, could be of no effect upon the operations of labor, or the taking care of the provisions & property in general. All this had to be left to Jem; and he well discharged his trust then, as he has continued to do full as well as could be expected, to this time. During my absence, he did the latter half of the thrashing & all the delivering to vessels of this large crop of wheat—having only the aid, at the two deliveries to keep the account of loads, of my son upon one occasion & a neighbor on the other. It so happened that during one of Julian's visits the vessel arrived, & he staid to attend to this business, which Jem. could not do, because not able to read. But neither of these aids served any other purpose than merely to write down the account of loads delivered. The facts of this crop being left to be thrashed & delivered, under the sole care & charge of my negro overseer, & that I could leave the farm without other superintendence for a visit to the Springs, caused nearly as much remark as did the amount of the crop of wheat then made.

The thrashing was long on hand, & consequently the heavy operation of fallowing two fields was late in being begun & in being completed. The clover field (West Field) had been ploughed by Sept. 17th, & the pea field then commenced. So rank was the cover of pea vines, that four-mule ploughs were required to cover them, & then it was a slovenly operation. A drought had much increased the labor of ploughing. At my return, only about half the pea land had been ploughed, & all the remaining vines had been killed by a previous (& unusually early) frost. A good rain soon softened the soil; & with the aid of that & the then brittle texture of the pea-vines, two-mule ploughs were sufficient for the remaining half of the field. If it had been a clover-fallow, the lateness of this ploughing would have very much reduced the production. But I was not able to see in the subsequent growth of wheat any certain loss from this cause, & from the pea-vines being dead & dry on all the land ploughed late.

The rapid increase of my crops to this time (1848) & especially the amount of the last wheat crop, induced my friend Willoughby Newton,[167] of Westmoreland, (himself a very successful improver, & a much better manager than myself,) to solicit me to furnish him, for publication, an estimate of the cost & profits. When first proposed to me, I refused, & had no thought of complying until after renewed & more urgent solicitations. At last I prepared the estimates, as well as I could, with the aid of the very full entries in my Farm Journal, but in the entire absence of all properly kept accounts of expenditures. However, though many of the items were necessarily stated by guess—& some omissions made by forgetfulness—I believe that if all such omissions of expenditures were correctly supplied, they would fall short of the receipts [on?] annual values also stated too low. But besides—the great omission made (by design) in summing up the net profits of my investment & the first five years operations on the farm is that nothing is allowed for the increased value of capital in the improvement of the land. And this increase would not only be in the intrinsic or productive value, but also in selling value, if my farm were now offered for sale. If that were the case, I think that not less than $13000 would be added to the amount of my purchase. And as all that increase would be due to the improvements made by me, of course as much ought fairly to be added to the fund of accumulated profits, & divided among the five years, & go to increase the net income of each year by one fifth of $13000.

The estimates which I furnished will present the most convenient &

concise statement of the financial department of my farming, & as such will be annexed & made part of these notes.[168]

Previous to the publication of these estimates, I had written nothing of agricultural matters for publication, with a single exception, since my return to a life of privacy & seclusion.[169] This condition I did not expect or desire ever to leave—& the strong disinclination I felt to again coming before the public, in any manner, was one of the several reasons for my reluctance to comply with Mr. Newton's request. But the statement of facts, (or supposed facts as to details,) made more impression on the public mind, & excited more interest & remark, than anything I had ever written & published before—though as I thought much of what had before been scarcely noticed, was of much more value for instruction than the last piece. The act of writing brought back something of my old habit of & fondness for treating agricultural subjects—& the continuance was strongly invited by the extensive notice & favor with which my late publication had been received. I had much of matter on hand—some written out, & some merely in rough materials—which I had expected to meet no other eye than my own during my life. I now, as leisure permitted, gave more time to these things. Especially I set about preparing what was designed for a last & posthumous edition of my Essay on Calcareous Manures. This though greatly extended, is still in slow & irregular progress, & probably will never be finished.[170]

The proprietor of The American Farmer of Baltimore,[171] to which paper Mr. Newton had sent my estimates, derived from the publication, as he stated, a very large addition to his subscription list, & especially from Virginia. At a later time he proposed to me to write another essay for his paper; & the proposition led to an arrangement for me to furnish him with a series of essays on different subjects of practical farming, to extend through a volume of his publication. This was done—& at the publisher's request, the arrangement is continued for such time & at such intervals as my leisure & convenience may permit.

The first of these essays, (which was continued through five monthly numbers,) was on Draining.[172] Throughout the whole, it was my continued effort to abridge, & to omit whatever could be spared. Still the essay is long—& might have been much longer with less trouble to amplify than I took to contract its extent. My own former & recent actual operations in draining supplied me with most of the facts & the rules there offered. This was also the case with the succeeding essays on other subjects. But the following this subject of my recent slight connexion with the agricultural press & with the public, has carried my remarks far ahead of the time of my farming operations, which make the main subject of these notes.

In the spring of 1849, & to the middle of April, my wheat crop, & especially that part on pea-fallow, promised well. It was thought by other persons, as well as myself, to be better than the growth of the preceding heavy crop. The great interest I felt, & the strong faith held in the effect of the green manuring of peas, made me more anxious for the result than my pecuniary interest. But my high hopes were to be blasted. On the 14th of April the weather became remarkably cold, & at 9.30 P.M. the temperature was 35°. On the 15th, at sunrise it was 28°—& on the 16th, 23½°. This was at my house, on the table land. But the temperature at night is always lower on the low-ground, as is evident from the different thicknesses of ice. The farm journal says— "Shallow water in ditches [on the low ground][173] was frozen nearly a quarter of an inch thick. Heavy white frost coated the leaves of wheat; & the globule of dew which usually hangs from the top of the highest blade, was solid ice. The young leaves of locust, walnut & ash trees in the yard, & of oak, hickory, poplar, persimmon & other trees in the woods, killed."—April 18th. Temperature at sunrise 25½°. The wheat then in all good land, was nearly or quite knee high, & nearly all the crop except that on poorest land, or otherwise very backward, had jointed. It seemed impossible that the stems could could escape destruction; & yet, though they ceased to grain, they did not die for two weeks. But finally every stalk perished that was then jointed. The only hope for a crop was in the poor land wheat, underling plants, & the suckers that would put out from the roots of the killed stalks. I would have taken 2000 bushels for my crop. But the product was much better. It amounted to 3375 bushels from 263 acres, or 12.83 to the acre. The price was good, & made this crop yield $4822, counting the value of the seed retained as equal to the wheat sold.

This loss of wheat by freezing, or, to [such?] great extent, was unprecedented in my farming life. May wheat (so called) I had known generally destroyed. But that kind I never raised. My kind which I have made & preferred since 1822, & continue to prefer, is the Early purple straw wheat.

There[174] were two parts of my crop which escaped this disaster. One was all my wheat following corn immediately—& which also was the latest sowing & on the poorest land. On this piece of 30 to 35 acres, the wheat was not forward enough to begin to joint, & it was not hurt by the freezing, & produced well for such land. The other piece which escaped nearly as well, was a knoll of dry & rich sandy loam, part of the pea-fallow, & on which the wheat at first had been as forward as any part of the crop. My sheep were allowed through winter & into March, to graze the wheat—& they were generally upon this knoll of about 10 acres, & kept the plants closely cropped, until they were removed. This wheat therefore was all of late growth, & this also nearly escaped all damage from the subsequent freezing weather. This disaster was general throughout my neighborhood & all lower Va & N.Ca. upon all wheat that was then jointed. But as not much was so forward in growth, that of the richer lands & also of early sowing, suffered much the most. The great body of the wheat of this region being still on land but little if at all improved, & all the late sowing, suffered but little from this unexampled cold weather.

My new rotation was now in full operation, with its two varieties of the crop following the corn. The six fields were each about 124 acres. Of the corn field (North F.) of 1848, the portion above referred to of 30 or 35 acres, was followed immediately by wheat. According to my rule, this part ought to have been sown in peas broad-cast, (at the last tillage of the corn,) & so a pea manuring, though of but inferior growth, would have been given to the wheat. But as I had not designated the part of the field early enough, this part had been not sown broad-cast, but planted with peas in the intervals between the corn, for seed; & the ripe peas had been gathered, & the vines taken off. So the secondary crop of peas here had the opposite to the manuring operation designed by the plan. This portion bore its wheat a year sooner, & then had to remain under clover two years, instead of one as in the case of the remainder of the field, which was under pea fallow, the year after the corn. And after the one year of full [grown?] clover of the latter portion, & two years of the former, the whole field would be ploughed together for the wheat on clover fallow—& so again make the culture regular.

This variation of crop, in the year after corn & the next, had some inconveniences. As the portion put in wheat immediately after corn was selected for its quality of soil, the outlines were irregular, & the quantity varying in different fields—both of which were objectionable. But the variation enabled me to try which was best of the two modes—& while both should be thus in operation, to give most of the clay soil to the longest growth of clover, & most of the sandy soil to pea fallow—to which crops these different soils were respectively best suited.

When planning this rotation, it had been to me a matter for doubt whether clover could keep possession of the land to the third year after the sowing. It was a general opinion that weeds would "eat out" the clover in the third year; & in consequence of this belief, on no previous system of culture or rotation in eastern Va. has clover been designed to stand longer than its second year. But from some land omitted, in the changes before made, I had found clover of the third year, though not so tall as in the second, to stand thicker & to make a better cover to the land. These observations encouraged me to found one branch of my rotation on the reliance that clover would stand (on my marled land) well through its third year. In this reliance, I have not yet been disappointed.

Early in 1849, I bought at private sale a neighboring tract of land, Larrey's, of 323 acres, of which the cleared land had been worn to the lowest state of exhaustion of which land is capable.[175] But it was for the woodland I bought it—some 100 acres being well covered with original forest growth, with the building & farm timber & fuel which my own farm so much needed. But except for my small use of the fencing timber, this purchase has been to me so far dead capital. The cost was a small fraction less than $5 the acre. In the summer of the same year, another tract of 300, Talley's, filling the interval between my late purchase & my farm, was offered at public sale; & I bought it at about $8.25 the acre.[176] This, though mostly extremely poor, was to me a very valuable acquisition, because its arable land was adjoining mine for more than a mile, & the dividing line was so crooked, that I could actually fence in the cleared part of this tract (Talley's) cheaper than I could leave it out of my general enclosure. Besides, its possession was necessary to the perfection of my plans for drainage. For in the higher parts of this land were some of the sources of springs which my covered drains ought to take in, & were defective without; & through the lowest land was the proper outlet, toward Totopotomoi creek, of the drainage of the western part of my low ground. All these schemes for more perfect drainage were subsequently carried through. The cleared land of Talley's was mostly so exhausted as to be of no value for cultivation, until improved. The improvement, by marling, I began in 1850, & by drainage in 1851. As I did not need more space for cultivation than I had before, I enclosed separately, all the highest (or table) arable land of Talley's & all its broken land & hillsides adjoining, & nearly all of the like kinds of my own farm, for a permanent pasture—which was much wanted. This pasture took in all the cleared land about my house (about 20 acres,) most of which I sowed with this view in grazing grasses. This part had before been well marled, & the parts sown in grass seeds was now well manured. But the wire-grass, which was either well set, or sprinkled, over most of the land enclosed, was in the beginning the principal reliance for grazing. This pasture contained about [*blank*] acres of cleared land, besides a smaller space covered with worthless growth of wood. This pasture will enable me to graze my fields only to such extent as will be deemed beneficial to the land, or rather to its culture & production. And when so grazed, it may be substituted by the pasture whenever bad weather would make it improper to expose the herd boys, or where the soil was so soft as to be hurt by the treading of live-stock.

The 20 acres of my farming land which this pasture took in, had served to make up the [*illeg.*] of West field. A larger space but of poorer land will be substituted, in the adjacent land of Talley's. Another part will go to extend Middle Field, & the remainder—North Field—to all of which the new additions will join. But neither of these new additions will at first give much more gross product to either field, & certainly no net product. Except 12 acres of forest land, requiring much labor to clear, all the other land to be added from the new purchase is exhausted & very poor.

The crop of wheat of 1850, on all my farm, & throughout all this region, was suddenly & unexpectedly struck with rust.[177] Within two days after the first observed appearance of the disease, it had so rapidly extended, that not a plant in my crop was entirely free from it. The wheat was then green enough to be destroyed—& its destruction was expected. But the progress of the disease was suddenly checked on the third day. Still, great reduction of the crop was expected in consequence of this disaster. No doubt damage was produced & lessening of quantity as well as of weight. But it was less than could have been supposed possible from so general visitation of the rust. My crop still yielded 4595 bushels from 238 acres, which was an average of 19.30 to the acre.

In 1848 & '49, my cultivation had been on the fields north & east of the belt of lowest land, in all which there is no spring-water to drain—& no under-draining had been done there, & but little in the other fields. In 1850, South Field was under clover, & to be fallowed for wheat. Some limited failures (by stoppages) of covered drains made in 1847 (& before referred to) were repaired, or the parts substituted by new cuts, & some new ones made. Still much more draining was obviously wanting for that field. The great defect of my former & extensive under-draining had been the want of sufficient depth of the drains, which was owing to the want of lower outlets—& this owing to the supposed deficiency of fall in the stream-ditches. But I had found that in the latter supposition I was mistaken. At different times of cleaning out the lowest & principal stream-ditches, more depth had been obtained; & in that August (1850) all the stream-ditches of South Field had been deepened a spade's depth (say 9 inches or more) throughout, & part double that depth. This lowering of the streams was a great direct aid to the drainage of the adjacent land. But the operation also showed that this improvement might be much more extended—& that thereby lower outlets, by 6 to 12 inches might be obtained for covered drains, & of course deeper & safer drains constructed. But to obtain these results, it would be necessary to first deepen (& also widen) the main stream ditch for its whole length, upward from its outlet, eastward into the neighboring farm. This would be a work of time, & could not be immediately begun. And until the general improvement of lowering the levels of the streams could be made, I post-poned the making of all other covered drains, which required greater depth than the then depth of the stream-ditches would afford. In consequence, much covered draining in South Field (for the succeeding wheat on clover fallow) & also in the next year's field for corn, (West Field) which was required, was not done—although the actual draining operations in both fields in these two years were very considerable. It was determined to lower the streams as soon as could be done. And a general system of lowering & sloping down the margins of all stream ditches was begun in 1850, on those of South Field. This operation was carried to considerable extent, & with much advantage that season, though mostly during my absence from home for more than 5 weeks, at the Springs.

I had been sick early in summer, because of improper exposure, & therefore had deemed it necessary, for me to visit the springs. But before the time arrived when I could leave home, I was so well, that but for disappointing my daughter Jane, who was to be my companion, for her pleasure & mine, I would have staid at home. I was absent from the 20th of August to the 28th of September. During that time my man Jem. Sykes had in charge & solely directed all the matters of the farm, under the general orders which I gave before leaving home; & as before finished the thrashing & the delivery of wheat.

For 1851, West Field was to be under corn. This required much covered draining. Nearly all that had been done here before continued to operate well. But many more drains still were wanting. Of these, the most important were those of which some of the remote sources were in the adjacent Talley's tract, which now I was able for the first time to command. And also, with the aid of another outlet through that land, towards Totopotomoi, I now determined to continue the main stream-ditch through both tracts, laying the course off to the best advantage through the middle ground, where there had been no connexion before, & deepening the old parts, as well as the new, so as to sink the level of the water 12 or 18 inches lower than even my previous deepenings had made. The objects were several: 1st. To give a lower & more effective discharge to rain-floods—not only by the deeper channel, but also by offering two outlets, at the two ends of the ditch: 2nd. By being able to shut out the main supply of water, in ordinary times, from either of the outlets, & emptying it through the other, first one half of the ditch could be cleaned out, or deepened, & then the other half, by diverting the water from the work. Before, no such cleaning or deepening could be done, except under the whole volume & current of the stream. 3rd. The deepening of the bottom of the main ditch, & lowering of its water, say 12 inches, would permit the mouths of the covered drains hereafter to be made, & emptying therein, to be that much deeper, & their whole courses also, without their having less fall:[178] 5th. By tapping the low-lying & water-glutted sand stratum, I hoped to drain that stratum, & even remote ground lying above it—& so dispensing with the necessity for many of the neighboring covered drains, required in the previous condition of the springs & the concealed under-water. The views which long before had led to the belief of this last-named facility—& the results of the practical trial will be stated hereafter. For the present, I will merely state the labors performed.

As before mentioned the main ditch had some years before been in some measure straightened, & also deepened throughout its then course. But it did not extend farther north than into the Sulphur Cove. Now the object was to extend it northward to my present outer line. With this view, the lowest parts of the land were found by the level, & the line for the ditch made where best would be combined the advantages of the lowest level & the shortest route. Through the new course, & in cleared land, a strip of 12 feet wide was ploughed out, with a 4-mule plough, & then the loosened earth (rich alluvial clay) moved off in carts, to manure the nearest sandy land. When this was done, another lower course of earth was cut by the plough, & in like manner the earth removed. When a heavy rain made the ground too soft for carting over it, I had to stop the carts, & merely throw out the ploughed layers with shovels on both sides, to remain until it should be convenient to remove the earth farther. Every layer cut by the plough brought in the bottom narrower—& after cutting about 2½ feet deep, the plough could no longer be used, & then the ditch was marked off accurately, & finished to the bottom by spades. The several parts of the work may be seen in the annexed cross section:

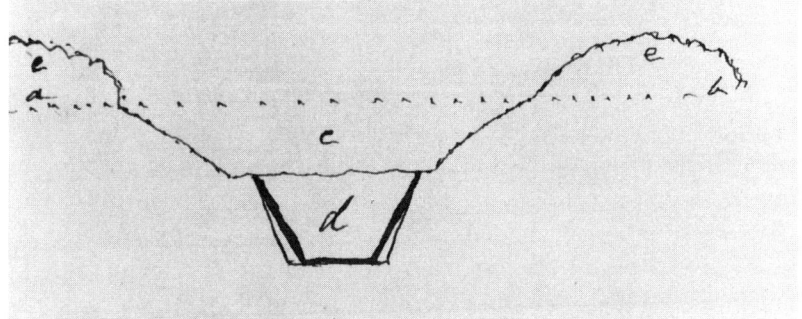

a to b, former surface.
c, the upper part cut by the plough & if not carted away, left in the banks, *e, e,* on each side
d, the lower part of ditch cut to lines by the spade.

Near opposite the Sulphur Spring is the summit level, or highest part of the route, from which there is a general but slight descent towards either end. Through Talley's tract I had to follow the old route of the shallow main ditch for that land, but deepened it from 18 to 24 inches more than had ever been done before. In this lowest digging some very bold boiling springs were reached, though this ditch had never before yielded a drop of spring water. And for some 200 yards along the new part of the route, near the Sulphur Spring, though the lower sand & its confined water could not be reached by the spade, it was done in many places by the auger, by boring 2 or 3 feet lower in the bottom of the ditch, & bursts of spring water drawn up. Any one of these bursts would have remained a permanent & bold spring if alone. But each one made, reaching the same glutted reservoir, of course gave freer vent to the confined water, & lessened the discharge from each of the previous apertures. Some continued, & some ceased to flow.

The opening of this deepened main ditch was a laborious work, & is not yet (in 1851) near completed. Much of the margins & banks of even the new part have not yet been carted off—& all the older part of the ditch is yet to be widened, all to be still more deepened, & all the margins to be lowered & removed. Already the obvious benefits produced are great. And if my extent of knowledge of the strata, & my territorial rights, had permitted this to have been done at first, it would have made the labor I have spent in other draining twice as effectual for the cost.

The deepening of this main ditch was waited for to empty therein the water from an extensive system of branch covered drains. Consequently it was late in the spring of '51 before the drainage was done, & still later before the low ground so drained was dry enough to be ploughed. Some of the important covered drains were moreover twice choked, soon after being covered, by very high & unusual overflowing floods from heavy rains. When the corn, late from these causes, was still very young, a long & severe drought began, which will reduce the crop of some 15 acres of this very rich low-ground (Sulphur Cove) to less than half what would have been obtained, even in the same season, from early drainage, & early & proper preparation of the land. Great as has been the expense of the draining, this amount lost of the crop from the delay would have doubly defrayed all the expense. This is one of the many cases of the omission or delay of an improvement being more costly than its best early execution. But my remarks have extended too far into what will best come together in a more general & also more detailed description of the drainage features & labors of the farm.

Peas, as a manuring & fallow crop.

Field peas have long been grown on some of the poorest lands of lower Va, as a crop for sale. With this view they were planted between the stations (or hills) of growing corn. If the peas did not produce much, in these circumstances, they cost little more than the planting; & the cultivators deemed the product as so much clear gain. The crop was better on poor sandy land than on rich, as in the latter case the plants would run too much to vine & leaf, & would produce less in grain than on poorer land. Such at least was the general opinion; & it was certain that most of the peas sent to market, or for sale, were produced on poor & badly cultivated lands.

Most good & reasoning farmers rejected this mode of raising peas among corn, because believing that whatever might be made in the peas would be just so much taken from the production of corn. That opinion kept me from making peas in this manner until after my stay in South Ca, where I saw the practice almost universal,[179] & no injury to the corn suspected. There are good reasons for believing that no such injury is caused by this secondary growth. The peas are planted so much later than the corn, that the latter crop finishes its growth before the former is much advanced. And if after the corn is perfected, the peas, should be ever so luxuriant, they only take the place of crab-grass, or other weeds which would have grown spontaneously, & taken possession of the ground. Thus I infer, from my later reasoning, & also from experiment sustaining the opinion, that the secondary growth of planted peas, does no harm to the more advanced growth of corn.

Again, it is now a well established scientific truth, that all pod-bearing plants, or peas, clover &c. take more of their support from the atmosphere, & less in proportion from the earth, than any other plants. And therefore, when their whole, or principal growth is left on the land as manure, their growth must be an enriching process, giving all to the land, while it had taken from the land but a small part of the vegetable product. No experiments have yet been made to show whether a broadcast & thick cover of pea-vines is equally harmless to corn. But there is no evidence to the contrary. If doing no harm to the corn, the heavier the cover of peas, the more it must be enriching to the land. These views led me to try this as a manuring crop—& not only as sown among growing corn, but also as a separate crop, having all the land & the sunshine to itself,—& which is much more productive, & consequently more fertilizing, than when peas are sown among growing corn.

Other farmers, long in advance of my practice, have desired to make pea-fallow a manuring & preparatory crop for wheat. Some few, from time to time, have sown wheat on pea-fallow; & we have had reports of fine wheat made by such preparation. But for some one or other reason, no such lucky experimenter ever continued long, if at all, to repeat the practice, or to begin to make it part of a practical & regular system or rotation. Some of our best improvers, who had planned the making pea-fallow a regular part of their rotation, did not carry the design into effect.

In 1839, when my son Edmund was about to take the direction of the Coggins farm, I wrote a series of articles on green-manuring, & schemes of rotation, which were published in the 7th & 8th vols. of Farmers' Register.[180] Pea fallow for wheat was one of the features of the preferred rotation; & this was pursued in our partnership farming for two years or more. The difficulty which caused the abandonment of the plan at that time, (though it latterly has been resumed there,) was that we could not raise the peas for seed, the seed we bought having been of a late kind,)[181] & there was then no certainty of being able to buy them. The second year, the whole field remained unsown, because of a disappointment in the expected supply, from N.Ca. This was an insuperable objection—which no longer exists. The increased demand for peas has made the supply regular & sufficient. Still the buying of so large a quantity as required to sow a field is a heavy expense—& the preparation & seeding is a heavy labor; & these are two important obstacles, which have mainly prevented the practice being persevered in anywhere.

I began to plant peas among corn, on a small scale, for experiment, the first year of my farming at Marlbourne, & gradually extended the planting. In 1846 I had a considerable space of my corn-field sown broad-cast in peas, as well as nearly all the remainder, of suitable soil, being planted. In addition, in 1847, another separate piece of land, where clover had failed, was also sown in peas, as part of the general fallow preparation for wheat. The succeeding crop of wheat on this piece especially, was so decidedly superior to the adjacent clover fallow, that I was induced to make the practice general; & I planned a rotation for the purpose of embracing the scheme of pea-fallow. This scheme of rotation has already been concisely mentioned, & will be more fully described hereafter.

In 1848, a whole field (South) which had been in corn in 1847, was under broad-cast peas. Though sowed too early for safety, for most years, as I afterwards found, the season was favorable, the stand good, & the growth excellent. That first success made me too confident, & incautious, & I have never since succeeded in having either a uniform good stand, or a good growth. Since, I have partially failed in obtaining full crops both by sowing too late & too early; but mostly by omitting to plough the land until near the time for sowing in peas, & then drought preventing either the ploughing of the land (if stiff,) or the coming up of the peas. The ploughing of land in May is eminently a cleansing process, as all the bad weeds for wheat are then well advanced in growth, & none yet in seed. The [*illeg.*] ploughing under then effectively destroys all the annuals then growing, & all the root weeds (as wild garlic) for that year. It was to have this benefit, as well as the freshest & cleanest seed-bed for the peas, that I postponed the ploughing until late in May. But this risk should not be incurred. Hereafter I shall plough at least all the clay land for pea fallow before April is over.

Owing to the partial failures of my pea [sowings?], I have never yet had wheat on a good pea-fallow throughout except the first time; & that wheat was the crop so nearly destroyed by the repeated freezings in April 1849. But the growths of wheat since have been fully equal to my previous high expectations for pea-fallow, wherever the manuring crop had grown well. Except that the early growth of peas is so precareous,

& so much dependent on warmth & sufficient & yet but moderate moisture, I have no other objection to the crop. When well started, it is as sure to grow well as any other crop, & is as little affected by excess of either drought or moisture.

Peas sown among corn in July, having a well pulverized & clean seed bed, generally start well—unless sown in or followed by drought so great that the seed either cannot sprout, or that they dry & perish after sprouting. But the shade of the corn so retards the growth of peas, that the latter is usually not half equal to the growth of a separate pea fallow. This year (1851) I gave much of my corn its last tillage in June, before & in wheat harvest, sowing peas at same time. All these peas have grown finely; & the only question as to the superiority of this plan, is in regard to the effect on the corn. No inferiority of its growth is however perceptible, in general appearance, so far.

Clover.

Uncertain as I have found the getting a good & general cover of peas, the growth of clover has been still more uncertain. The Pamunkey marl is especially favorable to clover—& much more so than is any merely calcareous marl—though the carbonate of lime is essential, & must be the foundation of all other improving or manuring substances for clover. To the sulphate of lime, which is certainly in this marl, much of its superior manuring effect on clover is due. Whether the green-sand is also beneficial is more than I know certainly. But notwithstanding the superior effect of this marl, I have been very unlucky in most of my clover crops. Either late severe frosts in spring, or summer drought, generally kills most of the young plants, of that spring's sowing—& sometimes scarcely any has escaped both these usual disasters. And when, rarely, a good stand has been obtained, if the summer of the next year should be very dry, still the growth may be very small. Thus, there has rarely occurred a good second year's crop, of a previous year's good stand of plants. My fields designed for clover fallow have sometimes had very little clover, & almost always more weeds than clover, over large portions, of the field.

On my system, nearly all my prepared manure, from stables, & winter cow & hog pens, has been applied as top-dressing on the clover, the year it was to be ploughed under in autumn. My views of this mode of applying manure have been published in a separate paper.[182]

Sulphate of lime (gypsum) so powerful a manure for clover elsewhere, has no effect on land marled with our eocene marl. This is easily accounted for, by the sufficient quantity of gypsum in the marl. But when some years shall have passed, I expect this first dose of gypsum will have been exhausted by the clover, or otherwise, & then that an application of gypsum will be beneficial.

My plan of clover-culture, & using the crop for hay & manure, has been before the public in an essay embracing the whole subject.[183]

Wide Beds.

Long ago I had formed the opinion that, where the bedding of land is required for its better surface drainage, that very wide beds would be preferable to narrow. I had before tried the plan successfully in practice on the few acres of arable low-ground I had on Coggins, & which was the only space then in my possession level enough for bedding to be required, or on which water-furrows would not have been actually injurious, by causing more washing. I had advocated the plan, for level lands, in different articles of the Farmers' Register. Very lately my views have been set forth more fully, in an essay published in the American Farmer.[184] This annexed paper will serve for full explanation, & enable me to dispense with any more in these notes.[185]

As soon as I had removed to this level farm, requiring bedding very generally, & which had been all cultivated in the narrow corn beds usual throughout this region, I determined to introduce my scheme of wide beds. But the altering the direction of old beds is a troublesome operation, rarely effected well in the first year, & injurious at first to drainage & to production, by the imperfection. Some early changes of this kind had been attended with these ill effects; & worse, because the change had not been properly digested, the direction had subsequently to be changed again. On this account, I submitted generally to follow the plan & direction of the bedding as I found it, for some years, before being well acquainted with the character & wants of the land, & deeming myself competent to choose the best directions for the wide beds. In 1848, I began to put part of the low grounds into beds of 27½ feet wide; & have continued since, as fields came under culture, to put them in beds of either 25 or 27½ feet. Nearly all the fields have now been ploughed in that shape. But though this shape is deemed best for drainage & for convenient cultivation, the deep water-furrows (& grips) are obstacles to carting across, (though less so than with the many more of narrow beds—) & will be still greater obstacles to the operation of machines for drilling the seed & for reaping wheat—both of which I wish to introduce on my farm. Therefore, though all the surface of each field will be kept laid off in the same general scheme of wide beds, I design, by reversing ploughing, or other changes of tillage processes, to keep the surface of all dry & sandy soil level enough not to make the obstacles referred to. The water-furrows through this kind of land will merely be visible, so as to serve as a guide for subsequent ploughing. One half or more of the surface of my farm is of pervious soil & subsoil, & does not need bedding—& I would never have any but level flush ploughing on such land, if it was in large spaces. But so spotted is the whole farm with soils of different textures & levels, that scarcely anywhere can a direction for ploughing & planting be chosen, in which some part of every row does not pass into either very stiff or low land. The manner of ploughing & of subsequent tillage could not be changed with all these frequent changes of soil; & hence the marking off the beds, & the extension of the rows, & the running of ploughs, must be continued through all kinds of land—except the little that is light & dry throughout the whole lengths of the rows, & that which is sloping or steep.

Corn culture.

Since putting my land into wide beds, I have as much as possible used flush or level cultivation. I use no mould-board plough in the tillage of corn, & raise no "hills" around the stalks with hoes. The land is broken well & deeply, & as early in winter as may be, & latterly 4-mule ploughs have mostly been used. The depth of ploughing is from 6 to 8 inches, & sometimes more in spots, or is designed to be as deep as the depth of soil will admit, if not too laborious for the team—or where the soil is not very deep, as in all the "black land." In the subsequent preparation & tillage—with large harrows at first, for covering the seed, & for smoothing the surface—cultivators for clear land—shovel ploughs, & even coulters, for more foul or stubborn ground—& one deep ploughing for all when the plants are from 6 to 15 inches high—with all, I aim to merely keep the surface clear of grass, & the soil well & deeply pulverized.[186] That is my whole rule for tillage, for every crop, after the soil has been made dry. But I must admit that I am not always as successful in the production of corn as many more careful cultivators, who work their crops more carefully & also longer than I do. But, I have not labor to spare from my wheat, & therefore cannot afford to give more to corn.

I doubt whether more is to be made by the usual greater labor, than will repay the greater expense.

If giving the last tillage to corn (& with it sowing the secondary crop of peas) can be done safely for the corn before wheat harvest—as I have done with all my forward growth this year—it will be a great saving of labor in corn culture, & also giving to the land much more benefit of the pea-manuring.

Wheat.

The product of wheat on my farm has risen above any hopes I had entertained a few years ago. On other farms in this neighborhood the present high rate of production is not less remarkable, & full as recent. Whatever may be the cause, there were no heavy crops of wheat grown in this neighborhood until recently. The main cause of the previous deficiency I think must have been the very light & insufficient applications of marl—& the very general use of green-sand earth for marl, or of beds very poor in carbonate of lime. Nearly all the marling farmers have latterly doubled, & some have tripled their former light dressings—& no one now uses the nearly non-calcareous green-sand bed, if he can obtain any more calcareous marl.

Judging only from the effects on wheat, I believe that this marl must contain a small proportion of phosphate of lime, which is so valuable & important a specific manure for wheat. It is certain, that latterly, not only are our products of wheat large for the land, but the quantity of grain is large in proportion to the straw—& my quantities of grain have latterly exceeded my estimates that had been made upon the appearance of the growing crop. This is precisely the difference which has heretofore been between the wheat crops of the best wheat soils in other regions, & ours. In the Genesee country of New York, & on other as well constituted wheat soils, a growing crop, which would actually yield 20 bushels to the acre, did not appear a heavier growth than our wheat which would make not more than 12 bushels.

Putrescent or prepared Manures.

The first winter & spring of my occupancy, the farm had been stripped of all litter as well as of all manure—& I had to purchase the remains of the straw-stack, & also collect leaves from the woods for the mules, horses, 4 oxen & a cow which then made the whole of my live-stock.

Since, the offal of my crops have made all the vegetable material for my winter-made manure. Latterly, more than half the corn stalk (by high cutting off,) has been left in the field, & as high stubble of the wheat as I could have left, without too much waste of the heads.

According to the plan advocated, I carry out the unrotted manure, in the latter part of winter & spring, & in dry weather, from stables, cowyard, & hog pen, & spread it as top-dressing on clover. I have made no experiments to test the comparative advantages of this mode of application; but I have pursued this practice now for about 17 years, & have been satisfied with the results. But even if more benefit could be obtained from the manure, by ploughing it under, I could not possibly be able to perform the labor. My manure for the whole year, such as it is, extends over 50 or 60 acres of clover land—& the whole labor of loading, carting, & spreading is sufficiently heavy.[187] If requiring to be ploughed under, & at times suitable for the crops, the labor would be very much increased—& the choice of times & weather as much contracted.

The penning of cattle for the nights, through summer, as usual on naked earth, & moving the pens as each space is enough manured, is costly in the exaction of labor, & very wasteful of the manure. But even this mode is less wasteful than to-pen on straw litter. In the latter case, the litter ferments so rapidly in summer, that it is mostly lost by decomposition, & serves to aid & is aided by the decomposition of the animal matter.

Hoping to avoid the worst of both these wasteful methods, I have for two summers penned my cattle on a thick bed of leaves from the woods, & mostly pine-leaves. These resist fermentation very strongly, & therefore are so much the better for this purpose. The first year, marl & salt were intermixed with the leaves—& once during summer the mass of leaves, then rotted at top & dry below, was hoed up & mixed. But this was a bad plan. While thus the rotted part was retained, & continued to rot & to waste, much remained unrotted until winter, & then was carted out as manure, because so intermixed with the rotted. This year I took a different & what seems a much preferable course. As before, the leaves were raked, heaped in the woods, & hauled in during wet spells in spring, when no other team work could be done. The pen, (about 34 yards square,) was filled with the leaves fully 4 feet deep at first, but which the treading of the cattle soon compacted to one foot & less. I had not then access to marl, & could not buy refuse salt—so that neither of these materials could be added to the compost. In August, when the earth was too wet for ploughing, the rotted upper layer of the bed was removed, & used to top-dress grass in the adjacent pasture land. This rotted layer was wet, compact in texture, though soft & almost miry, & seemed to be rich manure. It was easily separated from the compact & unrotted bed of leaves below—which, by being so stripped was made a firm & sufficiently dry bed for the comfort of the cattle. If such a removal had been made earlier, & oftener, the manure would have sustained less waste, & the cattle less dis-comfort. In this manner, I think the very putrescent animal matter will serve as leaven to promote the fermentation of the leaves; & both will be better economized than in any other way. Should there still remain a layer of the leaves unrotted, it need not be moved, but will serve for part of the litter for the next Summer's penning.

One important advantage of penning on this thick layer of pine leaves is that the beetles, so destructive elsewhere to fresh dung in summer will not meddle with this. The greatest destruction they commit is by eating the excrement, which is their only food. But they also roll off & bury balls of it, in which they have enclosed their eggs. Whether it is that the odor of the pine leaves is offensive to these insects, or that they know they cannot either roll off their balls, or bury them on the leaves— so it is, that they avoid the dung in the pen, while nearly all outside is devoured or removed by them. During the summer months, it seems as if three-fourths of all the dung of animals is utterly destroyed by these insects.

Live-stock.

My cattle have been gradually increased from about [*blank*] to now about 50 head—& my sheep are now about 50 in number. Until 1851, when a separate pasture had been enclosed, which has in part only supplied the grazing, all the cattle & sheep, after leaving the winter & spring pens, were herded & grazed upon the field which had the previous year borne wheat after clover. It was deemed beneficial to the crops (wheat & clover especially,) that the land should be grazed & trampled to some extent. The time for this grazing was when each field had borne wheat (on clover fallow) the preceding year, & was to be planted in corn the year succeeding the pasturing. But I doubt whether the *trampling* before the wheat crop, would not be better than before corn. Besides the regular grazing of this shift, I also had the cattle for a short time on the young clover, as soon as the wheat was removed. The trampling then, & perhaps also the preventing so much shade of weeds, is beneficial to the growth of the young clover.

Now, the permanent pasture, though mostly poor, & as yet having very little other than wire-grass, will enable me to have the cattle on the tillage fields no more than will be supposed best for their production.

The cattle were confined entirely to a well-littered pen, sheltered from the wind on the north & west sides, from the beginning of November to as late in April as they required dry food. They were driven to water twice a day. Their food was wheat straw at will—the few corn-shucks pulled off separately—& the shucks & fodder left on the stalks, after they had been a night in the stable, for the mules. Under this rough treatment, my cattle (exclusive of milking cows & working oxen,) have fared better than cattle usually do. They are usually in better condition than most other cattle in the spring; & not one has died at that time, or under any suspicion of death being caused by poverty.

My sheep have been kept to supply lambs & mutton to my family & partly for sale. They are more cheaply kept, & with less trouble than any other stock. When on a good pasture, though without an enclosure, they need scarcely any attention to prevent their wandering to the crops. Of late years, my sheep have been permitted through winter to graze on the wheat; & if permitted access only when the ground is not wet, & not suffered to stay too much in one place, I do not think their grazing is perceptibly injurious to the wheat, while their trampling is beneficial to both wheat & clover. No dry food has ever been given to my sheep, except during the short time that the ground is covered by straw—when they have fodder. They were penned at night, with the cattle, winter & summer, generally, before I had a separately enclosed pasture.

I have tried to have hogs to graze on clover, & on the wheat fields, after removing the wheat, but found it impossible to have them kept out of mischief. Hence, they have, of necessity, been confined to a pen, winter & summer, & fed almost entirely on corn. Even this bad plan I think has returned me some profit—& certainly more than if the hogs ranged in the woods, or in enclosed fields. But I cannot avoid their being neglected, & suffering sometimes both for proper supplies of food & water. I have heretofore raised nearly the whole of my supplies of pork. But I design to reduce the number of hogs to no more than will consume my offal grain. While western bacon can be bought at 5 to 7 cents, I think it bad economy to raise & feed hogs on good corn, fit for sale. The price however is sometimes much higher; & now it is from 11½ to 14 cents.

The year 1851 was remarkably favorable to the production of wheat. My crop had been seeded very imperfectly, though with great labor, because of the continued excessive drought, & great hardness of the land, during all October. Most of my good land was stiff, & all such was in hard clods. Scarcely more than half the number of plants stood that as much seed would usually produce. Yet the crop yielded more than 6000 bushels from 267 acres (by estimate of the land.) The crop of corn was very much shortened by severe drought in summer. With this year, & now as the amounts of the last products are precisely ascertained, I will exhibit the full statement, in tabular form, of all my grain crops raised on Marlbourne.[188] The products of peas, which even for the ripened seed, have been important in latter years, are not included. But a small proportion are saved, & the quantity measured. All the larger remainders are either ploughed under as manure, or fall & rot on the land, where not ploughed under, or are eaten during winter by stock. As manure, or for food, all are consumed on the farm, & more are annually bought, to make up the large quantity of seed (more than 200 bushels) latterly designed to be sown, so as to cover broadcast two of the six fields.

In 1850 a convention had to be elected to alter the constitution of Va. The radical changes designed were advocated by almost every aspirant, whether he really approved them or not, for the purpose of gaining popular favor.[189] The selection[s?] of candidates for seats in the convention, according to the corrupt usage which has latterly been introduced in Va, was done by self-constituted district conventions, in which but few persons acted except demagogues & office seekers—& if other more patriotic & disinterested persons entered, it was to see that they had no power to prevent the vote being the mere decree of a few managers, who acted entirely for their own base interests. Under such a system generally working & with the further evil principles of these caucuses being of party character, & making party creed the first ground for the choice of a body to frame or remodel a form of government—it was to be expected that the choice of members for this high service, would be generally as bad as could be made. And the result did not fall much short of this anticipation.

Statement of Marl applied, & Grain Crops made on Marlbourne Farm, from 1844 to [blank]

Year	Marl applied. Heaped Bushels	Wheat					Corn				Oats			Total Acres in grain
		Acres	Seed Bushels	Crop Bushels	Sold Bushels	Average to acre	Acres	Crop Bushels	Sold Bushels	Average to acre	Acres	seed	Crop	
1844	67,875	No land under wheat.					156	2830	1562	18.14	131	154	2000	287
1845	75,512	134	140	1977	1764	14.75	112	1600	796	14.28	92	120	1200	338
1846	35,545	201	213	2432	2162	11.42	120	3600	2508	30.	20		250	341
1847	42,575	235	270	3511	3287	15.32	175	4500	3060	25.71	16		200	426
1848	55,106	256	224	5127	4869	20.02	106	3080	1501	28.12	2	4	106	364
1849	56,169	263	258	3375	3115	12.83	140	5431	3753	38.79	0	—	—	403
1850	34,684	238	225	4595	4381	19.30	124	3500	1859	28.	0	—	—	362
1851	850	267	278	6072	5772	22.74	130	3600	2280	27.70	Peas gathered 285			
1852	23,228	259	302	5308	4736	20.45	124	5438	3823	43.85				
1853		255	306	4790	4807	18.80	136							

After both the opposing caucuses, of the two political parties, in this district, had made their respective nominations, some opposers of this mode of nomination assembled in public meeting, at a very late day, & nominated another ticket, in which my name was included. I knew that there was no possible chance for my being elected, in opposition to caucus organition, dictation & rule. But I gladly seized the opportunity afforded by this published nomination, to put forth, without the appearance of improperly obtruding them, my opinions of the expected changes of our government, & more especially of the caucus system of selecting representatives & public officers. I did not attend a single public meeting, or place, nor in any other way act the candidate. But in the few days which intervened between the publication & the day for the election, I had left home to visit the Springs. The votes given to me, under these circumstances, were more numerous than could have been expected—but of course did not serve to elect me.[190] I insert my answer to the call made upon me, as a concise statement of my sentiments upon the political questions under consideration.[191]

Throughout this year, 1851, I have done no marling. Mr. Carter Braxton, who had voluntarily offered to me the use of his marl for this farm, without limitation or conditions, & which offer was the operating inducement to buy the farm, in the course of time made sundry requisitions connected with my working the marl, which I had complied with, until they were made so burdensome to me, & yet of so little use to his own interest—indeed, in some respects, so absurd as well as unreasonable—that at last I was obliged to understand these demands as indirectly denying & withdrawing the privilege which he had freely, fully, & of his own accord & motion, given to me. Believing this, I complied with the last requisition, to its full extent, & then withdrew from all further use of Mr. Braxton's marl. When so quitting, the last uncovered body was not half worked out, & had enough marl all ready exposed & well drained for use, to cover 150 acres or more. Mr. Braxton's gift of the use of his marl was to me of great value—but not the slightest loss or cost to him, as he has marl in inexhaustible quantity, & easily accessible in various places; & all of it beyond his own demand is of no value to him. While I ought to be, & am, thankful to him for the kindness of feeling that prompted his original offer, I rejoice that his favor to me has cost him not a cent. On the other hand, by his profiting only partially by my example in conducting his marling operations, (which before were very slowly & badly executed, & yet at double cost,) & by better availing himself of the benefits afforded by marling for wheat culture, he has doubled his crops of wheat—&, at the very least, is richer by $10,000 than he was before, or would have been now, if I had not become his neighbor.

I have clea[r?]ed off the earth from part of the marl of Mr. J. W. Tomlin,[192] about a mile more distant, & have made the road ready for me, when I may have both spare labor & fit state of the roads, for this very long hauling. Since, by boring, I have found the extension of the same eocene marl on my own land, (near the Sulphur Cove,) but unfortunately covered by 13 feet of earth where nearest to the surface. This bed will be opened as soon as circumstances permit, & the thickness of the marl & the difficulties of the excavation, ascertained. Should I be enabled to work there advantageously, the locality is very favorable in vicinity to those parts of my land yet to be marled for the first time, & which are more remote from the marl which I have heretofore used, & also from the new uncovering on Mr. Tomlin's land.

The rapid & great improvement of my land, & increase of the crops, had seemed to add greatly to my capital. So that, notwithstanding the greatly increased outlay necessary to make stated & liberal allowances to my daughters, I found my funds more abundant than before my many & heavy losses previous to removing to my present residence. It had always been my designed policy to distribute to my children, as they arrived at sufficient age & discretion, such portion of capital of their designed patrimony, as I could spare without injury to the general farming capital, & the future benefit of all my children. Looking to my property as held in trust for my children, not only was I prompted by their interest, but by regard to my own ease & relief from labor & care, to place in each one's charge & management his or her respective portion. In this way, when it can be done, each son is put to work to nurse & increase his own share of capital—instead of drawing the income from the father's annual gifts or allowances. The first course, if the son is trustworthy, is the surest to make him industrious & economical—& the latter to make him idle, & prodigal, if not worse in his habits founded upon idleness. But though wishing to act upon this early approved (& yet very unusual) rule of conduct, the state of my family & my affairs did not permit me to carry out the plan fully, until lately. As my three older children came of age,[193] I gave to each property to the amount of $4000. After my wife's death, to my next four children, all daughters, when they severally left school, I paid annuities equal to the interest of $4000 for each, including a moderate charge for board &.[194] Thus, I was at last freed from my care about disbursements for their expenses, or having to exercise my judgment or direction in regard to their expenses. This procedure worked well; & in leaving them all, even when just having left school, to use their own income at will, in no case has either of my daughters exceeded the amount, or been wanting in proper prudence in expenditures.

At the close of 1850, (after some previous farther advances towards this end,) I thought I could pay off the entire estimated portions to my children of mature age, & provide for the same for the younger children[195] as fast as they should reach sufficient age, or be able to use their capital—& in the mean time to pay the full income, on interest of a share, to each one not still a minor. With this view, I made a rough estimate of the then value of my property, & found it, including the capital before given to my older children, full $81,000. This allowed a dividend of $9000 for each of my nine children. And this accordingly was then given, either in capital actually paid over, or in the interest of the like capital, to each of my children except the two youngest, then still at school.[196] It is true that I could not have then paid the capital to all the then distributees—as it would have left but the shares of the two youngest in my hands, & moreover would have required the sale of my land, & division of my slaves—& of course the cessation of all further accumulation by my own farming labors. But I charged myself with the quarterly payments of interest on as much capital—leaving the fourth distribution of the capital to be made after my death, or sooner if necessary.[197] In this manner, I did not the less divest myself of the whole portions of seven of my children, because for four of that number I retained & managed their capital, & paid to them the interest.[198] To facilitate these regular payments, I had latterly vested all my surplus income in government loans or other permanent 6 per cent. stocks.

In making the estimate of my property for this equal division, it is true that I took care that any error of amount should be in favor of leaving some surplus capital, after the final division, rather than to leave a deficiency, to be borne by the latest sharers. But with this exception, I designed so to share equally, & to distribute in succession, as required by age, the whole amount of my then possessions—not reserving for myself even an equal share, or any share.[199] I did this upon several grounds. I was certain that my own personal wants & uses for income would never be increased beyond the then moderate & yet ample amount. If I should live until my youngest child should be portioned in capital, or in its interest, I felt assured that before that time I could earn enough more to meet all subsequent demands; & if I should die before that time, of course no more would be wanted, except to complete the division.

In regard to these general estimates of property, & of other values of uncertain amounts which have been before stated, it should be understood that all are more or less conjectural, though as near accurate as my recollection & my belief would indicate. I have never kept any accounts as to my own pecuniary matters, in which the rights of or dues to other persons were not concerned—& have always been unacquainted with, as well as very neglectful of the keeping of accounts properly. I was very careful, however, in keeping accounts of my obligations or acquittances to other persons—as in regard to my wards formerly, & to the subscribers of the Farmers' Register subsequently.[200] But this was the extent of my care. At this time, & for years back, I have not any account book, nor so much as a memorandum of any debts due to me, (unless evidenced by bonds.) It is true, & it is the only & a poor excuse for such a neglectful course, that I have very few debts (except the very many that are desperate) due to me, & that I owe almost none—except to my commission merchant only, whose account is settled twice a year. For this neglect of keeping accounts, & vouchers for payments made, I have doubtless lost thousands of dollars in the course of my life. The course is indefensible—but my amendment at this late day is hopeless.

Since the death of my wife, my unmarried daughters have lived with me, & by their care & attention have conducted my household affairs with as much success as was possible for housekeepers so young & inexperienced. To the exemplary conduct of my affectionate & dutiful children I am indebted for all the comfort & happiness that I enjoy. And I have much of both to be thankful for. Though I have had to bear & still bear, some heavy afflictions, still in my family relations generally I have been unusually & eminently blessed.

The health of my family in general, at my new residence, has been good—and could not have been better, so far as regards diseases of locality or climate. For some years after my return from South Carolina, there remained to me symptoms of a determination of blood to the head, which though slight, were without cessation—& which made me look for apoplexy as my end.[201] But these symptoms have since disappeared—& more lately I am still more unpleasantly affected by bronchitis, or some other hopeless affection of the throat—which though unaccompanied by pain, is very troublesome & annoying, & is growing worse. In other respects, my health has generally been good. All my more temporary indispositions were induced by my habitual exposure to the heat of the sun, & often to other inclemencies of the weather or season. With some abatement, I am yet able to lead a life of generally active & (as most persons would deem it, even of laborious) pursuits—which course is essential to my happiness. But my condition of recent healthiness, & my activity & power to labor & to endure, after all, are such as might belong to a man of good constitution at 70 or 75 years of age. My naturally feeble constitution & physical powers, & the super-added ill-health of a large portion of my earlier life, have operated to bring upon me early infirmity & decay of both physical & mental powers. In my 58th year, I am in body & mind as if 12 or 15 years older. My power of memory has long been lessening—& now, scarcely at all retains the minute details of *recent* occurrences. In addition to thus speedily forgetting, of late I have almost lost the ability to acquire solid & useful information by reading or study. When it is so difficult to acquire new knowledge, & so easy & certain to lose any so acquired, no more profit, & but little & very transient pleasure, are to be obtained from new books or studies of truly solid & valuable information. I have almost ceased to make such attempts. I give as much of my leisure time as ever to reading, & glance over as many pages. But my reading is now almost confined to the lightest works of fiction—romances, the tales & scetches in magazines—agricultural & political periodicals & news papers—nearly all of this mostly light & useless matter is forgotten in a few weeks, if not in a few days, after being read.

These defects & infirmities, are the usual & inevitable effects of old age, & accompaniments of nearly exhausted mental powers. I do not mention them in a spirit of complaint, but merely to state facts having (perhaps) more or less bearing on my acts in recently passed years, (of which I cannot myself judge—) & I fear will have more on my remaining short term of life. May God protect me, even if early death be the means, from my living through an old age of great infirmity of body and imbecility of mind!

But as I now am, however lowered in physical & mental power, I still greatly enjoy life, without much regretting the probable speedy approach of its end. In my children it seems to me that my life is renewed & extended. Their well-doing is nearly all that concerns me personally for the short remainder of my life. For their benefit I can not do much more than I have already effected. In their present & prospective welfare, & especially in their good conduct, all my wishes & all my happiness rests. And in this, to me most important of all concerns,[202] I have sources for much happiness. Perhaps the calm enjoyments of my latest years of life are not less in measure than during my years of youth & early manhood.

To my Children.

For you I have prepared, & to your care & direction I entrust, the materials which I have written without care as to form & manner, but with every care to adhere to the truth, so far as enabled by a failing memory. Exactness has not always been attained in the details, especially as to dates & numbers. For in the haste of writing, I often either trusted to my memory, or otherwise left the amounts blank, to be corrected or supplied by future reference to my farm journals, or other papers. Should I not hereafter supply all such needed corrections, it may be done by another hand, by reference to the other named papers.[203]

These notes have been written in the leisure hours of a few months of 1851. They are not designed as an autobiography, nor for publication—for which, besides other & sufficient objections, this writing is entirely unfitted by its hasty preparation, & rough form. But even in this form, I presume that these notes, after my death, will be interesting & valued by my children, & more remote descendants. And should the incidents of my life, & results of my labors for agricultural improvement, be deemed worthy of being written for the public eye, he who may undertake the task may find some of the materials in this writing. For such purpose, & to that extent, I am willing that it may be used—but no farther. Even if I were to make every correction of form & manner as well as matter that my taste & judgment, & more mature deliberation could possibly suggest, I am too well aware of the difficulties of autobiography to attempt the task, certain as I should be of failing in the attempt.

INCIDENTS OF MY LIFE

Volume 3 (1853)

Private.

Incidents of my Life

3

1853

In Memoriam

1855

After an interval of more than two years since the writing of the foregoing pages, I resume the continuation of these notes. The motive for this resumption is to state the very different condition of things which has subsequently occurred & now exists, in regard to my position in the public mind & favor, compared to that which I supposed had been before assigned to me.

I had before stated in a few but strongly expressed passages the bitterness of my feelings for the slighting and ungrateful conduct of my countrymen in general, & the apparent forgetfulness of the agricultural public of Virginia of my services. Some striking examples & proofs were adduced. To my imagination, perhaps morbidly sensitive, & construing many things wrongly, every indication of the public action or non-action concerning me, served to show the general unconsciousness of the great majority, of my services. It is true that I never ceased to have many warm & grateful admirers & approvers. But these were remote, scattered, & their opinions not heard and mostly not known. Of those persons so near as to be in the sphere of personal intercourse & companionship, it seemed to me that there were many more who were either indifferent or more or less hostile to me, than truly friendly. Much of this latter position was doubtless my own fault. I never possessed what are known as popular manners—never courted popular favor—& on both these grounds, failed to obtain it. While it has been my good fortune to have the warm attachment of many intimate friends, & the high admiration of many who scarcely knew me personally, I have lost many of former approvers, & had around me in every place of long residence, more who disliked me, through envy, jealousy, or other causes, or were indifferent, than true friends. My admitted errors of conduct might have offered much ground for this rather hostile than friendly feeling of the neighboring population. But the main cause was my habit of uttering my opinions of men & things freely & strongly, & incautiously, as if every one I spoke before was a man of honor & my friend, instead of being, as often was the case, an enemy, a tattler & mischief-maker. Thus, whatever I thought was said—& whatever said was reported & generally with false additions, where the report could be most offensive, & do me most harm. I have long been fully sensible of my error in thus speaking freely, & of its ill consequences to myself. But I have not been able to correct myself. The only attempt to prevent the certain delinquency, was in my general course of seclusion from the public, & thus avoiding as much as possible the conversation of all other than my valued neighbors, or, more distant friends & well-wishers.

But lest I should leave a false impression by this general confession, I will add some necessary explanation. Among those persons who have at former times taken sides against me, & who after being friendly, became very hostile to me, there are some who are now among my warmest & devoted & I fully believe true friends. To these persons I had never given any indication of my being aware of their enmity, & did nothing to conciliate their favor. I merely by my general conduct (as I infer) *lived down* their prejudices, or out-lived their just causes of dislike. A general, but less marked condition of things like this, extends over my old county & more especially the immediate neighborhood of my early residence. The few friends left to me, & the many enemies I had in Prince George, made me the more willing to leave that county & without any desire to retain any connexion with it—which however was compelled by my property being there, & several of my children afterwards returning to reside there. But subsequently, & now, I am gratified to believe that I have as many friends & approvers, & as few enemies in that region, (& some enemies whom I would wish otherwise—) as I could possibly expect from my conduct, & almost equal to any desire.

The latter part of my editorial career, the disregard of the public of my latter publications, & the slighting course of the legislature & especially in the niggardly support, contemptuous treatment, & speedy extinction of the Board of Agriculture,[1] all conduced to bring me to the conclusion that the public of Virginia was wearied of me & my writing—& therefore that I would withdraw entirely from all connexion with the public in my native country. The high compliment which I then received from another country, in being appointed to the Agr. Survey of S.C.[2] while much soothing my wounded pride, served, by the contrast, still more to embitter me against & seclude me from the public of Virginia.

In Jan Feby 1845, a meeting was called in Richmond to organize a State Agricultural Society.[3] There was but small attendance, & few of those who attended were really farmers. However—by aid of some members of the legislature, & of other persons of note then in the place on public business, a society was organized, on a magnificent plan. I had not attended, because expecting nothing but wrong procedure, & speedy extinction of the Society, after the fashion of so many other predecessors—as well from my rule of seclusion. I was therefore not a little astonished when seeing in the newspapers, in the account of the last proceedings of the meeting that I had been chosen as the president of the Society.[4] My course was instantly decided upon. I could not act before receiving the official notice of my election, from the Executive Committee, which was received some week later—& accompanied by the request that I would prepare & deliver the first Annual Address. I wrote by return of mail to decline the office & service. Though my language was courteous, the act was ungracious—and at a later time, when this society, & also a suceeding one had died without doing anything of any use,[5] I did still more to give offence, to the founders & members, in making the reference to these abortions which will presently be quoted.

In 1850, I was invited by the Agricultural Societies of the Eastern Shore of Md. to deliver the Annual Address to these societies. Though I had declined more than one such application in Virginia, I consented to act. This region had furnished many subscribers & some able writers for the Farmers' Register. Intercourse entirely kind had subsisted between us. I had not a personal acquaintance in all this region, but, as I believed, some friends, & many approvers. These reasons, together with my wish to see an unknown agricultural region of remarkable & peculiar features, induced me to comply. I was received with most cordial welcome, & every attention that could be offered to an honored guest. My address had been written to condemn what I deemed the usual wrong procedure of agricultural societies, & to indicate a better course. The societies I was addressing necessarily came in (incidentally) for a share of my censure, which was taken in good part. The following extract[6] will show the manner of my reference to the Agricultural Societies of Va, which had recently lived but to die, as I then supposed. But it seemed the last one was not dead, though dormant. Soon after my address was published, as if it had galvanized the apparently dead body, a meeting of the Society was summoned & held. The President (my substitute) was Andrew Stevenson,[7] a lawyer of some note, & a corrupt & hacknied politician—a landholder & no farmer. By request, he delivered an address to the Society, which must have been even more worthless than such things usually are, as it was not published—& then the Society was no more heard of.[8]

After the last named State Agricultural Society had been organized, I sent in my name & subscription as a member—deeming it my duty to do so much to forward the work, but to have no more to do with it. My subsequent taunts, just quoted, might have been expected to arouse anger, & I well deserved that result. These occurrences seemed still more to surprise me with what followed.

In the beginning of 1852, there was the third recent attempt to establish a State Agricultural Society. And this time, I determined to co-operate personally, & to try whether (warned by recent failures,) a society could be established upon proper principles. Besides this reason, other occurrences of the last two years had served to soften my previous feelings, & to make me more willing to again mingle with my fellows for the public good.

During this time had appeared the different agricultural publications refered to formerly,[9] in a paper of Maryland—which had been received with more notice & applause by the public than anything I had before offered, except the "Essay on Calcareous Manures" & that long ago. Especially in Virginia were these papers valued. For while the general subscription to the Md paper (the American Farmer) was greatly increased, (the publisher said it was doubled by the publication of the first communication—) the subsequent increase was so much more from Va. as to make the subscription from that state greater than that of Maryland. I felt the value of this evidence of approval, as well as many others put in words. It seemed as if my existence had been almost forgotten for some years, & that my former services to agriculture were now first brought to light & fully recognized.

Another cause of my new notoriety, though not prompted in the least by myself, had my concurrence & aid in being put in operation: In 1851, I received a letter from the editor of De Bow's Review, (published in Charleston & New Orleans,) requesting me to supply a sketch of my biography, & my portrait, for the "Gallery of Enterprise," a series of which had been lately begun in that valuable & widely circulated periodical.[10] The name indicated the design. It was to present the labors of *working* men, who had been of eminent service to themselves & to their country. This plan had not then been abused as it was soon after, & extensively in other publications, presenting galleries of portraits of *nobodies*, & of any who would pay for a place, & were not ashamed to have their nothingness so prominently exhibited to public view & contempt. When the application came to me, it was a novelty, at least to my ignorance, & I esteemed it so high a compliment as to consent & comply. Upon consulting my friend Wm. Boulware[11] on the subject, he offered to be my biographer. No one was better qualified, & both as a literary man, & as being acquainted with me as a farmer & improver. I furnished him with written documents, before published, which were my chief works—& also notes of my personal & more private life. The hasty & concise notes then written for this purpose, induced me to extend them into this much more full account, & was the sole origin & cause of the writing these sheets.

Mr. Boulware was properly limited to small space, to suit the plan of the proposed publication. When his manuscript was finished, he submitted it to my eye. At my request, he abated the measure of his panegyric in some particulars, where I thought it exaggerated the facts of the value of improvements I had made. In other points where his estimates were his own opinions founded upon undisputed facts, he refused to lower his estimates—upon the grounds that he, & not I, was responsible for the deductions from facts, & he was assured that he had not stated them above their true measure.

This sketch made me much better known to numerous readers in other states. It was perhaps more impressive in Virginia, because having been sought & first appearing on such remote ground as New Orleans. The engraved portrait was bad. But it was enough a likeness to make me known when seen afterwards by strangers. My marked features & long gray hair served for such recognition, even by aid of a bad portrait.

Soon after this publication, I was invited by the authorities both of the Society & the town, to attend the annual meeting of the Southern Central Agricultural Society, in Macon Ga. The assemblage was numerous, from Ga, & other neighboring states—& my reception was most kind, complimentary, & gratifying to my feelings. I had never known the like in my own country. The planters of the south had profited little by my advice & my warnings. But if they had been as much my disciples & had profited as much by my example & instruction as had thousands in Virginia, they could not have appeared to consider me more as a their own & a public benefactor. And such evidences were offered not only by men, but in some marked cases by ladies. On the last day, I was called upon, & had to deliver an extemporaneous address—almost my first attempt. I had more self-possession than expected, & to my own satisfaction, succeeded well. My audience seemed well pleased.

When attending the meeting called at Richmond in Feby 1852, to organize a State Agricultural Society,[12] I met with a large & zealous assemblage. Among these were some of my old friends & contributors to the Farmers' Register, & many persons strangers to me personally, but who seemed, like the others, to be delighted to meet me. There was nothing like concerted or prepared or public compliment. It was a general cordial welcome, as if of old friends, & both by old & new acquaintance.

For the temporary organization of the meeting, I was chosen to preside. In the final & complete organization, the officers for the ensuing year were elected separately by private ballot. The ballots for president, except my own, all showed my name. But the deference paid to me in other respects, though less obvious, was much more substantial. My opinions as to the organization of agricultural societies, & their operation, had long been peculiar—& much opposed to the generally prevailing & popular opinions & usage. In these respects, the meeting adopted, without exception, every measure of change from former & usual measures I proposed.[13] In organization, in principle, & prospective policy, the society was made precisely as I advised. Thus, I was enabled to shut out some of the worst evils, which before had been enough to render useless, if not destroy, every previous effort. Before, as in most other such societies elsewhere, the election of a respected but inefficient president, alone served to put the society to sleep. The president could not be refused a re-election, because too much respected to be slighted; & he was continued until the society died under his incumbency. This I guarded against by the provision of annual rotation in office of the president. This was made a feature of the constitution. But this alone, of all I proposed, was afterwards repealed. The whole working power was thrown into the hands of the Executive Committee. But by forbidding more than two members (ex-officio or other) being residents of the same county or town, we prevented the whole management falling into the hands of men of the city of Richmond, as had been the case before, as near residents only could always conveniently attend the meetings. Thus was secured a healthy country & agricultural predominance in the Ex. Committee. The rules & principles also for offering & amending premiums were so changed, that they would work hereafter for the improvement of agriculture, or for instruction, instead of as generally heretofore & elsewhere, being either useless & absurd, or hurtful. But in this latter respect, though every principle & general rule was fixed as I proposed, & subsequently the details generally in conformity, in later practice, there were many premiums afterwards offered directly opposed to our stated policy & even to the constitution. This was done at later & thinly attended meetings of the Committee, when a member could, by watching his time, get passed measures deemed of minor importance, because not receiving due consideration.

But though our society at its first meeting was composed of excellent materials—embracing many good & zealous & highly intelligent farmers from various parts of Va, still we were miserably few, & poor, & weak, for our pretentions as a State Society. We had enrolled at the first meeting, (of three days' continuance,) not more than 130 members. And at the next annual meeting, after nearly a year of effort by the Ex. Com., we numbered only some 300 members, & had only a few hundred dollars, without having been able to have an exhibition or bestow a premium, or to make any other expenditure for our great objects. We had looked, & in vain, for aid from the legislature. In the longest session ever known of that body,[14] through parts of two years, it had not given time to consider the petition of the Society, or to hear read a bill for its aid. Nor even to pay the slightest attention to any interest of agriculture. This was no surprise to me, if so to others. Such had always been the course of that despicable assembly, (in all modern time) the legislature of Va.—& it had been recently rendered worse by the operation of the last change of the constitution, & the enlargement of the constituency to universal suffrage.

At the close of my year's service, (the duties of which I had assiduously & zealously performed,) I expected to retire from the presidency, under the constitutional exclusion. But this prohibition was then repealed—and I was then obliged to decline a re-election on the ground of my inability, because of my engagements & my infirmities, to continue to perform the duties, especially in the frequent meetings of the

Executive Committee. I was next urged at least to permit myself to be made 1st Vice-President, to show that I had not separated from the Society. This I consented to, with the understanding that I could not regularly attend the meetings of the Executive Committee, & undergo the exposure which neither my business nor my health permitted. Col. Philip St. G. Cocke was elected my successor.[15]

In the year of my service, I had attended every meeting of the Ex. Com. & the Society, had drawn most of the official papers, had made three elaborate agricultural communications, (of which two, on practical subjects, were offered for & took premiums at the first subsequent fair—) & also had prepared & read an Address at the Annual Meeting.[16]

The first few paragraphs of my official address to the Society, at the close of the first year, here annexed, will show that I kept no terms with the legislature. This address was delivered at night during the session, & in the Hall of the most numerous branch of the legislature—many of its members might have been expected to be among my hearers. But I do not think that half a dozen were there—& as most of them read nothing, probably my rebuke was known to not many more.

"Upon this occasion [pp. 3 & 4]—further the good work."[17]

Avowing that I could not continue to serve thus diligently, or at all in regular manner, I retired to comparative inaction. For the next year my service on the Committee had been more nominal than real, except at the long session at the next annual meeting & fair—or such other service as I could render at home. But though my influence in the action of the Society thus became much lessened, & null in some respects, & therefore the affairs of the Society are not necessary incidents of my memoirs, I will state the remarkable proceedings of the second Annual Meeting, & the change made to great prosperity.

In the beginning of the second year, stronger appeals were made to the members of the Society, & to the agricultural community. Gen. W. H. Richardson,[18] late Secretary of the Commonwealth, & one of the Ex. Com. was employed as our agent to traverse the state, obtain new members & their contributions, & to excite zeal for our aid. This measure, though costly, was highly successful, & beneficial. The members before the next Annual meeting had been increased to several thousand & the funds to more than $6000. An Exhibition & fair had been determined on. The city of Richmond had given the necessary grounds,[19] & erected requisite fixtures at an expense of nearly $10,000. Great interest & expectation were excited throughout the state. Most of the railroad companies offered free passage to all members going to & returning from the Fair, & to all animals & other subjects offered for exhibition. The Meeting of the Society, & of the Ex. Com. continued nearly through the whole first week of Nov. 1853, with unabated interest. Howmany thousands of members & other visitors then crowded Richmond beyond all example, I do not know. But such a concourse was never seen, nor imagined. The days were scarcely long enough for the sessions & other stated business of the Executive & other committees, the public addresses, & other parts of the ceremonies. And every night the Metropolitan Hall[20] was packed full of people, who remained in session & discussion to 10 or 11 o'clock, with untiring attention.

The great incident of the meeting occurred on the night of the 2nd of November. Lewis E. Harvie of Amelia,[21] one of the Vice-Presidents, had proposed to the Ex. Com. & by its instruction now offered the following resolutions.[22] These resolutions were adopted, unanimously by the Society, & then the members present were called upon to begin the subscription. It was begun with unexpected readiness & liberality. The enthusiasm excited was beyond all precedent & all previous calculation. In individual donations, subscriptions for life-memberships, (for many who were already members; & also for many others,) & in engagements of responsible members for their counties, there was subscribed that night $39,000. And in the meetings of the two next nights, the sum was increased to about $44,000. A plan had been adopted, in the resolutions passed, to apply in every county, by collecting committees. So that in addition to the sums pledged for many counties, a larger amount may be yet expected from the many individuals & counties not yet heard from.

Among the distinguished visitors were Gen. Wingfield Scott,[23] Ex-President Tyler,[24] & Wm. C. Rives,[25] all his life expectant-president in future. Deservedly as some of these commanded great celebrity & approval, & sustained as some were by strong political favor, it was as obvious as remarkable that political & military fame here took a subordinate station to agricultural merit. These gentlemen received much complimentary notice from the assemblage. But if I am not misinformed by report, & by all that fell under my own observation, my friend Willoughby Newton[26] & myself attracted much more attention (though not in noisy demonstrations,) than any who had derived importance from official station. Five of my children as well as many of my nearest friends, unknown in the crowd, had opportunities of hearing remarks made by numerous spectators, in ignorance of their presence, & in perfect freedom. And from the reports of such unquestionable witnesses, more than from the outward & loud demonstrations of the assemblage, I was made to believe that I especially was the chief object of interest, & the "observed of all observers." This belief was indeed to me a very high gratification.—I endeavored however to bear my honors meekly, & never to appear conscious of them except when it was unavoidable.

This recent position of mine, so remarkably opposed to that which existed but a few years past, is necessary to state, lest I should leave a false impression by my previous statements of my former & very different place in the public favor.

Newspaper & editorial notices of men, so often justly termed "puffs," are of little worth for estimating the value of the individuals so praised.[27] In many cases, of public characters, such editorial praises are begged or bought by the subject, or his partisans. In other cases, they are the dictates of corrupt political support for base motives. But, when such notices are of a person in private & almost recluse life—never seeking such favors, & having no reward to give for them—& when the praises proceed from strangers, & from editors of all political sides, & none of my own peculiar political views—it must be admitted that even if commendations thus bestowed are ever so much misplaced or exaggerated, they at least are evidences of the prevalent opinions of the intelligent portion of the community. As such evidence of the general favorable opinion & good-will now entertained for me, I will annex sundry editorial paragraphs cut out of newspapers recently—& which are not near all of such that have met my eye, though no more than these were preserved. With most of the editors here quoted, I had not the slightest personal acquaintance, & with not one of them anything like intimate relations.

Before offering more editorial notices, I will quote some extracts of like import from known sources, & higher authority. The following extract from a speech of G. W. P. Custis,[28] delivered in Washington, before the "National Agricultural Society" in 1852, is given at length in the volume of Transactions published by that body. The speech was preliminary to the speaker's motion to elect me an honorary member of that Society, which was done unanimously. I was the only one then elected who had not bought the honor by making a large donation to the Society.[29]

Besides the principal annual address,[30] there were two others prepared by distinguished gentlemen, (Ex-President Tyler, & Professor Maupin[31] of the U. of Va.), by request, & delivered before the great assemblage at the Fair. There was also an elaborate report, read by

N. F. Cabell esq.[32] Each of these writers, as well as Mr. Edmunds,[33] introduced my services in their remarks, with almost unmeasured eulogy.[34]

But enough of this second-hand self-praise—which may be tedious even to my children, & would be offensive or ridiculous to any other hearers.

The avowed reasons which I gave for positively declining a re-election to the office of president of the State Agr. Soc. were both true & sufficient. I had, during my year of service, faithfully performed my official duties, & to my great inconvenience both as to my business & my health. For every stay from home of a few days together always disordered my health—& if in Richmond, & during winter, gave me wretched cold, which troubled me much longer. As a member, I had written *all* of the truly agricultural & important communications to the Society, & as a member of the Ex. Com. had drawn, either principally or entirely, nearly all of the official writings of that body. I could have been content to persevere, & to expose myself still to labor, loss, & danger to health, if I had found zealous co-operation in many of my fellow members of the Society, or the sympathy & excited interest of the farming community. But there was neither, to the close of my year of service. There was no reason why I should continue to labor, almost alone & uselessly. Nearly all other persons who professed zeal in the cause, thought of the society's succeeding only by a full adoption of what I deemed the "humbug[35] policy—or operating by exhibitions & fairs, not confined to proper agricultural subjects, but extended to everything to make a show, & to attract a crowd. By my withdrawing, I gave full play to the advocates for this policy—& a very great infusion of it was added in the next year to our previous scheme of premiums, though in violation of our constitutional requirements. I will not say that this violation & change of policy, & the introduction of the most[36] illegitimate subjects for premiums did not have the important operation in drawing the immense crowd to the first fair, & thus exciting all the enthusiasm & zeal which were so conspicuous & effective.

Yet, after all, what has been done by the Society? The premiums which I had proposed, for experiments, for essays of practical instruction, had induced the sending in of some valuable papers (at the time of the fair,) besides mine sent more than a year earlier. The proper premiums had also brought out interesting & instructive reports of great entire crops, good & profitable farming—& had caused to be collected & displayed specimens of all the best agricultural implements & machinery. The proper stock premiums had also served to bring many fine animals, calculated to improve the stock & increase the profits of farmers. But all these probably did not so much excite interest & excite a crowd, as the other numerous humbug premiums, for other stock, fabrics, & even agricultural products which had no effect in promoting agricultural profits or improvement. I shall try to weed out these improper subjects from our list of premiums, & to extend the proper subjects, as much as may be without lessening the attraction of the fairs.

A stronger reason existed than any named above, for my withdrawing from the very conspicuous & responsible position of President of the Agr. Soc. & from all great efforts before the public eye. The decay of my memory had continued to increase, (as it still has since,) so as to alarm me lest I should have greatly impaired other mental powers, without my knowing it. By request of the authorities of the S. Ca. Institute, I had undertaken to prepare & deliver before the body in Nov. 1852, an agricultural address. The locality & the expected audience made this compliment doubly valued. The subject engaged all my interest. It was on the general exhausting culture of the southern states, & reasons for change, & means for remedy. I found great difficulty in the preparation. It was not for scarcity of ideas, or of ready flow of expression. As usual heretofore with me, when writing on any subject highly interesting to me, my ideas came faster than I could write them, rapidly as my pen moved. But the difficulty was that I could not remember on one day what I had written the day before. And when recurring to a branch of the general subject which had before been touched upon, forgetting that I had treated it but a day or two before, I would go over it again, in different words, but of like substance. Thus I had more trouble in correcting, & especially in comparing like passages, & rejecting & cutting out what could be spared, than ever before, & more than the labor of the first hasty & continued writing, with all that was repeated or superfluous. While so engaged, I regretted that I had undertaken the task. I feared that I was approaching the condition of the Archbishop of Grenada when after asking for, he rejected the friendly warning of Gil Blas, that he was no longer competent to write[37]—& I might not have such warning to save my credit. Therefore I resolved that the labor then on hand & another address required of me as President of the Agr. Soc. should be my last attempts to write anything other than plain & unpretending statements of agricultural practices or opinions.

The Address to the S. C. Institute, was delivered in Charleston, in Nov. 1852.[38] It was received with all respect, & appearance of approval. I was myself satisfied with it. I was received in Charleston with the most cordial welcome, & respectful attention. My stay there, (protracted by indisposition to near two weeks,[39] was a time of gratification & of triumph which then was to me without example.

From the termination of this scene, I hastened home, to prepare for closing my public duties. The address designed for that purpose, (& which has before been referred to, & appended,) was written in a very short time, while almost confined by the continuation of my severe indisposition contracted in Charleston.

Very recently there has come to my knowledge a strange & ludicrous circumstance in regard to my address delivered in Charleston. It was there heard by Mr. De Bow, who had it reprinted in his Review, properly omitting the preliminary part *only*, which had no relation to the main subject. In this paper, designed for a Charleston audience, I had expressed my *extreme* opinions as to southern wrongs & rights, & had denounced the northern states & people, & the government of the U.S. for sustaining northern aggressions, in my strongest language.[40] I had some doubts whether such remarks might not be improper to utter even in Charleston. I certainly would have withheld such, as unpalatable, in any city of Va., & would have deemed them highly offensive to any northern audience. Yet I lately learned that this entire paper, as republished by De Bow, & with his complementary introductory note, has been inserted in the Agricultural Report from the Patent Office for 1853![41] This annual volume is made up under authority of Congress, by U.S. officers, & more than 100,000 copies printed & bound at government expense, for gratuitous distribution throughout all the land. And so my bitter denunciations of the policy of government, & the wrongs perpetrated by the north, have thus been spread before all the people of the northern as well as southern states, by the action & at the expense of the U.S. government!

In the year since these (designed) last addresses were delivered, I have had to decline invitations to perform similar duties in three other cases. These were from the Agrl. Society of Edgecombe, N.C. of Rappahannock, Va, & of the Association of Southern & Slaveholding States, to meet in Columbia, S.C.

Before quitting the subject of my public action, I will refer to my only connexion with political events in latter time. I was strongly opposed to what were mis-called the "compromise" measures enacted in 1850— and preferred a separation of the southern from the northern states, as I still do, to submission to those measures of fraud & triumph of the north, & grievous wrong & humiliation of the south. While these measures were before Congress, & there yet remained hope that the southern states would not submit, I wrote a series of three articles on the subject, which will be here inserted. They were published in the Richmond Enquirer, & republished in a Georgia paper. Of course they were entirely useless.[42]

When passing through S.C. on my way from the Agrl. Meeting in Georgia, I wrote the following, which was published in the Charleston Mercury. This was nearly my last meddling with political matters—except as always, to express my opinions thereupon, in conversation, in the strongest terms, & without the least reserve.[43]

Before closing this last writing, I will concisely bring up the statement of my family & farming concerns to the present time, (Nov. 1853.)

Three others of my children have married within the last two years, making 5 in all.[44] Of these, 4 are settled on their farms in my old county Prince George.[45] Of the four younger children, remaining unmarried as yet, my three daughters continue to live with me at Marlbourne.[46] If they shall also all marry & be compelled to leave me for another home, I shall leave my present home also, for some other manner of life, for the short remainder of my days. If the kind of property which I hold was not incapable of division (for the land) I would before this time have made a final division of it among my children, reserving only a life annuity for myself—& thus relieving my latter days of labors & perplexities which are becoming more & more onerous & disagreeable as aged infirmities grow upon me.[47]

My youngest son Charles, I had desired to make a farmer, & to aid me in my business, & subsequently, upon just & proper conditions for all interests concerned, to take upon himself my whole farming business, with a full remuneration for managing all except his own share [proportion][48] of the property. But after trial, he did not then like the business. Subsequently, he took employment on the lowest grade of engineering on a railroad then in the course of construction.[49] After only 18 months service, he has lately risen to a sufficiently good salary, & fair prospects of further promotion. This business, for a young man, is one of the best schools for any other subsequent pursuit. I trust it will give to Charles the steadiness of purpose & also the disposition to become a good farmer, after some years service in his present labors.

There has been no other important occurrence in my family affairs, for good or for evil, except one grievous affliction. This was the death of my oldest grandson, Edmund Quintus Ruffin, (son of Edmund,) a noble boy of nearly 14 years old.⁵⁰ No son deserved to be more valued for his virtues, & character of solid worth. No one's death could have been more lamented. But while the excellent qualities of a child removed by death serve greatly to increase the amount of loss, & the distress of the parents, they also serve as the best source for consolation. Far better is it for the bereaved to remember the lost one for his virtues & good gifts, than for his vices or defects!

There has been very little of new or unusual occurrences in my farming since the last notice. My attention to my work has been much withdrawn, until but slight & general personal attention is given to the farm operations. Of course they are carried on with less economy of time & labor & materials, & with less effect & profit. Notwithstanding this growing & now considerable neglect, & worse management than formerly, my wheat crops have not decreased in average product, & the corn crops have increased. The fertility of the land has decidedly improved under my 6 field rotation. And the heavy growth of weeds, the result of increased fertility, is so great an impediment to good tillage, & has caused so much imperfect ploughing, as to have kept down the crops of wheat below their proper mark. Since 1850, the crops of which were the last known & entered on a foregoing page, (213,)⁵¹ the aggregate of the last 3 crops of wheat has exceeded the three preceding crops (of '48, '49, '50,) by 3193 bushels—yet with a continued decline in the last three years, from 6072 to 5308 & 4790. The decrease was owing partly to latter bad preparation, & for the last crop especially—while the aggregate increase is due to increased fertility. Of the corn crop, the last 3 years show an average increase, as well as an aggregate increase on the preceding 3 years. The crop of 1853 is not yet gathered, but is estimated, & I think fall low, as above stated. The last years crop (1852) was the largest ever made, (5438 bush. & 43.85 to the acre,) & this promises as much.

The marl bed, discovered but not opened before, has been excavated to considerable extent at favorable times in both 1852 & '53. But lying so deep under both earth & water, this marl cannot be worked except in summer & dry season, & in a large & continued operation. In summer, there is rarely the time of 4 or 5 weeks together to be spared—& therefore there have been but a few such operations. And still I am obliged to continue also to work J. W. Tomlin's marl,⁵² to use when I cannot haul from my own. What with the great labor & rare opportunities for working my own marl, & the great distance of the other, there has been not much marl applied. Nearly all the open land of Talley's (pasture as well as tillage land,) has been marled, & a small beginning made on the Larry tract.

The main ditch has been successively deepened, until now it is from 5 to 6 feet deep throughout. The lowering of the margins, & carting off the earth, also is much advanced, but not near completed. The principal tributary ditches have also all been deepened every year, until deemed now deep enough. The effect of this deepening is very important in better drainage of under-spring-water—& also of rain floods. Formerly, every heavy rain overflowed the stream ditches & considerable spaces of the lowest arable land. Now it very rarely occurs that any one ditch does not convey all the water thrown into it by the heaviest rain. The general drainage effects, in other respects, are greatly increased—notwithstanding many particular or partial failures of the underdrains, & repairs of the old as well as considerable new extensions being required every year. But the entirely new works of this kind are not so much required by old drains having failed to act, as to my own ideas of the necessity & profits of drainage being altered. In the beginning of these operations, drains were made only where indispensable to even a small production of land. Now I deem underdrains necessary for better tillage & production where formerly they were not deemed sufficiently required for the expense of their construction to be incurred.

Dec. 1853.

In Remembrance of Jane Dupuy

(1855)

In Remembrance of Jane Dupuy, formerly Ruffin.

BORN JANUARY 16TH, 1829.
MARRIED JANUARY 26TH, 1854.
DIED JULY 24TH 1855.

Marlbourne, July 27th. 1855

In writing these notes of incidents, & thoughts relating to the illness & death of my beloved daughter, (& in which task I ask to be aided by like notes of others nearest to her,) I aim not to preserve any regular order, or to be careful in the choice of either subjects or manner of expression. I will write, as I hope some of my children will do, as if we were conversing with each other, & with the same freedom & scope as we would thus speak. No strange or careless eye will see this unstudied & mournful record of things which we wish not to forget, & which would be interesting to none, except those who greatly love & revere the memory of the dead. Still, there are others of near relatives now too young to have fully known what we know of the excellent qualities of my deceased child. Especially, her babe, if spared to live, & to revere her mother's memory, may derive instruction & support, as well as nourishment to filial affection & reverence, from these details. Therefore, it will be not improper, & may be useful, for us to state qualities of the dear departed one, which would not be necessary to be mentioned to those who now most deplore her loss, as they have nothing to learn in regard to the traits of disposition & character which made her so dear to all her family, & even to all who knew her.

My daughter Jane, from her childhood, had been remarkable for her uniform gentleness & docility, & affectionate kindness of manner &

correctness of conduct. Yet, with the absence of all the usual heedlessness & errors of childhood & early youth, & with the most perfect obedience to her parents, & to every proper rule of conduct, she was always gay, light-hearted, & joyous. These dispositions continued through girlhood to womanhood. She seemed never to have had a gloomy or unhappy thought, except for the sake of others' sorrows. And while always as cheerful & gay as any one could be, she was not the less thoughtful of all she owed to other persons. Totally unselfish, affectionate to her friends, kind & benevolent to all, she attracted regard on slight acquaintance, & secured permanent love & esteem from all who knew her well. A parent is a too partial judge of the merits of his child—& especially of personal qualities to which we are accustomed by time & continued companionship, & therefore are more ready to be deceived into too favorable opinions by love. But endeavoring to guard myself from such self-deception, I do not think that I erred in supposing my Jane to be highly attractive in personal appearance & in manners, as well as much more estimable for the qualities of her mind & her sound principles, & pure & strict moral conduct. If she had a defect of temper, or an evil propensity, or had committed any offence, or entertained a hostile or unkind feeling towards any human being, I am ignorant of either. Nor were her's merely such negative virtues, consisting in the refraining from positive vices. In her smooth & flowery path through life, for so short a course, she has had as little acquaintance with the miseries as with the vices of the world—& but few claims have been presented to her requiring great sacrifices. But so far as required by circumstances few have been more ready to feel for & to aid others, whenever she saw the need to exist. Kind & considerate regard for others always marked her conduct, & was so habitual, & so devoid of all counteraction by selfishness, or the desire of self-indulgence, that such promptings & the effects were seen throughout her last illness, & even to the last day of her life.

Though her frame was small & delicately formed, & indicating to a first view fragility of body & constitution, such was not the case. She had uncommon strength of body, an excellent constitution, & had never suffered any serious illness previous to the last. Her mind was good, & well cultivated, & furnished with much instruction from general miscellaneous reading, though pursued for amusement & not instruction. Her fondness & taste for music were of high order, her voice, for singing, though not of great compass or power, was remarkably sweet & melodious—& her performance on the piano, though not extended to pieces of very difficult execution, & mostly confined to accompaniments to her songs, was correct, in good taste, & highly pleasing. Until her marriage removed her from her father's house, she had been the first voice of our little family choir of four. Her place could not be filled—& in that one respect, unimportant as it was compared to her loss otherwise, all of us, & especially her father, felt a privation, & a void made in the daily pleasures of the family, which had not been diminished by lapse of time, when all the connected & greater blessings which her life had brought to us, were cut off by her death.

With such qualities, & the effects seen in her manners—(for her manners were naturally the result of her feelings & principles, which directed her wishes & her conduct—) while yet a child in years, she was a woman in modesty, discretion, & correctness of deportment, & in avoidance of the usual errors of early age & of animal spirits, giddiness, heedlessness & levity. And in her mature womanhood, she still retained the uniform gayety of childhood, & the natural & unaffected graces of early youth. Her youthful personal appearance aided the delusion of her new acquaintance, who almost always supposed, & without doubt, that she was but some 18 years of age even when she had reached 22 and more.

She had married Dr. John J. Dupuy, the son of my half-sister.[1] The losing her from my own dwelling was felt as one of the greatest privations of my life, & of my personal sacrifices. I have other children not less loved or valued, & who, because of greater age & longer trial, & extended family ties, are of more utility. But Jane's presence was to her father as the light of the sun to his old age, & which all other blessings & values could not compensate or substitute.

On April 6th, 1855, her illness & great danger commenced. On the 8th she gave birth to a female infant, & still continued for some days longer in great peril of life. Then hope deceived us for a time—& at various other intervals. But more generally we feared or despaired. She continued to suffer most usually & greatly—often in great agony—sometimes comparatively free from pain—but always prostrated in strength, & gradually more & more wasted in flesh, & changed in appearance, by emaciation. I cannot pursue the details of her long sufferings. Perhaps they may be supplied by others, to some extent, in connection with the instances of meek resignation & courageous endurance of the sufferer, even when others suffered most for her, or despaired—

[Extracts from the separately written notes of E. S.][2] [When I began to write these notes, I requested of others of our family to do the like. My daughter Elizabeth Sayre afterwards did so in the form of a letter to a common & dear friend to all the parties—; but owing to our distant residences, I did not see her writing until long after mine had been finished. From it, I will here make some extracts of passages which will supply some of my omissions, or describe scenes & incidents which I was unable or unwilling to attempt. The following first extract begins with her arrival, on her first visit to her sister.]

"—I went first to her room while she was asleep to accustom myself to her appearance—but I had to leave immediately. I was shocked to find her so emaciated. I am sure I should not have known her if I had seen her elsewhere than at Beechwood. As soon as I could compose myself, I went to see her again. She was then awake, & had been told of my arrival. She greeted me with a smile—as she did every one who entered her room—but a smile so different from her own bright, joyous smiles of brighter days. I remained with her [then][3] a fortnight—& I pray that I may never forget her patience, her gratitude & gentleness. It was indeed a privilege to be with her. Of course, she had to be waited upon like a helpless infant—& amid all her suffering, she never forgot to say "I thank you," or "You are so kind—What should I do without you?" She never forgot others—was always considerate as to their comfort. I will give you a few instances of her unselfishness, & her thought for others. Our sister Ella was sick in the next room, though then not sick much, as we thought—& often in our great anxiety to do something for Jane, Ella would be left alone—& sister Jane would be the first to remind us of it, & ask one or more of us to go to Ella. Again, she loved much to hear the pattering of the rain on the tin roof, & seemed to listen to it with great pleasure. It actually seemed to lull her to sleep. During my first visit to her, Brother Edmund [the proprietor of Beechwood][4] was in his wheat harvest, & it rained almost every day. She would then say, "Oh! how I love to hear the rain! But I am so sorry it is raining, for Brother will lose by it." Numerous other little circumstances could I mention, to show you how thoughtful of others she was. And in everything that was going on she evinced some interest. For though so very ill, she did not think she should die. Sister Mary [Edmund's wife][5] received a sewing machine, which Brother had ordered. Jane insisted that it should be brought into her chamber that she might see it. Father bought for her, & brought with him, a Melodeon, the music of which instrument she had formerly so much loved, at Marlbourne. That also was taken to her room for her to see it—& I shall never forget the pleasure & gratitude which were exhibited in her face, & the manner in which she thanked Father for the gift. It was then taken down to the parlor, where we would play & sing for her, her favorite hymns & chants.

"After remaining with her nearly two weeks, I returned to my home, hoping she was better, though I did not think she would ever be well again—leaving with all at Beechwood the injunction, to send for me immediately if she grew worse. I heard from Father that she was slowly improving; but the next day, received a summons to see the last of her. I went up the day following, & found her evidently sinking." E. S.

Throughout her long illness, of more than fifteen weeks continuance, except when most suffering pain, or in the greatest prostration of strength, she never lost her natural cheerfulness, & which rose to gayety in the intervals of freedom from pain, of apparent improvement, & of renewed hope to all. And her still more remarkable hopefulness of recovery never even intermitted, or abated, until a few days before the close, when, all hope being lost, her sister Mildred deemed it her duty (& in compliance with a prior request of & pledge to Jane,) to inform her that she was in the greatest peril, & her recovery a bare possibility. Even then, & afterwards to the end, though hope was extinguished, or, for a time, barely existed, calm resignation & submission to the will of God immediately assumed the place;—& with but a very transient appearance of sinking, or of mental agony, she passed from cheerful & undoubting hope of life, in calm & quiet resignation, to the certainty of speedy death. Few of the boldest & strongest men, in mind & heart, even when in all the vigor of unbroken health, & with every inducement to appear courageous, or unfeeling, could have so borne this trial, & sudden sentence of death. And yet all her sufferings had not made her weary of life, or the more willing to die. She had in a loved & loving husband, father, brothers, sisters & all others of a numerous family connections, many & the strongest ties to the world, a bright prospect of happiness in life, & she greatly wished to live. But as soon as made to understand that she must die, she submitted quietly & calmly, & without a murmur. Thenceforward, she endeavored to make every necessary preparation, in directions to her sister & husband, as to the division of her little personal possessions among her numerous friends—not forgetting in these respects, even the servants who had kindly waited on her—& affectionate messages, as it were, from the entrance to the grave, to distant friends, & some who would never have expected to occupy her thoughts at such a time. But these & such directions were [often] & in the intervals of the more important attentions to her religious duties.*

---

*Some weeks after the writing of the above, & also of my daughter Elizabeth's separate notes of the same scenes, some omissions of both were supplied by the more full statement of Mildred, made to me for this purpose, & noted as follows:

At an early time of Jane's illness, she had asked of both her husband and Mildred, & obtained their solemn promises of compliance, that should her recovery be deemed hopeless, they would so inform her. At different times, afterwards, & when the sufferer still was altogether hopeful, her friends around her had almost despaired. Still until utterly despairing, they on whom this afflicting duty was imposed could not bear to crush her still bright & cheerful hopes, & not only to produce the distress of mind to be expected from such a communication, but probably, by that distress, to increase the power & depressing effects of disease, & so hasten the fatal end. But at last the time came when the promise made must be redeemed. After consultation between her husband & sister, the latter consented to perform the painful duty, & at the earliest opportunity. But before that occurred, Jane had suspected the truth of her condition, from seeing the appearances of grief & tears, which with every effort, could not always be concealed from her by her deeply afflicted friends & attendants. Thus it was that, as soon as they were together alone, she asked Mildred if John (her husband) did not think that she was much worse. Mildred answered in the affirmative, and proceeded to say that she was undoubtedly in extreme danger. As soon as she took in, & could realize the full purport of the words, (& rightly construing the meaning to extend farther than the words so reluctantly uttered,) she was, for a few minutes, greatly agitated, & her tears began to flow. Her first words were, "And must I die?" which were followed by broken expressions of fervent prayer, asking that God would make her prepared for death, & resigned to his will. She then asked Mildred to pray for her. But her sister was then not enough able to command her voice or feelings—& she asked Jane if she would not prefer to have Mr. Murdaugh,[6] the pastor of the parish, (& who lived very near,) not only to pray, but to converse with her. To this she eagerly assented. The minister was sent for. Very soon, Jane, in appearance & manner restored to composure, continued to converse with Mildred in regard to directions required by her near approaching death & in that conversation, & still more in others succeeding, with her husband &

with Mildred, she made dispositions for everything requiring attention—& as to many things, all indicating affectionate consideration & regard for others, which were so trivial of themselves, that no one could have expected them to occupy any thought of one who was awaiting, & looking at, the sure & speedy approach of death. In the few days which intervened, though on proper occasions she spoke of her approaching death as being fully understood, & kept in mind, such allusions were rare & transient, & never accompanied by any indications of grief or terror. She continued throughout calm & resigned to her inevitable destiny.

["—Before[7] their interview ended, she told sister Mildred exactly what disposition to make of everything of her own. She left some memento to each one of us—& messages of love to absent friends. Even the servants at the old home were not forgotten—to them she sent her love—& a hope that they would meet with her in heaven. Before the extremity of her illness, she had told Sister Mildred, that she wished her to take her child in the event of her death. Sister Mildred told her she would, with Cousin John's [her husband's][8] consent. On this sad occasion, after naming a gift for all others she most loved, she turned to Sister Mildred & said, "And now, my dear, dear sister, what can I give you—you who have watched over me & nursed me so tenderly?" This was Mildred's reply: "Sister Jane, I would rather have your baby than ought else in this world." She spoke not—but putting her arms around Mildred's neck, she wept tears of gratitude."—E. S. [Extract from Notes of E. S.][9]

*This incident occurred, not in this interview, but in another soon after, as I have since learned from Mildred. E. R.[10]

My daughter Mildred was with her sick sister from the beginning of her illness, & remained in her chamber, & in attendance, almost day & night, to the close. The only exceptions to these continued watchings & services, were for a few days & nights together, when Mildred was herself so sick as to be compelled to let her place be substituted—& a few other separate nights, when some dear friend & near relative acted as chief attendant for a night, & so permitted Mildred to sleep undisturbed. Such close attention & service so long continued, strange to say, did not break down the nurse by fatigue, or illness—& it seemed that her bodily powers were sustained by, & made to obey the determined mind & will. It was not that enough of other persons, & even of near relatives & friends, did not offer, & were not ready & willing to share the burden of waiting upon the sufferer. But almost entirely helpless as was she throughout, she needed frequent attentions which her delicacy would have been pained to receive from any but a sister; & also, so considerate was she always of the comfort of others, & so unwilling to call on them for the services which they offered to perform, & would gladly have been permitted to perform, that she would have suffered for the want of many necessary attentions & services for her temporary relief, rather than ask them of any other than her sister who had always also been her most intimate friend & companion. This unwillingness to cause trouble or inconvenience to those in attendance, was marked & enduring throughout. Even in the few last hours, before she had become unconscious of everything, when she knew she was about to die, & when frequent changes of posture were needed to afford temporary rest & relief to her wasted & sore body, she expressed her regret for so "tiring" those who were waiting upon, & lifting her—& who would have been glad to perform any ten-fold greater services & labors, to afford her even the slightest relief. Never was more strongly shown the absence of selfishness, & regard for the good or comfort of others.

At the first notice of her illness, (though she was then deemed safe from the earliest danger,) I hastened from my residence, Marlbourne, to visit my daughter. On several occasions, when she was much better, I returned home, but soon came back. Twice, Jane was thought recovering with so much certainty, that arrangements were made by me for Mildred to go home—as her long stay had been unforeseen, & was attended by great inconvenience. But in each case, she feared to leave her sister, & refused to go home. On the last of these occasions, Jane had urged Mildred to go, by every reason of expediency which she knew to exist—& without intimating the slightest objection of her own to her departure. But when Mildred remained deaf to her persuasions to leave her, & refused positively to leave her at all, while her illness lasted, Jane's joy at retaining her sister's company & aid was most touchingly evinced. She had been earnestly urging, for the sake of her sister & of others, the removal from herself of her most valued companion & nurse, & greatest comfort in her nursing. There never was more kind & unremitting attention bestowed—& never was such care more highly appreciated by a suffering invalid, & more gratefully felt & acknowledged.

I also was attendant for the greater portion of the time, though useless to her, except in gratifying her feelings by my presence. On several times of supposed improvement I had returned home. But the regular reports by the mails were so slow, that the delay kept me anxiously uneasy—& on the first bad report I hastened again to the sufferer. Finally, when I heard of the most alarming & prostrating turn of her illness, & did not expect to find her alive, I went determined to return no more until the final result was certain. All her sisters & brothers who had distant residences, had been to visit her at different times. Some days before her death, all the then absent were notified, by express, of the increased & great danger—& all hastened to, & remained with, the loved sufferer, to the closing scene.

Early in her illness, when we yet had sanguine hopes of recovery in no long time, I planned & proposed to Jane, that, as soon as she should be strong enough I would carry her to visit her sister, Mrs. Sayre, where she could have salt bathing, (on Elizabeth River,) & afterwards to the Springs in the mountains. These journeys she looked forward to with sanguine hope, & with delight in anticipation. Nor did she cease to hope confidently for these benefits & pleasures, until she had learned that there remained no hope for her life. Until then, these expected journeys occupied pleasantly much of her thoughts & words, when at ease—& her plans in these & other matters, were spoken of by her not only with hope, but as cheerfully as if she had been already restored to health.

For the earlier & longer portion of her long illness, & before the later extreme emaciation of her frame had been produced, the change of appearance of her face was remarkable. The bloom & roundness of her features indeed were gone. But the then but slight reducing of the fulness of health had even increased her beauty, though greatly changing its character. Her face, when at rest, seemed as if of the purest white & polished marble, & the countenance was of angelic sweetness of expression & feature. Even some former slight natural defects of her features were removed. The nose, straight & well-formed, had in health been too delicate in out-line, & the eyes were too small, & the eyebrows so small as to be almost indistinct. Now, by the actual measure of emaciation of the face, the nose had comparatively been made more prominent, & very slightly aquiline—the eyes were more full—the eyebrows more manifest on the purely white skin—and altogether the face had gained in dignity & beauty of expression & in impressiveness, as much at least as it had lost in bloom & brightness. At particular times, this remarkable beauty struck every observer. Yet how different from her former self! It was not the beauty of earth, but of one already belonging to heaven. At such times, even when I was hopeful of her recovery, I wished greatly to obtain her portrait as she then appeared, in such strong contrast, & yet not inferior in beauty, to the daguerreotype likenesses, taken in her blooming health. How much is that wish now increased by her death!

Few persons, suffering long & painfully from disease, can always preserve the same good temper, & consideration for others, as they would have exhibited when happy & in health. All would expect some such deficiencies, & be ready to excuse their occurring frequently & habitually. But in all the long illness of my angel child—of prostration, of strength, & mostly of total helplessness—of great continual privation, & the pain of wearysome constraint & of soreness from long lying, & great emaciation—& frequently suffering pain even to agony—even when not gay, as sometimes—or cheerful, as in all the intervals of comparative ease & quiet—she never had drawn from her any expression of murmuring or complaint, or fretful discontent—& never other than words & thoughts of kindness, love, & gratitude to all who aided in ministering to her wants & soothing her sufferings. If she had not, in her previous days of health & joy, gained the love & esteem of all who now attended to her through sickness & suffering, she would have [*illeg.*] still better claims in this latter time. If she had lived to enjoy it, she would have been still more the object to all of love, & of admiration for her rare excellencies. Dead—she now appears to my mind & feelings as a heavenly being who was allowed to remain a while on this earth. In her sojourn here, I believe, (& great is my comfort in believing,) that she was as happy as any resident on earth can well be. There were but few occurrences in her peaceful passage through life to cause her pain or sorrow—none for remorse, & scarcely any for regret. And her benevolent, pure, & affectionate heart, her kind disposition & sweet temper, her cheerful & joyous temperament, & the fruits of these offered in the love of all around her—all served to strew her path with flowers, & to make her always happy. Even in her most painful passage from this world—in which she had to bear so much & so long—her agonies were softened & made endurable by her cheerful & hopeful disposition, & by the love & loving attentions of friends, & by the kind interest for her displayed by all others who could not have access to her, or be permitted to see her on her bed of death. Even in & through this her only time of great distress & suffering, I trust that she found, & was comforted by many sources of great enjoyment & happiness.

[Throughout[11] her illness, Jane was at no time delirious, or out of her right mind. But on some occasions, & mostly in her last days, her thoughts wandered, as if dreaming, when not asleep. But when speaking under the influence of such thoughts, it was but for a few words & moments, & she quickly recalled her perfect & clear understanding. It was perhaps the effect of the opium which made part of her daily medicine. This ingredient she was greatly opposed to taking, & especially when near to her death, because, as she said, she wished that nothing should then cloud or bewilder her mind, or understanding. And in submitting to continue to take a medicine to which she was so averse, she exhibited one of the many evidences of her gentle & dutiful disposition. At more than one of the times when her thoughts thus wandered for a moment, it was to music, which she so much loved. The night preceding her last, a change was seen, before daybreak, which her attendants thought was the beginning of her dying. It was soon after this that she asked for all the family to be summoned, and she took leave of each one, in words affectionately & especially addressed to each. Previously, but late in the night, she was aroused, as she thought, by hearing sweet music accompanying the words of a familiar & favorite hymn, of which, in evidence of her having just heard them plainly, she repeated the first lines. Her full conviction of having heard this music, with her perfect clearness of mind otherwise, in her then apparent close approach to death, all produced on my sister Dupuy[12] (then present) the belief that it was no delusion of a sick & wandering mind, but that, in truth, the departing spirit already heard the voices & harmony of heaven—the inviting & welcoming voices of sister angels.]

[Extract from the notes of E. S.][13]

["—When she had, for some days been gradually sinking, on Monday, the 23rd, about daybreak, we were all called up, [at Jane's request] by those who had[14] with her during the night. Soon we were all in the room, (and, Thank God! we *all* were there—). Jane asked Brother Julian to pray for her—which he did—solemnly committing her soul to God. Then followed a scene which I cannot describe. She bad each one farewell, in the most impressive manner. When our youngest brother went to her, she put her arms around his neck, & said—(Oh! I can never forget her tone of voice—) "Charley! Charley! I hope I am going to heaven—Charley, won't you meet me there? Won't you love your Savior? Good b'ye." "Now where is my dear Father?[15] Father approached & knelt at her bed-side. She put her arms around him, & said "My dear, dear Father, won't you love your Savior? For your dying child's sake look to Jesus—he will love you. Oh! Father, meet me in Heaven."[16] She continued to hold him to her, now & then saying "My poor Father—my poor Father—don't grieve for me too much." Last of all she called her husband—and what she said to him I did not hear, until she came to tell him "Good b'ye". She then clasped her hands, & said "Now, my Savior, receive my soul". I have heard & read of many such scenes—but it has never been my privilege to witness the like. After this, she revived sufficiently to receive the communion—& after that, was so much better, that hope sprang up in the hearts of many of us—& we continued to give her nourishment & medicine. On Tuesday morning, about 10 o'clock, she asked for music; & as Sister Mildred had gone, at our urgent request, into another room to go to sleep, I went down & played while Mr. Murdaugh & others sang the two pieces which Jane selected, "I will arise, & go to my Father," & the hymn, "How firm a foundation". Those who remained with her said she seemed to follow, in the spirit, the singing—& when the last line of the hymn was sung, "I'll never, no never, forsake"—she seemed to feel it very much. About 12 o'clock, while our sister Mrs. Beckwith,[17] Mildred & I were waiting on her, they at her back, & I in front of her, I stooped to do something, when she looked me full in the face, & said "I can't see you plainly—Ah! I know this is the last. Put everything straight, & call them all in—for the mist of death is coming over my eyes." The pupils of her eyes were then so much dilated that they covered the entire iris. Once more all were gathered around her bed. She did not again bid us adieu. It seemed as though she had done that, & would spare us the pain of repeating it. She merely said "I know this is the last—" & commenced to repeat that beautiful hymn, "Prayer is the soul's sincere desire," but her strength failed—when Sister Mildred took it up, but she was not equal to the task—& Lotty, Brother Julian's wife[18] finished it. And thus we were watching when she again revived—but I believe after that she never saw distinctly. For I observed, as one & another would leave the room & come in again, she would look at them, but never seemed to recognize them. About half after 1, her pulse again sank, & there was no doubt that she was passing away. For a time she seemed to suffer pain, which grieved us the more—for we had hoped that her last hours would be quiet. Oh! it seemed as if every groan of hers entered our souls. But her husband [Dr. J. Dupuy][19] told us that he believed she was not at all conscious of pain. I staid with her as long as I could—& finally left her. Sister Agnes [Beckwith][20] Sister Mary, Lotty, & Cousin John[21] remained with her. She gradually became more & more quiet, until she gently breathed her last, at 4 o clock, P.M. For two hours before her death, she was entirely unconscious, & did not speak.

Thus passed away from earth this loved one—& deeply as we feel our bereavement, we all thank God that he has released her from her sufferings. Death has taken from us our brightest gem. Her place can never be refilled. Her songs we shall never again hear—and Oh! she sang so sweetly!"—

—"In our sad bereavement, we have much to comfort us. It is a gratification to us to know that every attention & comfort that physicians & friends could bestow, she had—that all who were nearest & dearest to her were around her—that the hands of love performed every act that went to alleviate her pains—& at last smoothed her dying pillow. We are all deeply grieved; but my poor father & Cousin John are most to be pitied. May God help them! Sister Mildred was her most devoted nurse, for nearly four months—& never did a mother more tenderly nurse her little babe, than she nursed our departed sister. She will meet with her reward. I never looked on death with the same feelings as I then did. It seemed to be robbed of all its terrors. After our beloved sisters body was prepared for burial, we went to take a last fond look. You will be surprised when I tell you that it was with real feelings of pleasure we gazed upon her form. On her face was the sweetest calmest look—& her lips being slightly parted, gave the appearance of a smile. Indeed, as there she was lying, she seemed to sleep, & to smile in a dream. We gathered around her, one after another—& you would have been touched to see my father, with her tender babe in his arms, stoop down to kiss her brow & lips. Oh! it was sweet to be there! And when I placed on her bosom a bunch of pure white flowers & evergreens, & Sister Mildred repeated the lines—

"Bring flowers, pale flowers, o'er the bier to shed,
A crown for the brow of the early dead—"

Father knelt down by the body, & wept aloud—& said, "The Lord hath given, the Lord hath taken away—Blessed be the name of the Lord!" I am sure that that scene was witnessed from on high, & that blessed spirits smiled upon it—For it seemed as though we were near Heaven then."] E. S.

The[22] body had been laid out on the bed where she had died, & arrayed by affectionate hands in the simple & solemn attire for the grave. The dimmed eyes were closed as in quiet sleep. The previous constrained posture of the body & dark tints of the face had disappeared. The lips slightly parted, seemed to indicate the beginning of a smile. The slight elevation of the knees, from the still remaining contraction by the disease, added to the natural & life-like appearance of the countenance—increased still more by the covering sheet being frequently moved by the breeze. There was no appearance to produce painful or worse feelings in the nearest friends who stood around. The countenance was placid, gentle, & engaging as when alive. The only difference, besides the pallor of death, was that apparently the wear of full fifteen years had been produced in the wasted form & face by long sickness, & great sufferings. The calm & happy countenance was a comfort to us, who had grieved for her sufferings, &, in despair of their cure, until, even in the new out-burst of mourning for the extinction of life, we had still felt thankful that she was relieved by death.

Her babe, who now will bear the mother's maiden name, was brought in. I placed its smiling lips to the mother's rigid cheek. This scene, in connection with other occurrences, will be told to this child hereafter, & may serve the more to impress on her mind & heart, the bright example of her angelic mother.

This infant, is now an object of great interest to all of us. Deeming that the solemn occasion would serve the more to connect every one with the motherless infant, it was suggested, & heartily concurred in, that its baptism should immediately precede the burial service for the mother.

In the afternoon of the next day, when nearly all the company had assembled in one of the two connected sitting rooms, & the corpse, in the coffin, had been placed near the wide opened partition. The nearest relatives & connections only of the infant, all assembled in the other apartment. They made a considerable number. And every one, who had made a profession of religion, acted as sponsor—I being one of the only two adults of all the near connections, not of that class. The baptismal service was never performed more solemnly & more affectingly. The duty of sponsors, as guardians & friends, was never more strongly impressed than on the many who then undertook the service of friends & supports to the motherless babe, who then occupied a position so interesting to all who witnessed the service. The face of the babe, as bright, joyous, as her mother's had formerly been, & laughing repeatedly during the ceremony, presented a touching contrast to the solemnity of the service, the awful presence of death, & the tears of a large portion of the mere auditors as well as the more interested assistants.

The assemblage of neighbors & friends of the family was greater than could have been looked for, where the notice had been so short. Before the hour appointed for beginning the burial service, there had been thunder, & dark clouds, & there was threatened rain which would be a great evil, & cause great exposure of the attendants, when there could be no postponement of the ceremony. The first portion of the service (of the Episcopal church) was read, the coffin was placed in the hearse, & the visiters & some of the family hastened to their carriages to proceed to the old family grave yard, on the Point.[23] The hearse & next following carriages had just moved on. The sun had again shone out brightly—& a sudden & then unexpected light shower of rain fell, & continued but for a few minutes, the drops glittering like brilliants as they fell through & reflected the bright sunshine. A perfect rainbow appeared, & remained visible, until hidden from view by the high river hills, as the procession descended to the beach. The signs in the sky had most touchingly accorded with the circumstances & the feelings of the occasion.

The beauty & the solemn conformity of the lower & natural scenery could not have been more striking, if planned by art, & produced by the most prodigal expense for the display of pomp, & pageantry. The roadway at first was along the brink of the high table land, & over looking the lower-lying & beautiful & picturesque skirt of forest growth, which has always been so much admired & loved by some of us—through the various noble trees of which the calm water of the broad bay was seen in varying glimpses, bright under the opposite & reflected evening sun light. Descending the hill, the procession next reached the river beach, & passed over its broad & firm sand & gravel, & partly through the shallow water of the river. Another portion of the passage was through the Grove, & its venerable oaks, exceeding any known in this region, in such great number together, in age, great size, & magnificent & solemn appearance.

The body was lowered into the grave, & the solemn religious service resumed & concluded. Rarely is the burial of a private individual, in like circumstances, so numerously attended. Perhaps no death, of one intimately known to so few, in her then but recent place of residence, was more sincerely lamented by all. Yet there were visible no loud outbursts of lamentation from any, & but few & silent outward demonstrations of grief, other than in the calm, solemn & respectful silence & attention of all. The deceased had been prayed for, by name, at the neighboring church,[24] for three successive days of public worship, held at intervals of two weeks—& with every evidence of the deep sympathy & sorrow of all who then prayed for her life & welfare. The long continuation of her great sufferings, & latterly, despair of her recovery, or of any relief on earth, had prepared all the neighbors, as well as the family, to find in her relief by death, a sense of gratification, mingled with that of sorrow. We, who had most grieved for her, while she was suffering & while hope yet remained, felt, when death arrived, the most profoundly how much the sufferer had therein received merciful relief. And though, since her death, all have shed many tears, few of them have been because of her death—or even afterwards in seeing the mortal remains of the departed spirit. These trials, in other cases, the usual producers of most overwhelming sorrows, & outbreakings of lamentation, we could & did bear, with comparative calmness. It was generally in minor matters, & incidents of comparatively slight importance, which caused tears to flow, & renewed feelings & expressions of welcome sorrow, when bringing to mind some loved quality or trait, or characteristic, or affection of the beloved dead, or something that brought forcibly before us the sense of what we had lost. And these are many—& I would not desire to lose their impression in forgetfulness. The grief they bring is mingled with solemn pleasure. Whatever she most loved, or acted in connection with, or whatever most interested her during her confinement to her bed of death, will be remembered by us with especial interest. Among such things, are some pathetic songs & pieces of music, which she had often formerly sung or played, & of which she, & I, when hearing her, had been very fond—& of which some, of sacred music, she had asked to be played on her melodeon, & sung for her, even as late as the last forenoon of her life, & but a few hours before its close. These pieces will hereafter have for me a sacred character, that will give to them a new & great appreciation, & cause them to afford me, more than formerly, pleasure, though a mournful pleasure in hearing them. But I shall wish no witness of their performance except of those who know & feel the connection of the present with past occurrences & feelings. I could not hear any of these songs or airs in ordinary mixed company, & on ordinary occasions, without a painful feeling of the profaning of the most solemn & sacred affections. They should be heard, in company only by ourselves, or dear friends who will never cease to feel the connection of the music with the dead, & with joys extinguished with her life—or still more appropriately, in solitude and deep in the night, & in moon light. In the latter circumstances, I feel the most like invoking & inviting to communion with me the released & happy spirit of my dead child. Of these pieces which she so especially loved, two are *"Carolan's Lament"*, & *"I will arise & go to my Father."* The last she had asked (of her sisters Elizabeth & Mildred, & once especially of myself—) to be played & sung several times during her last few days of life—& the latest time of its performance, together with the hymn

"*How firm a foundation*" also designated by her request, was on the day of her death. Other and as impressive reasons have I to remember, & to love for her sake, "Then you'll remember me" & the simple song "*Bring flowers*," which were among those which I had most delighted to hear her sing, & which in former days, of joy & happiness, I had so often heard from her sweet & touching voice. Particularly I had been pleased by the pathetic images presented in two of the stanzas, of the last, long before I could connect them with any actual events, or suspected that they both, however strong in contrast, would be precisely applicable to the then joyous & happy one who gave them musical utterance, & with profound impression on those who heard her, unsuspicious of any such real woes to affect both. These stanzas will here be copied—(from Mrs. Hemans'.)[25]

"Bring flowers, fresh flowers, for the bride to wear!
They were born to blush in her shining hair.
She is leaving the home of her childhood's mirth,
She hath bid farewell to her father's hearth.
Her place is now by another's side—
Bring flowers for the locks of the fair young bride!

———

"Bring flowers, pale flowers, o'er the bier to shed,
A crown for the brow of the early dead!
For this through its leaves hath the white rose burst,
For this in the woods was the violet nursed.
Though they smile in vain for what once was ours,
They are love's last gift—bring ye flowers, pale flowers!"

Extracts From Carolan's Prophecy. (Mrs. Hemans)
"Voice of the grave!
I hear thy thrilling call;
    x x x x x x x x x x
  I hear thee O thou voice!
And I would thy warning were but for *me*,
  That my spirit might rejoice.
    But thou art sent
  For the sad earth's young and fair—
For the graceful heads that have not bent
    To the wintry hand of care!

>   x x x x x x x x x
> There's a young brow smiling near,
>   With a bridal white-rose wreath—
> Unto *me* it smiles from a flowery bier,
>   Touched solemnly by death!
>   x x x x x x x x x
>   Silence and dust
>   On thy sunny lips must lie—
> Make not the strength of love thy trust,
>   A stronger yet is nigh!
>   x x x x x x x x x
> And the bitterness I know,
>   And the chill of this world's breath—
> Go, all undimmed, in thy glory go!
>   Young and crowned bride of death!
>
> Take hence to heaven
>   Thy holy thoughts and bright,
> And soaring hopes, that were not given
>   For the touch of mortal blight!
> Might I follow in thy track,
>   This parting should not be!
> But the spring shall give us violets back,
>   And every flower but thee!"

"O my son Absalom! Would God I had died for thee, O Absalom, my son, my son!"—(Samuel II. Ch. XIII.33.)[26]

"The Lord gave—the Lord hath taken away—blessed be the name of the Lord!"

All-merciful God! I heartily thank thee that my beloved child's sufferings are ended—and that she is at rest, even though her relief has been brought by death. I thank thee that I no longer grieve for *her* afflictions, but only for myself, and for others who greatly loved her—and because of our loss, never to be compensated. And especially we thank thee for our belief that our loss is her great gain.

Merciful God! while suffering under this heavy affliction, I thank thee for the consolation afforded in the great value of the blessing I have enjoyed, though now lost. I thank thee for the precious recollection, that, from early childhood to her hour of death, my child has never offended me—nor has ever, by any misconduct, brought to her father either sorrow or anger—and that all of pain or grief which she has ever caused, has been in the fear or anticipation of misfortune to her, & anguish for her recent and great sufferings. I thank thee, that her short life has been as happy as it was blameless. I thank thee, Merciful Father! for the portion of my life which has been smoothed and brightened, and my happiness greatly increased, by the intimate companionship & confiding love of my deceased child—while she was the joy of my heart, and the light of my household. I thank thee that, to all who loved her, (and they were all who knew her,) she dispensed joy and pleasure, as well as derived them continually from her kindly and affectionate heart, & its promptings in her every impulse & action. Great God! whose mercies I acknowledge throughout the heaviest chastisements, I thank thee that, in the long illness and severe suffering with which thy will directed that my child's life should close, there did not fail or intermit any portion of her kindly & affectionate consideration for others—scarcely anything of her accustomed cheerfulness & hopefulness—and even when without a remaining hope of continuing in this life, to which she had so many and strong ties, that her calm resignation to thy will was perfect.

Merciful God! I entreat thee to bless the young babe of my departed daughter. Make her to be like to & equal to her mother, in person, in loveliness of disposition, in purity of heart, & in principles and conduct conforming thereto.[27]

Merciful God! in my great affliction for the withdrawal of one of my chief blessings, let me not forget to acknowledge, with much thankfulness, that thou has also blessed me greatly in other children who yet remain to me—and, much beyond the lot of most parents, that my blessings and happiness as a father have far exceeded my troubles and sorrows, even with this now added, the greatest affliction of all. Continue, Merciful Father! to bless me in my remaining children—and bless them all, in health of body & of mind, in their conduct and condition. And if it shall be thy will that death shall strike down another of the dearly loved remaining props of my old age, whether in the bloom & bright promise of youth, or in the more tried & useful & more valuable prime or maturity of life, Oh God! in thy mercy spare me this sorrow, by my being first called & removed by death.

Beechwood, July 26th, 1855

IN REMEMBRANCE OF ELLA RUFFIN

(1855)
―――――――――――――――――――――

In Remembrance of Ella Ruffin.

Born September 10th 1832.
Died August 24th 1855

Marlbourne, August 27th 1855.

Within one month after the death of my Jane, another beloved daughter, another pure spirit, has been taken from me by death. I have no heart or power to describe the circumstances in detail. But, as I have written so much of my sense of the loss of one of my children, if the speedy repetition of a like infliction were not even mentioned in like manner, the omission might seem to indicate a want of due application & of feeling for the last bereavement. I would wish to prevent there being drawn from my silence this inference—unjust to the living, & still more unjust to the dead.

Ella, my youngest daughter, early in the summer, had been indisposed, but was not supposed to be seriously sick. She had not been confined at home, or had (as supposed) needed medical attention. I thought her entirely well, except for remaining weaker than before being sick, when she went with me from our home to Beechwood, mainly for the purpose of aiding to attend on Jane, & to relieve her sister Mildred of part of her almost continued services as attendant & nurse. The fatigue & exposure caused by this journey of 30 miles across the country, made Ella worse, & showed that we had been in error in the previous supposition of her restored health. She was very soon placed under medical care, for continued slow fever, which was pronounced to be typhoid. Her fevers did not yield to medicine; & under both, she continued to become more weak. Still, while there, she was never confined to her chamber by sickness. And so much were we all more deeply interested in the then much greater sufferings & danger of her sister, that, in comparison, little was thought of Ella's sickness—& her danger had not been even suspected, by any but her physician.[1] And no one more than Ella herself, felt this greater interest for her dying sister. And in this respect, as generally, even Jane was not Ella's superior in the absence of selfish feeling; & could not have felt more devotion to a sister's greater sufferings & danger. They occupied neighboring apartments, on the same floor. And when fatigue & weakness kept Ella on her bed, as usual latterly for the greater part of every day, she was generally or frequently left alone, because of the greater anxiety of all to attend to Jane. This comparative neglect was regretted by all except by Ella herself. For so far from complaining, or showing discontent for herself, she seemed always to think that she required nothing & ought to have no share of any attention that could be given to her sister. Her anxious care & thought were so given to her sister, that Ella, even more than others, thought little of herself, & her sickness. It was not until after Jane's burial, that I learned, from the attending physician, that Ella had a disease of the heart. For this incurable, & probably at some future & uncertain time, also deadly disease, of course it was hopeless to attempt any remedy. But for the benefit & improvement of her health in other respects, I proposed to carry the invalid to the mountains & the medicinal springs & baths—& was so advised to do so by her physicians. For this, we hurried the necessary preparations, including our necessary return home. Every available precaution was used, then & afterwards, to prevent all fatigue & exposure of travel that was not inevitable. During the necessary & but short delay at home, Ella had the attendance of our family physician, Dr. Curtis,[2] & the aid of his opinion & directions. We reached the Red Sweet Springs, without much suffering from fatigue, or other inconvenience to the invalid—at which place, in quiet, I designed to remain through the season. But other distressing symptoms had then begun to show, & soon threatened other danger—cough, & dropsical swelling of the feet &c. Our kind friend & physician, Dr. Withers,[3] advised me that my daughter's remaining at the Springs would be useless, if not hurtful—& that an unfavorable & expected turn of her disease would render her removal hopeless for a long time—for ever, I readily inferred. He therefore advised me to use the earliest interval of sufficient improvement to convey her to our home. By his medical treatment & care, the dropsical symptoms were soon abated; & she seemed improving so much, that Mildred (& also other friends) thought she ought to remain longer. But the kind & urgent advice of Dr. Withers, & my dread of the awful result of long lingering illness, even if not terminated by death, among strangers, & far from all the comforts of home, made me use the then time of improvement & strength to return with my child—to die at home, & in the bosom of her family. But she was not spared, even for this alleviation of her end, & of our sorrows.

Our first day's journey (by stage coach,) was to Fincastle, the fatigue of which Ella bore well. The succeeding night, or through all the early & middle part, she rested unusually well, & without any complaint. Near to day-break, she was struck by paralysis, which rendered her whole left side incapable of motion. She suffered no pain. She was still able to speak, though not always distinctly & fully. She made no murmur, or complaint, at this addition to all her previous afflictions. For though she did not suspect the extent of the calamity, she was obliged to know that she was much worse & more helpless than previously. And thus she continued, until, quietly, gently, & silently she breathed her last—at 2 P.M. the same day. She died, without a pang of bodily or mental suffering—and as she had lived throughout her long & distressing illness, (& latterly hopeless herself, as we believed, though she never uttered it—) calm, & meekly submissive & resigned to the will of her Creator.

For weeks before I had known that her recovery was hopeless—& latterly had expected that her death was not far remote. But this last & most horrible disease, paralysis, (when the sufferer still continues to live,) threatening, & usually producing, total helplessness & prostration of body & mind, was sent in mercy to enable me to submit, & ever to rejoice in the midst of my overwhelming sorrows, & heartily to thank God that my child had been removed so soon by death, from a fate far worse than death.

We were at a public hotel, & total strangers to every one near. But the kindest attentions were offered by many, & rendered by some, whose services were accepted as being indispensable, who knew nothing of us, but our affliction, & deplorable situation. Especially to Mrs. Price,[4] our hostess, & to her daughter, Mrs. Nelson,[5] were we indebted for much kindness—and to many strangers, encountered on the several railway trains, in the next day's dismal journey, when bringing the coffined body of my child homeward. But with all these kind attentions & aid, without which I do not know what would have become of me—or whether I should have retained my mind, (if indeed I have entirely—) under the pressure of my difficulties—these two last days were days of horror unspeakable—far more than doubled in pain & distress beyond what would have been the mere effect of the main cause alone, the death of my child, if that had occurred at home.

With all the great difficulties of the first day's journey, & unexpected & unavoidable delay in Richmond through the night, we reached home the next morning, Sunday 26th. The appearance of the approaching hearse gave to the other members of our family the first information of the death of another sister.[6]

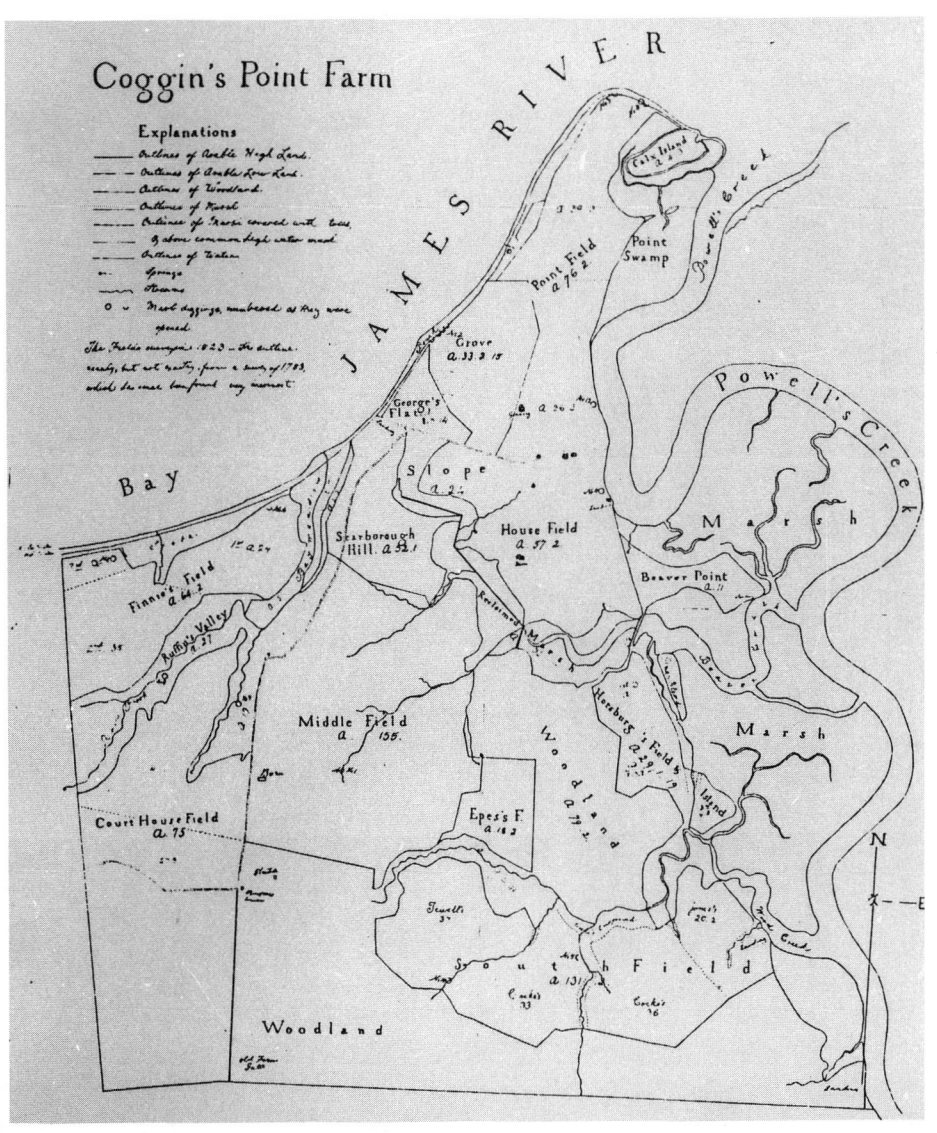

Coggin's Point Farm, Prince George County, 1823, with annotations by Edmund Ruffin. (*Courtesy of James Skelton Gilliam*)

Shellbanks, Prince George County. (*Virginia State Library and Archives*)

Marlbourne, Hanover County. (*Virginia State Library and Archives*)

Low-ground fields and main ditch at Marlbourne. (*Photograph by David F. Allmendinger, Jr.*)

Drainage ditch at Marlbourne. (*Photograph by David F. Allmendinger, Jr.*)

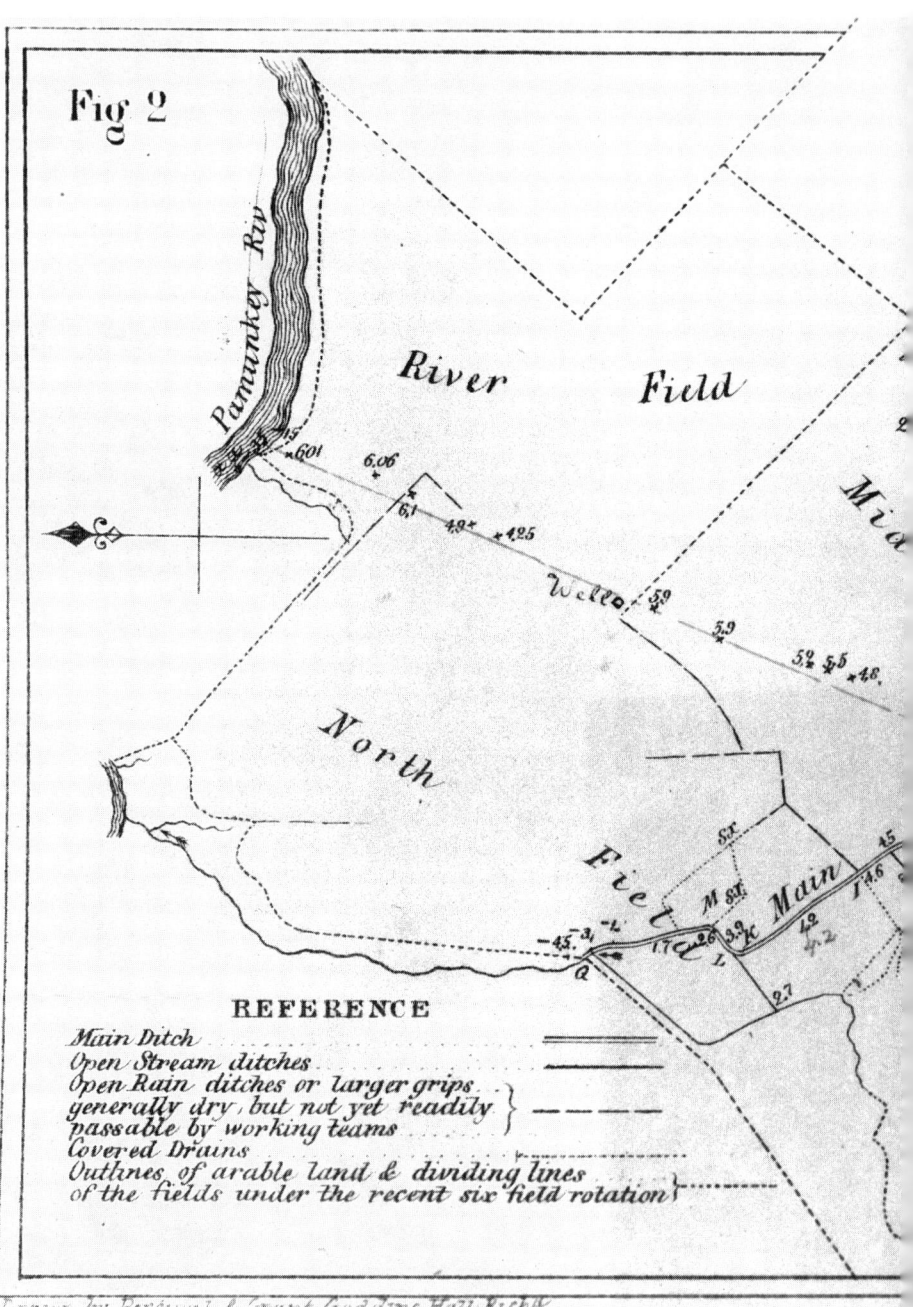

Map of Marlbourne Low Grounds With the recent drainage from 1845 to 1855, from Ruffin's "Account of the Draining of Marlbourne Farm" (1857). (*Virginia Historical Society*)

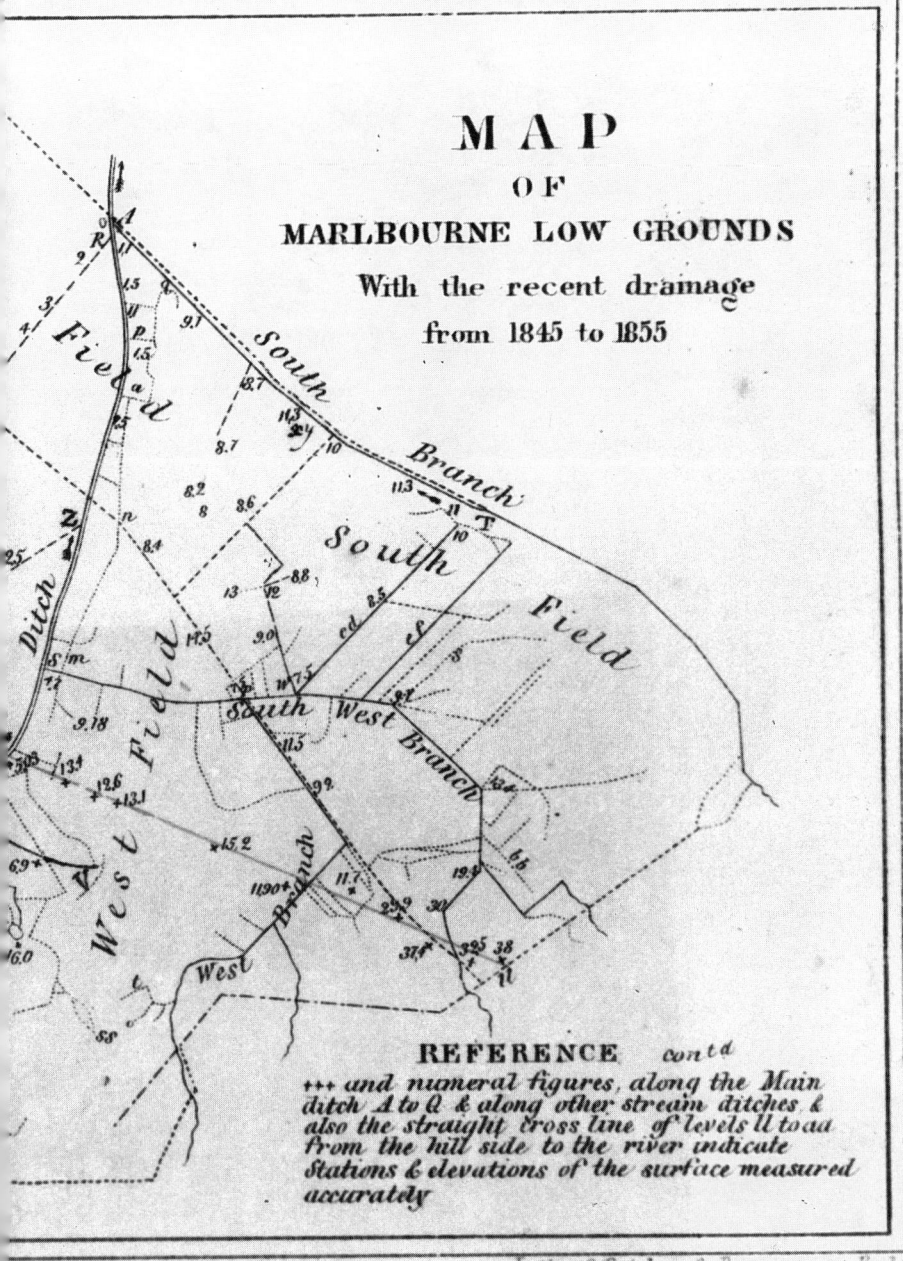

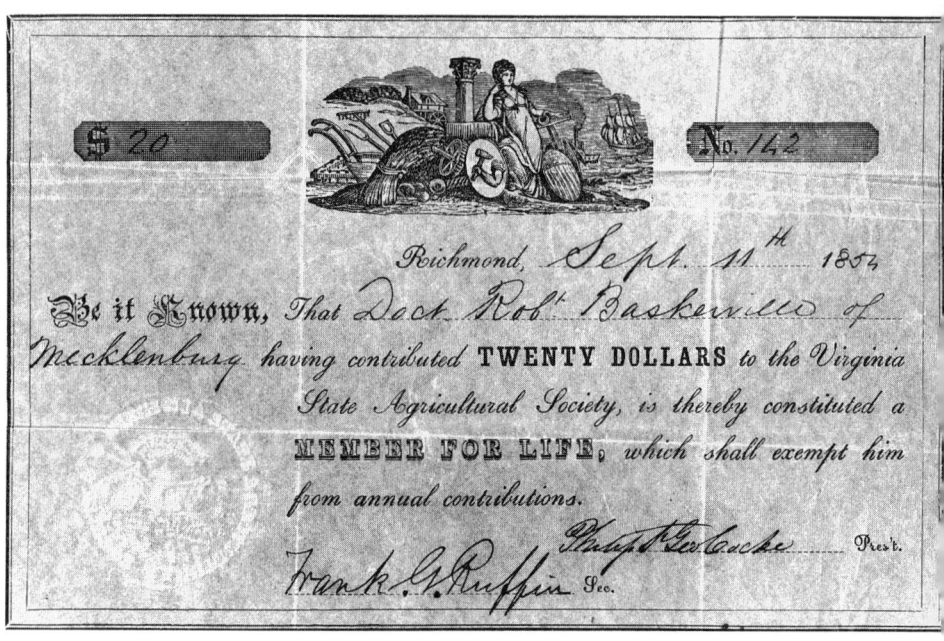

Robert Dortch Baskervill's lifetime membership certificate in the Virginia State Agricultural Society, 1854. (*Virginia Historical Society*)

Beechwood House, Prince George County, where Jane Ruffin Dupuy died. (*Photograph by David F. Allmendinger, Jr.*)

Edmund Ruffin with his children Julian, Ella, Charles, and Mildred, 1851. (*Virginia Historical Society*)

Edmund Ruffin's portrait from *De Bow's Review*. Ruffin called the engraving "bad" but noted "it was enough a likeness to make me known when seen afterwards by strangers." (*Virginia Historical Society*)

The ruins of Tarbay, Thomas Cocke's home in Prince George County at the time of his suicide. (*Photograph by David F. Allmendinger, Jr.*)

Court House Field at Coggin's Point Farm, near the site of Ruffin's first marl pit. (*Photograph by David F. Allmendinger, Jr.*)

Appendices

Appendix 1

Edwin Ruffin, of Virginia, Agriculturist, Embracing a View of Agricultural Progress in Virginia for the Last Thirty Years. With a Portrait.

[By William Boulware]

The subject of this sketch was born January 5, 1794, in the county of Prince George and state of Virginia. In youth and throughout life he has suffered much from a feeble constitution and delicate organization. But neither his debility nor the delicacy of his structure has prevented the most untiring industry in whatever interested him, and the exhibition of an energy, physical and intellectual, which would seem to have required a strong frame, and a hardy and powerful nervous system.

His father, a gentleman of fortune, afforded him all the opportunities for a most liberal education; but he was a little erratic at that period, devoting himself sometimes with great diligence to his studies, and sometimes utterly neglecting them. Yet he was always fond of intellectual pursuits, and though his text book may have lain unopened, he was still occupied, and most frequently, with history, fiction or general literature. As he read for amusement and not improvement, fiction engaged much of his time. In the sixteenth year of his age he was sent to William

Source: [William Boulware], "Edwin Ruffin, of Virginia, Agriculturist . . . ," *De Bow's Review* 11 (1851): 431–36. Ruffin identified Boulware as the author of this sketch in Ruffin, "Incidents" 3:228–29. He supplied Boulware with documents and notes for this sketch. The title of the article in the original journal contained the error in Ruffin's first name.

and Mary College. At first he applied himself with assiduity, and advanced with great rapidity. He was especially successful in geometry, for which he manifested much fondness and decided talent. The first examination was passed by him with distinguished credit.

But soon he relaxed in his studious habits, and was finally suspended from the institution for continued neglect of the duties of his class.

His father being now dead, he was left by an easy guardian to the indulgence of his own tastes and disposition. He returned home to a kind stepmother, without any definite object in view or any determination as to what should be his career in life. But war had now been declared with Great Britain, and at the first muster at which he was enrolled, having reached the military age of eighteen, he enlisted in a volunteer company,[1] and soon after entered on active service. He marched with the first regiment called out from Virginia to the town of Norfolk, and served as a private from August, 1812, to Feb. 1813. He then returned home, and was permitted by his guardian to take possession of his estate. In the division of his father's land he had received, as his share, the farm called Coggin's Point, situated in the county of Prince George, on the waters of James River, and now celebrated throughout this state from the extraordinary improvements made there by Mr. Ruffin. He entered with industry and enthusiasm into the practical business of agriculture, though only nineteen years of age. Yet he did not suffer this occupation to monopolize his attention, for before the end of the year he was married.[2]

Agriculture in Virginia had then reached its lowest point of depression. Under the exhausting system of cultivation which had prevailed from the first settlement—a system which was truly a systematic destruction of the country—adopted in the first instance by emigrants, to obtain the largest immediate profit, and who were utterly regardless of its ultimate effects, and continued by their descendants, when the same cause which had induced it had ceased to exist, the land, for the most part, no longer paid the expenses of cultivation. As a patient who has undergone a long and rapid process of depletion, and who has little blood left to yield to the Sangrado practitioner, such was the tide-water section of Virginia. With such culture—such impoverishment—and the prospect of a population thus situated, society was rapidly declining. It was well said by Mr. Ruffin, in an address to the people of his county,[3] that at that time—

"Almost every man was growing poorer, or the prospects of his family becoming worse. The grade of society had been, and still continued to be, on the decline. The proprietors having no hope of the improvement of their lands, or of being remunerated for ever so great industry and devotion to their business, thought it was well to bestow very little. Accordingly, like the inhabitants of a city ravaged by the plague, they thought more of present enjoyment than of providing for future wants; and there prevailed generally, habits of idleness and improvidence, of pleasure-seeking, and of neglect of business, with all their necessary consequences." The population fled from the country to seek a better fortune in the distant West. He continues: "There was scarcely a proprietor in my neighborhood, and deriving his income from cultivation, who did not desire to sell his land, and who was prevented only by the impossibility of finding a purchaser, unless at half of the then very low estimated value. All wished to sell—none to buy. If a stranger had been inclined to settle among us, he might have chosen almost any farm in the county, and would scarcely have failed to find the owner glad to sell, and at a low price."

The county of Prince George differed but little from all the lower part of Virginia. There seemed no refuge from poverty but emigration. Many of the aristocratic mansions of this hospitable and generous population were now abandoned to silence and ruin, and their former inmates, with the remains of their dilapidated fortunes, made their melancholy way to the wilds of the West. Many a field which had descended from generation to generation of the same stock, for long years, and which had offered to successive heirs green prospects and rich harvests, now thinly clad in broom-straw and the tiny hen-grass, was given up to the encroaching forest.

In this state of things, the subject of our sketch entered on his career as a farmer. He was totally inexperienced, and had no knowledge, either theoretical or practical, of his business. But in this he differed but little from older men of the same period in Virginia. He gave himself up with enthusiasm to his pursuit, labored most industriously, yet labored in the dark, and, of course, often went astray; sometimes in pursuit of one "ignis fatuus," and sometimes of another. He saw clearly that the prevailing systems and practices of culture were wrong, and wandered from experiment to experiment to discover what was true. Often mistaken in views adopted "a priori," he soon tested them by careful experiment and rigid induction. Many investigations, thus pursued for a series of years by one whose logical power equalled his industry, naturally and inevitably led to great results. "Labor vincit omnia," says the Mantuan farmer.[4]

The estate of Coggin's Point was, at that time, extremely poor, the larger part not averaging more than ten bushels of corn per acre, nor more than six bushels of wheat, on the better half of the land.[5] Bordering it, on the river, was a tide marsh of 300 acres, covered by water when the tide was up, but left free when the tide was low. One of the first of Mr. Ruffin's experiments was, to reclaim a part of this marsh. He limited his efforts to about 32 acres, the most favorably situated, as he believed, for success. After five long years' exertions, he succeeded in draining this small section, and bringing it into good culture. It produced three very large crops of corn, then three others less and less in quantity, when the vegetable soil had so rotted away that the level of the land was now too low for cultivation, and it was abandoned to its former element. Such has been the fate of every effort of a similar kind on soils of the same character.

About the year 1813, Captain John Taylor, of Caroline, published his "Arator."[6] It was received with enthusiastic eclat. There was a general belief that he had discovered the great secret of improving Virginia soils, and many anxious farmers now rejoiced, as the tempest-tossed sailor on the first sight of land after a perilous voyage. Here was presented a cure for their misfortunes; they might remain on their old homesteads and retrieve their shattered fortunes. The principal feature in his system was the protection of the land from grazing, and making the vegetable serve as manure. Another, and secondary idea, was to throw the land into high beds, in cultivating the corn crop, by deep ploughing. Mr. Ruffin became an ardent admirer of "Arator," and adopted his opinions and precepts. He had not yet learned that the inorganic elements of soils, the mineral ingredients, are often deficient; that sometimes one or more are exhausted by cultivation, sometimes not furnished by nature to the virgin lands, and that their vegetable growth will not furnish them. He at once carried into practice the new ideas, and subjected them to the test of experiment. For four or five years he used all the means of improvement recommended, and found them, as he states, "either profitless, entirely useless, or absolutely, and in some cases, greatly injurious."

What then was to be done?[7] He was not the man to despair, save in a desperate case. But circumstances seemed singularly to concur in establishing the belief that any permanent improvement was hopeless. Putrescent manure, when applied, disappeared in the course of two or three years, and left not a vestige behind. The country seemed destined to sterility. Indeed, Nature had made barren a large portion of the tidewater country, and her decree was irreversible, with the present elements of the soil. The virgin land, when first stripped of the primeval forest, would in many localities scarcely pay the expenses of cultivation. And yet this soil had received the dropping foliage and the decaying timber from the time of the flood. It is not too much to say, that 100 feet in depth of putrescent matter had been piled on its surface, and had rotted there in the lapse of years, and yet the soil had remained still poor. In this exhibition of Nature herself, was found an answer to Colonel Taylor's theory. An application of vegetable matter might restore the soil to its original productiveness, but no more. To make an improvement beyond this point, some change must be made in its mineral constituents.

But at that period little was known in this country of the science of agriculture. The investigation of its chemistry had just commenced in England by Sir H. Davy, who had entered as a pioneer the vestibule of the science, and raised his torch to dispel the dense darkness which had thus far enveloped the whole subject. While Mr. Ruffin was meditating on the last remedy for sterile lands, removal to the West, he obtained a copy of Davy's "Agricultural Chemistry," which had been just published in this country.[8] He read it with peculiar interest, though not acquainted with chemistry. It was obvious that, at least, the true philosophical mode of examining questions of agriculture had been reached. In the perusal of this author, there was one statement which appeared to afford some hope. As an illustration of the chemical defects of land and their remedies, he adduces an example of a soil of good apparent texture which was sent him from Lincolnshire by Sir Joseph Banks,[9] as remarkable for sterility. Upon analyzing it, he found that it contained sulphate of iron, the copperas of the shops; and he offered the obvious remedy of top-dressing with lime, which converted the poisonous substance into a manure.

It occurred to Mr. Ruffin that the soils of his section might be like the specimen of Sir Joseph Banks. They were of "good apparent texture," and they were sterile, and they had always been so. Putrescent manure made no permanent improvement. Might not the same poisonous substance exist in them? He immediately applied a proper test, but it disclosed no sulphate of iron. This supposition, then, must be abandoned. But might not some other substance, equally deleterious exist? Might there not be some acid? He was induced to present this question to himself, and to incline to believe the affirmation from several circumstances. He says:

"These were, first, that certain plants known to contain acid, as sheep sorrel (the rumex acetorus) and pine, preferred these soils and indeed were almost confined to them, and grew there with luxuriance and vigor, proportioned to the unfitness of the land for producing cultivated crops. Second: That of all the soils supposed to be acid, which I examined by chemical tests, not one contained any carbonate of lime. Third: That the small proportion of my land and of all within the range of my observation, which was shelly, and of course, calcareous, was entirely free from pine and sorrel, and moreover was as remarkable for great and lasting fertility, as the land supposed to be acid for the reverse qualities. Shells or lime would necessarily combine with and destroy all the previous properties of any acid placed in contact; and therefore, if acid were present universally, and acting as a poison to cultivated plants, it seemed plain enough why the shelly lands were free from this bad quality, and by its absence had been permitted to grow rich and continue productive. Still I could obtain no direct evidence of the presence of acid, either free or combined, by applying chemical tests to soils, nor were there any authority in my oracle, Davy's 'Agricultural Chemistry,' nor in any other work which I had read, for supposing vegetable acid to be present in any soil."

But without any authority from chemistry, and in spite of his own failure to detect any such element in soils, by means of the imperfect analysis which he attempted, he felt a very strong confidence that such did exist, and that it was the cause of the sterility of the lands and their incapacity for durable improvement. If his views were true, lime furnished the appropriate remedy. Fortunately, the beds of fossil shells which underlie nearly all the tide-water section of Virginia and the adjacent states, presented the material at hand to test the truth of his theory.

He began operations in February, 1818, and applied between 125 and 200 bushels from one of these beds per acre, to 2½ acres of land. His anticipations were sanguine, and he watched with anxious interest, the progress of the experiment. The marl, as it is commonly called, contained 33⅓ per cent. of carbonate of lime. The land was planted in corn, and when the plants were only a few inches high, their superiority over the adjacent corn was manifest. This continued and increased as the crop advanced, and when the corn was gathered, it was found that the increase was fully forty per cent. That of the wheat crop, which succeeded, was still more. This success on a small area was followed by extensive applications of marl from year to year; and each application testified to the truth of his theory. The acidity of the soil was neutralized, the acid plants and acid pines disappeared, the land improved from year to year. The lime afforded food to the plants, medicine to the soil, and gave permanence to the manures. The retentive capacity which had been inferred from the fact that the most fertile and durable soils known were highly calcareous, was manifested by the marled land, more and more clearly each succeeding year. Mother earth changed her face, and changed her constitution, under the healing influences of this salutary medicament, and now presented an appearance as different from her former self, as the healthy and robust man from the lingering and hectic victim of consumption. Verdant fields and abundant harvests were the monuments of his discovery. Broom-straw (andropagon) and poverty grass (aristida gracilis) gave place to luxuriant clover, and a poor, thin and stunted vegetation, disappeared from the now smiling landscapes.

When[10] Archimedes, in his bath, discovered that a body immersed in a fluid loses as much in weight as the weight of an equal volume of the fluid, and detected by means of it, how much alloy an artist had fraudulently added to a crown, which King Hiero had ordered to be made of pure gold, he is said to have been so overjoyed, that "accoutred as he was," he plunged into the street, crying "Eureka, Eureka, Eureka!" Dr. Rittenhouse,[11] when he saw the transit of Venus over the sun's disc, fainted with excitement. Dr. Franklin, when he discovered with his little kite the identity of lightning and electricity, is said to have experienced emotions of great intensity. The Virginia farmer had greater cause for rejoicing, excitement and exultation than either, for he had not only extended the boundaries of science, but had made a discovery which would add millions to the productions of his country—which would arrest the declining fortunes of his state—which would feed the hungry, give comfort to the indigent, and afford the means of improving the condition of thousands of his race.

In 1818, Mr. Ruffin made a communication to the Prince George Agricultural Society on the subject of his discovery,[12] which formed the basis of his work entitled, "An Essay on Calcareous Manures;" published in 1832. It is to be regretted that the limits of this sketch will not permit the insertion here of that communication. It is the nucleus of the essay. In the latter production, the principles maintained, and which were then for the first time promulged in an independent work, and supported by facts and arguments, are the following:—

1. The capacity of soils for being enriched permanently by putrescent manures is only equal to their original or natural degree of fertility.

2. The absence of carbonate of lime almost universally in the soils of

the Atlantic slope of Virginia, and by inference of most of the other states; and most frequently even in what are called limestone soils.

3. The general presence of some vegetable acid in all the naturally poor soils in the district above referred to, acting as a cause of sterility.

4. The application of carbonate of lime to neutralize the acid, and by that and other effects to prepare the land for speedy and profitable improvement.

These principles were maintained with great ingenuity and ability, and made their way rapidly into public favor. They are now generally received as true, and form the basis of agricultural improvement throughout the extensive section of country for which they were intended. The chemists have detected humic acid in the soil; carbonate of lime is acknowledged to be generally wanting in the slope of the Atlantic states; and it is equally admitted that a considerable mixture of the calcareous element is an essential ingredient in all fertile and durable soils.

The Essay was soon eagerly sought—everywhere discussed—and wrought a powerful effect on the convictions and practices of the proprietors of Eastern Virginia. It passed through three editions. Though the cultivators of the soil are proverbially slow in changing their usages, in this instance the new ideas were rapidly diffused, and, in a short time, large numbers were engaged in marling. Men who before had made only a few hundred dollars from their annual crops, were now found counting up their thousands. Agriculture had become profitable—a prospect was presented of comfort and wealth to the farmers of the country; energy and enterprise succeeded to indolence and idleness, and now it was no longer necessary to look for homes in the western forests for themselves and their descendants.

In an appendix to the "Essay on Calcareous Manures," is an extract from the journal of Coggin's Point Farm, showing the annual crops made from 1813 to 1842.[13] From this source we learn, that in 1818, when the first experiment in marling was made, the crop of wheat on that estate was 450 bushels, and that of corn, 2,670 bushels. In 1843, the product of wheat was 4,725 bushels; that of corn, 4,675 bushels. The quantity of arable land in the beginning was 472 acres, but this was afterwards increased, by clearings of extremely poor land, to 632 acres, which diminished the general product per acre.

In continuation of these details of success, we avail ourselves of the most reliable information to present some evidence of the increase of products on the Marlbourne estate, on which Mr. R. now resides. This land is, for the most part, an alluvial plat on the shore of the Pamunkey, originally fertile, but reduced by injudicious tillage to a state of great impoverishment. In 1844 Mr. R. removed to this estate. We are informed that the ordinary crop of wheat, for a considerable time previous, did not exceed 1,000 bushels, but we have no information as to the corn. In 1845, after an application the year previous, of 67,875 bushels of marl, the crop of wheat on 134 acres, was 1,977 bushels; that of corn on 112 acres, 1,600 bushels. In 1848, after the lapse of only three years, the wheat crop reached 5,127 bushels on 254 acres, and that of corn, 3,080 bushels on 106 acres. This vast improvement—much more than a duplicate of product, indeed, nearly triple—was effected without any other fertilizing substance but the marl, the manure furnished by the crops and clover sown upon the land. The profits upon this estate, including price of land, labor, stock, and everything necessary to its cultivation, were in '47, within a fraction of 23 per cent on the whole investment; in '48, a little upwards of 20 per cent. Nothing being said in this estimate of the increase in the value of the farm, which is, certainly, now worth three times as much as it was four years ago.

It is necessary now to go back and make some reference in this sketch to the labors of Mr. Ruffin, of a different character, though this reference may be a mere synopsis.

He has the honor or the misfortune, according to the different opinions of the two political parties, of having been the author of the first popular effort to resist the restrictive system, or the system for the protection of domestic industry, as its friends loved to designate it. He conceived and organized a plan for the formation of an extensive and numerous association of county agricultural societies, to protect the rights and interests of agriculture, as well as to promote its improvement. In 1818, the society was formed in his own county. The affiliated societies presented to Congress, in the session of 1819–20, the first petition ever offered against the protective policy.[14] This fact and the novelty of a remonstrance on the part of the agricultural interest, produced a profound sensation at the time. There was then no appropriate committee to whom it could be referred, and the Committee of Agriculture was for the first time established and took charge of this petition.[15] That session, the bill for increasing the protective duties of 1816, was lost in Congress by one vote only.[16] The next session the societies again presented their united remonstrance; and the third session, in a petition prepared by Mr. Ruffin, they asked a reduction of the duties on imports to the revenue standard.[17]

In 1824, Mr. Ruffin was elected to the senate of Virginia, and remained in that body for three years, when he resigned his place and abandoned political life.[18] With too much of patriotism and rigid unbending principle to be a supple partizan, he has ever had but little kindness for either of the political parties which divide and distract our country. He has freely denounced both, when wandering, as he believed, from those principles which should control the government of this confederacy. It can never be said of him, as of Burke, that he "to party gave up what was meant for mankind."

In 1832, Mr. Ruffin engaged in the publication of a new agricultural periodical, called the "Farmer's Register," which was well received and sustained by the public. It was a journal of high order of merit, edited with ability, and numbered among its contributors many of the ablest men of the South.[19] In form, size, as well as substance, it rather resembled the English Quarterlies of agriculture than any paper among us at present devoted to this subject. It exerted great influence in diffusing rich stores of scientific and practical information, and particularly in extending the use of calcareous manures. Virginia, Maryland and North Carolina are much indebted to this work for the amelioration of their systems of culture, and the great advance they have made upon their former modes of cultivation and the present general prosperity of the farmers of these states. Their energies were aroused and lethargy dispelled by the pictures presented of the results of judicious agriculture, and facts demonstrating the large profits to be made in this department of business. The noble science of agriculture was exhibited in all its attractions, and intellect and taste were enlisted in its development and practice. He conducted this journal for ten years, when he left it, and soon after it expired.

While engaged in the "Farmer's Register," he published, for a short time, a periodical of another kind, but intimately connected with the interests of the cultivators of the soil. This was the "Bank Reformer," devoted to an exposure of the defects of the banking system of that state, and a bold and imposing denunciation of what he believed to be its corruptions.

In 1841 he was appointed a member of the "Board of Agriculture," established by a law of Virginia, and became its secretary.

From this position he retired upon being appointed Agricultural Surveyor of the State of South Carolina. This appointment, conferred most unexpectedly by a state in which Mr. Ruffin had scarcely any personal acquaintance, was highly flattering and honorable to him; and he determined to accept it, though at a great inconvenience and loss. The appointment was for two years, but he would only consent to take it for one; and as the labor for so short a period could not possibly be sufficient for one twentieth part of the important subjects claiming investigation, he directed his efforts for the most part to discovering and examining the beds of marl and other calcareous deposits, and urging their use upon the people of the state. The marl was abundant beyond all expectation, and universal ignorance prevailed on its value. After spending a laborious year, and making an extended and valuable report, he closed this career and returned to his family.

He then removed to his farm at Marlbourne, which had been purchased for him by his directions during his absence, and commenced those rapid and remarkable improvements, of which some little information has been already given. He here has had green sand marl with which to improve his land, a much more fertilizing and valuable substance than at Coggin's Point. He now lives in the midst of his devoted family, still ardently engaged in his favorite pursuit, with his energies unrelaxed, and a vivacity and activity remarkable in one of his age.

He has seen his efforts crowned with success. It is principally due to his exertions that Virginia is going through a process of rapid improvement, such as has been rarely, if ever before, witnessed. Emigration has for the most part ceased; her sons may now find abundant sources of prosperity at home. The census of 1850 shows an increase in the value of the lands of Eastern Virginia since 1837 of 23 millions of dollars.[20] Nor is even this amount a fair estimate of the real enhancement. The high price of labor, regulated by the southern markets, keeps down the profits of the farmer upon the capital invested, and, of course, depresses the value of the lands.

In an address of Mr. Ruffin to his friends and neighbors of Prince George, in 1843, who had assembled to do him honor in the presentation of a service of plate, he contrasts their present condition with what it was twenty-five years before. The former part of the picture has been before adverted to in this sketch; in the latter part he says—

"In all of this time, my old neighborhood, and, so far as I know, through the whole county, not one individual, after beginning to marl, has emigrated or desired to emigrate." "The prices of lands here have greatly increased, though less than their true value. But I know not how to estimate the rate of increase, because sales are now more rare than ever formerly, though for the opposite reason. Then it was that nobody would buy; now, nobody will sell."

"I know nowhere a more industrious and steadily thriving community than is exhibited in the present occupants of these lands. Among them, I believe, it would be difficult to find a young landholder who is not attentive to his business, industrious, and thriving in his operations; and of seeking pleasure less than his predecessors, finding it far more successfully in steady attention to the cultivation and improvement of his farm. And his change, and all the results and benefits, economical, social and moral, are mainly owing to this one circumstance, that every man has now presented to him, in certain prospect, a full and sure reward for his labors." What is here affirmed of the county of Prince George, is, to a very great extent, true of all Virginia below the mountains.

Mr. Ruffin has thus enriched his state by his labors—enriched his friends, his neighbors and himself. His indelible impress is made on Virginia, and time must strengthen it. His monument is truly more lasting than brass, for it is the soil of his state. He has cause to be conscious that he has deserved well of his country. His memory will be cherished with gratitude, when many of those who occupy so much of the public attention, and who are ever parading before the popular gaze, shall cease to exist in the recollection of man, when their evanescent honors shall have passed away with the excitement that gave them birth, and like the consumed candle, their light shall have vanished forever.

Appendix 2

Statement of the closing scenes of the life of Thomas Cocke.

Feby. 25. 1840.

The lapse of time in the last two days, instead of lessening the acuteness of pain caused by the circumstances which just before occurred, seems to add weight to the first shock. This has always been my singular disposition. The heaviest afflictions which have ever been brought upon me by the death of dearest & most valued objects, have been scarcely realized by my mind upon the first sudden communication of the event—& some days have passed away before the entire lost value seemed to be estimated, or the full force of the stroke felt. Thus it is now. At a time when others may begin to forget their grief, & to receive some consolation for their misfortune, most afflicting & horrible as it was, my at first dull & torpid feelings become sensitive, & the hardness of heart—the almost absence of feeling, with which I reproached myself—is more & more changed to the frame of mind & of heart which might have been expected in me at first. My thoughts are continually brought back to the source of pain, & my grief even partakes something of remorse. I feel strongly impelled to write down the strange & horrible circumstances which have just occurred, & thus to record & preserve, even if but for my own eye, the many minute details which would otherwise soon fade away from a frail memory.

On the evening of the 18th inst. I went to visit my son Edmund & his family at their residence at Beechwood Cottage;[1] &, as always, gave

> Source: Edmund Ruffin, "Statement of the closing scenes of the life of Thomas Cocke," 25 Feb. 1840, Ruffin Papers, ViHi. For biographical information on Cocke, see volume 2, note 7.

a considerable proportion of the time of my visit to my oldest & best friend, Thomas Cocke, their very near neighbor, at Tarbay. I spent the greater part of the next day with him, & also about two hours of the evening of the succeeding day, when I took that leave of him which subsequent developments showed that he knew to be the last. Next morning, (21st) early, I returned to my residence, in Petersburg. On the night of the 22nd, at 8 o'clock, an express messenger arrived, with a hurried note from my daughter-in-law,[2] stating that Mr. Cocke had that forenoon put an end to his existence!

Grieved I was indeed—but not to compare with what I now feel; surprised & shocked too, but perhaps less than any other person; for I had long suspected the coming to this issue, & our recent conversations had confirmed my opinion that by this awful & horrible means he would seek release from his severe bodily pain & mental wretchedness.

I aided that night in enforcing my son's directions, sent by a second messenger, for the making & sending the coffin; & early the next evening I rode to the scene of the dreadful catastrophe. The hearse with the coffin, arrived about an hour after. At 3 o'clock the few persons present—comprising however in their number all those in the vicinity who knew him best & loved him most—placed the mangled corpse in the grave.[3] There was no ceremonial service of any kind. The deep regrets of his friends, the tears of his few relatives, & of his assembled slaves, & the awe-stricken feelings of all, made the simple & naked service of returning what was now earth to earth, more solemn & affecting than any ceremonial could have produced.

And now, before stating the circumstances of the last act of this tragedy, I will here attempt to sketch something of the singular characteristics of this remarkable man—of whom, whatever were his defects, I can conscientiously say in this solemn hour, that no stronger mind, no nobler heart, have animated any human being whom I have ever known. In the thirty years of our intimate acquaintance, dating from my boyhood & his mature age, I have never known him to do or to design injury to any fellow creature, nor to seek his own benefit unjustly at the cost of others. Yet was his gigantic intellect left always useless, because directed to no proper & noble end, & his virtuous feelings & impulses led to no good—save that the first served to minister to the temporary pleasure, & the last to command the love & esteem of the very few persons who knew & properly appreciated him.

His life had been that of a recluse, from his early youth. For even when afterwards thrown into society, he found no companionship in all the early part of his life. When his connexion in marriage (after middle age)[4] required, he endured common society, without taking pleasure in it. The death of his wife, & subsequent pecuniary losses & misfortunes caused him to withdraw again to his early hermit-like life. He saw very few persons, & wished to see yet fewer. There were very few in whose association he took any pleasure. With all his benevolence for mankind, he had for them neither love nor admiration. If not a misanthrope, at least he heartily despised his fellow man.

From having pursued a most active & indeed laborious life as a farmer, induced by the desire for occupation & not for its ultimate objects, disease & infirmity had for several years confined him almost to his apartment. His greatest pleasure, indeed almost his sole pleasure latterly, continued to the last to be found in books. But the decay of his memory from age, & as he maintained (though in that he was mistaken,) the prostration of all vigor of mind & reasoning power, destroyed the greater part of pleasure to be derived from reading, & was a matter of mortification to his pride as well as of diminution of his pleasure. So situated, his lonely life could scarcely be otherwise than a regular succession of one wretched day added to another. The youthfulness of his two children, devotedly attached as he was to them, rendered them unsuitable companions; & the care of their education required one or both of them to be from him except at rare intervals, until very recently. Thus he was almost entirely alone, & his mind permitted to be continually brooding over his real & his imaginary causes of unhappiness. An apoplectic attack which occurred some years ago, & which was very near producing death, aggravated all these evils, by leaving bodily feebleness, lethargy, torpor, difficulty of breathing, & a state of general suffering, too heavy to bear, & which made the coming of death to him the most desirable of all earthly events. But longed for & expected for years, death seemed as far off as ever; and except for his increasing weakness & painfulness, of which the sufferer alone was sensible, he appeared to be in excellent health, & to withstand the attacks of time & old age astonishingly. At 64 years of age, his still full head of hair was as black as in his youth. No touch of gray was visible, even if a white hair was to be found.

I visited him on the 19th at noon, & remained with him until near sunset; & again on the afternoon of the succeeding day. He seemed, as at all times, delighted to see me; & notwithstanding his pain, & though intermixed with complaints of his intolerable sufferings, & of woes unutterable & indescribable, he was generally cheerful & even as gay as I have ever known him to be. Indeed I saw no change, save an increase of the disposition which I had witnessed for years, to express his anxiety to die. In referring to his bodily sufferings, he several times closed his remarks with these words: "I cannot bear it—& I *will not* bear it." He also seemed at other times inclined to remark upon & to discuss the general question of suicide. I tried to avoid the subject, & to change the conversation. Though then strongly suspecting the tendency of such language, or rather the state of mind which prompted the utterance, I could not bring myself to acknowledge to him, to let him know fully, that I comprehended the drift of his dark expressions, & suspected his design. It seemed to me, that to do this, would have removed one obstacle in his way. I affected to be ignorant of the import of his expressions, & merely observed that suicide must always be the effect of temporary insanity. I thought that if he could believe that the world would attribute the act to insanity, that his pride would revolt at the sentence—that he might therefore hesitate & delay—& delay would prevent the dreaded result altogether. His only answer to that remark was, "In that, you are *altogether* mistaken." Since the awful & speedy fruition of my expectation, I have been visited by self-reproach approaching to remorse, that I did not use my privilege of a confidential friend—the only one as he told me that day, & had often told me before, in whose presence he permitted himself to "think aloud,"—& combat his opinions & try to change his design. But though feeling thus self-condemned, I am as perfectly satisfied, now as then, that all such efforts would have availed nothing with a man of such strong mind, who had reasoned with himself in solitude for years, & had considered & measured the subject in every aspect.

It was not difficult to draw him to gayer subjects, as was my endeavor, & he readily entered upon them. I had designed when commencing this writing, to note down all that was remembered of these last & long private & unreserved conversations held under such remarkable circumstances. But I cannot do so. It would seem shocking even to my own feelings & sense of propriety, to intermix with the deeply tragical & horrible result, the gay, the trifling, & even ludicrous manner which marked his expressions as well as mine, many times during these two days.

At other times, as heretofore, his words were replete with wisdom, & with interest to his hearer. His well stored mind enabled him to discuss ably & eloquently the many subjects on which our conversation ranged. Among various other things we talked of general & of party politics, (of the latter but with bitter scorn & contempt) of morals, of religion. I was struck with the force of one of his expressions. He was telling me of advice which he had recently given his young son, in regard to his general conduct through life. "I told him," said he, "whenever you are urged by passion or interest to commit any act which your judgment condemns, or makes you suspect the perfect propriety of, pray to God, my son, immediately & earnestly, to strengthen & sustain you in the right course, & it will be the best possible mode of avoiding evil."

He ridiculed the pomp & expensiveness of the usual modes of burying the dead, & cited the example of his youngest brother,[5] for whose corpse the coffin cost $70. "And what folly the attempt to prevent the designed operation of the universal law of nature, by burying our dead 6 feet deep. The Chinese are wise enough to forbid graves being deeper than 18 inches." "But," said I, "whether at our depth or theirs' the final result is the same; & the flesh passes into grass." "True," said he, "but that proper & natural result is much longer delayed. It is not frustrated however. Grass grows & receives its bulk & substance from the man's buried body; the ox or the hog eats the grass, & what was first man's flesh, & next grass, becomes part of the brute, which when killed & eaten, again becomes part of man again. Thus, there is a perpetual round of changes; of greater or of less extent & duration." He stated his wishes as to the plainness of the burial of his own body, & requested me to come & aid the simple & essential services required. "I have given my directions particularly to James (his nephew)[6] & will have no parade or formalities over my body."

At another time he said—"Have you not remarked that there are many individuals of the human family who in their dispositions & mental qualities strikingly resemble the general characters of certain species of brutes? Some men show precisely the disposition, & kindred propensities to those of the fox—others of the hog—others of the wolf &c. Some possibly have the noble qualities of the lion; But how few are the human lions, compared to the numbers of the human cats, & foxes & hogs, & hyenas!" In answer to a remark of mine, he answered, "Yes, I heartily despise my fellow creatures."

My second visit on the next evening was limited to about two hours, & closed with my taking leave of him, as I was to return home early the morning after. He was even more cheerful though this time. When it was necessary for me to bid him farewell, he urged a longer stay so strongly, that I am sure it had reference to his then near approaching end, & that he wished me to be at hand when it was consummated. But though his words & conduct indicated *to me* so strongly his general design, he did not let escape him a word to betray any immediate purpose or settled plan. My last words to him stated that my designed arrangements now would bring me often to the neighborhood, & that I should visit him again soon & often. He did not intimate, as might have been supposed, in any way that he knew it would be our last meeting in this world.

Things went on through the next day (the 21st) so far as observed, in the usual & almost unvaried way.[7] On the 22nd, (Saturday) after breakfast, he shaved himself; which was so unusual on that day, that it attracted his servants' notice. His son, as usual, had gone to attend to his farming operations, recently commenced, at Aberdeen,[8] about 5 miles off. Mr. Cocke had ordered the dinner & directed of what it should consist, as he did usually. When dinner was ready, about 2 o'clock, he was not in or about the house, which, as it was very unusual for him to walk outside of the yard, caused surprise & uneasiness to his servants, which increased with their unsuccessful search for him in every place that he could be supposed to have reached in walking. At last, about 4 o'clock, one of his men thought of entering a thicket on the side of a deep valley. When he reached to within some short distance of a large oak tree, he saw seated at its foot the object of his search, a bloody headless corpse. Horror-struck, he fled to tell what he had seen, & to send for the son & the nearest friends of his master. My son was the nearest, & he was quickly there, the first who reached the horrible scene—for the slaves dared not approach until assured by his presence & commands. The corpse was seated upright, in a natural posture, the back resting against the body of the tree. All of the front part of the head above the lower jaw was gone, & what remained of the back part with the gray locks, hung down & spread over on each shoulder. The gun, the instrument of destruction rested between his knees as it naturally fell, after having been fired into his mouth. The right hand, blackened with the burnt gunpowder showed that it had grasped the gun near the muzzle, & the shoe of one foot was off, & the[9] end of the stocking had been cut, so as to use the toe to push back the trigger. The body did not seem to have been moved in the slightest degree, either by the tremendous concussion, or by any struggle of the body in the act of death. The effect must have been instantaneous. Pieces of the scull, some of them black from the burnt powder, and the brains, were scattered all around. After my arrival the next morning, I aided in the gathering up as many of these widely scattered fragments as could be found.

The body remained seated upright, braced against & supported by the tree, & the limbs in the natural & seemingly easy position that had been first assumed, & which presented in stronger & more horrible contrast the work of death in the bloody remains of the shattered head. Long will it be before the vividness of that object will be erased from the memory of those who saw it! I thank God that I did not see it. For even from the description, it is continually coming before my mental vision. I am as perfectly free from all belief in supernatural visitations, or appearances, as is any man on earth, & from my childhood to mature age, never has any such fear crossed my imagination, nor has my reason treated such fears as otherwise than too absurd & ridiculous for serious thought. But it is not reasoning, nor even any distant approach to belief, but my painful feelings & shattered nerves, that make me, as I write, alone & in the depth of night, feel almost afraid to look around, lest the object which so dwells on my mind's eye should be more palpably present, & thus demand of me more strongly & sternly than does my own heart, "Why did you to make no effort to prevent this deed?"

To return.[10]

Another neighbor arrived in a few minutes after Edmund, & they, with the assistance of some of the negroes, laid the corpse upon a blanket, & bore it to the house. Soon the son arrived, overwhelmed with grief & horror. The considerate care & influence of Edmund prevented by persuasion, his young friend from seeing the corpse of his father. The nephew, James B. Cocke, & several other neighbors followed, & the always painful &, to me, most revolting task of undressing & dressing the dead, was commenced by cutting off the blood stained garments from the stiffened limbs. Edmund was spared his share in that service, by being engaged in another scarcely less painful, that of writing to the son-in-law of the deceased, to inform him of the event.[11] The daughter of the deceased had been married about a year, & had resided since in New York.

Almost as soon as the corpse had been brought into the home, Edmund saw a written sheet of paper on the table of the parlor, laid open, is if for observation. It was in the following words:

"During the last two or three years my existence has been only an endurance of intolerable sufferance. When I look forward, even *hope itself* suggests no relief. I find myself not only a burthen on myself, but entertain no hope that my permanence in this world can essentially aid my dear children. Thus situated—desperation prompts me to put an end to my existence, and to confide in the Mercy of Heaven.

"My body can be found under or near the large oak below the multicaulis planting.

I consider the summons of a jury unnecessary, as this paper announces the fact of my exit by my own operation."

Th. Cocke
10 o'clock, 22 Feby, 1840"

This writing was indeed clearly & awfully explicit, even if the visible results had left any doubt as to the cause & manner of the deed. I have read and heard of many remarkable cases of firm & desperate determination in the procedure of other unhappy beings who have laid violent hands on their own lives. But neither in real life nor in fiction, not even in the wildest imaginings of romance writers, has there occurred a suicide to compare with this, in long deliberation & preparation of the plan, & in the regulated & cool determination with which it was executed. No doubt the sufferer was long constrained & long withheld from the act, by the far more weighty considerations of his duty to society, to his children, & far greatest of all, to God. But these being silenced, it does not appear that the natural shrinking of humanity from the pains & terrors of death had the slightest weight on his determination o[r] his action. Many circumstances, which had occurred without exciting observation before his death, when viewed in connexion with it, proved a settled purpose & plan previously & perfectly arranged. I have no doubt but that he had long before fixed the place, the day, the very hour, for the deed. Why he should by such delay of a fixed purpose, have added ten-fold to his own difficulty in its execution, & to its horrors, is more than I can imagine. For having once determined on the act, the most fearless & careless of all self destroyers would have acted on the first determination, & not have made every minute that passed a living death, in the painfulness of anticipation, for days, if not for weeks, before the final consumation. I cannot even surmise the cause. It is absolutely certain that the studied delay was not the effect of any shrinking from the execution of the awful design.

I will state some circumstances, in addition to those already mentioned, which go to show a pre-arranged & particular plan, & the coolness with which it was arranged & completed.

Some time before, he requested his son to send out the young negro man who waited on table, to shoot wild ducks. This had been continued by his own order to the servant part of nearly every day afterwards. Such an order, & directed to so inexpert a gunner, was thought strange, but only as a whim, that attracted no consideration. This was doubtless designed for the purpose of having the gun always at hand, & ready for use, which might not be secured otherwise without causing observation & arousing suspicion of the object. About a week before, he sent over to my son for some percussion caps, as if for his servant's use, & three of these caps were found in his pocket after his death. This was another precaution against not finding the gun ready, & against its missing fire, even if ready. The day before his death, he had directed the servant to wash out the gun carefully; another precaution to secure its more certain effect. He had certainly selected the spot for the execution, with previous & careful observation, & considered the possibility of every contingency. The large oak I believe had been to him a favorite resort, in long past & happier times. It stands on a hill side about ten yards below the edge of the cultivated ground, (which is the planting mentioned in his note,) & on the other side of the tree, & immediately from it, the hillside is precipitous to the stream which is about 15 feet lower, in a narrow ravine. Any convulsive struggle in death, that would have caused the body to be thrown from the position taken on the upper side of base of the tree, would probably have thrown it down the almost perpendicular descent into the ravine. And this contingency was no doubt in his mind, when he wrote that his body could be found "under *or near*" the oak tree.

The writing which he made so short a time before his hour had arrived is executed with unusual care, & shows a steady hand. Part of the same forenoon he had been reading one of the newspapers which I had carried to him & my son found the papers as if thrown carelessly on one side of his seat on the sofa, & his spectacles on the other, as if he had but just left his seat, & in usual manner. He was missed from the house by his servant before 12 o'clock; but no importance was attached to it, as he sometimes, though rarely, walked out, & as I now know, had recently visited the oak. For during my last visit to him, when speaking of his extreme feebleness, he had described it by stating the great difficulty & fatigue caused to him not long before by a walk to & from a spot which he named, & which was very near the oak. His route was afterwards traced by my son, following his foot prints on the soft earth. It was plain that he had cautiously concealed himself from the view of his servants at the kitchen,[12] by keeping the dwelling house between him & them, for which purpose he left the direct course, & reached the spot circuitously. He took with him his razor, obviously to finish the deed, if the gun should by possibility fail. The razor was laid upon the ground by his side.

    I venture no comment upon this awful deed. It is not for man to judge of, but for God—and may the merciful God judge of it in mercy! But while I cannot attempt to justify, & will not try even to offer excuses in mitigation of the last & greatest offence of his life, neither will I in any manner join in the universal cry of condemnation, which in all such cases, proceeds not only from the moral & the pious, & from those who hold in reverence the laws of God, but also from those whose opinions & acts are altogether different from & opposed to, those of a virtuous life. When death calls me from this world, may my dread account of sins over-balancing virtues, be not greater than that of my self-slaughtered friend!

Edmund Ruffin

Appendix 3

First Views Which Led to Marling in Prince George County.

By the Editor.

Among the persons who have read with interest the 'Essay on Calcareous Manures,' and have received as sound the novel theory and doctrines there maintained, several have expressed their curiosity which had been excited to learn the earliest facts, or the train of reasoning, which led to the imputed cause of the effect of naturally barren soils, and the remedy. Such inquiries have been made of the writer by persons of investigating and well informed minds, but of very different education and pursuits; and they were all pleased to say, in regard to the concise verbal answers made to their inquiries, that they deemed the details likely to be interesting to many, and that if given to the public, they might serve better to induce the consideration and enforcement of the doctrines, than had been done by the mere arguments which had been already published, convincing as they considered the arguments to be.

Though, without these reasons and solicitations, the writer might have still refrained from touching this subject, it was not that he had not held the same opinion—and, except in his own case, would have urged the same course. It is certain, that the tracing of the steps by which any new discovery, or improvement, is reached, must always be interesting in proportion to the admitted importance of the results; and indeed such

Source: Edmund Ruffin, "First Views Which Led to Marling in Prince George County," *Farmers' Register* 7 (1839): 659–67. Ruffin referred to himself as "the Editor."

a statement seems almost necessary to induce the reader to accompany the author from his first premises to the remote conclusion, and which otherwise is only reached through a devious and tedious passage, and by a course of reasoning which is wanting in interest, because the application and tendency of the arguments and proofs are not seen when they are first presented. The objection which restrained the writer from before pursuing a course which he would have highly approved in others, was, that such a narrative of opinions and facts would be indeed a personal narrative, and therefore obnoxious to the charge of egotism throughout. The statement of the reasoning which led to the successful use of fossil shells on the poor lands of lower Virginia, would be incomplete if not accompanied by a narrative of early labors, and the early as well as latest results and effects. In the whole of this, there would be scarcely any thing but statements of what the writer thought, and reasoned, and performed. But the subject must be so treated, or not at all; and having consented to give the narrative, the writer will throw aside all scruples and objections, and endeavor to enter as much into detail, as he, if a reader of others' agricultural improvements and practical operations, would desire to find.

With the beginning of the year 1813, when barely nineteen years of age, the easy indulgence of my guardian gave to me the possession and direction of my property; which consisted of the Coggin's Point farm, with the necessary and yet very insufficient stock of every kind. It is scarcely necessary to add that, at my very early commencement, I was totally ignorant of practical agriculture; and such would have been the case, according to the then and now usual want of training of farmers of Virginia, even if my farming labors had been postponed to a mature age. But I had always been fond of reading for amusement, and the few books on agriculture which I had met with had been studied, merely for the pleasure they afforded, at a still earlier time of my boyhood. The earliest known of these works was an English book, in four volumes, the 'Complete Body of Husbandry,'[1] of which I have not seen the only known copy since I was fifteen years old. This work was probably a mere compilation, and of little value or authority; but it gave me a fondness for agricultural studies, and filled my head with notions which were, even if proper in England, totally unsuitable to this country. 'Bordley's Husbandry' next fell into my hands, and its contents were as greedily devoured.[2] This was indeed written in America, and by an American cultivator; but as he drew almost all his notions from English writers, his work is essentially also of foreign materials.

Thus prepared, I commenced farming, ignorant indeed, but not in my own conceit. The agriculture of my neighborhood, like all that I had ever witnessed, was wretched in execution, and as erroneous as well could be in system, whether subjected to the test of sound doctrine, or the improper notions which I had formed from English writers. I was right in condemning the general practice of my neighbors—but decidedly mistaken in my self-satisfied estimate of my own better information and plans.

Just about the time that my business as a cultivator was commenced, Col. John Taylor's 'Arator' was published;[3] and never has any book on agriculture been received with so much enthusiastic applause, nor has any other had such widespread early effects in affecting opinion, and stimulating to exertion and improvement. The ground had before no occupant, and therefore this work had to contend with no rival. The larger landowners, of lower Virginia especially, had previously treated their own proper employment, and their only source of income, with total neglect; and very few country gentlemen took any personal and regular direction of their farming operations. It was considered enough for them to hire overseers, (and that class then was greatly inferior in grade and respectibility to what it is now,) and to leave the daily superintendence to them entirely. The agricultural practices, and also the products, were consequently, and almost universally, at a very low ebb. The work of Taylor appeared when these evils had become manifest; and it was received with a welcome which in warmth was proportioned to the magnitude of the evil, and to the exaggeration of the promises of speedy and effectual remedy which the author made, with so much good faith no doubt, but which proved any thing but true to the great majority of his sanguine followers.

Of course, I was among the most enthusiastic admirers of 'Arator;' and not only received as sound and true every opinion and precept, but even went beyond the author's intention, (perhaps,) and applied his rules for tillage to lands of surface and soil altogether different from the level and originally rich sandy soils of the Rappahannock, where his labors and system had been so successful. However, this error was by no means confined to myself; for his other disciples fully as much misunderstood the directions, and misapplied the practices.

It was my main object to enrich my then very poor land; and, for that, Taylor offered means that seemed to be sure and speedy. According to his views, it was only necessary to protect the arable land from all grazing, and thus let the vegetable cover of the land, when resting, serve as manure—to plough deep, and in ridges—to convert all the cornstalks and other offal to manure, and plough it under, unrotted, for the corn—to put the farm under clover, as fast as manured—and the result would be sure. I hoped at first to be able to manure, say 10 to 15 acres a year, very heavily, with the barn-yard manure, and expected that such manuring would give a crop of 50 bushels of corn to the acre. The space, so enriched when in the succeeding crop of wheat, would be laid under clover—and its acquired productiveness be made permanent, by the lenient rotation of two crops only taken from the land in four years. But utter disappointment followed. The manure was put on the poorest (and naturally poor) land; and it produced very little of the expected effect in the first course of crops, and was scarcely to be perceived on the second. Clover could not be made to live on land of this kind; and even on much better, or where more enriched, was a very precarious crop, and which, where the growth was best, certainly yielded the entire occupancy of the ground to natural weeds after one year. The general non-grazing of the fields under grass, or rather under weeds, produced no visible enriching effect, and the ploughing of hilly land (as mine mostly was,) into ridges, caused the most destructive washing away of the soil by heavy rains. These results were not speedily made manifest; and before being convinced of their certainty, I had labored for four or five years in using these means of supposed improvement of the soil, but all of which proved either profitless, entirely useless, or absolutely and in some cases greatly injurious. And even after trying to avoid the first known errors, and using all other supposed means for giving durable and increasing fertility to my worn and poor fields, at the end of six years, instead of having already achieved great improvement, I was compelled to confess that no part of my poor land was more productive than when my labors commenced, and that on much of it, a tenfold increase had been made of the previously large space of galled and gullied hill-sides and slopes.

When more correct opinions had been formed in after time of the actual condition and requirements of such poor soils, it seemed an astonishing delusion that would have been altogether ludicrous but for its serious effects, that I should have counted on so much improving such a soil, and by such means. With the exception of a small part near the river banks, (perhaps one-fifth of the then cleared and cultivated land,) which had been originally of very fine quality, and, however abused and exhausted, was still good land, the farm generally consisted of a soil of sandy loam, usually about three inches deep, and through which a single-horse plough could easily penetrate and turn up the barren and more sandy subsoil. Grazing the fields, when not under tillage, had been the practice, and under it, very little growth was to be seen except the light and diminutive "hen's nest grass," which formed the almost universal cover of the poor fields of lower Virginia, in the intervals between tillage. Add to these circumstances of very poor and shallow soil, and barren and sandy subsoil, and almost no vegetable cover to turn under, that every field was more or less hilly, and liable to be washed by heavy rains—and the judicious reader will see nothing but false confidence and ignorance displayed in my bold adoption of Taylor's system. Nor was I convinced of my error until after nearly all the fields had been successively thrown into ridges by two-horse ploughs, and all the hilly and more slightly inclined surface had been awfully washed and gullied, by the exposure of the loose subsoil to the action of the streams of rainwater.

While these my supposed measures of improvement were in progress, I was in habits of frequent and familiar intercourse with my oldest and best friend, and former guardian, Thomas Cocke, who resided then on his Aberdeen farm, and since and now on Tarbay, adjoining my own land.[4] My friend was a man for whose mind and mental cultivation I could not but entertain a very high estimation. But, though all his life a practical and assiduous cultivator, and finding his greatest pleasure in his farming labors, he yet was a careless, slovenly, and bad manager, and of course an unprofitable farmer. Therefore, on this subject I held in but light esteem the opinions which he held opposed to my own. One of these, (and which he had first gathered from some old and ignorant, but experienced practical cultivators of his neighborhood,) was the opinion that our land which was naturally poor could not "hold manure," to any extent or profit, and therefore could not be enriched. For years I heard this opinion frequently expressed by him, and the evident inference therefrom, that the far greater part of our lands, and of the whole country, was doomed to hopeless sterility; and, as often as heard, I rejected it as a monstrous agricultural heresy—as treason, indeed, to the authority of Taylor, and of every other author on agriculture whom I had read or heard of. But at last, I was compelled, most reluctantly, to concur in this opinion.

What was then to be done? I could not bear the idea of pursuing the general system of the country in continuing to lessen the already small productiveness of my fields, by their course of cultivation. The whole income, and more, was required for the most economical support of a then small but fast growing family; and for any increase of income or net profit, there was no hope, save in the universal approved resort, in all such cases, of emigrating to the rich western wilderness. And accordingly such became my intention, fully considered and decided upon, and which was only prevented being carried into effect by after occurrences.

Just before this time Davy's 'Agricultural Chemistry' had been published in this country;[5] and I read it with delight, notwithstanding my then total ignorance of chemical science, and even of chemical names, except as learned by its perusal. There was one passage in this author which seemed to promise to afford both light and hope on the point in which disappointment had led me to despair. As an illustration of defects in the chemical constitution of soils, and of the remedies which proper investigation might point out, he adduced the fact of a soil "of good apparent texture," which was steril, and seemed incapable of being enriched. The fact which struck so forcibly on my mind was presented in the following concise passage of Lect. iv. "If on washing [for analyzing][6] a steril soil, it is found to contain the salt of iron, or any acid matter, it may be ameliorated by the application of quick-lime. A soil of good apparent texture from Lincolnshire, was put into my hands by Sir Joseph Banks[7] as remarkable for sterility. On examining it, I found that it contained sulphate of iron; and I offered the obvious remedy of top-dressing with lime, which converts the sulphate into a manure."

Much the greater part of my land, and of all the land of lower Virginia, seemed to me just such as Davy described in this single and peculiar soil. It was certainly of "good apparent texture," that is, it was neither too clayey or too sandy, nor had it any other apparent defect to forbid its being fertile in a very high degree. Yet it was and had always been steril, and, as my experience concurred with that of my older friend in showing, it could not be either durably or profitably enriched by putrescent manures. Could it be possible that the sulphate of iron (copperas) which Davy found in this soil, and which he evidently spoke of as a rare example of peculiar constitution, could exist in nineteen-twentieths of all the lands of lower Virginia? This could scarcely be; and yet, in despair of finding other causes, I set about searching for this one.

It was not difficult, even for a reader so little instructed in chemistry, to apply the test for copperas. It was only necessary to let a specimen of the suspected soil remain soaking in pure water, until any copperas, if present, would be dissolved; then to separate the fluid by pouring off and filtration, and then to add to the fluid some of the infusion of nut-galls. If copperas had been held in solution, the mixture would produce a true *ink*, of which the smallest proportion would be made visible in the before perfectly transparent water. But all these first attempts were fruitless, and I was obliged to conclude that the great defect, or impediment to improvement, in most of our soils, was *not* the presence of the salts of iron. But though not a salt, of which one of the component parts was an acid, might not the poisonous quality be a *pure* or *uncombined acid*? This question was raised in my mind, and the readiness produced to suppose the affirmative to be true, from several circumstances. These were, 1st, that certain plants known to contain acid, as sheep-sorrel and pine, preferred these soils, and indeed were almost confined to them, and grew there with luxuriance and vigor proportioned to the unfitness of the land for producing cultivated crops. 2nd. That of all the soils supposed to be acid which I examined by chemical tests, not one contained any calcareous earth.[8] 3rd. That the small proportion of my land, and of all within the range of my observation, which was *shelly*, and of course calcareous, was entirely free from pine and sorrel, and moreover was as remarkable for great and lasting fertility, as the lands supposed to be acid, for the reverse qualities. Shells, or lime, would necessarily combine with, and destroy all the previous properties of any acid placed in contact; and therefore, if present universally, and always acting as a poison to cultivated plants, it seemed plain enough why the shelly lands were free from this bad quality, and by its absence had been permitted to grow rich, and to continue productive. Every new observation served to add strength to this notion; and in our tide-water region generally, and even in my own neighborhood, there were plenty of subjects for observation and comparison, both in small shelly and fertile spots, and a vast extent of poor pine and sorrel-producing lands. Still, I could obtain no direct evidence of the presence of acid, either free or combined, by applying chemical tests to soils, (as was tried in many cases,) nor was there any authority in my oracle, Davy's 'Agricultural Chemistry,' nor in any other work which I had read, for supposing *vegetable acid* to be present in any soil. Though Davy adds to the supposition of the presence of the "salt of iron," "or any acid matter," it is clear from the whole context that he had in view the possible and extremely rare presence of a *mineral* acid (as the sulphuric,) and not *vegetable* acid, which my views required, and my proofs were afterwards brought to maintain. Sulphuric acid is sometimes found in certain clays, and in combination with iron is also in peat soils; but these facts have no application to ordinary soils of any country. Of course, this absence of authority would, to most inquirers, have seemed fatal to the position of an acid principle being *generally* present in the soils of Virginia, and in great quantity and power of injurious action. This was, indeed, a great obstacle opposed to the establishment of my newly-formed opinion; but it was not yielded to as insuperable. Diffident as I then was of any such views of my own, and holding the dicta of Davy as the highest authority, and even his omission of any position as evidence that it was untrue, or unknown, still I was not daunted, and supposed it possible that the soils of this country might vary essentially in composition, in this respect, from those of England; or *barely possible* that even the great chemical philosopher might not have observed the presence of vegetable acid in the comparatively few cases of its existence in English soils. The later observations of subsequent years added much to my evidences of the existence of acid in soils; and still later and scientific investigations of chemists have served to establish that there *is* an acid principle in most soils, in the *humic* or *geic acid*. But these discoveries of chemists had not been published in 1817, (if indeed known to any) nor had my own observations reached to all the proofs which I afterwards (in 1832) published in the first edition of the 'Essay on Calcareous Manures,' and which were still in advance of the now generally received opinions of the geic or humic acid. It must therefore be confessed, that if I reached a correct conclusion, it was not on sufficiently established premises, and known chemical facts. However, reached it was, whether by right or wrong reasoning; and however little supported by direct proof or authority, I was almost sure, in advance of any known experiment, first, that the cause of the unproductiveness and unfitness for being enriched of most of our lands, was the presence of acid, and secondly, and consequently, that the application of lime, or calcareous earth, would, by taking up and destroying the poisonous principle, leave the soil free to receive and to profit by enriching manures.

But even if this theoretical position had been demonstrated, still it might furnish no *profitable* practical remedy. For admitting that the application of calcareous matters would relieve the soil of its great evil, and make it capable of receiving subsequent improvement, yet after being so relieved, the land, I supposed, would be still as poor as before, and would require all the manure, labor and time necessary to enrich any very poor soil; and these might be so expensive, that the improvement of the land would cost more than it would afterwards be worth. These considerations served to lessen my estimation of the utility of the theoretical truth, and to make my earliest applications of the theory to practice hesitating, and very limited in extent.

Having settled that calcareous matter was the medicine to be applied to the diseased or illy constituted soil, I was luckily at no loss to find the materials. In some of the many ravines which passed through my land, and on sundry parts of the river bank, were exposed some portions of the beds of fossil shells, which underlie nearly all the eastern parts of Virginia and several other southern states; the deposite which then had obtained in this region, though unproperly, and still retains, the name of *marl*. I began operations in February 1818, at one of the spots most accessible to a cart. The overlying earth was thrown off, and a few feet in width of the marl exposed, in which a pit was sunk to the depth of but three or four feet. When night stopped the digging and throwing out of the marl, the slowly oozing water filled the pit; and as no proper plan of draining had been adopted, the first shallow pit was abandoned, and another opened. In this laborious and wasteful manner there was as much marl obtained as I was then willing to apply. It served to give a covering of 125 to 200 bushels per acre, to 2½ acres of new-ground. The wood on the land had been cut down three years before, and suffered to lie and rot until cleared up for cultivation in 1818. Though poor ridge land, and of what I deemed of the most acid class of soils, still the previous treatment had given to it so much decomposed vegetable matter, that its product would necessarily be made the best of which such a soil was capable of bringing. And because of the superabundance of food for plants then ready to act, this was not a good subject to show the earliest and greatest benefit of neutralizing the acid. However—notwithstanding this circumstance, and the small amount and poverty of the marl, (which contained but one-third of calcareous matter,) the improvement produced was greater and more speedy in showing than I had dared to count on. When the plants were but a few inches high, and before I had hoped to see the slightest improvement, (indeed none had been expected to show in the first year,) the superiority of the marled corn was manifest, and which continued to increase as the growth advanced. My high gratification can only be appreciated by a schemer and projector—but such a one can well imagine my feelings and sympathise in my triumph. The increase of the first crop, corn, I stated, by guess, in reporting the experiment, to be fully 40 per cent., and that of the wheat which succeeded was much greater. Subsequent measurements of other products of experiments induced me to believe I had underrated the amount of increase in this first application. (This experiment is the first stated, and at length, at page 37 of 'Essay on Calcareous Manures' 2nd Edition.)[9]

Great as had been the labor of this application, and small its increased product, (comparing both with later operations,) the results served to completely sustain my theoretical views, and also, showed the remedy for the general evil to be far more quick, and more profitable, than I had dared to count on. Another person would probably have despised this small increase to the acre, if supposing the effect to be but temporary; and this all would have inferred, whether judging by comparison with all other manures known in practice, or even if by the authority of books. For the best informed of the old writers (even Lord Kaimes,[10] for example,) while claiming for the effects of marl great durability, still consider that at some period, say 20 or 100 years, the effects are to cease. But my views were not limited within any practical experience, or authority, but by my own theory of the action; and that theory taught me to infer that the benefit gained would never be lost, and that, under proper cultivation, the increase of product would still more increase, instead of being lessened in the course of time. In thus fully confiding in the permanency of the improvement, I was at once convinced of the operation being both cheap and profitable. All doubt and hesitation were thrown aside, and I determined to increase my labors in marling to the utmost extent of my views. Still the want of spare labor, and the established routine of farm operations which occupied all the force, retarded my operations so much that no more than 12 more acres (for the next year's crop) were marled in that year.

It forms an essential part of the character of an enthusiastic and successful projector, and especially an agricultural projector, to be as anxious to inform others as to profit himself. Of course I tried to bestow upon, and share my lights with, all my neighbors and other farmers whom my secluded life permitted me to meet. This disposition also caused my earliest attempt at writing for even so small a portion of the public as constituted a little agricultural society which I had induced to be established in my neighborhood.[11] To show my earliest opinions and statements on this subject, I will here quote the material part of a communication made to that society, and which was written in October of the year of my first experiment.[12] I copy the extract just as it then stood, and with all its defects of form and of substance. I then shrunk in fear from the greater publicity which the press would have afforded, and had not the remotest anticipation that my first effort, then made, would lead me to the extent of intercourse since established and maintained with the public, both by writing and printing.

"We should be induced to infer from the remarks of those writers who have treated on the improvement of land, that a soil artificially enriched is equally valuable with one which would produce the same amount of crop from its natural fertility; and that a soil originally good, but impoverished by injudicious cultivation, is no better than if it never had been rich. If this conclusion be just (and the contrary has not been even hinted by them) it is in direct contradiction to the opinion of many intelligent practical farmers, with whom my own observations concur, in pronouncing that soils naturally rich, (although completely worn out,) will sooner recover by rest—can be enriched with less manure—and will longer resist the effects of the severest course of cropping, than soils of as good apparent texture and constitution, and in similar situations, but poor before they were brought into cultivation. Should the latter opinion be correct, it is of the utmost importance that the subject should be investigated; as the only conclusion that can be drawn from it, is, that such land must have some secret defect in its constitution, some principle adverse to improvement; and until this is discovered and corrected, it is an almost hopeless undertaking to make a barren country permanently fertile, by means of animal and vegetable manure.

"That *inclosing* has but little effect in improving land naturally barren, is sufficiently proved by poor wood-land. This has had the benefit of inclosing for, perhaps, thousands of years, and is yet miserably poor. It may be said that leaves are not to be compared in value to grass or weeds; but surely leaves ought to improve as much in a thousand years, as grass or weeds in twenty. Besides, it is well known, that leaves taken from this very land, and applied elsewhere, have produced much benefit; and the advocates of inclosing must agree with me in ascribing to this cause, the natural fertility of the most valuable land.

"As to manure, there are but few farmers who have not, like me, experienced complete disappointment in endeavoring to improve land so little favored by nature. In the usual method of summer manuring, by moveable cow-pens, the most negligent farmers give the heaviest covering, by suffering their pens to remain stationary sometimes six or eight weeks. I have known the surface in this manner to be covered an inch thick with the richest of manures, and yet, after going through the same course of crops and grazing with the adjoining unmanured land for six years, could not be distinguished. * * * * * [13]

"If any one principle should be always found in one kind of soil, and as invariably absent in the other, we might reasonably infer that *that* was the cause of fertility or barrenness. Judging from my very limited observations, it appears evident that calcareous earth constitutes a part of every soil rich in its natural state, and that whenever a soil is entirely or nearly deficient, it never can become rich of itself, and if made so by heavy doses of dung, will soon relapse into its former sterility.

"Let us observe how facts coincide with this opinion. The lower part of Virginia is generally poor; narrow stripes along the rivers and smaller water courses are nearly all the high lands that are valuable, and in this class, exclusively, shells are seen so frequently, and in such abundance, that it seems highly probable that they are universally present, but so finely divided as not to be visible. When we know the change produced by calcareous earth in the color and texture of soil, and in a field of an hundred acres, all of the same dark colored mellow soil, shells may be seen in only a few detached spots, yet we cannot but attribute the same effects to the same cause, and allow calcareous matter to be present in every part.

"The durable fertility of land which contains shells in abundance is so wonderful, that I should not dare to describe it, were not the facts supported by the best authority. The calcareous matter for ages has been collecting and fixing in the soil such an immense supply of vegetable matter, that near two centuries of almost continual exhaustion have not materially injured its value. I have seen fields on York, James, and Nansemond rivers, now extremely productive, which are said to have been under cultivation for thirty and forty years, without any aid worth mentioning, from rest or manure.

"The same cause operates on low lands, formed by alluvion, and situated on streams accustomed to overflow. Such land is, with very few exceptions, of the first quality; and it is made so by the calcareous matter which the currents must necessarily convey from the strata of marl through which they pass; and which being intimately mixed with sand, clay, and vegetable matter, is sufficient to form the finest and deepest soil. All the rich low grounds which I have had an opportunity of observing, have marl on some of the streams which fall into them, and I have not heard of any on those few which are poor. Not a solitary instance of shells being found in poor land of any description has come to my knowledge.

"If these premises are correct, no other conclusion can be drawn from them but that a proportion of calcareous earth gives to soil a capacity for improvement which it has not without; and it also follows, that by an application of shell-marl, the worst land would be enabled to digest and retain that food, which has hitherto been of little or no advantage."

* * * * * 14

"The property of fixing manures is not more important in marl, than that of destroying acids. The unproductiveness of our lands arises, not so much from the absence of food as the presence of poison. We are so much accustomed to see a luxuriant and rapid growth of pines cover land on which no crop can thrive, that we cannot readily see the impropriety of calling such a soil absolutely barren.

"From the circumstance of this soil being so congenial to the growth of pine and sorrel, (both of which are acid plants,) it seems probable that it abounds in acidity, or acid combinations, which, (although destructive to all valuable crops,) are their food, while living, and product, when dead. The most common forest trees are furnishing the earth with poison as liberally as food, while it depends entirely on the presence of the antidote, whether one or the other takes effect. I have observed a very luxuriant growth of sorrel on land too poor to support vegetables of any kind, from green pine brush having been buried to stop gullies; and it is well known how much land on which pines have rotted is infested with this pernicious plant. Marl will immediately neutralize the acid, and this noxious principle being removed, the land will then for the first time yield according to its actual capacity: sorrel will no longer be troublesome; and, by a very heavy covering, I have known a spot rendered incapable of producing it, although the adjoining land is quickly set to the edge. Pines do not thrive on shelly land, whether fertile or exhausted. To this cause I attribute the great and immediate benefit I derived from marl on new-ground: the acid produced by the pine leaves is destroyed, and the soil is capable of supporting much heavier crops, without being (as yet) at all richer than it was."—*Com. to Pr. Geo. Agr. Soc.*

Before proceeding to state later experiments, and general practice and results, it will be necessary to recur to some other connected branches of the subject. The reader will pardon the apparent digression.

So well established and general has the opinion now become that this *marl* is a manure and a most valuable one, that it may seem strange that I should have only arrived at such an opinion, indirectly, by the train of reasoning indicated above. There were hundreds of persons who afterwards said, "Oh! *I* never doubted that marl was a good manure;" but not one of whom had been induced to try its operation. But passing by these *postponing* believers, and all others who confessedly never attached any value to this great deposite, it may require explanation why I had not learned its value from English works which treat so extensively on marl, even though I had then had access to but few of them. It was precisely because I *had* read attentively some of the English accounts of marl that I was *deterred* from using our *marl*, which agreed with it (apparently) in nothing but name. Struck with the importance attached to marl in England, I had earnestly desired to find it, and had searched for it in vain, years before the early beginning of my farming. The name induced a close examination of what was called marl here; but the "soapy feel," the absence of grit, the crumbling and melting of lumps in water &c., which were the most distinguishing characteristics of the marl of the English writers, were in vain looked for in our shell beds—of which the earth was generally sandy, never "soapy," and of which the lumps were often of almost stony hardness, and if not, at least showed nothing of the melting disposition of the English marls. I had before this, however, found in the American edition of the 'Edinburgh Encyclopedia,'[15] more modern and correct views of marl, and had thereby learned to prize *calcareous matter* in general, as an ingredient of soil whether natural or artificial. But still, even admitting that the shelly portion of our marl would slowly decompose, and gradually furnish some manure to the soil, still it seemed that there was little prospect of its operating as the English marl, of such very different texture and qualities. I then supposed that the shells which had resisted decomposition, even where exposed on the surface of the beds, for centuries, would be as slow to dissolve, and to act as manure, if laid upon the fields. Still, notwithstanding these grounds of objection, the general idea of the value of calcareous manures would have induced me earlier to try fossil shells, but for being *deterred* therefrom by the only actual facts then known of use. When speaking of my thought of trying marl to my friend, Mr. Cocke, he told me that it was not worth the trouble; that he (attracted merely by the name,) had made several small applications, in 1803, on soils of different kinds, and that he had found almost no visible benefit; and he had attached so little importance to the trial, that he had never thought to mention it, until induced by my remark. This communication was enough to check my then slight disposition to try marl. The old experiments of Mr. Cocke, as well as some much older, and like his, considered worthless by the makers, and almost forgotten, are stated at page 36 of 'Essay on Calcareous Manures.'

As soon as I was satisfied that I had found in marl a remedy for the general and fixed disease of our poor lands, it became very desirable to know the strength of different beds, and of the different parts of the same bed. The rules of Davy, for determining the proportion of carbonate of lime, were easy to apply; and having provided myself with the necessary tests, and other means, I was soon enabled to analyze the specimens with ease and accuracy. This was a delightful and profitable direction of my very small amount of chemical acquirements, and served to stimulate to further study. The amount of knowledge was indeed very small—and is still so, with all later acquirements added. But little as I had been enabled to learn of chemistry, the possession led me to adopt my views of the constitution of soils, and enabled me to double the product, and to much more than double the clear profit and pecuniary value of my land, in the course of a few years after.

Though my own doubts as to the propriety and profit of marling had been removed by my first experiments, it was not so with my neighbors. Small applications were indeed made by two of them only, in the next year after my first trial. But either because the land had been kept too much exhausted of its vegetable matter by grazing as well as cropping, or because the experimenters could not think of the operation of the manure as different from that of dung, or for both these reasons, it is certain that they were not encouraged by the results to persevere. They stopped marling with this one trial, until several years after, when both recommenced, then fully convinced of the benefit, and were afterwards among the largest and most successful marlers. One of these persons was the late Edward Marks,[16] of Old Town, and the other my old friend Thomas Cocke—who though he had led me to find the disease, could not be speedily convinced of its true nature, or of the value of the remedy. As late as 1822, when he walked with me to an enormous excavation which I was then making in carrying out marl, he said to me, that, "In future time, if marling shall then have been abandoned as unprofitable, this place will probably be known by the name of '*Ruffin's Folly*.'" For some years, my marling was a subject for ridicule with some of my neighbors; and this was renewed, when in aftertime the great damage caused by improper applications began to be seen, and which will be described in due order.

Having had in view from the beginning the true action of marl, and fully believing that its good effects would be permanent, and even increasing with time, under a proper system of tillage, I was no more discouraged by what some deemed small profits, than I was annoyed by the incredulity and ridicule of other persons. Almost all the farms in the neighborhood except mine, were regularly and closely grazed, when not under a crop, and, of course, they had not stored up in the soil much either of inert vegetable matter, or its acid product. Mine had not been grazed since 1814, and had been rested 2 years in every 4; and 3 years in 4 on the poorest land. And though, in truth, no increased production had been obtained by this lenient treatment, inasmuch as the increase of acid counterbalanced the increase of vegetable food, still when marl was applied, the acid was immediately destroyed, and the food left free to act. The effect of marling was generally shown most plainly on the first crop of corn, and the limits could be easily traced, by the deep green color of the plants before they were five inches high; and the increased product of the first crop, on acid soils, rarely fell under 50 per cent., was most generally 100, and has been known to be 200 per cent. But even such increase was not satisfactory to many persons, until the action of marl came to be better understood, and the permanency of the effects were credited. In five or six years after my commencement, there were few if any of those of my neighbors, who had marl visible on their lands, who had not begun to apply it. And though it has been injudiciously as well as insufficiently applied since, and not one-fourth of the full benefit obtained, still the general improvement and increased products of the marl farms of Prince George have been very great. The existence of marl, too, which was known at first but on a few farms in my own neighborhood, has been since discovered in many and remote parts of the county; and wherever accessible, it is valued and used. The like observations will now apply to most of the other counties of lower Virginia. Wherever the effects of marling could be seen for a few years, the early incredulity not only disappeared, but most persons were even too ready to believe in marl possessing virtues to which it has no claim. Thus, ignorant or careless of its true mode of operation, they crop the marled lands more severely than before; and if they are not thereby soon reduced as low as their former state of sterility, they are made to approach it as nearly as possible, and at a sacrifice of nine-tenths of the profit from marling which a more lenient and judicious system of cultivation would have insured.

In 1819, the second year, my marling was increased to 62 acres, but most of it at too thin a rate. In 1820, only 25 acres, though at 600 heaped bushels or even more to the acre. Up to this time I had done as most other persons have, that is, attempted to marl "at leisure times," and without making it a regular employment for a certain additional force, or reducing the amount of cultivation, or of other operations on the farm. No person will ever marl to much advantage, who does not avoid this error; and this year's labors showed the necessity of an alteration. The next year, two horses and carts, with the necessary drivers and pit-men, were appropriated to marling at all times when weather permitted, except during harvest, thrashing, and wheat-sowing times. Viewing marling too as the most profitable operation, except the saving of a crop already made, it was made a fixed rule of the farm that marling was to be interrupted for nothing else. My corn shift for that year was reduced in size one-half—so that one-half could be marled while the other was under cultivation. By these means, I marled 80 acres this year, 1821, (and too heavily,) and had all the lessened corn-field on marled land. The product of the half was equal to what the whole had brought before, and I was enabled thereafter to have every field marled over in advance of its next cultivation. In 1822, the land marled was 93 acres, 100 in 1823, and 80 in 1824, which served to cover nearly all of the then cleared land requiring marling. The next three years' marling amounted respectively to 50 acres, 24 acres, and 27 acres, being principally upon land subsequently cleared and brought into cultivation. Since then, there has been no marling on the farm, except on wood-land, not yet cleared, and on small spots formerly omitted, and of which no account was taken. With the exception of such spots, (and some such still remain, because of their inconvenient position,) all the land which was not naturally calcareous, or too wet or too steep for carting on, had been marled by 1827; and none has required any additional dose, though some of the thinnest covered places had been re-marled long before that time, so as to bring them to a proper constitution.

In 1824, I first observed, (and had never before suspected such effect,) the injury caused by having marled acid soil too heavily. To show my first impressions, I will copy the words of my farm journal, written on the very day on which the discovery was fully made.

"June 13th, 1824. Observed a new and alarming disease in a large proportion of my corn—and what makes the matter much worse, the evil is certainly caused by marling. The disease seems to have commenced when the corn was from 6 to 10 inches high, and to have stopped its growth. Its general color is a pale sickly green, and the leaves appear so thin as to be almost transparent: next they become streaked with rusty red, and then begin to die at the upper ends. Several pulled up, showed no defect, or injury from insects, among the roots. All the land marled from pits Nos. 7 and 9 (both yellow)[17] from 1820 to 1822, is so much diseased as to promise not more than half a crop. The corn is twice as large as on the spaces left for experiment without marl, yet looks much worse; though 3 weeks ago its superiority in color and vigor was even more than in size. With but few exceptions, the land *newly* marled from the same pits, and the old marling from Nos. 1 and 8,[18] (both blue) as well as that not marled, are free from this disease. The parts most affected are those which were dryest and poorest, and of course were least covered with vegetable matter. Yet though the corn on this old marling is generally so bad, it is yet evident that the land is more benefited by the manure than at first: flourishing stalks of corn, 18 to 24 inches high, are seen frequently within a few feet of those most hurt by this disease."

Subsequently, when the whole extent of injury could be seen, the following remarks were written in the journal, at the date below.

"October 15th. The damage caused by marl to this crop I suppose to be about one-third of what the land would otherwise have made, judging from the present and former measurements of the same land, where experiments were made.

"Nearly all the heavy marling in Finnies (at 800 bushels,) about 20 acres,[19] suffered by it; the poorest and lightest most injured, here and in Court-House Field."[20] The few rich spots escaped, as did most of the piece plastered (on the heavy marling) in 1820. The marks of this experiment were destroyed, and the superiority was not so regular as to enable me to trace the outlines of the gypseous earth—but an acre of corn might be taken which certainly was plastered, better than any other acre in the old land. This at least proves that *gypsum* contained [if any][21] in the marl has not caused the disease. The poor land lightly marled in 1819, showed but little of the disease, and none was found in the piece not marled, nor in any marled since the last crop [or now first cultivated since being marled.][22]

"In Court House Field, the injury was confined to 19 acres, the poorest part of the field, which was in corn in 1821,[23] marled and fallowed, 1822, and in wheat 1823, corn 1824. The remainder of the old land, which had not been cropped so severely, and was covered as heavy with *blue marl*, brought a fine crop, quite free from the disease. The new-ground was mostly marled very heavy (800 bushels of 45/100)[24] and this and all my former clearings, (some marled equally heavy,) were also quite free. These facts satisfy me that it was not the quality, but the over quantity of marl which has caused the evil; and that the land which has escaped, owes its safety to its containing more vegetable matter. I forgot to state that on some of the lightest spots of South Field, the wheat was much injured, though blue marl was used there.

"If I had followed my own advice to others, "to put no more marl at first than would but little more than neutralize the soil, and repeat the dressing afterwards" this evil would not have fallen on me. The present loss is not much; but it makes me expect the same on all similar land, marled as heavily. I shall endeavor to avoid it, by giving vegetable matter to the soil—either by manuring, or by allowing 1 or 2 more years of grass in the first term of the rotation. *Why* the quantity of marl applied should do harm in *any* case, is more than I can tell; but I draw this consolation from the discovery—if a certain quantity, (say 500 bushels per acre) is too much for present use of the soil, it proves that it will combine with more vegetable matter, and fix more fertility in the soil, than I had supposed. That the second crop should be injured, and not the first, is owing to the unbroken state of the shells at first, and, by their being reduced, twice as much calcareous matter is in action after a few years."

Thus it will be seen, from these entries made at the time, that I took a correct view of this great and unlooked-for-evil, and was by no means discouraged, or induced to lessen my efforts in marling. But in all after operations, on poor land, the quantity was lessened from 500 and 600 bushels, (and even more of the poorest marl,) to about 300 bushels. With this alteration, the operation was continued with as much zeal as before; and also at a later time on another farm (Shellbanks) purchased afterwards, where I marled upwards of 400 acres.

When this injury was first discovered, about 250 acres of very similar land had been marled so heavily that the like mischief was to be looked for in the next crop, and thenceforward, if not guarded against. For a more full account of this disease, and my opinions thereon, I must refer to what has been before published, (Essay on Cal. Man. p. 51.) It is sufficient here to say that by pursuing the means there advised—in allowing more rest from grain crops, furnishing vegetable matter to the land, in its natural cover of weeds, in clover, and farm-yard manure so far as the limited supply sufficed—that no very great loss was subsequently suffered, except in the field where the disease was first discovered, and which was marled in 1819. This field was too remote and inconveniently situated, to be manured from the barn-yard; and from that and other causes, (including the failure of clover,) that field, only, still shows injury from marling in the present crop (1839); so much diminished, however, that its general average product this year is fully twice as much as the land could have brought before being marled.

The results of many particular experiments made during the progress of marling this farm were stated in the 'Essay on Calcareous Manures,' and the general benefits and improved products were described in a later publication. (page 112 of vol. vii, Far. Reg.).[25] It is not necessary here to repeat these statements. But as this article may come under the notice of some readers who have not access to the others, the general results, as produced in the whole period of twenty-two years, from the earliest experiment to the last product, will be here very concisely and generally stated.

The many and extensive old galled parts of sloping land, wherever dressed with marl, and even without the further help of barn-yard manure, are now nearly all *skinned over* by a newly formed soil; and though such soil is both poor and thin, and may yet long remain so, the *whole* of its present productive power is due to marling; as such galled land was, before, naked, entirely barren, and irreclaimable by other manures. Where much or rich putrescent matter has been also applied to galls, with or after marl, both rich and durable soil has been formed, though at great cost.

The more level parts of the old and greatly exhausted fields, and the newly cleared wood-land, both kinds being naturally poor, thin, and acid soils, are the only lands which have enjoyed anything like the full beneficial effects of marling. These have been increased in product from 5 and 10 bushels of corn per acre (which may be considered the usual minimum and maximum rates,) to at least 20, and in some cases to 35 bushels, even without the aid of barn-yard manure. Where putrescent manures have been also applied, they have raised the products higher; and these manures are now as durable and as profitable, as formerly they were fleeting and profitless in effect.

The before poor and light soil which formed the greater part of the old arable lands, and which was not above three inches in depth, (and scarcely two inches, when in its natural forest state,) is now seven inches and more, and required three-horse ploughs to break it to proper depth, where the one-horse ploughs formerly would frequently reach and bring up the barren subsoil.

The valuable operation of marl has increased with time, even where the effects were also the most speedy.

The soil, which before was totally unable to support red clover, is now (except on the most sandy spots) well adapted to the growth, and capable, according to the grade of fertility, of receiving the great benefit which is offered by that most valuable of improving crops.

And generally—notwithstanding all the many and great errors committed in my marling, (for want of experience,) and of still worse general farm management—and though a considerable portion of the old land was either but little or not at all fit to be improved by marling—and though the land added since by new clearings was all very poor, and worthless for its natural producing power—still the general annual grain products of the farm have been increased from three to four-fold, and the net profit of cultivation and the intrinsic value of the land have been increased in a still greater proportion.

Appendix 4

Queries to Ascertain the Action and Effects of Shell Marl as Manure, and Answers as to the Oldest Marled District in Prince George County, Va.[1]

1. When was the use of marl as manure commenced on your farm?
2. Whose property was the farm, and under whose direction was its general management, (if not your own,) then, and since?
3. What was the quantity of cleared land on the farm then ready for and subject in its turn to cultivation of any kind, exclusive of all waste ground?
4. What is the quantity since added, by new clearings of forest land, or other waste spots brought into tillage? And, generally, was the land thus added richer or poorer than the present average quality of the farm?
5. What was the rate of progress in extending the marling—and, altogether, how many acres have been now marled?
6. What was the usual strength of the marl used, or its proportion per cent. of carbonate of lime, or pure shelly matter?
7. Was there any peculiar quality or ingredient, besides the carbonate

> Source: Edmund Ruffin, "Queries to Ascertain the Action and Effects of Shell Marl as Manure, and Answers as to the Oldest Marled District in Prince George County, Va.," *Farmers' Register* 8 (1840): 489–97. The questions appear on pp. 489–91; Ruffin's own responses are on pp. 496–97. The questionnaire and the responses of Ruffin's neighbors (the latter being omitted here) appear after Ruffin's analysis of the survey, "Observations on the Earliest Marled District of Prince George County," pp. 484–89. This edited document contains Ruffin's account of the earliest known experiment with marl, together with evidence on Ruffin's early farming.

of lime, that served to give additional value to the manure—as "green sand," or gypsum, or a large proportion of fine clay, &c.?

8. Or was there any thing that served more than usually to lessen the value, as stony hardness of many shells, or of masses of marl, &c.?

9. What have been the usual quantities of marl applied to the acre?

10. Have there been made trials of any *much lighter dressings* of marl than the usual quantities—and if so, what were the results, compared to the usual quantities?

11. Have there been made trials of any *much heavier dressings* than the usual quantities—and with what comparative results?

12. Was the cropping and general management of the land, *for a few years immediately previous to its being marled*, such as might be considered *meliorating* or *improving*, (or at least as *preserving* its degree of fertility,) or was it *impoverishing*, and wasting of fertility in general? State the rotation of crops, if known.

13. The same question as to the few years immediately after marling, and since.

14. What have been the usual and general results of the applications of marl, on the increase of the crop next following, on land in different conditions—and afterwards to the present time?

15. Have the earliest fertilizing effects of marl (or the increased product of the first crop, or first course of crops in the rotation,) been subsequently increased or diminished by lapse of time—and in either case, under, and in proportion to, what circumstances?

16. Is it your opinion, whether founded on experience or observation, that the early increased product of your marled land (say for the first three or four crops, or of any number you have yet made thereon,) will be subsequently diminished, under any rotation of crops, or course of cultivation, that would not have been decidedly exhausting and injurious to the land, if marl had not been applied?

17. Has sterility, or other damage, been caused on any part of the land, by applying marl too heavily, or in any other manner—and under what circumstances of soil, tillage, &c.?

18. Has it been found that any other manures, either vegetable and putrescent, or mineral, are more efficacious, or durable, on poor natural soils *after* marling them?

19. What do you suppose was the average productive power, in corn, per acre, of all your now arable and cultivated land, before marling?

20. What do you suppose is the present average productive power of the same in corn?

21. What was the usual or average quantity of the crops of wheat made annually on the farm before marling, and recently?

22. Taking such general grounds for the estimate as may be satisfactory to your own judgment, state what you suppose to be the annual value of the present *general* or *average gross product* of grain, or other marketable products of the fields in cultivation, of the land marled, caused by, and owing to marling—per acre, and also in total amount annually from the whole farm?

23. Does your experience or observation serve to contradict any of the important theoretical opinions in regard to the action of marl, or statements of actual results in practice, as presented in the "recapitulation" embraced in pages 53 to 56 of 'Essay on Calcareous Manures'[2]—and if so contradicting, in what particulars?

I. *Answers to the foregoing queries, by James B. Cocke, of Bonaccord.*[3]

Answer to query 1st.—In 1820 or '21, as a regular business. A small experiment had been made by my grandfather, James Cocke,[4] and all knowledge of it forgotten many years before.*

*This very old experiment, made nearly or quite seventy years ago, and deemed a failure and forgotten until within the last twenty, was stated as below, at page 89 of 'Essay on Calcareous Manures.'[5] Within the last few weeks the reporter revisited this spot, and saw that it still exhibited a decided superiority over all the immediately surrounding land, which, with the farm generally, had been marled, and all very much enriched, since the first published account of this curious and valuable fact.—ED.

"The two old experiments described at page 36,[6] though the only applications of fossil shells known to me, previous to the commencement of my use of this manure, were not all which had been made, and which being deemed failures, had been abandoned and forgotten. Another, within a few miles of my residence, was brought to light and notice afterwards, by an old negro, who was perhaps the only person then living who had any knowledge of facts. After I had found enough success in using this manure to attract to it some attention, Mr. Thomas Cocke of Aberdeen was one of those who began, but still with doubt and hesitation, to use marl to some considerable extent. One of his early applications was to the garden. The old gardener opposed this, and told his master that he knew "the stuff was good for nothing, because when he was a boy, his old master (Mr. Cocke's father) had used some at Bonaccord, and it had never done the least good." Being asked whether he could show the spot where this trial had been made, he answered that he could easily, as he drove the cart which carried out the marl. The place was immediately sought. It was on the most elevated part of a very poor field, which had been cleared and exhausted fully a century before. The marled space (a square of about half an acre) though still poor, was at least twice as productive as the surrounding land, though a slight manuring from the farmyard had been applied a few years before to the surrounding land, and omitted on this spot, which was supposed to have been, from its appearance, the site of some former dwelling house, of which every evidence had disappeared except the permanent improvement of the soil usual from that cause. A close examination showed some fragments of the hardest shells, so as to prove that the old man had not mistaken the spot. This, like other early applications, had been made on a spot too poor for marl to show but very small early effects; and as only one kind of operation of any manure was then thought of, (that which dung produces,) it is not strange that both the master and servant should have agreed in the opinion that the application was useless, and have remained under that opinion until almost all remembrance of the experiment had been lost."

XI. *Answers by Edmund Ruffin, in regard to Coggins' Point farm.*
Answer to query 1st.—On Coggins' Point farm, on James river, in January, 1818.[7]

2d.—My own property, and under my personal direction from 1813 to 1832; afterwards under my overseers, until 1839, and since in possession and charge of my son, Edmund Ruffin, Jr.

3d.—In 1818, about 540 acres, of which 68 had been cleared since 1813.

4th.—About 197 acres added, principally by new clearings, making 737 of tilled land now. Nearly every new acre added since 1813 was poorer than the present general average, and without exception as to the clearings since 1817. The average quality of all the new land was poorer than the present general average of the whole farm, by nearly one half.

5th.—In 1818 marled 15 acres.
      1819   62
      1820   25
      1821   80
      1822   93
      1823   100
      1824   80 when nearly all the then open land which was

supposed to need marl had been covered. By 1830, the marled surface had been increased to 670 acres of cultivated land, and since, to 51 acres more, of pasture and wood-land not cleared.

6*th*.—Most of the marl used contained from 37 to 40 per cent. of shells, or carbonate of lime. Another kind averaged about 45 per cent. Another, (the marl of the broken river banks,) used perhaps for 100 acres, had from 20 to 25 per cent., the remainder of its contents being coarse sand. The bed of peculiar appearance, and greatest strength, under the north end of the peninsula, contains 61 per cent. This, being distant, was used for about 60 acres only.

7*th*.—None, except the last-named in last answer. This contains also a very small proportion of gypsum, some "green-sand," and a very small proportion of some soluble saline matter.

8*th*.—Only the usual degree of hardness of the shells, and the proportion of earth not calcareous being, as usual, principally of silicious sand.

9*th*.—For first three years, generally 500 to 600 bushels. Afterwards 300 to 400.

10*th*.—As little as 96 bushels have been used. The early effects much less than of larger quantities. This and other light dressings being deemed quite too small, were added to, in a few years, so as to be made equal to what was then supposed a proper and sufficient rate.

11*th*.—As much as 1200 bushels were tried, and without injury, or perceptible greater early benefit than 600 produced on adjacent ground. This land then newly cleared, and since also well manured from the barn-yard. The lighter marlings, say from 3 to 400 bushels, as productive on the second round of crops, if not on the first, and more profitable than any heavier—except where much vegetable matter was also given to the ground, then or afterwards; in which case, more marl was required, and in proportion; and was used profitably, if given heavily at first.

12*th*.—The four-shift rotation (1st, corn, 2d, wheat, where not too poor to bring it, and 3d and 4th, the natural grass and weeds, not grazed,) had been pursued since 1814; and this very lenient rotation was barely enough improving to compensate for the injury caused by washing, the land being generally hilly.

13*th*.—The same rotation continued after marling, and then it became decidedly improving. Some years afterwards, clover sown on all wheat. For the last 10 years, the course of cropping has been more severe (by taking an additional wheat crop on the best land under clover, or in the second year of rest,) and also partial grazing permitted. Still, the system of cultivation is improving to the land, though less so than before, when milder.

14*th*.—On newly cleared poor and acid land, but full of rotten vegetable matter, and in its best state for producing, the increase from marling on first crop about 50 per cent. or more. On old and previously much exhausted land, the first increase from 80 to 120—and in some cases more than 150 per cent. On the same lands, now, 10 to 20 years after marling, the increase upon the original product is from 200 to 400 per cent. and generally fully double the earliest increased crop, next after the marling. On poor stiff soil, the increase and profit of marling less than on poor light soils. On neutral soil, naturally rich, but impoverished, the early increase much smaller, but growing with time. On calcareous land, no benefit.

15*th*.—Increased always, when of any benefit at first, except where much "marl-burning" was caused by the dressing having been too heavy.

16*th*.—No general diminution expected, and none believed to be possible, under a mild and judicious rotation of crops.

17*th*.—Only as above stated, from marling too heavily; and that was the more readily produced, (when the marling was alike,) in proportion to the poverty of the land and the severity of its tillage. The disease of "marl-burning" prevented or removed by giving vegetable matter in proportion to the excess of marl. A large space has been thus diseased; but by rest, and vegetable matter, the injury has been almost every where cured, or prevented.

18*th*.—Putrescent manures believed to be more efficacious at first, and certainly more lasting in effect, and far more profitable, on marled land. Gypsum, and also "green-sand" generally having more or less effect on clover after marling, on acid land, and *always* quite inoperative there before marling.

19*th*.—Certainly not exceeding 12 bushels; I incline to think not more than 10. All cleared since 1818 was marled before being cultivated.

20*th*.—From 25 to 27 bushels per acre. The largest crop yet made was in 1839, amounting to 4500 bushels. Of this crop one entire field of 112 acres which had been all originally of poor and mean soil, and all, both new and old land, quite poor when marled, was supposed to have averaged 30 bushels to the acre.

21*st*.—The general average of my six first years' crops, immediately preceding marling, was 637 bushels. The average product per acre, in the first three years, was 5⅔ bushels, on the richest half of the land—wheat not being sown on the poorest half. The greatest crop made before marling was 896 bushels. The greatest since, in 1831, was 2500. This year, (a very short crop here and generally) the quantity made was nearly 2000 bushels. Allowing for the recurrence of all the usual measure of diseases and disasters to which this latterly very precarious crop has been subject, the actual average annual product of wheat is estimated at 1800 bushels. This is believed to be greatly below the productive power of the several shifts. The causes of usual and greatly reduced product are principally the ravages of insects.

22d.—I suppose $8 per acre, on all the land each year under marketable crops; and for the quantity of land usually under tillage, about $3200.

23d.—No answer requisite, from this source.

Appendix 5

Statement of Marling and Crops, on Coggins Point (now Beechwood) Farm

Statement of marling and crops, on Coggins Point (now Beechwood) Farm**

Year	Acres Marled	WHEAT.			CORN.			Acres in Cotton	Bales of Cotton
		Acres in Wheat.	Product in Bushels.	Average to acre.	Acres.	Bushels.	Average to acre.		
1813	0	145	810	5.58	125	2250	18		
1814	0	110	550	5.	163	1340	8.18		
1815	0	78	520	6.67	136	1955	14.38		
1816	0	104	896	8.61	144	2300	16.90		
1817	0	79	595	7.52	188	2050	10.90		
1818	15	63	450	7.14	160	2670	16.68		
1819	62	132	1015	7.69	137	2000	14.59		
1820	25	119	1020	8.57	164	2780	17.		
1821	80	160	1049	6.56	77	1775	23.		
1822	93	154	1627	10.56	114	2250	19.73		
1823	100	139	1475	10.61	158	3000	19		
1824	80	194	1850	9.54	156	3405	21.80		
1825	50	195	1452	7.45	70	1254	17.91	48	
1826	24	170	1390	8.17	138	2275	16.48	70	
1827	27	151	1366	9.04	104	1665	16	76	37
1828	.0	153	936	6.12	112	1750	15.62	90½	55
1829	.0	134	908	6.78	133	2300	17.37	96	
1830	50	—	—	—	—	—	—	50½	33
1831	0	—	2160	—	—	—	—	0	

Statement of marling and crops, on Coggins Point (now Beechwood) Farm** *(continued)*

Year	Acres Marled	WHEAT.			CORN.			Acres in Oats.	Acres in roots, vines, &c.
		Acres in Wheat.	Product in Bushels.	Average to acre.	Acres.	Bushels.	Average to acre.		
1832	0	—	—	—	126	2830	22.46		
—	—	—	—	—	—	—	—		
1835	—	—	—		4000				
1836	10	184	394	2.17		4415			
1837	0	147	2056	13.98		2620			
1838	0	150	2117	14.11		2070			
1839	2	167	1252	7.49	190	4500	23.68	30	
1840	12	228	1942	8.61	143	3540	24.40	50	5
1841	32	212	2475	11.62	146	3800	25.33	10	10
1842	30	250	3377	13.50	155			50	10
1843	4 / 13	307	4725	15.39	166	3380	20.36		
1844	15	270	4600	17.04	100	2500	25.		
1845	5 / 17	270	3600	13.33	100	1600	16.		
1846	70	290	3000	10.34	140	3115	22.25		
1847	90	234	2571	10.99	144	5070	35.20		
1848	5	274	3544	12.93	150	4625	30.83		
1849	40	225	2600	11.55	170	5010	29.47		
1850	90	321	4112	12.81	110	3150	28.64		
1851	10 / 25	263	4420	16.81	118	3750	32.61		

**After 1827, I ceased to keep a regular farm journal, as had been done before. Hence the blanks in the table which appear afterwards to 1836. The occupancy and direction of the present proprietor, Edmund Ruffin, jr., began with the year 1839.

Source: Edmund Ruffin, *An Essay on Calcareous Manures* (5th ed.; Richmond, 1852), p. 184. The table is presented here without Ruffin's extensive explanatory notes.

ABBREVIATIONS

NOTES

INDEX

Abbreviations

CSmH	Henry E. Huntington Library, San Marino, Calif.
DAB	*Dictionary of American Biography*
DLC	Library of Congress, Washington, D.C.
DNA	National Archives, Washington, D.C.
DNB	*Dictionary of National Biography*
NcU	Southern Historical Collection, University of North Carolina, Chapel Hill
Vi	Virginia State Library and Archives, Richmond
ViHi	Virginia Historical Society, Richmond
ViU	University of Virginia Library, Charlottesville
ViW	Earl Gregg Swem Library, College of William and Mary, Williamsburg, Va.
VMHB	*Virginia Magazine of History and Biography*
WMQ	*William and Mary Quarterly*

Notes

Introduction

1. Edmund Ruffin, *An Essay on Calcareous Manures* (Petersburg, Va., 1832).
2. Studies of Ruffin's life and career in agricultural reform include Avery Craven, *Edmund Ruffin, Southerner: A Study in Secession* (1932; reprint ed., Hamden, Conn., 1964); Betty L. Mitchell, *Edmund Ruffin: A Biography* (Bloomington, 1981); J. Carlyle Sitterson, "Edmund Ruffin, Agricultural Reformer and Southern Radical," Introduction to Edmund Ruffin, *An Essay on Calcareous Manures*, ed. J. Carlyle Sitterson (1832; John Harvard Library ed., Cambridge, Mass., 1961), pp. vii–xxxiii; William Kauffman Scarborough, "Introduction," in William Kauffman Scarborough, ed., *The Diary of Edmund Ruffin*, Library of Southern Civilization (3 vols.; Baton Rouge, 1972–89), 1:xv–xlv; W. M. Mathew, "Planter Entrepreneurship and the Ruffin Reforms in the Old South, 1820–60," *Business History* 27 (1985): 207–21; William M. Mathew, *Edmund Ruffin and the Crisis of Slavery in the Old South: The Failure of Agricultural Reform* (Athens, Ga., and London, 1988); David F. Allmendinger, Jr., "The Early Career of Edmund Ruffin, 1810–1840," *VMHB* 93 (1985): 127–54; and David F. Allmendinger, Jr., *Ruffin: Family and Reform in the Old South* (New York and Oxford, 1990).
3. [William Boulware], "Edwin Ruffin, of Virginia, Agriculturist . . . ," *De Bow's Review* 11 (1851): 431–36 (printed as appendix 1). Ruffin identified Boulware as the author of this sketch in Edmund Ruffin, "Incidents of my Life" (2 vols.; 1851–53), 3:228, Edmund Ruffin Papers, ViHi.
4. Ruffin, "Incidents" 3:228.
5. Edmund Ruffin, Jr., to Edmund Ruffin, 21 Jan. 1852, Ruffin Papers, ViHi.
6. This volume is not among Ruffin's papers at the Virginia Historical Society, and family members have not been able to trace it. It may have been lost with Ruffin's journals for Coggin's Point Farm during Union occupations of Beechwood Farm after 1862. Ruffin discussed losing the farm journals in Edmund Ruffin, "Account of the Draining of Marlbourne Farm," note following date of 20 Mar. 1865, p. 97, Ruffin Papers, ViHi. No volumes of the "Incidents" were described in the inventory of Ruffin's personal manuscripts that his daughter-in-law Jane M. Ruffin ordered in 1889 (Frank G. Ruffin to Jane M. Ruffin, 4 Jan. 1889, photocopy of typescript in possession of Marion Ruffin Jones, Walkerton, Va.). Recently Steven Colvin has found a possible clue concerning the missing volume. Ruffin's great-granddaughter Anne Ruffin, who died in 1985, once recalled to Colvin that as a girl she had seen among Ruffin's diaries at least

one volume in her ancestor's handwriting, "possibly the story of his life." Children in the family, she remembered, were fond of playing with this old volume, which was never located after her childhood (Steven Colvin to the editor, 31 May 1988).

7. Ruffin, "Incidents" 2:115, 123. The third reference (p. 110) was to a speech Ruffin delivered in 1818 to the Prince George County Agricultural Society.
8. Edmund Ruffin, Jr., to Edmund Ruffin, 21 Jan. 1852, Ruffin Papers, ViHi. Similar, if shorter, farm histories appeared regularly in the *American Farmer* between 1819 and 1831. See, for example, John Singleton, "Land by the use of Shell-Marle," *American Farmer* 2 (1820–21): 114–16; William M. Barton, "Mr. Turner's Premium Farm," ibid., 7 (1825–26): 305–6.
9. Edmund Ruffin, "First Views Which Led to Marling in Prince George County," *Farmers' Register* 7 (1839): 659–67 (printed as appendix 3). See also Edmund Ruffin, "The Former Poor and Exhausted Condition, and Earliest Subsequent Improvements, by Marling, of Coggin's Point Farm," ibid., 7 (1839): 112–16.
10. Ruffin, "Incidents" 3:228.
11. Evergreen comprised 968 acres in 1790, when it was still owned by Ruffin's great-grandfather. By 1806 George Ruffin had enlarged the farm and its affiliated properties to 1,205 acres (Prince George County, Va., Land Book, 1790, p. 13, and Land Book, 1806, p. 18, Vi [microfilm]). By 1831 the farm had grown to about 1,600 acres; a description of the house and land appears in George H. Ruffin to Harrison Henry Cocke, deed, 1831, Cocke Family Papers, ViHi. The large Georgian house now standing on the farm was built about 1807–8, after Ruffin was born (Calder Loth, ed., *The Virginia Landmarks Register* [3d ed.; Charlottesville, 1986], p. 346).
12. Pauline Pearce Warner, *Benjamin Harrison of Berkeley, Walter Cocke of Surry: Family Records I* (Tappahannock, Va., 1962), p. 167; Edmund Ruffin, will, 28 Nov. 1789, proved 14 June 1791, Prince George County Deed Book, 1787–92, Part 2, pp. 530–32, Prince George County Court House, Va.
13. Ruffin's biographers have identified his mother by name, but her origins have remained obscure until recently. Ruffin himself supplied only her name when he completed his genealogical chart in 1856 and indicated no kin for himself through his mother's family (Craven, *Ruffin*, p. 3; Sitterson, "Edmund Ruffin," p. viii; Edmund Ruffin, "Ruffin Family Genealogy, Compiled May 1, 1856 at Beechwood, Prince George Co., Va.," ViHi). The identity of Jane Lucas Ruffin was established firmly in *Lucas v. Lucas*, 29 May 1794, Surry County Order Book, 1789–94, p. 492, Vi (microfilm), and *Lucas et al. v. Harris*, 28 May 1805, Surry County Order Book, 1804–7, p. 194, Vi (microfilm). George Ruffin married his second wife, Rebecca Cocke, in 1799 (Surry County Marriage Register, 1768–1853, 29 Aug., 19 Sept. 1799, p. 54, Surry County Court House, Va.; see also Catherine Lindsay Knorr, comp., *Marriage Bonds and Ministers' Returns of Surry County, Virginia, 1768–1825* [Pine Bluff, Ark., 1960], p. 72).
14. John Bennett Boddie, *Southside Virginia Families*, 1 (Baltimore, 1966): 158.
15. They were Jane Skipwith Ruffin Dupuy (1800–1870), Juliana Ruffin Coupland Dorsey (ca.1806–1876), Elizabeth Ruffin Cocke (1807–1849), and George Henry Ruffin (b. 1810). Two other children, George R. (b. ca.1802) and Rebecca S. (b. ca.1804), apparently died in infancy (Dupuy family Bible records, 1763–1910, ViHi; Edmund Ruffin to Rebecca Cocke

Ruffin Woodlief, 23 Mar. 1823, fall 1823, Ruffin Papers, ViHi; extracts from the will of Juliana Dorsey, 20 June 1876, Dorsey and Coupland Papers, ViW; Elizabeth Ruffin to Edmund Ruffin, 18 Feb. 1828, Juliana Ruffin Coupland Dorsey to Edmund Ruffin, 13 May 1849, Ruffin Papers, ViHi). Ruffin's half brother, George H., was still living at the start of the Civil War; see Scarborough, ed., *Diary* 2:301 (11 May 1862). The year of George H. Ruffin's birth is confirmed in U.S. Census, Population Schedules, Prince George County, Va., 1850, p. 61a, DNA (microfilm).

16. *Petersburg Intelligencer*, 19 May 1807; Anne Bryant Arritt, comp., "Marriage and Death Notices Printed in 'The Visitor' (Richmond), 1809–1810," *Virginia Genealogical Society Quarterly* 7 (1969): 61. The date of death for Ruffin's paternal grandmother, Jane Skipwith Ruffin, has not been discovered. In 1783 she feared she had consumption and that her life was hanging "by a very slender thread" (Jane Ruffin to Peyton Skipwith, 14 Apr. 1783, Skipwith Family Papers, ViHi).

17. In 1860 Ruffin met in Kentucky a former fellow student at William and Mary, Charles S. Todd. This was one of the few times he welcomed an old schoolmate. Throughout his adult life Ruffin knew well only one of his classmates, William C. Rives, whom he disliked (Scarborough, ed., *Diary* 1:460 [7 Sept. 1860], 2:10–11 [26 Apr. 1861]). The draft of a letter Ruffin addressed to an acquaintance in 1857 describes his resolution in his "youth & early time of manhood" to abstain from drinking through "self control." Undoubtedly the letter referred to his days at William and Mary, and it underscores the impression he gave of feeling isolated in college (Edmund Ruffin to unidentified correspondent, 1 June 1857, Ruffin Papers, ViHi).

18. William Boulware wrote that Ruffin was sent to the college "in the sixteenth year of his age," which would have been 1809 ([Boulware], "Edwin Ruffin," p. 431). College records do not indicate when Ruffin enrolled. The fact that he knew Charles S. Todd, whose last year of attendance was 1809, indicates that Ruffin was enrolled for a time during both years (*A Provisional List of Alumni, Grammar School Students, Members of the Faculty, and Members of the Board of Visitors of the College of William and Mary in Virginia, from 1693 to 1888* [Richmond, 1941], p. 40).

19. [Boulware], "Edwin Ruffin," p. 431; Prince George County, Va., Land Book, 1814, p. 41, Vi (microfilm).

20. In 1815 Ruffin owned thirty slaves aged nine and older, according to county tax lists, which omitted all the younger children. In 1820 children aged fourteen and younger accounted for nearly half the slave population (or twenty-four of fifty-two people) at Coggin's Point. See Prince George County, Va., Personal Property Tax List, 1815, p. 22, Vi (microfilm); U.S. Census, Manuscript Schedules, Prince George County, Va., 1820, p. 54, DNA (microfilm).

21. Edmund Ruffin, note concerning the fragment of a petition, 1858, and note concerning an electioneering squib, 1858, Edmund Ruffin Papers, Manuscripts Department, ViU.

22. Notice of Champion Travis's death appeared in the Richmond *Enquirer*, 4 Sept. 1810; it is reprinted in Virginia Genealogical Society, comp., *Marriages and Deaths from Richmond, Virginia, Newspapers, 1780–1820*, Special Publication no. 8 (Richmond, 1983), p. 154. The exact date of the marriage has not been established.

23. For an account of Agnes Ruffin Beckwith's feud with her father, see Suzanne Lebsock, *The Free Women of Petersburg: Status and Culture in a Southern Town, 1784–1860* (New York, 1984), pp. 61–63.
24. For vital records of Ruffin's children, see William K. Scarborough, "The Ruffin Family: Children and Grandchildren of Edmund Ruffin," in Scarborough, ed., *Diary* 2:xxiii–xxvi. The date for Agnes Ruffin Beckwith's death appears in Margaret Stanly Beckwith, "Personal Reminiscences, 1844–1865" (3 vols.), 2:35, ViHi.
25. Ruffin, "Incidents" 2:220.
26. For an analysis of this period in Ruffin's career, see W. M. Mathew, "Edmund Ruffin and the Demise of the *Farmers' Register*," *VMHB* 94 (1986): 3–24.
27. These traditions are treated in William R. Taylor, *Cavalier and Yankee: The Old South and American National Character* (New York, 1961), pp. 37–94, 145–62. Ruffin's personal account differs from the evidence on other southerners discussed in Bertram Wyatt-Brown, *Southern Honor: Ethics and Behavior in the Old South* (New York, 1982), pp. 117–48, 178, and in Eugene D. Genovese, *The World the Slaveholders Made: Two Essays in Interpretation* (New York, 1969), pp. 151–94. Taylor, Wyatt-Brown, and Genovese all interpret Ruffin as an exceptional figure in the antebellum South. Ruffin was driven by an ambition similar to that of the young William Wirt, as interpreted by Taylor. Although Ruffin was from the Tidewater and though he did not view the accumulation of slaves as a means of social mobility, he had much in common with the middle-class masters described in James Oakes, *The Ruling Race: A History of American Slaveholders* (New York, 1982), pp. 57–68.
28. Ruffin did draw a genealogical chart of his family in 1856, but in 1851 he had not yet begun that project (Ruffin, "Ruffin Family Genealogy," ViHi; Scarborough, ed., *Diary* 1:259 [27, 29 Dec. 1858]).
29. Ruffin has received more sympathetic treatment in works dealing with the history of agriculture than in those dealing with the history of the South and slavery. See Avery Craven, *Soil Exhaustion as a Factor in the Agricultural History of Virginia and Maryland, 1606–1860*, University of Illinois Studies in the Social Sciences, 13 (Urbana, 1926), pp. 134–44; Lewis C. Gray, *History of Agriculture in the Southern United States to 1860*, Carnegie Institution of Washington, Publication no. 430 (2 vols.; Washington, D.C., 1933), 2:780–81, 915–16; Albert Lowther Demaree, *The American Agricultural Press, 1819–1860*, Columbia University Studies in the History of American Agriculture, no. 8 (New York, 1941), pp. 65–69, 359–63; Charles W. Turner, "Virginia Agricultural Reform, 1815–1860," *Agricultural History* 26 (1952): 83, 88–89; Paul W. Gates, *The Farmer's Age: Agriculture, 1815–1860* (New York, 1960), pp. 107–8, 341–42.
30. Ruffin, "Incidents" 2:139.
31. Edmund Ruffin, *An Essay on Calcareous Manures* (5th ed.; Richmond, 1852), p. 185.
32. In the "Incidents" Ruffin said the family first made Shellbanks its permanent home in 1829. In an essay closer to the event, however, he wrote that they had lived temporarily at Shellbanks during the summers of 1828, 1829, and 1830 and that they moved to Shellbanks permanently in 1831 (Edmund Ruffin, "Desultory Observations on the Police of Health in Virginia—As It Is, and As It Ought to Be," *Farmers' Register* 5 [1837–38]: 159).

33. Ruffin, "Incidents" 2:104, 108–9, 135–36, 139.
34. Ibid., 2:162, 193.
35. U.S. Census, Manuscript Schedules, Prince George County, Va., 1820, p. 54, 1830, p. 46, 1840, p. 106, U.S. Census, Manuscript Schedules, Dinwiddie County, Va., 1840, p. 67, U.S. Census, Slave Schedules, Hanover County, Va., 1850, p. 151, Hanover County, Va., 1860, p. 424, DNA (microfilm); see also Allmendinger, *Ruffin*, pp. 77–79. In 1823 Ruffin drew up a table summarizing his first eleven years at Coggin's Point; he listed the number of his "labourers" at sixteen in 1813, twenty-two in 1823. This is the earliest surviving statistical summary by Ruffin of his farming and slaveholdings ("Table of Crops made on Coggin's Point Farm," 16 Sept. 1823, Blow Family Papers, ViW). Ruffin kept records concerning his slaves in his farm journals; those for Coggin's Point he turned over to his son (Edmund Ruffin, Jr., to Edmund Ruffin, 13 Mar. 1847, Ruffin Papers, ViHi).
36. Ruffin, "Incidents" 2:116, 131, 184–85, 200–206. Ruffin consistently underestimated the value of machinery he owned, probably because he did not understand how it worked. He put the value of his machines (excluding plows and cultivators) in 1848 at $376 (Edmund Ruffin, "Farming Profits in Eastern Virginia: The Value of Marl," *American Farmer* 5 [1849–50]: 4). In the 1850 census he estimated the value of his machines at $100 (U.S. Census, Agriculture Schedules, Hanover County, Va., 1850, p. 21, DNA [microfilm]). Edmund, Jr., objected that Ruffin's estimate for 1848 was too low; see Edmund Ruffin, Jr., to Edmund Ruffin, 10 Apr. 1849, Ruffin Papers, ViHi. On Ruffin's machines, see also Edmund Ruffin, Jr., to Edmund Ruffin, 16 June 1849, 18 June 1852, and Elizabeth Ruffin Sayre to Edmund Ruffin, 4 Sept. 1860, ibid.; Edmund Ruffin, "Essays on Various Subjects of Practical Farming: On Clover Culture, and the Use and Value of the Products," *American Farmer* 6 (1850–51): 291–93.
37. Ruffin, *Calcareous Manures* (5th ed.), pp. 338–53; Ruffin, "Farming Profits," p. 3.
38. Edmund Ruffin, "Essays on Various Subjects of Practical Farming: No. I.—On Draining," *American Farmer* 6 (1850–51): 181; Ruffin, "Incidents" 3:257.
39. On the role of friendship among southern intellectuals, see Drew Gilpin Faust, *A Sacred Circle: The Dilemma of the Intellectual in the Old South, 1840–1860* (Baltimore and London, 1977), pp. 2–3, 6–7, 13, 17, 48, 145–46. Ruffin's preoccupation with the causes of his own failures has invited the interpretation that he was an alienated man, as Faust and William R. Taylor characterize him. Faust has seen the sources of his alienation in a flawed institutional setting that provided little support for antebellum southern intellectuals. Ruffin's "Incidents," however, reveals that at least one institution—the family—played a significant supporting role in his intellectual career.
40. Edmund Ruffin to unidentified correspondent, 10 Apr. 1835, Edmund Ruffin Papers, NcU. To this correspondent Ruffin wrote, "*Shellbanks* is merely a farm, on which my family, servants, & printers reside, & where a Post Office is kept. My printing office is in my yard, & its labors given almost exclusively to my own publications."
41. Ruffin, "Incidents" 2:187–88, 196.
42. Ibid., pp. 164–66, 186–87, 196–99, 211; Ruffin, "Essays: On Draining,"

pp. 177–81; Ruffin, "Essays: Clover Culture," p. 258. Ruffin only rarely recorded the precise tasks assigned to individuals in his farm journal.
43. Ruffin, "Incidents" 2:131.
44. For an instance of a slaveholder who apparently placed greater value on mastery than did Ruffin, see Drew Gilpin Faust, *James Henry Hammond and the Old South: A Design for Mastery* (Baton Rouge, 1982), pp. 3–4, 69–104. Ruffin, though more secure in his sense of origins than Hammond, shared Hammond's ambition for acclaim and success, as well as Hammond's desire to improve the health of slaves. Ruffin, however, simply was not driven by ambition for a place at the top of the master class.
45. Ruffin's emphasis on success as well as his self-criticism could be interpreted as betraying an underlying fear of failure, a possibility reinforced by his suicide. Most of his passages containing self-criticism, however, represent merely candid assessments of what succeeded and what did not. Throughout the text he sustained an attitude indicating that he considered his career a great success. For interpretations emphasizing Ruffin's failures, see Eugene D. Genovese, *The Political Economy of Slavery: Studies in the Economy and Society of the Slave South* (New York, 1965), pp. 124–31, and W. M. Mathew, "Agricultural Adaptation and Race Control in the American South: The Failure of the Ruffin Reforms," *Slavery & Abolition: A Journal of Comparative Studies* 8 (1986): 129–47.
46. The date of Ruffin's death is a matter of uncertainty. Ruffin's biographers disagree, Betty Mitchell choosing 17 June 1865, and Avery Craven, 18 June. See Mitchell, *Ruffin*, p. 255; Avery Craven, *DAB* 16:214–16. Craven avoided pinning down the date in his book on Ruffin. The uncertainty originated in a discrepancy between the final entry of Ruffin's diary and Edmund, Jr.'s letter about the suicide (the former indicating 18 June, the latter, 17 June). Richmond and New York newspapers of 1865 also differed on the date. See Edmund Ruffin, Diary, p. 4089 (16, 17, 18 June 1865), DLC; Edmund Ruffin, Jr., to George and Thomas Ruffin, 20 June 1865, in "Death of Edmund Ruffin," *Tyler's Quarterly Historical and Genealogical Magazine* 5 (1923–24): 193–95. For a discussion of evidence on the suicide, see the interpretations in David F. Allmendinger, Jr., and William K. Scarborough, "The Days Ruffin Died," *VMHB* 97 (1989): 75–96.
47. Ruffin, "Incidents" 2:103. In these passages Ruffin quoted entries from his farm journals of 1827 to 1829, which sustained his memory about feeling despondent.
48. Edmund Ruffin, "Statement of the closing scenes of the life of Thomas Cocke," Ruffin Papers, ViHi (printed as appendix 2).
49. Scarborough, ed., *Diary* 1:368–71 (2 Dec. 1859).
50. Allmendinger, "Early Career," pp. 150–54.
51. For comparisons between the two deaths, see Ruffin, "Closing scenes," pp. 4–11; Ruffin, Diary, pp. 4089–4100 (16, 17, 18 June 1865), DLC; "Death of Edmund Ruffin," pp. 193–95; Craven, *Ruffin*, pp. 93–94; Sitterson, "Edmund Ruffin," p. xxxii; Richmond *Whig*, 20 June 1865; Allmendinger, *Ruffin*, pp. 176–85.
52. Ruffin's son had feared his father might take his own life in the spring of 1865 but apparently was unaware of the range of Ruffin's thinking on suicide until after the event; see "Death of Edmund Ruffin," pp. 193–95. Accounts in the Richmond newspapers attributed the suicide to Ruf-

fin's despondency over the outcome of the Civil War; see Richmond *Daily Times*, 20 June 1865, and Richmond *Whig*, 20 June 1865.
53. Edmund Ruffin, Jr., to Edmund Ruffin, 3 Dec. 1855, Ruffin Papers, ViHi; Edmund Ruffin, "In Remembrance of Jane Dupuy, formerly Ruffin," 1855, pp. 15–17, and separate note inserted at p. 9, ibid. (printed elsewhere in this volume).
54. Apart from Ruffin's memoirs the principal evidence on these illnesses appears in family correspondence: Edmund Ruffin, Jr., to Edmund Ruffin, n.d. [1855], 24 Aug., 18 Oct., 29 Nov., 3, 7 Dec. 1855, Mildred Ruffin to Edmund Ruffin, [29 Apr. 1855], Julian C. Ruffin to Edmund Ruffin, 24 Aug. 1855, Agnes R. Beckwith to Edmund Ruffin, 29 Nov., 2 Dec. 1855, Ruffin Papers, ViHi. Ruffin registered the cause of Ella Ruffin's death as heart disease; see Hanover County, Va., Register of Deaths, 1853–71, p. 10, Hanover County Court House, Va.

Volume 2

1. The tariff of 1824 was a protective measure enacting Henry Clay's notion of building a home market by protecting manufactures. The tariff increased duties on cotton, woolen, and iron goods and on hemp, raw wool, coffee, sugar, molasses, and salt. Voting on this bill in Congress followed sectional lines; southern delegations lined up in opposition.
2. Brackets in original.
3. Brackets in original. No punctuation follows this sentence.
4. For the Virginia usury law, see William Waller Hening, ed., *The Statutes at Large; Being a Collection of All the Laws of Virginia* . . . (13 vols.; Richmond, etc., 1823), 12:337–38; *Acts of the General Assembly of Virginia, Passed at the Session Commencing 4th December 1843, and Ending 15th February 1844* . . . (Richmond, 1844), p. 54.
5. On efforts to combat rust, a plant disease caused by fungi, see Gates, *Farmer's Age*, pp. 163–64.
6. Ruffin reluctantly accepted a definition of *marl* as the natural mixture of fossil shells and clay extracted from sedimentary deposits underlying most of the Tidewater. When farmers spread this mixture over their fields they created *marled land;* carbonate of lime from "decayed sea-shells" neutralized acidity of the soil (Edmund Ruffin, "On the Composition of Soils, and Their Improvement by Calcareous Manures," *American Farmer* 3 [1821–22]: 319–20; Edmund Ruffin, "On Lime as a Manure," ibid., 8 [1826–27]: 105; Ruffin, *Calcareous Manures* [5th ed.], pp. 110–11). On the meaning of the word *manure* in Ruffin's time, see Sitterson, "Edmund Ruffin," p. xiv, n. 14.
7. Thomas Cocke (1774–1840) became Edmund Ruffin's guardian in 1810. He was Ruffin's neighbor, closest friend, and collaborator in soil experiments during the early years at Coggin's Point. Cocke committed suicide in 1840 (Claiborne Thweatt Smith, Jr., *Smith of Scotland Neck: Planters on the Roanoke* [Baltimore, 1976], pp. 197–99; Boddie, *Southside Virginia Families* 1:151–53; Allmendinger, "Early Career," pp. 127–54).
8. Ruffin was referring to his stepmother, Rebecca Cocke Ruffin Woodlief (1771–1837) (Benjamin B. Weisiger III, *Prince George County, Virginia: Mis-*

cellany, 1711–1814 [Richmond, 1986], pp. 68, 74; Boddie, *Southside Virginia Families* 1:158).
9. "Latter" is interlined without indication of an insertion.
10. He was referring to his move to Shellbanks, three miles south of Coggin's Point.
11. The author intended to begin a new paragraph with this sentence but forgot to indent the first word at the top of his page.
12. Ruffin moved to Petersburg.
13. The table was omitted, and no table of this description appeared in the second edition of the *Essay* (1835). A table of Ruffin's crops between 1813 and 1842 did appear in the third edition, but it omitted 1833–35 entirely; on page 184 of the fifth edition (1852) Ruffin included a table of crops between 1813 and 1851. For this table, drawn up in the year he wrote most of the "Incidents," see appendix 5.
14. Ruffin's measures against malaria and intestinal disease appear to have had some effect; nine of his and Susan Ruffin's eleven children survived infancy. "Bilious fever" in France eventually was identified as typhoid; see Jean-Pierre Peter, "Disease and the Sick at the End of the Eighteenth Century," in Robert Forster and Orest Ranum, eds., *Biology of Man in History: Selections from the Annales . . .* (Baltimore, 1975), p. 108. On the unhealthy environment confronting Tidewater residents, see Darrett B. Rutman and Anita H. Rutman, "Of Agues and Fevers: Malaria in the Early Chesapeake," *WMQ*, 3d ser., 33 (1976): 31–60; Carville V. Earle, "Environment, Disease, and Mortality in Early Virginia," in Thad W. Tate and David L. Ammerman, eds., *The Chesapeake in the Seventeenth Century: Essays on Anglo-American Society* (Chapel Hill, 1979), pp. 96–125; and F. J. Spencer, "Epidemics and Eubiotics: The Physical Health of Virginians," in Roscoe D. Hughes and Henry Leidheiser, Jr., eds., *Exploring Virginia's Human Resources* (Charlottesville, 1965), pp. 107–29.
15. Ruffin labeled this area the "Reclaimed Marsh," immediately south of House Field on his 1823 map of Coggin's Point Farm.
16. The reference here is probably to Ruffin, "Farming Profits in Eastern Virginia," pp. 2–10; see also his study of the extent of marling in Edmund Ruffin, "Communication to the Virginia State Agricultural Society: Some of the Results of the Improvements of Land by Calcareous Manures . . . ," *Southern Planter* 12 (1852): 258–71.
17. Ruffin taught that marl had more permanent effects on soil than vegetable or animal manures.
18. An ink smear blurs some words on this page of the manuscript.
19. In 1828 Ruffin bought 390 acres of the farm that became Shellbanks from the estate of Charles Eppes; it was assessed at $4 per acre (Prince George County, Va., Land Book, 1828, p. 24, Vi [microfilm]).
20. In 1830 he purchased 203.5 acres bordering the original Shellbanks tract from Sally Harrison (ibid., 1830, p. 22, Vi [microfilm]).
21. The tenant has not been identified.
22. The reference is to Ruffin, "On the Composition of Soils," pp. 313–20. Ruffin provided no closing quotation mark.
23. Ruffin's 1818 address to the Prince George Agricultural Society was his first public statement; extracts from the address appeared in Ruffin, "First Views Which Led to Marling," pp. 663–64 (see appendix 3).
24. Five editions of Edmund Ruffin's *Essay on Calcareous Manures* appeared

in his lifetime. The first edition, containing 241 pages, was published in Petersburg by J. W. Campbell in 1832; it was printed by L. R. Bailey in Philadelphia. The second edition was published at Shellbanks by Ruffin at the *Farmers' Register* office in 1835; it was issued as a supplement to volume 2 of the *Register*. The third edition was published in Petersburg by Ruffin in 1842 as a supplement to volume 10 of the *Register*. The fourth edition was published in Philadelphia by Laurens Wallazz in 1844. The fifth edition was published in Richmond by J. W. Randolph in 1852. Randolph issued a second printing of the fifth edition in Richmond in 1853; this printing bore the imprint of E. B. Mears, stereotyper of Philadelphia. The author enlarged the work for the second edition and again for the third, in which he deleted an appendix containing criticism of slavery. He further enlarged the book in the fifth edition, which contained 493 pages. Over Ruffin's lifetime, the *Essay* more than doubled in length.

25. These political writings were early statements against the tariff. See Edmund Ruffin, "Memorial of the United Agricultural Societies of Virginia, Jan. 10, 1820," *American Farmer* 1 (1819–20): 347–49. Ruffin also may have written "An Address to the Public from the Delegation of the United Agricultural Societies of Virginia," ibid., 2 (1820–21): 57–59, and "The Petition of the Delegates of the United Agricultural Societies of Prince George, Sussex, Surry, Petersburg, Brunswick, Dinwiddie, and Isle of Wight," ibid., pp. 339–40. Ruffin was a delegate from Prince George when these societies met at Petersburg in December 1820 and was chosen secretary of the delegates.

26. The manuscript no longer survives in any of the collections of Ruffin's papers. The first edition of the *Essay on Calcareous Manures* was printed in Philadelphia but published in Petersburg.

27. Among these works was M. Puvis, *Essay on the Use of Lime as a Manure*, trans. Edmund Ruffin (New York, 1836).

28. Ruffin did not provide the years of this winter; he probably issued the prospectus in the winter of 1832–33.

29. Ruffin did not close the quotation.

30. John Taylor of Caroline (1753–1824) advocated farming reforms that influenced the young Ruffin. The enclosing system entailed creating meadows and using pens or fences to prevent livestock from grazing on arable land (John Taylor, *Arator: Being a Series of Agricultural Essays, Practical and Political* . . . , ed. M. E. Bradford [1818; Liberty Classics ed., Indianapolis, 1977], pp. 130–44, 234, 243–44; Craven, *Soil Exhaustion*, p. 101; and Freda F. Stohrer, "*Arator:* A Publishing History," *VMHB* 88 [1980]: 442–45). On Ruffin's encounter with Taylor's theories, see appendix 3, pp. 191–93.

31. Ruffin occasionally gave the same meaning to *marl* and *lime*. In 1826 he drew a distinction between the two, defining *marl* as the bed of fossil shells like those at Coggin's Point; *lime* was the substance formed by burning limestone. Both were calcareous manures, containing calcium carbonate. Marl (or "mild lime") had more durable and valuable effects than lime (or "caustic" or "quick" lime) because it absorbed acid more slowly. See Ruffin, "On Lime as a Manure," pp. 105–7; Ruffin, *Calcareous Manures*, ed. Sitterson, p. 8.

32. Ruffin defined "putrescent manures" as "those formed of vegetable and animal matters," including weeds and stable manure. These were differ-

ent from calcareous manures, chemical substances derived from limestone, chalk, or shells, containing "carbonate of lime" (Ruffin, *Calcareous Manures*, ed. Sitterson, p. 10, n. 4; Ruffin, "On the Composition of Soils," p. 319).

33. Point Field was a long, narrow piece of arable land on high ground stretching from the tip of Coggin's Point southward toward the two small houses Ruffin occupied in 1813. It contained 76.2 acres.
34. Ruffin was introducing an increasingly elaborate scheme of alternating different crops on specific fields, taking care to fallow a field between crops of grain. (Fallow land has been plowed but not seeded, allowing it to rest at least one season.) Eventually, at Marlbourne, he developed a six-field system that included clover and peas. On rotation systems, see Gray, *History of Agriculture* 2:807–10.
35. Here Ruffin provided a clue to the contents of his missing volume 1.
36. These plowing methods represented efforts to control erosion and to preserve soil fertility. Instead of harrowing the soil flat, Ruffin plowed it deeply into ridges; instead of plowing up and down hillsides, he plowed horizontally across slopes. George Washington experienced similar discouragement in such efforts; see Craven, *Soil Exhaustion*, pp. 87–88. See also Gray, *History of Agriculture* 1:448.
37. Ruffin introduced new implements, but by 1851 he viewed these particular ones disdainfully. A cultivator was a horse-drawn implement used to break the soil before planting; by 1860 it consisted of a harrow frame with plow handles and metal cutting blades, or shares, of various shapes. Ruffin described the trowel plow as the most common plowing implement in Virginia between 1817 and 1842. It was drawn by horses or mules and was held upright by the plowman; its trowel-shaped cutting blade cast a thin layer of earth on both sides of the share. A moldboard is the curved metal plate of a plow that turns over the earth into a furrow. See Edmund Ruffin, "Report to the State Board of Agriculture, on the Most Important Recent Improvements of Agriculture in Lower Virginia—and the Most Important Defects Yet Remaining," *Farmers' Register* 10 (1842): 263–64; Gray, *History of Agriculture* 2:794–95; Willard W. Cochrane, *The Development of American Agriculture: A Historical Analysis* (Minneapolis, 1979), pp. 190–96; and Leo Rogin, *The Introduction of Farm Machinery in Its Relation to the Productivity of Labor in the Agriculture of the United States during the Nineteenth Century*, University of California Publications in Economics, no. 9 (Berkeley, 1931), pp. 52–57, 66–68. Ruffin bought his first threshing machine in 1845 (Edmund Ruffin, Marlbourne Farm Journal, p. 142 [9 July 1845], Vi).
38. Wire grass (*Cynodon dactylon*) is Bermuda grass, an important pasture grass of the South. Bluegrass is a forage grass; Ruffin was referring specifically to *Poa compressa*. Greensward is Kentucky bluegrass (*Poa pratensis*). See Ruffin, *Calcareous Manures* (5th ed.), p. 173; A. S. Hitchcock, *Manual of the Grasses of the United States* (Washington, D.C., 1935), pp. 106, 112–14, 483–84.
39. Shirley and Westover plantations lay across the James River from Coggin's Point in Charles City County. Their owners, Hill Carter and John A. Selden, respectively, had introduced these rotation plans. See Scarborough, ed., *Diary* 1:194 n. 42, 2:386 (24 July 1862).
40. Ruffin was familiar with known principles of the nitrogen cycle.
41. Ruffin here recalled an event of 1813.

42. The author omitted the opening parenthesis.
43. The reference is probably to Edmund Ruffin, "Desultory Observations on the Application and Action of Putrescent Manures," *Southern Planter* 6 (1846): 135–42.
44. The author crossed over this abbreviation, apparently by mistake.
45. Ruffin intended to begin a paragraph with this word but forgot to indent at the top of his page.
46. In recalling this failure, Ruffin provided another clue to the contents of volume 1.
47. See Ruffin, "Essays: On Draining," pp. 5–8, 33–38, 90–95, 128–31, 177–82.
48. Ruffin undertook draining projects at Marlbourne, too; his son Edmund, Jr., continued those at Coggin's Point, which he renamed Beechwood.
49. The author forgot to indent the first word of this paragraph.
50. Ruffin's handwriting often makes it difficult to discern whether he meant *cleaning* or *clearing;* the most common usage in his published essays has been followed here whenever his handwriting is not distinct.
51. [Edmund Ruffin], "On Draining: Addressed to Young Farmers," *Farmers' Register* 1 (1833–34): 385–90, 705–10.
52. The word "all" is interlined above the word "my."
53. Andrew Nicol (1805–1858), born in Perthshire, Scotland, was Ruffin's overseer between 1835 and 1839. He later became a dealer in farm implements and joined Thomas S. Pleasants in editing the *Southern Farmer* (Edward A. Wyatt IV, comp., *Preliminary Checklist for Petersburg, 1786–1876*, Virginia Imprint Series, no. 9 [Richmond, 1949], p. 296).
54. Robert B. Bolling (1805–1881), a wealthy Petersburg resident, obtained Sandy Point in Charles City County through marriage to Sarah Melville Minge ("Genealogy: The Cocke Family of Virginia," *VMHB* 4 [1896–97]: 329, 331). For Nicol's work on the Sandy Point estate, see William K. Scarborough, *The Overseer: Plantation Management in the Old South* (Baton Rouge, 1966), pp. 160–62.
55. At this point in the manuscript there are three and one-half blank pages apparently intended for material dealing with the founding of the *Farmers' Register.*
56. Thomas W. White (1788–1843) of Richmond was the first printer of the *Farmers' Register;* in 1834 he founded and published the *Southern Literary Messenger* (Russell Benson Devine, "Thomas Willis White," *Southern Literary Messenger* 1 [1939]: 503–7).
57. The printer probably was Robert Ricketts, whose name appears on the copyright page of Edmund Ruffin, *An Essay on Calcareous Manures* (2d ed.; Shellbanks, Va., 1835). See also Wyatt, *Preliminary Checklist for Petersburg*, pp. 246–47.
58. Ruffin published the *Farmers' Register* at Shellbanks from 1833 through 1835. He must have moved the shop to Petersburg at the end of 1835, because he printed the remaining issues of volume 3 in that city, beginning with that for January 1836. He abandoned the *Register* after completing volume 10 in December 1842. See Earl G. Swem, *An Analysis of Ruffin's* Farmers' Register, *with a Bibliography of Edmund Ruffin*, in *Bulletin of the Virginia State Library*, 11 (Richmond, 1918): 45. The correct month of the first publication in Petersburg appears in Wyatt, *Preliminary Checklist for Petersburg*, p. 247.
59. Ruffin's granddaughter identified the tutor of Edmund, Jr., and Agnes as

Mr. Holsbrook, who must have been Julian's tutor also (Beckwith, "Personal Reminiscences" 1:3b). Young Edmund once referred to him as "Mr. H" (Edmund Ruffin, Jr., to Julian C. Ruffin, [ca.1829], Ruffin Papers, ViHi). Ruffin himself also gave instruction to his sons in their early years (Scarborough, ed., *Diary* 2:436 [31 Aug. 1862]; Ruffin, Diary, p. 3158 [16 Jan. 1864], DLC). After their tutoring at home, all of the Ruffin children were sent to schools in Richmond, Petersburg, and—in the case of Edmund, Jr.—New Haven, Conn.

60. Edmund Ruffin, Jr. (1814–1875), completed his studies at the University of Virginia in 1833; Julian Calx Ruffin (1821–1864) graduated from the College of William and Mary in 1839 (Maximilian Schele De Vere, comp., *Students of the University of Virginia: A Semi-centennial Catalogue, with Brief Biographical Sketches* [Baltimore, 1878]; *Provisional List of Alumni of the College of William and Mary*, p. 35).

61. Ruffin did not identify the female teacher, and neither did his children. Ruffin neglected to mention that his youngest son, Charles (b. 1832), would have to be educated; the episode with the governess may have occurred before Charles was born.

62. Ruffin did not supply the precise year, though earlier in the manuscript he twice recorded the year as 1835 (Ruffin, "Incidents" 2:105). In April 1835 Ruffin still was living at Shellbanks and gave no indication that he was about to move; by July 1836 he was living in Petersburg (Edmund Ruffin to unknown correspondent, 10 Apr. 1835, Edmund Ruffin Papers, NcU; Edmund Ruffin to Thomas Ruffin, 19 July 1836, Thomas Ruffin Papers, NcU). Ruffin probably moved his family to Petersburg in the spring of 1836.

63. The author probably neglected to delete "condition" after inserting the preceding three words.

64. These rail lines undertaken in the 1830s linked Richmond and Petersburg with cities to the north and south. The Richmond, Fredericksburg, and Potomac Railroad was chartered in 1834 and was under construction by the end of that year; Edmund, Jr., must have worked on the fifty-eight-mile section between Richmond and Fredericksburg, completed in 1836 (Moncure Robinson, "Present State and Prospect of the Richmond, Fredericksburg, and Potomac Rail Road," *Farmers' Register* 2 [1834–35]: 525–26; John Lancaster, "Report to the Third Annual Meeting of the Stockholders of the Richmond, Fredericksburg and Potomac Rail Road Company," ibid., 4 [1835–36]: 345–47).

The Greensville and Roanoke Railroad ran eighteen miles between Hicksford (Emporia), Va., and Gaston, N.C. Chartered jointly by the two states in 1833, the road was a branch of the Petersburg and Roanoke Railroad that enabled that line to compete with the Portsmouth and Roanoke Railroad for trade on the upper Roanoke River. The Greensville line was surveyed in 1835 and began regular service on 30 March 1837 (Edmund Ruffin, Jr., "Account of the Greensville and Roanoke Railway," ibid., 5 [1837–38]: 9–13).

The Raleigh and Gaston Railroad, incorporated in 1835 and completed in 1839, ran ninety-five miles northeast from Raleigh to Gaston, N.C. There it joined the Greensville line of the Petersburg and Roanoke (Charles Clinton Weaver, *Internal Improvements in North Carolina previous to 1860*, Johns Hopkins University Studies in Historical and Political Science, ser. 20, nos. 3–4 [Baltimore, 1903], pp. 81–82, 86–89; Charles F.

Garnett, "Raleigh and Gaston Rail-Road," *Farmers' Register* 7 [1839]: 388–90).
65. Railway mania struck Ruffin himself. His enthusiasm for railroads was evident from the earliest days of the *Farmers' Register;* between 1833 and 1840 he published numerous articles on railroad companies, often boosting Petersburg roads. In 1838 he published the annual report of Petersburg's rival, the Portsmouth and Roanoke Railroad, including its account of calamities: a "melancholy accident" near Suffolk, in which an excursion train collided head-on with a lumber train; the discovery that portions of the track near Weldon, N.C., were decaying; and a second accident, "not less fatal in its consequences," involving a derailment and "a dreadful crush of all the coaches which were next to the engine" (Arthur Emmerson, "Sixth Annual Report of the President and Directors of the Portsmouth and Roanoke Railroad," *Farmers' Register* 6 [1838]: 330).
66. The panic of 1837 and its resulting depression kept receipts low for new railroads in eastern Virginia and North Carolina (Peter C. Stewart, "Railroads and Urban Rivalries in Antebellum Eastern Virginia," *VMHB* 81 [1973]: 6). See the curious annual report and letter of resignation by Walter Gwynn, general agent and civil engineer of the Portsmouth and Roanoke Railroad ("To the President and Directors of the Portsmouth and Roanoke Railroad Company," *Farmers' Register* 6 [1838]: 333). Gwynn maintained receipts had not declined during a year he described as "unparalleled in commercial distress," bringing forth "the prostration of every branch of industry." His company had prospered, he insisted; and in conclusion, he resigned. On the panic of 1837 and its financial ramifications in Virginia, see James Roger Sharp, *The Jacksonians versus the Banks: Politics in the States after the Panic of 1837* (New York and London, 1970), pp. 215–73, and Larry Schweikart, *Banking in the American South from the Age of Jackson to Reconstruction* (Baton Rouge and London, 1987), pp. 120–27.
67. Mary Cooke Smith (1816–1857) was the daughter of Thomas Gregory Smith and Anne Dabney Smith of King and Queen County. An orphan when she married Edmund, Jr., in 1836, she had inherited her parents' valuable farm, Bellevue, and their slaves (Scarborough, ed., *Diary* 2:xxiii; Steven A. Colvin, *On Deep Water* [Verona, Va., 1983], pp. 52, 56). Mary Cooke Smith and Edmund, Jr., had met before they were ten years old (Ruffin, Diary, p. 359 [6 June 1858], DLC).
68. The author must have been thinking of one of the two old, small houses in House Field.
69. Beechwood House was completed in 1849; the family moved there in November 1849 from a smaller cottage (built about 1839) nearby in the yard, where Ruffin took up residence in 1860 (Mary C. Ruffin to Edmund Ruffin, 17 Nov. 1849, Ruffin Papers, ViHi; Scarborough, ed., *Diary* 1:297–98 [14 Apr. 1859], 504–5 [27 Nov. 1860]).
70. Ruffin favored hard money and opposed banks and their paper currency. For views similar to Ruffin's among Tidewater Whigs and Democrats, see Sharp, *Jacksonians versus the Banks*, pp. 260–61.
71. On the moneylending and investments of other southerners, see Jane Turner Censer, *North Carolina Planters and Their Children, 1800–1860* (Baton Rouge and London, 1984), pp. 12–15.
72. Ruffin probably meant to write "debtors."
73. Rebecca Cocke Ruffin (who married Peter Woodlief after Ruffin's father died) named Ruffin guardian for his younger half sisters Juliana and Eliz-

abeth and his half brother George in the early 1820s. Ruffin's eldest half sister, Jane Ruffin Dupuy, had married in 1817 (William Jones Dupuy family Bible records, 1763–1910, ViHi; Edmund Ruffin to Rebecca Cocke Ruffin Woodlief, 23 Mar. 1823, Ruffin Papers, ViHi).

74. Ruffin's animus toward banks inspired him to issue publications devoted to the banking controversy; these included the short-lived periodical *The Bank Reformer* (1841–42) and an anonymous pamphlet written by Ruffin, *Desultory Observations on the Abuses of the Banking System: Addressed to the Consideration of the Agricultural Classes* (Petersburg, 1841). Concerning his campaign in Petersburg against the banks, see Mathew, "Ruffin and the Demise of the *Farmers' Register*," pp. 12–13.

75. Ruffin's grandfather, the second Edmund Ruffin (1745–1807), was the first member of the family to own Coggin's Point (*Virginia Gazette* [Purdie], 30 Oct. 1778; Edward Lewis Goodwin, *The Colonial Church in Virginia: With Biographical Sketches of the First Six Bishops of the Diocese of Virginia* [Milwaukee, 1927], p. 155; Edmund Ruffin, "The Blackwater Guerilla: A Tradition of Revolutionary Times," 1851, Ruffin Papers, ViHi).

76. One of the first railways in the South, the Petersburg and Roanoke Railroad was chartered in 1830. It ran south from Petersburg to Blakely, N.C., four miles below the falls of the Roanoke River. Construction on this sixty-mile road began in January 1831 and was completed thirty-one months later, in 1833 (Weaver, *Internal Improvements*, pp. 76–77; Stewart, "Railroads and Urban Rivalries," pp. 3–6; Edmund Ruffin, Jr., "Account of the Greensville," p. 9; "Progress and Condition of the Petersburg and Roanoke Rail Road," *Farmers' Register* 1 [1833–34]: 758; M. Robinson, "Public Works for Facilitating Transportation: Petersburg Rail Road," ibid., pp. 53–55).

It was on the Petersburg and Roanoke in 1840 that Ruffin began his first long train ride and his first trip to Charleston, S.C. He departed Petersburg at 1 A.M. on 14 April and arrived (after changing trains) in Wilmington, N.C., at 7 P.M. the same day. He had traveled 181 miles. On the sixteenth he boarded a steam vessel belonging to the Wilmington Rail Road and sailed for Charleston (Edmund Ruffin, "Notes of a Steam Journey," *Farmers' Register* 8 [1840]: 243–44).

As late as 1856 Ruffin still owned $2,500 worth of stock in the Petersburg and Roanoke (Edmund and Julian Ruffin, Ledger and Accounts, 1828–30, 1855–65, p. 174, Vi).

77. Ruffin insured four properties in Petersburg in 1844. One of these, a three-story brick house, stood on the northwest corner of High and Market streets. This was the building he occupied in January 1836 and purchased in the winter of 1839–40. Here he and Robert Ricketts printed the *Farmers' Register*. In addition, Ruffin owned an adjoining three-story dwelling on the north side of High Street, a kitchen to the rear of that building, and a two-story brick "lumber house" on the west side of St. Paul's Lane, between Bank Street and Old Street (*Farmers' Register* 3 [1835–36]: 576; Edmund Ruffin to unknown correspondent, 24 July 1840, Ruffin Family Papers, CSmH [microfilm]; Mutual Assurance Society of Virginia, Revaluations 13911 and 13912, Edmund Ruffin, 1844, Vi [microfilm]). Ruffin's daughter Agnes and her husband, T. Stanly Beckwith, may have lived for a time in one of these tenements (Elizabeth Ruffin to Susan Travis Ruffin, n.d. [ca.1840], Ruffin Papers, ViHi). Ruffin's house

on the corner is no longer standing, though evidence of its existence is clearly visible on the wall of the adjoining house, which was apparently one of those he insured. The "lumber house" on the lane is gone.

78. Ruffin published his subscribers' names in "Supplement to Vol. I. of Farmers' Register: List of Subscribers," *Farmers' Register* 1 (1833–34): 769–76.
79. The *Cultivator*, a leading farm paper of the period, was published in Albany between 1834 and 1865; its founder was Judge Jesse Buel (1778–1839). See Demaree, *American Agricultural Press*, pp. 340–44.
80. Most Virginia banks suspended specie payments in 1837, in violation of their charters. The legislature passed a relief measure delaying enforcement of charter forfeiture for nearly a year; it later extended the period of relief (Schweikart, *Banking in the American South*, p. 124).
81. Abel P. Upshur (1790–1844) practiced law in Richmond and owned a farm in Northampton County. He was secretary of the navy and then secretary of state under John Tyler. Ruffin published two of his pamphlets, one on federalism and one on credit, in 1840 (Robert Sobel, ed., *Biographical Directory of the United States Executive Branch, 1774–1971* [Westport, Conn., 1971], pp. 325–26). See also Claude H. Hall, *Abel Parker Upshur: Conservative Virginian, 1790–1844* (Madison, Wis., 1963).
82. Nathaniel Beverley Tucker (1784–1851), professor of law at William and Mary and author in 1836 of two novels, *George Balcombe* and *The Partisan Leader*, was an early advocate with Ruffin of secession (J. V. Ridgely, "Nathaniel Beverley Tucker [1784–1851]," in Robert Bain and Joseph M. Flora, eds., *Fifty Southern Writers before 1900* [Westport, Conn., 1987], pp. 483–91).
83. Thomas R. Dew (1802–1846) became professor of political law at William and Mary in 1826, then president of the college in 1836. His criticism of Van Buren's subtreasury system caught Ruffin's eye in 1840, as had his *Review of the Debate in the Virginia Legislature of 1831 and 1832* (1832) (Stephen Scott Mansfield, "Thomas Roderick Dew at William and Mary: 'A Main Prop in that Venerable Institution,'" *VMHB* 75 [1967]: 429–42).
84. Two issues only of the *Southern Magazine and Monthly Review* were published by Ruffin and his son Julian in 1841.
85. An insertion is indicated here but appears to have been cut from the manuscript.
86. Controversy erupted in 1840 when Governor Thomas W. Gilmer of Virginia demanded the return of three black seamen, New York citizens who had tried unsuccessfully to help a slave escape from Virginia. William H. Seward, governor of New York, refused to deliver the three. The dispute continued through 1842, involving executives and legislatures of both states (Glyndon G. Van Deusen, *William Henry Seward* [New York, 1967], pp. 65–66; Margaret Vowell Smith, *Virginia, 1492–1892* [1893; Port Washington, N.Y., 1972], pp. 350–51).
87. Ruffin omitted the closing quotation mark after "Disguise."
88. Condy Raguet (1784–1842) was a Philadelphia author and editor who advocated states' rights and free trade. His book *A Treatise on Currency and Banking* (1839) caught Ruffin's attention (*DAB* 15:325–26).
89. Theodorick Bland (1742–1790) was born in Prince George County, studied medicine at Edinburgh, and practiced briefly in Prince George before turning to farming. He was an American officer during the Revolution,

voted against the federal Constitution in the 1788 state convention, and became a member of the first House of Representatives (*DAB* 2:356–57). Ruffin published Bland's papers (Theodorick Bland, *The Bland Papers: Being a Selection from the Manuscripts of Colonel Theodorick Bland, Jr. . . .*, ed. Charles Campbell [2 vols.; Petersburg, 1840–43]).

90. On 24 June 1837 the General Assembly passed "An Act for the temporary relief of the Banks of this Commonwealth, and for other purposes," suspending previous acts that had subjected banks to forfeiture of their charters for "failing or refusing to pay or redeem" their "notes or debts in specie" (*By-Laws of the Bank of Virginia: To Which Are Appended, the Act Establishing General Regulations for the Incorporation of Banks, and Subsequent Acts respecting the Banks of This Commonwealth* [Richmond, 1840], pp. 56–58). This temporary relief was then renewed in subsequent sessions of the legislature. In addition to their serial publication in *Acts of the General Assembly of Virginia*, all banking acts between 22 March 1837 and 18 March 1840 were collected and printed in *By-Laws of the Bank of Virginia*, pp. 29–68.

    In its general banking act of 22 March 1837, the legislature authorized banks to issue negotiable notes in denominations of not less than $10 ("An Act Establishing General Regulations for the Incorporation of Banks," *By-Laws of the Bank of Virginia*, pp. 32–34). In the session of 1841–42, the legislature placed a minimum of $5 on such notes (*The Code of Virginia: Second Edition, Including Legislation to the Year 1860* [Richmond, 1860], p. 342).

91. The general banking acts of March 1837 expanded the capital of state banks by $5 million and permitted banks a circulation of five times their reserves. Critics like Ruffin felt this would encourage irresponsible lending (see Schweikart, *Banking in the American South*, p. 121; "An Act Increasing the Banking Capital of the Commonwealth," 25 Mar. 1837, *By-Laws of the Bank of Virginia*, p. 46). Though the banking act required payment on demand, Ruffin obviously felt that once banks had been allowed to suspend payments they would never feel obliged to redeem their notes.

92. The last four letters were omitted by Ruffin.

93. Quoted from "Editorial Remarks in Reply," *Farmers' Register* 9 (1841): 617.

94. John Stuart Skinner (1788–1851) founded the pioneer farm journal, the *American Farmer*, in Baltimore in 1819. Skinner was its editor until 1830; he published Ruffin's first paper on soils in 1821 (Demaree, *American Agricultural Press*, pp. 23–38; "Melancholy Death of John S. Skinner, Esquire," *American Farmer* 6 [1850–51]: 348).

95. The cryptic quotation is a reference to the first and last words of a long passage concerning Skinner, free trade, and banking in Edmund Ruffin, "The Currency—As Connected with the Interests of Agriculture," *Farmers' Register* 9 (1841): 157–58. Brackets in original.

96. The controversy did find its way into the newspapers, though in an unexpected way. Editors of the *Richmond Compiler* and *Lynchburg Virginian* felt Ruffin's discussion of banking was inappropriate in a farming periodical such as the *Farmers' Register*. Ruffin was defended, however, by the Petersburg *American Statesman* (Edmund Ruffin, "The Farmers' Register, and Its Course in Regard to the Banks," *Farmers' Register* 9 [1841]: 372–

75). The editor of the *American Statesman* at this time was Ruffin's close friend Charles Campbell (Wyatt, *Preliminary Checklist for Petersburg*, p. 274).

97. Ruffin indicated he wanted to insert three pages into the text with the heading "Insert at p. 154." He did not specify a point of insertion, but this appears to be the appropriate place.

98. For the act of 1838, whose suspension provisions Ruffin disliked, see Virginia General Assembly, *Acts of the General Assembly of Virginia, Passed at the Session of 1838* (Richmond, 1838), chap. 106, pp. 78–79.

99. For the text of the statement Ruffin printed about bank notes, see Craven, *Ruffin*, pp. 69–70; see also a broadside printed by Ruffin, "Legalized Swindling System," enclosed in Edmund Ruffin to James Henry Hammond, 11 Nov. 1845, James Henry Hammond Papers, DLC.

100. The insertion on banks ends at this point. On a loose sheet of paper inserted in volume 2 is the draft of a public toast Ruffin offered at about this time in Petersburg. On one side of the sheet Ruffin wrote: "Toast offered by me at the public dinner given to B. W. Leigh at Petersburg— & responded to with enthusiasm by the company—all whigs—& the paper-money party." On the reverse side of the sheet is Ruffin's toast: "The Bank of the United States, & the banks of all the twenty four states—the first not authorized, & the last prohibited by the Federal Constitution. *Some* confidence might be placed in the new born zeal & professed hostility of political leaders against the *paper money system*, if, while they are crushing the former of these great yet countervailing evils, they made any effort to put down, or to restrain the abuses of the latter." Benjamin Watkins Leigh (1781–1849), an attorney in Petersburg and Richmond, was senator from Virginia between 1834 and 1836. A prominent Whig, he nearly became the party's vice-presidential nominee in 1840 ("Letters from William and Mary College," *VMHB* 29 [1921–22]: 156, n. 25).

101. Six issues of the *Bank Reformer* appeared at Petersburg between 4 September 1841 and 5 February 1842.

102. For an assessment of this explanation, see Mathew, "Ruffin and the Demise of the *Farmers' Register*," pp. 3–24, and Mathew, *Edmund Ruffin and the Crisis of Slavery*, pp. 27–32.

103. Ruffin's final issue appeared in December 1842.

104. On 20 March 1841 the General Assembly passed legislation establishing the Board of Agriculture; the text of the bill appears in "Board of Agriculture," *Southern Planter* 1 (1841): 42–43. Governor Thomas W. Gilmer signed the bill and appointed the board's first members. Ruffin was one of two delegates from the Tidewater district and became corresponding secretary; James Barbour was president. Other delegates were James M. Garnett, Richard Sampson, Edward Watts, Nathaniel Burwell, Peter H. Steinbergen, and Joseph Johnson. Delegates met for the first time in Richmond on 6 December 1841 (Edmund Ruffin, "The Board of Agriculture," *Farmers' Register* 9 [1841]: 688).

The board assigned itself the task of gathering "a full account of the agricultural statistics of the State," reflecting Ruffin's major interest in his late years at the *Register*. The board divided the state into eight districts and assigned a member to circulate a list of printed questions in each area. C. T. Botts, editor of the *Southern Planter* in Richmond, saw this as his major interest, too, and joined in the friendly race for information; Botts predicted that one "long-legged strider" on the board would provide strong competition ([C. T. Botts], "Virginia Board of Agriculture," *Southern Planter* 2 [1842]: 39–40).

105. Ruffin, "Report on the Most Important Recent Improvements of Agriculture in Lower Virginia," pp. 257–66; Edmund Ruffin, "Report to the State Board of Agriculture on the Brandon Farms," *Farmers' Register* 10 (1842): 274–82; Edmund Ruffin, "Report to the State Board of Agriculture of Virginia, In reply to their inquiry as to the 'Obstacles to improvement, including the operation of the laws, or governmental regulation'" (extracts), ibid., pp. 512–17; and Edmund Ruffin, "Description and Account of the Different Kinds of Marl, and of the Gypseous Earth, of the Tide-Water Region of Virginia," in Ruffin, *Calcareous Manures* (5th ed.), pp. 427–93. These reports also appeared in Virginia Board of Agriculture, *Report to the Senate and House of Representatives* (House Journal and Documents), doc. 12 (1842–43), pp. 55–116.

106. See pp. 67–68, 70.

107. Among the small number of printed works published separately from the *Farmers' Register* was Charles Campbell's edition of *The Bland Papers*. To keep his shop busy, Ruffin printed in the *Register* the seventh edition of John Taylor's *Arator* (Petersburg, 1840), and he edited the first publication of William Byrd II's *Westover Manuscripts* (Petersburg, 1841). He also published two editions of his own *Calcareous Manures* (1835, 1842).

108. The contents of the Petersburg shop are listed in an 1843 indenture, revealing what Ruffin had required to run a first-class printshop: "Two printing presses and fixtures, 1 standing press and boards, 2 imposing stones, 10 chases, 8 stands, 68 cases, 2 racks job type, 2 desks, 1 stove and drum, 2 founts Bourgeois, 1 fount long primer, 1 fount brevier, 2 founts Nonpareil, 1 fount of double pica, 1 of great primer, 2 of pica, 28 sorts small job letters, a quantity of leads, brass rules, old metal letter boards, wetting boards, furniture, 2 racks and galleys, and other articles incidental to a printing establishment" (indenture between Laurens Wallazz, Peter P. Batte, and Edmund Ruffin, 26 Dec. 1843, Petersburg, Va., Hustings Court Deed Book 13, 1842–43, pp. 231–32, Vi [microfilm]; see also Wyatt, *Preliminary Checklist for Petersburg*, p. 249).

109. Laurens Wallazz (b. 1809) came to Petersburg from Philadelphia; he purchased Ruffin's printing equipment in January 1843 but returned to Philadelphia by the end of May that year. He is listed as publisher of the third edition of Ruffin's *Essay on Calcareous Manures* in 1842 and issued the fourth edition in 1844 in Philadelphia. By 1850 he had returned to Virginia and was teaching school in Prince George County (Wyatt, *Preliminary Checklist for Petersburg*, pp. 249–50; *Farmers' Register*, new series, 1 [1843]: cover sheets; U.S. Census, Manuscript Schedules, Prince George County, Va., 1850, p. 72, DNA [microfilm]). In 1845 he visited for a few days at Ruthven (Elizabeth Ruffin to Julian C. Ruffin, 14 June 1845, Ruffin and Meade Family Papers, NcU). His estate is mentioned in the text of a Virginia law passed in the legislative session of 1857–58 governing enclosures and animals. He is listed there as deceased (*Code of Virginia: Second Edition*, p. 494).

110. Thomas S. Pleasants (1796–1871) had a career associated with farm papers. He recovered from his failure as Ruffin's successor and in 1854 became editor of the *Southern Farmer* (Lester J. Cappon, *Virginia Newspapers*,

1821–1935: A Bibliography with Historical Introduction and Notes [New York, 1936], p. 153; Wyatt, *Preliminary Checklist for Petersburg,* p. 296).

111. When Ruffin insured the house on the corner in 1844, it was the dwelling and grocery of a tenant, William Nash (Mutual Assurance Society, Revaluation 13911, 1844, Vi [microfilm]).
112. Ruffin meant to say that the amount he actually received fell short of $600 and that his final receipts did not approach the $8,000 due him.
113. Ruffin's appointment as state agricultural surveyor for South Carolina came in December 1842.
114. James Henry Hammond (1807–1864), elected governor of South Carolina in 1842, formed a friendship with Ruffin through their shared ideas on agricultural reform and banking. It was Hammond who introduced Ruffin to influential circles in South Carolina. See Mitchell, *Edmund Ruffin,* pp. 44–48; Faust, *James Henry Hammond,* pp. 126–28, 236–38.
115. Edmund Ruffin, *Report of the Commencement and Progress of the Agricultural Survey of South Carolina for 1843* (Columbia, 1843).
116. Edmund Ruffin, Diary as Agricultural Surveyor in South Carolina, 1843, Ruffin Papers, ViHi.
117. Julian was living at Ruthven, his farm in Prince George County.
118. Almost certainly the Petersburg paper was *The Republican,* which circulated between 1843 and 1849 (Wyatt, *Preliminary Checklist for Petersburg,* pp. 250–53).
119. Extensive excerpts also appeared in a Philadelphia journal; see "Ruffin's Agricultural Address," *Farmers' Cabinet* 8 (1843–44): 270–72.
120. Ruffin here inserted the text of the proceedings at Garysville on 28 December 1843, printed as a four-page pamphlet by the Charleston *Mercury.* For the original account, see Charleston *Mercury,* 5 Feb. 1844.
121. Theron Gee purchased most of Shellbanks (593.5 acres) from Ruffin in 1839 (Prince George County, Va., Land Book, 1839, p. 13, Vi [microfilm]).
122. In 1840 Ruffin inspected the immediate neighborhood of his future property in Hanover County while analyzing soil samples from adjoining fields at Newcastle Farm. His narrative of this tour makes plausible Ruffin's assertion that he began looking for a farm before giving up the *Register*; it reveals, too, that he knew beforehand the character of the land he bought in Hanover. See Edmund Ruffin, "Remarks on the Soils and Marling of the Pamunkey Lands: Introductory to the Queries and Answers Thereon," *Farmers' Register* 8 (1840): 679–91.
123. Ruffin adopted Charles Lyell's terms for geologic time. Both major classes of marl came from the Cenozoic era. Eocene marl was the oldest deposit, characterized by fossil shells and their great degree of disintegration. Miocene marl, a bed of which lay immediately above eocene marl at Coggin's Point, was a more recent deposit and contained larger numbers of preserved shells. Ruffin first found miocene marl in 1818 at Coggin's Point; he found eocene marl in 1819. See Ruffin, *Calcareous Manures* (5th ed.), pp. 436–38, 450–52.
124. The previous owner was Bartholomew McCarty Tomlin, who acquired the property in 1833 through his wife, Mary Elizabeth Bolling Blakey Tomlin. Tomlin built a new house on the farm in 1840, then fell into debt. Formerly known as the Blakey estate, the property was advertised for sale in September 1843. See Colvin, *On Deep Water,* pp. 18, 129 n. 38; Richmond *Enquirer,* 5 Sept. 1843.

125. The main ditch at Marlbourne passed through the middle of the low grounds and probably occupied the bed of an older stream. It remains visible where it crosses under U.S. Highway 360.
126. A *main ditch*, in Ruffin's usage, was "the lowest, deepest, & most capacious ditch of all, into which all others empty, & through which they are all discharged into some still lower outlet" (Ruffin, "Account of Draining," note to p. 8, Ruffin Papers, ViHi).
127. Here the author wrote in the margin, "Insert on p. 166, general description of natural features & soils of the farm." He did not provide the insertion.
128. Spring Garden bordered Marlbourne on the west. A farm of eight hundred acres, it had a large brick house built in the eighteenth century. When Ruffin moved to Hanover County, Spring Garden was owned by William Henry Roane; after 1845 it belonged to John A. Meredith (Hanover County Historical Society, *Old Homes of Hanover County, Virginia* [Hanover, Va., 1983], pp. 49–51).
129. Carter Braxton (1789–1855), grandson of the signer of the Declaration of Independence, had acted as trustee of Bartholomew Tomlin's estate when the farm was offered for sale in 1843. His brother, Dr. Corbin Braxton, was a friend of Ruffin. The Braxton and Ruffin families became entangled in several ways. Carter Braxton's wife, Mary Grymes Sayre Braxton, had two younger brothers, each of whom married a Ruffin daughter against Ruffin's wishes; William Sayre married Elizabeth Ruffin in 1852, and Burwell Sayre married Mildred in 1859. See Richmond *Enquirer*, 5 Sept. 1843; Colvin, *On Deep Water*, pp. 23–29; "Sayre Family," *VMHB* 3 (1895–96): 96; Ruffin, Diary, insert following p. 722 (12 Aug. 1859), DLC.
130. Ruffin once gave the overseer's name as N. Talley (Ruffin, Marlbourne Farm Journal, p. 82 ["Sick List, kept from 10th of July to 10th of Decr.," following entry of 12 Sept. 1844], Vi). The overseer—described by Ruffin as "young" in the farm journal—was reassigned from Marlbourne to Julian C. Ruffin's farm in Prince George County in 1846, when Julian moved to Marlbourne for a time. Another young man, twenty-year-old Richard Spratley, then came to Marlbourne "as a farming pupil, & partial assistant in the direction of the farm operations" (ibid., p. 172 [22 Apr. 1846], Vi).
131. "Report" is interlined above "understanding."
132. Corbin Braxton (1793–1852), brother of Carter Braxton, was a physician, member of the Virginia legislature, and general in the Mexican War. He lived near Marlbourne in King William County. See Colvin, *On Deep Water*, pp. 24–25, 27, 62; David L. Pulliam, *The Constitutional Conventions of Virginia from the Foundation of the Commonwealth to the Present Time* (Richmond, 1901), p. 102; U.S. Census, Population Schedules, King William County, Va., 1850, p. 244, DNA (microfilm).
133. Greensand earth, a deposit of black granules containing gypsum, was first called "gypseous earth" by Ruffin, who objected to classifying it as a marl. He always considered it an inferior, short-lived manure because of its low percentage of carbonate of lime. See Ruffin, *Calcareous Manures* (5th ed.), pp. 454–82.
134. William Barton Rogers (1804–1882) was a leading geologist of the antebellum South. He taught at William and Mary from 1828 to 1835 and at the University of Virginia from 1835 to 1853. He was head of the Virginia state geological survey from 1835 to 1842, in which role he earned Ruffin's

criticism. In 1834 Ruffin published one of Rogers's first articles, which dealt with greensand marls. See William Ernst, "William Barton Rogers: Ante Bellum Virginia Geologist," *Virginia Cavalcade* 24 (1974–75): 13–20; *DAB* 16:115; Michele L. Aldrich and Alan E. Leviton, "William Barton Rogers and the Virginia Geological Survey, 1835–1842," in James X. Corgan, ed., *The Geological Sciences in the Antebellum South* (University, Ala., 1982), pp. 83–104.

135. "Impressed" is interlined above "possessed."
136. In his first speculations about calcareous manures Ruffin had thought of their effects primarily in relation to acid soils; by the time he owned Marlbourne he had become more confident that they would improve neutral soils also (Ruffin, *Calcareous Manures* [5th ed.], pp. 143–47).
137. See Ruffin, "Account of Draining," Ruffin Papers, ViHi.
138. Brackets in original.
139. The ferruginous clay Ruffin mentioned was a layer of clay containing iron below the surface soils in this section of Marlbourne. A diagram depicting what was probably this particular stratum appeared in Ruffin, "Essays: On Draining," p. 128.
140. Talley's tract, which took its name from a previous owner, belonged to John Pate's estate and was purchased by Ruffin in 1849. The sale apparently was not recorded in the land tax book, though Pate's estate was identified as possessing property bordering Ruffin's (Hanover County, Va., Land Book, 1850, p. 19, Vi [microfilm]; Ruffin, "Account of Draining," p. 40, Ruffin Papers, ViHi).
141. Ever the editor, Ruffin improved the following long passage when he transcribed it from the journal. The changes involved small matters of style, not meaning; and he fell victim to his own handwriting, overlooking a few of his minute commas (Ruffin, Marlbourne Farm Journal, p. 120 [14 Mar. 1845], Vi).
142. "A grip," Ruffin wrote, "is a narrow & shallow rain-ditch, opened by one or two plough furrows in one track, & finished by spade & shovel, to about 12 inches wide & as much of average depth—which will be filled with loose earth by every crop ploughing, & require shoveling out immediately after" (Ruffin, "Account of Draining," note to p. 8, Ruffin Papers, ViHi).
143. "Beds" are the raised land, or "ridges," on which crops are planted between furrows, or drainage depressions. Planting in beds, or in a "ridge and furrow" system, was essential, Ruffin believed, where land was too level to permit rainwater to flow from the surface (Edmund Ruffin, "Essays on Various Subjects of Practical Farming: The Advantages of Ploughing in Wide Beds, Compared to the Ordinary Narrow Beds," *American Farmer* 7 [1851–52]: 20).
144. By "under-furrow" Ruffin probably meant a small furrow ("grip-furrow"), dug along the bottom of an existing depression "with a few extra runnings of the plough" (Ruffin, "Essays: On Draining," p. 7).
145. Brackets in original.
146. "Coultering" is the working of soil with a plow blade or disc that makes vertical cuts.
147. Brackets in original.
148. Ruffin here inserted the following marginal note, written in 1851: "This was a great error, caused by my then ignorance. The great evil of *all* the

low land was its suffering from the quantity of *under-water*—& which was the especial cause of the rain-water lying on the surface & the great need (as then supposed) for mere surface draining."
149. Edmund Ruffin, "The Excavation of Marl Pits, and Carrying out and Applying of Marl," *American Farmer* 7 (1851–52): 208–11, 239–42. Each edition of the *Essay on Calcareous Manures* also contained descriptions of Ruffin's procedure.
150. Ruffin evidently was referring to ridges of land between water furrows; balks usually are ridges left unplowed.
151. The author intended to begin a paragraph here but neglected to indent its first word at the top of his page.
152. Edmund Ruffin, "Essays on Various Subjects of Practical Farming: On Harvesting Corn-Fodder—Different Methods Compared," *American Farmer* 6 (1850–51): 422–26.
153. N. Talley was the overseer; see note 130.
154. In 1844 sons Edmund, Jr., and Julian lived on their farms in Prince George County, and daughter Agnes Ruffin Beckwith lived in Petersburg. Rebecca, Elizabeth, Mildred, Jane, Ella, and Charles remained in Ruffin's household.
155. The author had consulted his farm journal. He took these figures from one of the rare entries mentioning particular slaves by name (Ruffin, Marlbourne Farm Journal, p. 82 ["Sick List"], Vi).
156. Additional evidence for Ruffin's assertions about health appeared in 1849, when he published his costs for medical expenses for slaves in this period (Ruffin, "Farming Profits in Eastern Virginia," p. 5, table III).
157. Susan Travis Ruffin (1793–1846), daughter of Champion and Elizabeth Boush Travis of Williamsburg, married Ruffin in 1813. Her children often begged her to write, but few letters documenting her life or her final illness have survived (Robert J. Travis, *The Travis [Travers] Family and Its Allies* [Savannah, 1954], p. 68; "Marlbourne," Hanover Historical Society *Bulletin*, no. 7 [1972]: 2–3; Agnes Ruffin to Edmund Ruffin, 17 Nov. 1833, Edmund Ruffin, Jr., to Edmund Ruffin, 12 July 1830, n.d. [1833], 7 Jan. 1846, Ruffin Papers, ViHi).
158. Nine of Ruffin's eleven children survived childhood and were still alive in 1851. Five of Ruffin's six daughters remained at Marlbourne in 1851, but disaster was about to strike the family. In 1855 Jane, Ella, and Rebecca all died; in 1860 Elizabeth died, followed in 1861 by Mildred. Julian was killed in battle in 1864.
159. Ruffin's Marlbourne Farm Journal (1844–51) survives in the Virginia State Library and Archives, Richmond.
160. Ruffin, "Essays: On Clover Culture," pp. 257–60, 291–93. Before Ruffin introduced his revised practices, clover was left in the ground and tilled directly into the field. Ruffin believed it was more profitable to harvest, stack, and cure the clover. He devised skewered cocks out of tall stakes driven into the ground. Grass was heaped around the bottom of each stake and then stacked to the top of the stake. Outer layers of grass sheltered the rest of the cock from sun and rain and permitted curing.
161. Ruffin, "On Harvesting Corn-Fodder—Different Methods Compared," pp. 422–26.
162. The scheme appeared as "Proposed schemes of Rotation of Crops," in Ruffin, Marlbourne Farm Journal, p. 254 (following entry for 13 May 1848), Vi.

163. In Ruffin's terminology a "division fence" separated arable fields within a farm.
164. The plan and diagrams were included in "Covered Drains for the corn field of 1847," in Ruffin, Marlbourne Farm Journal, p. 244 (following entry for 1 May 1848), Vi.
165. These terms all referred to small ditches for surface drainage. "Water-furrows" were simply drainage channels dug by plowing between beds. "Cross-grips" were "small ditches about 12 inches wide and a little deeper than the water-furrows," which were "cut across the beds at every small depression which otherwise would retain puddles of rain water" (Ruffin, "Essays: On Draining," p. 7). "Rain ditches" were shallow channels, normally dry at the bottom, designed "to carry off temporary accumulations of water, or to prevent the hurtful accumulations from rain, on the surface of the land"; "grips" were a type of rain ditch (Ruffin, "Account of Draining," note to p. 8, Ruffin Papers, ViHi).
166. Jem Sykes was a member of the original colony of slaves transferred to Marlbourne on 29 December 1843, before the Ruffin family arrived. From the start of the enterprise Ruffin referred to him as foreman, and Sykes's name (and "little" Jem's) appears occasionally—not routinely—in the Marlbourne Farm Journal. The experiment of leaving the farm in charge of Jem Sykes began in the summer of 1847, when Ruffin visited his children in Prince George for nine days. "My foreman, left to himself, has done better than I had feared," he wrote (Ruffin, Marlbourne Farm Journal, pp. 1 [1 Jan. 1844], 12 ["General Description of the Farm" (1844)], 278 [30 Aug. 1847], 364 [4 Apr. 1849], 420–21 [20 June 1850], Vi). Sykes also appears periodically in Ruffin's personal diary (Scarborough, ed., *Diary* 1:86–87 [4 July 1857], 391 [12 Jan. 1860], 2:317 [26 May 1862], 367 [4 July 1862]). He disappeared from Marlbourne and Hanover County after 1864. He and his brother John were present at the farm as late as 29 May 1864. John Sykes had fled with Union raiders on a previous occasion, and Jem had caught him stealing hogs. In June 1864 Ruffin wrote an autobiographical account of Marlbourne in which he recalled Sykes's role at the farm (Ruffin, Diary, pp. 3386, 3397–98 [29 May, 4 June 1864], DLC).
167. Willoughby Newton (1802–1874) served one term as a Whig member of Congress, 1843–45. One of Ruffin's closest friends, he shared an enthusiasm for agricultural reform and the secessionist cause; he was a member of the executive committee of the Virginia State Agricultural Society (U.S. Congress, *Biographical Directory of the American Congress, 1774–1961* [Washington, D.C., 1961], p. 1387).
168. Here Ruffin inserted an offprint of his article "Farming Profits in Eastern Virginia," *American Farmer* 5 (1849–50): 2–11; the article also appeared in the *Southern Planter* 9 (1849): 226–37. This essay, which gained Ruffin wide attention in Virginia and Maryland, contains quantitative evidence and some personal history about the first five years at Marlbourne.
169. The exception Ruffin had in mind was his essay "Desultory Observations on the Application and Action of Putrescent Manures," pp. 135–42. In fact, he did not withdraw completely; in 1845 he was editing an agricultural column for the Richmond *Enquirer* (Edmund Ruffin to James Henry Hammond, 17 May 1845, Hammond Papers, DLC). The *Southern Planter* essay of 1846 appeared first in this column, on 24 May 1845. See also [Edmund Ruffin], "Marl," *Southern Planter* 5 (1845): 99–100.
170. In 1851 Ruffin was working on the fifth edition of *Calcareous Manures*,

which appeared in 1852. His gloomy thought about not finishing this edition might have resulted from momentary frustration in assembling materials. It also was a typical expression of Ruffin's depression after the death of his wife in 1846. He often wrote that he anticipated an early death for himself. Despite the gloom, he still loved writing and editing; he handed the revisions to J. W. Randolph thirteen years before expiring.

171. Samuel Sands (1800–1891) was editor of the *American Farmer* when Ruffin resumed his writing for the public. From Sands's first apprenticeship in 1811 until his death, he worked as a printer and publisher in Baltimore; it was Sands who, in 1814, first set in type the verses of "The Star-Spangled Banner" ("Death of Samuel Sands," *American Farmer*, 10th ser., 10 [1891]: 175). Sands's delight at Ruffin's contributions is evident in his editorial comments (Samuel Sands, "The New Volume—Mr. Ruffin, of Va.," *American Farmer* 6 [1850–51]: 16, and "To Correspondents," ibid., p. 49; Demaree, *American Agricultural Press*, p. 37, n. 65).

172. Ruffin, "Essays: On Draining," pp. 5–8, 33–38, 90–95, 128–31, 177–82.

173. Brackets appear here in the "Incidents" but not in the Marlbourne Farm Journal. In this passage Ruffin combined his journal entries for 16 and 17 April and thoroughly rewrote them. At some point he consulted a calendar and became aware that he had misdated these entries in 1849; the temperature he gave originally in the journal for 18 April was actually recorded on 17 April (Ruffin, Marlbourne Farm Journal, pp. 356–57 [16, 17 Apr. 1849], Vi).

174. The author intended to begin a paragraph here but did not indent the first word at the top of the page.

175. "Larrey's" tract was transferred to Ruffin by James Larry (Hanover County, Va., Land Book, 1850, p. 21, Vi [microfilm]).

176. The reference is to the 300 acres purchased from the estate of John Pate (Hanover County, Va., Land Book, 1850, p. 19, Vi [microfilm]; Ruffin, Marlbourne Farm Journal, pp. 385–86 [8 July 1849], Vi). The property was advertised by Ezekiel S. Talley, commissioner for Pate's estate, in the summer of 1849. The 300 acres, Talley boasted, adjoined "the land of Mr. Edmund Ruffin, the rapid improvement and increased value of whose plantation, by the use of marl, within a very few years, are exciting the admiration and wonder of the natives of old Hanover" (Richmond *Enquirer*, 24 July 1849).

177. See note 5 above.

178. The fourth item on this list was omitted.

179. In his 1843 report Ruffin wrote approvingly of growing peas among corn, a practice he witnessed during his year as agricultural surveyor. "The length and heat of summer in this region, greatly increases the value of the pea crop," he wrote. "Being generally planted among the growing corn, and at a late period of its growth, the peas have enough time and sun to cover the ground well, and to mature, after the corn ceases to grow or to shade the land. This peculiar benefit of a southern climate, in regard to peas, is generally appreciated and availed of; and in this, some approach is made to an alternation of crops" (Ruffin, *Report of the Agricultural Survey of South Carolina*, p. 80).

180. [Edmund Ruffin], "On the Manuring of Arable Lands by Their Own Vegetable Growth—Rotation of Crops," *Farmers' Register* 7 (1839): 561–64; 8 (1840): 7–10.

181. The author did not supply an opening parenthesis.
182. Edmund Ruffin, "Application and Action of Putrescent Manures," *American Farmer* 5 (1849–50): 70–75.
183. Ruffin, "Essays: Clover Culture," pp. 257–60, 291–93.
184. Ruffin, "Wide Beds," pp. 20–22, 49–51.
185. The paper was not inserted.
186. On farm machines and implements of the antebellum period, see Gray, *History of Agriculture* 2:792–800, and Rogin, *Introduction of Farm Machinery*.
187. A table summarizing the amount of labor performed in marling by pitmen and one mule appears in Ruffin, *Calcareous Manures* (5th ed.), p. 338.
188. Ruffin inserted the table after this paragraph; it appears on p. 112. He published the table with slightly different data in the fifth edition of *Calcareous Manures*, p. 188.
189. The Constitution of 1851, produced by what is called the "Reform Convention of 1850–51," extended the franchise to all adult white males. It also reapportioned the legislature and provided for popular election of the governor, judges, county officials, and members of the Board of Public Works. Delegates from the eastern half of the state managed to keep tax rates on slaves at a minimal level (Charles Henry Ambler, *Sectionalism in Virginia from 1776 to 1861* [Chicago, 1910], pp. 261–71; Jack P. Maddex, Jr., *The Virginia Conservatives, 1867–1879: A Study in Reconstruction Politics* [Chapel Hill, 1970], pp. 15–16).
190. Results of the district vote appeared in the Richmond *Enquirer*, 3 Sept. 1850. Ruffin placed tenth in a field of eleven, gaining 134 votes; Dr. Corbin Braxton, who placed first, received 389 votes.
191. Ruffin here inserted his statement clipped from the Richmond *Enquirer*, 9 Aug. 1850. The statement was indeed a concise summary of Ruffin's political views. In it he opposed much of what the forthcoming convention would adopt. Although he said he no longer saw harm in expanded white suffrage, he still favored certain requirements for voting—a long period of residence, payment of state tax, and service in the militia. He accepted popular election of county magistrates but opposed direct election of all higher officials. He saw evil in the caucus system, political patronage, long sessions of the legislature, and borrowing by the state except for defense and war. He addressed this statement to a committee composed of Benjamin R. Blake, Edward C. Pollard, William S. Fontaine, Martin Drewry, Thomas Roane, P. H. Aylett, C. Shelly, N. Talley, D. H. Gregg, "and others." Ruffin's district for this election included King William, Hanover, Caroline, and Spotsylvania counties.
192. John Walker Tomlin (1809–1862), uncle of the man who owned Marlbourne before Ruffin, was a farmer and neighbor of Ruffin in Hanover County (Colvin, *On Deep Water*, p. 51; U.S. Census, Population Schedules, Hanover County, Va., 1850, p. 408, DNA [microfilm]).
193. Edmund, Jr., Julian Calx, and Agnes. In 1842 Agnes Beckwith's furniture was sold at public auction to pay for her husband's debts; Ruffin bought the furniture and loaned it to Agnes, "in consideration of the natural love and affection" he had for her. Agnes's money problems led to later conflict with her father. For an inventory of the furniture, see Indenture by Edmund Ruffin, 3 Jan. 1843, Petersburg, Va., Hustings Court Deed Book 13, 1842–43, pp. 185–86, Vi (microfilm).

194. These daughters were Rebecca, Elizabeth, Mildred, and Jane. Ruffin forgot to provide the *c* in "&c."
195. These were the twins, Ella and Charles.
196. In 1849 and 1850 Ella was attending the school conducted by Moses D. Hoge (1818–1899) in Richmond. Hoge was minister at the Second Presbyterian Church; he later became chaplain of the Confederate Congress and after the Civil War was moderator of the General Assembly of the Southern Presbyterian Church. His boarding and day school for young ladies, at the corner of Franklin and Fifth streets on Shockoe Hill, offered instruction in a range of subjects, for which costs could reach $400 a year.

    Ella Ruffin received highest marks at the end of 1849 in all her courses, including mental philosophy, rhetoric, algebra, geometry, French, Bible recitation, history, spelling, and penmanship. She wrote to Ruffin that she had a "very good report" to send him; she pleaded with her father not think her grades were better than she deserved, for she tried hard "to get perfect ones" (Ella Ruffin to Edmund Ruffin, 15 Dec. 1849, M. D. Hoge, Semi-Monthly Report for Ella Ruffin, 8 Dec. 1849, Ruffin Papers, ViHi; M. D. Hoge, "Boarding and Day School for Young Ladies," pamphlet [1849], ViHi; John Miller Wells, *Southern Presbyterian Worthies* [Richmond, 1936], pp. 105–39).

    Charles apparently was another matter. No record of his school has been found, though Ella reported she had received a letter from him, presumably written at school. "I think he is behaving very well now about writing," she noted. "Does he write any oftener home now?" (Ella Ruffin to Edmund Ruffin, 15 Dec. 1849, Ruffin Papers, ViHi).
197. Ruffin considered this 1851 division of his estate the third distribution. The first occurred when he gave $4,000 to each of the three eldest children between 1835 and 1842; the second followed the death of his wife in 1846.
198. The four were Rebecca, Elizabeth, Mildred, and Jane, for whom Ruffin established rudimentary forms of trust funds. He retained the capital also of Ella and Charles, still minors in 1851; and by that year he had determined not to give Agnes Ruffin Beckwith any more of her portion in fee simple, not trusting the competence of her husband (Ruffin, "Incidents" 2:215–16; Agnes Ruffin Beckwith to Edmund Ruffin, 14 Nov. 1847, Thomas Stanly Beckwith to Edmund Ruffin, 21 Aug. 1854, Edmund Ruffin to Thomas Stanly Beckwith, 25 Sept. 1854, Ruffin Papers, ViHi). On the function of trust funds, and for a discussion of the Ruffin-Beckwith feud, see Lebsock, *Free Women of Petersburg*, pp. 54–86. On Ruffin's estate and the conflicts that erupted in his family, see Allmendinger, *Ruffin*, pp. 79–84, 90–105.
199. Eventually, in 1856, Ruffin did reserve for himself and a granddaughter a portion of his estate worth $32,500, whose capital was managed by Edmund, Jr., and Julian and whose interest provided his retirement income (Edmund Ruffin, Distribution of Estate, 1 Mar. 1856, with codicil dated 4 Sept. 1862, photocopy of typescript in possession of Marion Ruffin Jones, Walkerton, Va.; Scarborough, ed., *Diary* 1:5–6).
200. One small book of Ruffin's accounts does survive (Edmund and Julian Ruffin, Ledger and Accounts, 1828–30, 1855–65, Vi).
201. Ruffin's complexion was described as "florid" in 1862 (Samuel R. Borum, District of Norfolk, pass issued to Ruffin, 28 Mar. 1862, Edmund Ruffin Papers, ViU).

202. Ruffin crossed out "earthly" before "concerns."
203. A few blanks were filled by pencil in Ruffin's hand. The rest were left as they stood.

Volume 3

1. See pp. 63–66, and volume 2, note 104. Ruffin attacked state legislators for their reluctance to pay travel and subsistence expenses for board members and for their impatient criticisms of the board's first meeting (Edmund Ruffin, "The Board of Agriculture, and Its Designed Action," *Farmers' Register* 10 [1842]: 1–2; Edmund Ruffin, "Remarks on the Legislative Debate on the Board of Agriculture," ibid., 10 [1842]: 217–18).

    Ruffin's affiliation with the Board of Agriculture cannot have lasted beyond November 1842, when the third of his three reports to the board was published in the *Farmers' Register* (Edmund Ruffin, "Report to the State Board of Agriculture of Virginia, in Reply to Their Inquiry," ibid., 10 [1842]: 512–17; Swem, *Analysis of Ruffin's* Farmers' Register, p. 132). The board itself appears not to have survived beyond 1842; there were no more notices of meetings after that date.

    The manuscript record of the board's first meeting survives ("Journal of the State Board of Agriculture, First Session, Dec. 6–10, 1841," in Ruffin, Marlbourne Farm Journal, pp. 1–7, Vi). Some of this document was published in "Report of the Board of Agriculture to the General Assembly of Virginia," *Farmers' Register* 9 (1841): 688–90.
2. A reference to his appointment as agricultural surveyor of South Carolina. See pp. 67–68.
3. Ruffin inserted "Feby" after writing and smearing "Jan." The meeting to establish the Virginia State Agricultural Society took place in the State Capitol on 20 January 1845, with 115 delegates present. They drafted a constitution and resolved to raise a permanent fund yielding $1,200 annually ([C. T. Botts], "Farmers' Convention," *Southern Planter* 5 [1845]: 41–45). This new Virginia agricultural society was incorporated in 1845, but it probably did not survive the year; it appears not to have met in 1846. P. D. Bernard of the *Southern Planter* lamented in March 1849 that no state society existed in Virginia and recalled that the one established in 1845 "failed very soon" ([P. D. Bernard], "Virginia Agricultural Society," *Southern Planter* 9 [1849]: 86–89).

    In 1820 Ruffin took part in the founding of the United Agricultural Societies of Virginia ("An Address to the United Agricultural Societies, and a Petition to Congress," *American Farmer* 2 [1820–21]: 337–38; "Constitution of the United Agricultural Societies of Virginia," ibid., p. 340). An earlier Agricultural Society of Virginia came briefly into existence in 1819, with John Taylor as president and Dr. John Adams as secretary (Edmund Ruffin, "Remarks on the Legislative Debate on the Board of Agriculture," *Farmers' Register* 10 [1842]: 218; "From the Memoirs of the 'Society of Virginia, for Promoting Agriculture,'" *American Farmer* 1 [1819]: 126). Ruffin later recalled that this early society survived about eight years; he apparently did not recall the papers it published in the *American Farmer* on grains and manures (Edmund Ruffin, "A Lecture on

the Promotion of Agricultural Improvement . . . ," *American Farmer* 6 [1850–51]: 221–31).
4. Ruffin here inserted a clipping about the proceedings (Richmond *Enquirer*, 24 Jan. 1845).
5. A second society, the Virginia State Agricultural Society, was formed at a convention in Richmond on 20–21 February 1850. Edmund Ruffin, Jr., became one of its vice-presidents. Though the senior Ruffin did not attend the convention, he served in 1851 as chairman of one of its committees ("Agricultural Convention," *Southern Planter* 10 [1850]: 78–81; "Petition," ibid., 11 [1851]: 65–73). The society met again on 18–19 February 1851 and reelected Andrew Stevenson as president ("Meeting of the Virginia State Agricultural Society," ibid., pp. 86–87). It was merged almost silently into the third society, initially called the State Agricultural Society of Virginia, which was organized in 1852 ("Virginia State Agricultural Convention," ibid., 12 [1852]: 81–82; "State Agricultural Convention," ibid., pp. 87–88; Scarborough, ed., *Diary* 1:30 [30 Jan. 1857]).
6. The address was published (Ruffin, "A Lecture on the Promotion of Agricultural Improvement . . . ," pp. 221–31). The great error in southern agricultural societies, Ruffin said, was their unthinking adoption of New England notions about societies and their fairs. He wanted to shift the emphasis on livestock and household manufactures to subjects more pertinent to the South. In South Carolina, for example, he would have emphasized rice culture.
7. Andrew Stevenson (1784–1857), a lawyer and politician, was Speaker of the House of Representatives from 1827 to 1834 and minister to Great Britain from 1836 to 1841; he owned a farm in Albemarle County and sizable acreage in Hanover County at the time Ruffin moved there (U.S. Congress, *Biographical Directory*, p. 1654; Hanover County, Va., Land Book, 1845, no page, Vi [microfilm]).
8. Here Ruffin inserted a one-page printed excerpt from his Maryland address from a source other than the *American Farmer*.
9. The reference was to the series of articles Ruffin published in the *American Farmer* between 1849 and 1851. See pp. 92–94.
10. James Dunwood Brown De Bow (1820–1867) began issuing *De Bow's Review* in 1846. The sketch of Ruffin that De Bow commissioned, the ninth in the "Gallery of Industry and Enterprise" series, is printed as appendix 1.
11. William Boulware (1810–1870), styled Lord Boulware by some contemporaries, was a Princeton graduate (class of 1829) and became professor of languages at Columbian College (now George Washington University). At his marriage he gained possession of Traveller's Rest, a farm in King and Queen County; in 1841 he became minister to Naples. He and Ruffin became close friends after the latter moved to Marlbourne, just twelve miles from Boulware's farm (Ann Todd Rubey, *Speaking of Families: The Tod[d]s of Caroline County, Virginia, and Their Kin* [Columbia, Mo., 1960], p. 1830; *General Catalogue of Princeton University* [Princeton, N.J., 1908], p. 141; Scarborough, ed., *Diary* 2:11–12, n. 3).
12. This was the successful Virginia State Agricultural Society (first called the State Agricultural Society of Virginia), which took over and reorganized its predecessor at a convention in Richmond on 19–20 February 1852. The executive committee was composed of L. E. Harvie, William Boulware, Edwin G. Booth, William G. Overton, and William H. Richardson.

(Of these men, only Richardson had served the previous year on the executive committee of the second society.)

The society thrived until 1861. It established permanent offices in Richmond at the southwest corner of Main and Twelfth streets, upstairs (M. Ellyson, comp., *The Richmond Directory and Business Advertiser, for 1856* [Richmond, 1856], p. 261). It conducted a successful annual fair, promoted research on farming conditions, and encouraged membership among Virginia farmers on an unprecedented scale. Ruffin was its president in 1852, 1857, 1858, and 1859 ("Virginia State Agricultural Convention," pp. 81–82; "State Agricultural Convention," pp. 87–88; Scarborough, ed., *Diary* 1:10, 12, 244, 352 ["Introduction to the attempt," 2 Nov. 1858, 2 Nov. 1859]; Virginia State Agricultural Society, *Journal of Transactions for the Years 1856–57* [n.p., n.d.], p. 28; Edmund Ruffin, "Report of the Agricultural Commissioner," *Southern Planter* 15 [1855]: 5–7; Allmendinger, *Ruffin*, pp. 115–16). The society continued to meet through 22–24 October 1860 and held its fair in October that year ("Journal of Transactions of the Virginia State Agricultural Society," *Southern Planter* 20 [1860]: 737–56). It disappeared from the public record in 1861.

13. Ruffin objected to the role played in earlier societies by nonfarmers, and he favored a research function for such societies. In published statements Ruffin had called for one-year terms for the presidents. He wanted to require members to conduct agricultural experiments and to submit written reports each year, and he proposed appropriating at least half of a society's funds to premiums for "careful and well conducted experiments on subjects of practical agriculture" (Edmund Ruffin, "Plan and Constitution of a Working Agricultural Society," *Farmers' Register* 9 [1841]: 719–20). He thought these proposals would discourage city men from taking over the societies. His emphasis on gathering statistics and conducting research was evident in the new constitution (approved 16 December 1852), which provided premiums for inquiries into agricultural conditions.

    The constitution as finally published did not forbid a second term for the president ("Virginia State Agricultural Convention," p. 81; "Constitution of the Virginia State Agricultural Society," *Southern Planter* 13 [1853]: 17–18). In resigning the presidency to avoid a second term, Ruffin pleaded "ill health and advancing age" ("The State Agricultural Society," ibid., p. 16). His successor, Philip St. George Cocke, served successive terms.

14. The 1852–53 session of the General Assembly was the longest session between the Revolution and the Civil War. It adjourned on 11 April 1853 after nine and one-half months (excluding a summer recess). The Richmond *Enquirer* praised this "working legislature" for dealing with a wide range of public business and passing more than 600 bills, compared to 475 at the previous session ("Final Adjournment of the Legislature," Richmond *Enquirer*, 12, 25 Apr. 1853; Cynthia Miller Leonard, *The General Assembly of Virginia, July 30, 1619–January 11, 1978* [Richmond, 1978], p. 448).

15. Philip St. George Cocke (1809–1861) served as president of the society from 1853 to 1856. One of the wealthiest men Ruffin knew, Cocke owned plantations in Virginia and Mississippi. He was a West Point graduate and in 1861 became a brigadier general in the Confederate army, taking part in the first battle at Bull Run (Manassas). In December 1861 he commit-

ted suicide at his home, Belmead, in Powhatan County (*National Cyclopaedia of American Biography* 4: 181–82; William H. Harrison to Edmund Ruffin, 10 Jan. 1862, Edmund Ruffin Papers, ViU).
16. In his presidential address Ruffin revealed his acceptance of the doctrine that slavery was morally good as well as a profitable system of labor. Though he conceded there had been evil in the slave trade, he insisted that slavery in the South had fostered a refined culture among a "master race" by confining drudgery to the "inferior race," whose condition had been improved in involuntary servitude. He also rehearsed arguments that northern wage labor was a harsh form of slavery. In this address Ruffin acknowledged the influence on his thinking of Elwood Fisher (1808–1862), a proslavery apologist and author of the *Lecture on the North and the South, Delivered before the Young Men's Mercantile Library Association of Cincinnati, Ohio, January 16, 1849* (Portsmouth, Va., 1849). The text of Ruffin's address also appeared in a supplement to the *Southern Planter* 13 (1853): 8–16.

    Among the other communications and essays in this highly productive period of Ruffin's life was a statistical study comparing nine selected Virginia counties (Edmund Ruffin, "Some of the Results of the Improvements of Land by Calcareous Manures on Public Interests in Virginia, in the Increase of Production, Population, General Wealth, and Revenue to the Treasury," Virginia State Agricultural Society, *Journal of Transactions*, 1 [Richmond, 1853]: 10–23). See also Edmund Ruffin, "New Views of the Theory and Laws of Rotation of Crops, and Their Practical Application," ibid., pp. 23–39; Edmund Ruffin, "The Profitable Improvement of Poor Land, and Either Mainly or Entirely from Its Own Resources," ibid., pp. 40–49; and Edmund Ruffin, "Facts and Testimony of Greatly Increased Production from the Use of Miocene Marl on Lands Naturally Poor," ibid., pp. 182–87.
17. Brackets in original. The cryptic quotation refers to the opening and closing words of a section at the start of Ruffin's address. The text inserted here was Edmund Ruffin, *Address to the Virginia Agricultural Society, on the Effects of Domestic Slavery* . . . (Richmond, 1853).
18. William Harvie Richardson (1795–1876) was secretary of the commonwealth from 1832 to 1852 and, as adjutant general of Virginia in 1841, helped to organize an enlarged state militia. An experimental farmer and owner of a farm west of Richmond, he played a role in organizing the state agricultural society founded in 1852; as agent of the society he canvassed the state, increasing membership from 339 to over 5,000 (Charles W. Turner, "William H. Richardson, Friend of the Farmer," *Virginia Cavalcade* 20 [Winter 1971]: 14–20).
19. The fairgrounds were in Monroe Square (now Monroe Park), one mile northwest of Capitol Square (Paul S. Dulaney, *The Architecture of Historic Richmond* [2d ed.; Charlottesville, Va., 1976], p. 157).
20. An auditorium on Franklin Street, between Thirteenth and Fourteenth streets, Metropolitan Hall was formerly the First Presbyterian Church. It was remodeled in 1853 by Robert A. Mayo and accommodated 1,500 people (Virginius Dabney, *Richmond: The Story of a City* [Garden City, N.Y., 1976], p. 144).
21. Lewis E. Harvie (1809–1887), a developer of the Richmond and Danville Railroad, became president of the line in 1856. He accompanied Jefferson Davis on the train to Danville after the evacuation of Richmond in April

1865. A resident of Amelia County, he was a member of the Virginia House of Delegates from 1841 to 1850 and a prosecession delegate to the state secession convention in 1861 (William H. Gaines, Jr., *Biographical Register of Members, Virginia State Convention of 1861, First Session* [Richmond, 1969], p. 43). Ruffin, who spent his final days in refuge at Redmoor Farm in northern Amelia County, reported Harvie's return to the county in the spring of 1865 (Ruffin, Diary, p. 3983 [24 Apr. 1865], DLC).

22. Ruffin inserted the resolutions as they appeared in the Richmond *Whig*, 3 Nov. 1853. Harvie's three brief resolutions dealt with subscriptions for a permanent fund for the society.

23. Winfield Scott (1786–1866), general-in-chief in the Mexican War, was the Whig candidate for president in 1852. Ruffin disliked Scott and in spelling his first name insisted on retaining the *g*, which he accused Scott of dropping (Richard B. Morris, *Encyclopedia of American History* [New York, 1953], pp. 712–13; Scarborough, ed., *Diary* 1:106–7 [21 Sept. 1857]).

24. John Tyler (1790–1862), tenth president of the United States, was one of the few major political figures with whom Ruffin remained on consistently friendly terms. Ruffin's account of a visit at Tyler's home in Charles City County, across the river from Coggin's Point, was recorded in Scarborough, ed., *Diary* 1:122–33 (11–14 Nov. 1857), 617–20.

25. William Cabell Rives (1792–1868) attended William and Mary, where he and Ruffin were "fellow-lodgers." Rives became a congressman and senator from Virginia and was twice minister to France. With John Tyler and Judge Thomas Ruffin of North Carolina, Ruffin's distant cousin, Rives attended the peace convention of 1861 in Washington. Ruffin despised him. See U.S. Congress, *Biographical Directory*, p. 1524; Scarborough, ed., *Diary* 2:10–11 (26 Apr. 1861).

26. See volume 2, note 167.

27. At this point Ruffin inserted newspaper clippings (which he dated by year only) from the Richmond *Whig*, 6 Apr. 1852; Petersburg *Southside Democrat*, n.d. [1852]; Washington, D.C., *National Intelligencer*, 29 Oct. 1853; and Fredericksburg *News*, n.d. [1852].

28. In the earlier years of the century, George Washington Parke Custis (1781–1857), grandson of Martha Washington, stepgrandson of George Washington, and father-in-law of R. E. Lee, had been an active promoter of agricultural reform through such writings as *An Address to the People . . . on the Importance of Encouraging Agriculture . . .* (Alexandria, 1808) and through annual agricultural fairs held on his northern Virginia estate, Arlington (Sara B. Bearss, "The Farmer of Arlington: George W. P. Custis and the Arlington Sheep Shearings," *Virginia Cavalcade* 38 [1988–89]: 124–33). On Custis's address to the United States Agricultural Society, which took place in 1853, not 1852 as noted by Ruffin, see George W. P. Custis to Francis Nelson, 30 June 1853, George W. P. Custis Papers, ViW. In acknowledgment of Custis's remarks, Ruffin presented him with a copy of the latest edition of his *Essay on Calcareous Manures* (George W. P. Custis to Francis Nelson, 24 Apr. 1854, ibid.).

29. Here Ruffin inserted an undated newspaper clipping about Custis's remarks (Washington, D.C., *National Intelligencer*, 29 Sept. 1853). He also inserted an extract from an address to the Virginia State Agricultural Society by John R. Edmunds of Halifax County on 2 November 1853, printed in an unnamed newspaper. Accounts of Edmunds's address appeared in most Richmond newspapers as well as the society's transactions;

Ruffin probably got his clipping from an edition of the Richmond *Whig*, 3 Nov. 1853.
30. Ruffin here reverted to his discussion of addresses delivered before the Virginia State Agricultural Society in November 1853.
31. Socrates Maupin (1809–1871) became professor of chemistry at the Richmond Medical College in 1846 and assumed a similar position at the University of Virginia in 1853 (*National Cyclopaedia of American Biography* 13:134).
32. Nathaniel Francis Cabell (1807–1891) practiced law briefly in Prince Edward County and after 1832 lived on his farm in Nelson County, where he collected documents on the history of agriculture in Virginia (Alfred J. Morrison, *College of Hampden Sidney: Dictionary of Biography* [Hampden-Sydney, Va., 1921], pp. 262–63).
33. John R. Edmunds (1812–1873), farmer and lawyer from Halifax County, was a member for three terms of the Virginia House of Delegates and served as president of the agricultural society (David L. Pulliam, *The Constitutional Conventions of Virginia . . .* [Richmond, 1901], p. 105).
34. Ruffin here inserted unidentified clippings containing extracts from the report of the Committee on Honorary Testimonials and from John Tyler's speech to the society. The testimonials appeared in the Virginia State Agricultural Society, *Journal of Transactions*, 1 (Richmond, 1853): 118; Tyler's speech appeared in ibid., p. 131, and was reported in the Richmond *Examiner*, 8 Nov. 1853.

Two pages of newspaper clippings follow in the manuscript, all bearing testimony to Ruffin's contributions. Ruffin did not identify the source of the first clipping; it appears to be from the Petersburg *Daily Express*. A second clipping, "Mr. Ruffin's Address," was taken from an unnamed North Carolina newspaper. The third clipping has no identification; the fourth was an editorial in the Richmond *Examiner*, 1853. A fifth undated clipping, giving an account of the Virginia state fair in 1853, came from the Washington, D.C., *National Intelligencer*, 19 Nov. 1853. Finally, Ruffin included an editorial lauding his discoveries taken from the Fredericksburg *Virginia Herald*, n.d. [1853].
35. The author forgot the closing quotation mark.
36. The author here inserted an imperfect copy of his *Address on the Opposite Results of Exhausting and Fertilizing Systems of Agriculture, Read before the South-Carolina Institute at Its Fourth Annual Fair, November 18th, 1852* (Charleston, 1853). His reference to this address follows two paragraphs later.
37. Ruffin was referring to Alain-René Lesage, *Gil Blas de Santillane* (1715–35).
38. A report of the address appeared in the Charleston *Mercury*, 19 Nov. 1852.
39. Ruffin did not close the parenthesis.
40. In a marginal note here Ruffin referred the reader to pp. 14, 19, and 22 of his address, which he had inserted into the manuscript after p. 244.
41. Edmund Ruffin, "Southern Agricultural Exhaustion, and Its Remedy," U.S. Senate, *Report of the Commissioner of Patents for the Year 1852*, Part 2: *Agriculture*, 32d Cong., 2d sess., 1852, Executive Document 55 (Washington, D.C., 1853), pp. 373–89.
42. Ruffin here inserted newspaper clippings containing the printed text of his anonymous article "What Will Be the Results of the Northern Aboli-

tion Action?" from the Richmond *Enquirer*, 22, 25 Jan., 2 Apr. 1850. The installments were signed by "A Virginian."
43. Ruffin here inserted the text of his article "The Armed Truce" from the Charleston *Mercury*, 7 Nov. 1851. The article was signed "A Virginian." In fact, Ruffin continued to write on political matters for the newspapers through the first year of the Civil War.
44. Rebecca Ruffin married John T. Bland in October 1851, Julian Ruffin married Charlotte S. Meade in May 1852, and Elizabeth Ruffin married William Sayre in October 1852, bringing to five the number of his married children.
45. The exception at this time was Elizabeth, who was living near Norfolk with her husband, William Sayre. The other four—Edmund, Jr., Agnes, Julian, and Rebecca—were living in Prince George.
46. Ruffin referred to Mildred, Jane, and Ella. Jane married John J. Dupuy in 1854 and died in 1855; Ella died unmarried in 1855; Mildred married Burwell B. Sayre in 1859 and died in 1862.
47. Ruffin was fifty-nine and would live until 1865, aged seventy-one; he would observe his sixtieth birthday on 5 January 1854.
48. "Proportion" is interlined above "share."
49. Charles abandoned his studies in 1852 at the Virginia Military Institute and began to search for employment as an engineer on railroad construction projects; eventually he, too, settled on a farm in Prince George County (Virginia Military Institute, *Register of Former Cadets* [Lexington, Va., 1927], p. 8; Edmund Ruffin to Jefferson Davis, 27 Aug. 1861, Ruffin Papers, ViHi).
50. Edmund Quintus Ruffin (b. 1839) died 21 March 1853 of a disease diagnosed as typhoid fever by his uncle, Dr. T. Stanly Beckwith; Edmund Quintus's older sister Virginia (b. 1837) died in 1844 at the age of seven (Edmund Ruffin, Jr., to Edmund Ruffin, 16 Apr. 1853, Ruffin Papers, ViHi; Scarborough, "The Ruffin Family: Children and Grandchildren of Edmund Ruffin," p. xiii).
51. The reference is to a page containing the "Statement of Marl applied, & Grain Crops made on Marlbourne Farm." See p. 112 above.
52. See volume 2, note 192.

In Remembrance of Jane Dupuy

1. John J. Dupuy (1822–1898), a physician in Prince George County, was Ruffin's nephew, son of William J. and Jane Ruffin Dupuy; he married Ruffin's daughter Jane in 1854 (William Jones Dupuy family Bible records, ViHi; Scarborough, ed., *Diary* 1:45).
2. Brackets in original. Here Ruffin inserted two pages of notes by his daughter Elizabeth Ruffin Sayre ("E.S."), who lived near Norfolk. He copied her notes in his own hand and introduced them with a paragraph of his own in brackets.
3. Brackets in original.
4. Brackets in original; this was probably Ruffin's intrusion.
5. Brackets in original.
6. Edmund Christian Murdaugh (b. 1822), an alumnus of the College of William and Mary, was the Episcopal minister in 1855 at Brandon Church

in Martin's Brandon Parish and Grace Church in Southwark Parish (*Provisional List of Alumni of the College of William and Mary in Virginia*, p. 29; Peyton Harrison, "Letter from Peyton Harrison, Visits to Berkeley, Etc.," *VMHB* 37 [1929]: 343; *Journal of the Sixty-first Annual Convention of the Protestant Episcopal Church in Virginia* . . . [Richmond, 1856], p. 149).
7. In this paragraph Ruffin shifted back to Elizabeth Sayre's notes. Brackets in original.
8. Brackets in original. This was probably an intrusion by Ruffin.
9. Brackets in original.
10. Here a loose piece of paper, one-third the size of sheets in volume 3, was inserted. On one side appears a note in Ruffin's hand, written in pencil after Ella Ruffin's death in August:

"Would it were, for my consolation, & for much better reasons, that I possessed that perfect & undoubting faith & clear perception, which others enjoy, of the future life & happiness of the virtuous & pious dead. But if the all-just & all-merciful God has ordained perfect & eternal happiness to be the reward for any of his creatures—sinful even when most free from sin—then no one can be more confident than I am that, both my beloved children are enjoying heavenly happiness. And if it be possible that the measure of such happiness could be increased, how much must that increase have been, by the meeting of the pure spirits of these loving sisters, so soon after their mournful separation on earth!"

On the reverse side the following notes appear, also in pencil and in Ruffin's hand:

"M. S. Notes, written by E. S. & E. R.—or extracts.
Prayer.
Extracts from
Bring 'Bring Flowers'—& fragments of 'Carolan's Prophecy.'
Music
I will arise
Bring Flowers
Carolan's Lament

One or more of
The last rose of Summer
I'll remember thee
Roslin Castle"

At the bottom of this sheet, upside down and encircled, are these figures:

"132.50
84.28
$ 48.22 = Check"
11. Brackets in this long paragraph are in the original. The paragraph was written in the voice of Ruffin, from his point of view.
12. The reference is to Ruffin's half sister Jane Ruffin Dupuy, who was both aunt and mother-in-law to Ruffin's daughter.
13. Brackets here and in the following paragraph are in the original text.
14. Ruffin omitted the word *been*.
15. Ruffin omitted the closing quotation mark.
16. Here is evidence that Charles and Edmund Ruffin had not joined other members of the family in experiencing religious conversion.
17. The reference is to Agnes Ruffin Beckwith.

18. Charlotte Meade Ruffin (1833–1918) had married Julian C. Ruffin in 1852; as a widow after the Civil War she owned and managed the portion of Marlbourne on which Ruffin's house stood (Colvin, *On Deep Water*, pp. 55, 93–95).
19. Brackets in original.
20. Brackets in original.
21. Dr. John J. Dupuy, Jane's husband.
22. Ruffin's own narrative resumes in this paragraph.
23. The graveyard is in a wooded area above the west bank of Powell's Creek, between Point Field and Point Swamp. It is downstream (north) from the old landing, at the point where the creek bends to the northeast.
24. The prayers probably were offered at Brandon Church; the reference, however, could have been to Merchants Hope Church (William Meade, *Old Churches, Ministers, and Families of Virginia* [2 vols.; Philadelphia, 1857], 1:437–38). Meade's account of the parish drew on notes by Ruffin.
25. Felicia Dorothea Brown Hemans (1793–1835) published *Songs of the Affections* (Edinburgh, 1830).
26. Ruffin inserted this quotation on a quarter-sheet of paper and bound it into the volume. The correct chapter number is 18.
27. Ruffin's granddaughter Jane Ruffin Dupuy died of diphtheria on 12 August 1864, at the age of nine (Ruffin, Diary, pp. 3543–44 [entry for 17 Aug. 1864], DLC).

In Remembrance of Ella Ruffin

1. Ella's physician at Beechwood may have been John J. Dupuy, husband of her sister Jane. Dupuy certainly attended Jane during her long illness. T. Stanly Beckwith, husband of Agnes Ruffin Beckwith, also may have been consulted; he offered at least one assessment of Jane's condition, and he attended Rebecca Ruffin Bland at her death in November 1855 (Edmund Ruffin, Jr., to Edmund Ruffin, [1855], Agnes Beckwith to Edmund Ruffin, Jr., 29 Nov. 1855, Agnes Beckwith to Edmund Ruffin, 2 Dec. 1855, Ruffin Papers, ViHi; Ella Ruffin, note in Elizabeth Ruffin to Julian C. Ruffin, 26 Apr. 1855, Ruffin and Meade Family Papers, NcU).
2. Probably Henry Curtis (b. ca.1792), a Hanover County doctor later attached to the First Virginia Regiment (Wyndham B. Blanton, *Medicine in Virginia in the Nineteenth Century* [Richmond, 1933], p. 319; U.S. Census, Population Schedules, Hanover County, Va., 1850, p. 413, DNA [microfilm]).
3. The advice probably came from Thomas F. Withers (b. ca.1791), a physician of Fauquier County, Va., who lived a short journey from the springs (U.S. Census, Population Schedules, Fauquier County, Va., 1850, p. 221, DNA [microfilm]). On the day Ella died, Julian C. Ruffin wrote to his father at Red Sweet Springs that he doubted Ella was as ill as Dr. Withers indicated (Julian C. Ruffin to Edmund Ruffin, 24 Aug. 1855, Ruffin Papers, ViHi).
4. Eliza Price (b. ca.1805) was the Fincastle hotel keeper who offered compassion to the travelers (U.S. Census, Population Schedules, Botetourt County, Va., 1850, p. 134, DNA [microfilm]; U.S. Census, Population Schedules, Botetourt County, Va., 1860, p. 132, DNA [microfilm]).
5. The daughter who helped the Ruffins was Martha S. Nelson (b. ca.1828),

wife of Robert B. Nelson (b. ca.1823), a young physician of Fincastle (U.S. Census, Population Schedules, Botetourt County, Va., 1850, p. 125, DNA [microfilm]; Botetourt County, Va., Register of Marriages [1770–1853], Part 2, p. 464, Vi).

6. Ella Ruffin was buried in the family plot at Marlbourne.

Appendix 1

1. The dates of Ruffin's service in the War of 1812 indicate that he volunteered with a Prince George company in the Fourth Virginia Regiment. This regiment served between 1 August 1812 and 31 January 1813, before the British fleet arrived in Hampton Roads; the regiment was stationed the entire six months at Fort Norfolk (Stuart Lee Butler, *A Guide to Virginia Militia Units in the War of 1812* [Athens, Ga., 1988], pp. 17–19, 178–79, 227; see also Scarborough, ed., *Diary* 1:42, 460 [1 Mar. 1857, 7 Sept. 1860]).

    Ruffin's later recollections of the War of 1812 indicate that he served also during crises of 1813 and 1814, when the local militia was called to meet threats from the British fleet on the James River. Ruffin recalled in particular the loyalty of slaves to their masters during that war. See Edmund Ruffin, "Consequences of Abolition Agitation," *De Bow's Review* 23 (1857): 551–52. This account reappeared in Edmund Ruffin, *Anticipations of the Future, to Serve as Lessons for the Present Time* (1860; Freeport, N.Y., 1972), pp. 392–93. A brief, early version appeared in the Richmond *Enquirer*, 25 Jan. 1850; Ruffin pasted this version into the "Incidents" (see Ruffin, "Incidents" 3:254).

2. Boulware must have taken material for the preceding paragraph from Edmund Ruffin, "First Views Which Led to Marling," p. 659 (see appendix 3).

3. Ruffin obviously supplied Boulware with the text of his 1843 address in Prince George County, as published in the Charleston *Mercury*, 5 Feb. 1844. Excerpts also appeared in "Ruffin's Agricultural Address," *Farmers' Cabinet* 8 (1843–44): 270–72.

4. Boulware's reference was to Vergil (70–19 B.C.), Roman poet, author of the *Aeneid*. In his *Georgics* he envisioned a golden age of rejuvenation in the agriculture and population of rural Italy. According to Vergil, it was actually love, not labor, that conquers all (*Omnia vincit Amor* [*Eclogues* 10.69]).

5. This paragraph indicates Boulware was drawing also upon the third edition of *Calcareous Manures* and Ruffin, "Former Poor and Exhausted Condition," pp. 113–14.

6. At this point Boulware drew again upon Ruffin, "First Views Which Led to Marling," pp. 659–60.

7. The wording closely follows Ruffin's in "First Views Which Led to Marling," p. 661. "What was then to be done?" asked Ruffin. Much of the following material is from this page, including the quotations. Ruffin spoke of Davy's book as his "oracle."

8. Humphry Davy, *Elements of Agricultural Chemistry, in a Course of Lectures for the Board of Agriculture* (Fredericksburg, Va., 1815).

9. Joseph Banks (1743–1820), president of the Royal Society, was a leading patron of science in Britain (*DNB* 1:1049–53).

10. Here Boulware was writing his own prose.
11. David Rittenhouse (1732–1796) of Philadelphia, astronomer and inventor, made calculations of the transit of Venus in 1769 and discovered the atmosphere of that planet. His surveys of colonial boundaries included a calculation later accepted by Mason and Dixon. He was the first director of the United States Mint (*DAB* 15:630–32).
12. This was the 1818 address to which Ruffin referred in his memoirs (see p. 28, above).
13. The table appeared in the third edition of *Calcareous Manures* (1842), p. 254. It had its origin in the table Ruffin drew for George Blow in 1823 (Edmund Ruffin, "Table of Crops made on Coggin's Point Farm," 1823, Blow Family Papers, ViW). It was first published in Ruffin, "Former Poor and Exhausted Condition," p. 114. It reappeared in expanded form in the fifth edition of *Calcareous Manures* (1852), p. 184, with data through 1851. Boulware's figure for 1843 corn production (4,675 bushels) differed from the figure Ruffin eventually determined (3,380 bushels) (see appendix 5).
14. The petition certainly was among the earliest received by Congress on the tariff but not the first. On 3 January 1820 a petition from another agricultural society in Virginia was read in Congress and referred to the Commerce Committee ("Remonstrance of the Virginia Agricultural Society of Fredericksburg," *American Farmer* 1 [1819–20]: 332–33). The petition from the United Agricultural Societies of Virginia was drawn up on 10 January 1820; among its signers was Thomas Cocke (ibid., pp. 347–49). For another reference by Ruffin to the petitions of 1820, see volume 2, note 25, above.
15. The House of Representatives established its Committee on Agriculture in 1820; the Senate waited until 1825.
16. The tariff of 1820 passed by a vote of 91 to 78 in the House; it failed by a single vote in the Senate.
17. "An Address to the Public from the Delegation of the United Agricultural Societies of Virginia," *American Farmer* 2 (1820–21): 57–59; "An Address to the United Agricultural Societies of Virginia," ibid., pp. 337–40; "Report on the Navigation Laws," ibid., 3 (1821–22): 321–25. Earl G. Swem did not attribute any of these petitions to Ruffin with certainty, but Ruffin was involved in their composition; see Swem, *Analysis of Ruffin's* Farmers' Register, p. 127.
18. Ruffin represented the district including Sussex, Surry, Southampton, Isle of Wight, Prince George, and Greensville counties during three sessions of the legislature, 1823–24, 1824–25, and 1825–26. He served on the Committee on Internal Improvements and opposed creation of new counties in western Virginia as well as the rechartering of the Farmer's Bank of Virginia (Henry G. Ellis, "Edmund Ruffin: His Life and Times," *John P. Branch Historical Papers of Randolph-Macon College*, 3 [1910]: 104–5; Leonard, *General Assembly of Virginia*, pp. 318–36). Boulware's reference to 1824 reflects Ruffin's faulty recollection of the date his first session began (1 Dec. 1823).
19. For Ruffin's list of contributors, see J. G. de Roulhac Hamilton, ed., "Writers of Anonymous Articles in the *Farmer's Register*," *Journal of Southern History* 23 (1957): 90–102. Publication began in 1833, not 1832.
20. Tidewater lands had increased in value by $17,260,521.31 between 1838 and 1850, according to tax records cited by Governor Joseph Johnson in his message of 12 January 1852 (Richmond *Enquirer*, 13 Jan. 1852). Boul-

ware was accepting a thesis Ruffin had developed that an agricultural rejuvenation in Tidewater Virginia had occurred, leading to an increase in population (including slaves) and land values. Ruffin supported the thesis through a study of nine counties, using census returns and assessment records at the state auditor's office in Richmond. He, in turn, accepted the figures in Johnson's address (Edmund Ruffin, "Communication to the Virginia State Agricultural Society: Some of the Results of the Improvements of Land by Calcareous Manures," *Southern Planter* 12 [1852]: 258–70; Ruffin, "Southern Agricultural Exhaustion, and Its Remedy," p. 375).

The thesis of a successful agricultural adjustment is supported by Emmett B. Fields, "The Agricultural Population of Virginia, 1850–1860" (Ph.D. diss., Vanderbilt University, 1953), pp. 81–83, and Craven, *Soil Exhaustion*, pp. 142–61. For a skeptical treatment of marling and diversification as causes of agricultural rejuvenation, see Mathew, *Edmund Ruffin and the Crisis of Slavery*, pp. 105–9, 123–26; Mathew does concede that marling raised land values. Paul W. Gates indicates that although land values were comparatively low in Virginia, the state had made a "notable agricultural comeback" by 1860 (Gates, *Farmer's Age*, pp. 112–13).

Appendix 2

1. In 1840, before Beechwood House was built, Edmund Ruffin, Jr., and his family lived in the small cottage now in the yard of the larger house.
2. Mary C. Ruffin, the wife of Edmund, Jr.
3. Cocke was buried at Tarbay.
4. Cocke married Sarah Colley (b. 1793), a woman nineteen years his junior, in 1810; they had two children, Nathaniel Colley Cocke (1820–1863) and Martha Cocke, who married James Cocke (Smith, *Smith of Scotland Neck*, p. 197).
5. Benjamin Cocke (1781–1836) died insolvent. His son, Richard Eppes Cocke (1824–1896), after inheriting Appomattox Manor in Prince George County from a maternal uncle, changed his name to Richard Eppes in 1840 at the request of his mother (Eppes family Bible records, Eppes Family Muniments, ViHi).
6. This was James B. Cocke, owner of Bonaccord, in Prince George County.
7. Ruffin here placed an asterisk without indicating an insertion into the text.
8. Cocke still owned Aberdeen, which his son, Nathaniel, was managing.
9. At this point Ruffin attached nearly a full page of manuscript to the top of manuscript page 8, revising his original text slightly by crossing it out and pasting over it. He thereby deleted one sentence in which he had written, "Death must have been instantaneous."
10. At this point Ruffin concluded the revisions he attached to the top of manuscript page 8.
11. The son-in-law also was named James Cocke (Smith, *Smith of Scotland Neck*, p. 199).
12. A detached kitchen stood on the west side of the house at Tarbay; Cocke must have walked toward the deep ravine to the east (Mutual Assurance Company of Virginia, Revaluation no. 2184, Nathaniel Colley, 5 Aug. 1816, Vi [microfilm]).

Appendix 3

1. Ruffin had studied Thomas Hale, *A Compleat Body of Husbandry: Containing Rules for Performing, in the Most Profitable Manner, the Whole Business of the Farmer and Country Gentleman* (4 vols.; London, 1758–59).
2. John Beale Bordley, *Essays and Notes on Husbandry and Rural Affairs* (Philadelphia, 1799).
3. John Taylor, *Arator; Being a Series of Agricultural Essays, Practical & Political: In Sixty-One Numbers* (2d ed.; Georgetown, D.C., 1814). This edition, the first to appear under Taylor's name, may have been the one Ruffin examined initially. An earlier anonymous edition appeared in 1813; it gathered together a series of newspaper essays (Freda F. Stohrer, "*Arator:* A Publishing History," *VMHB* 88 [1980]: 442–45). Ruffin certainly owned a copy of the third edition of *Arator* (Baltimore, 1817), for he referred to "strongly marked passages" of that edition in *An Essay on Calcareous Manures* (1st ed.), p. 35. (The quotations he took from the third edition contain minor inaccuracies.) Ruffin himself published the seventh edition of *Arator* in the *Farmers' Register* 8 (1840): 703–72.
4. Cocke was still alive when this essay was written; Tarbay bordered Ruffin's farm on the west.
5. Humphry Davy, *Elements of Agricultural Chemistry, in a Course of Lectures for the Board of Agriculture* (Fredericksburg, Va., 1815).
6. Brackets in original.
7. See appendix 1, note 9.
8. [Ruffin's note]: I was not then aware, of the important and novel fact which I afterwards ascertained and established, and now fully received (with very slight acknowledgement of its source) by the geologists of this country, that *almost all the soils* on the Atlantic slope of this country, and even including nearly all limestone soils, are also entirely destitute of *carbonate* of lime, though that ingredient seemed universal in all the good soils of England, and the continent of Europe.
9. All such references in this essay are to Ruffin, *Calcareous Manures* (2d ed.).
10. Henry Home, Lord Kames (1696–1782), Scottish judge, produced several works on agricultural improvement (*DNB* 9:1126–28).
11. The Agricultural Society of Prince George must have formed about 1818, when Ruffin delivered his address. Similar societies were forming then in other Tidewater counties. Though the Prince George society was still functioning at the end of 1821, it appears to have disbanded shortly after that time (Ruffin, "On the Composition of Soils," pp. 313, 316). A new society formed in Prince George in the spring of 1842 (Edmund Ruffin, "First Labors of a Working Agricultural Society," *Farmers' Register* 10 [1842]: 523–24).
12. Ruffin was referring to his 1818 address to the Agricultural Society of Prince George (see volume 2, note 23, above). The following quotations, taken from passages in that address, indicate that Ruffin still had the text in his possession in 1839. They did not appear in the text of his 1821 essay for the *American Farmer*, "On the Composition of Soils," which clearly was composed in 1821 and may have been a thorough revision of his 1818 remarks. The quotations he inserted here may be the only surviving fragments of Ruffin's first writing on the subject of calcareous manures.

13. Asterisks are in the original publication.
14. Asterisks are in the original publication.
15. Ruffin referred to *The American Edition of the New Edinburgh Encyclopedia: Conducted by David Brewster* (21 vols., Philadelphia, 1813–32). Brewster issued the first volumes of this multivolume work in Edinburgh in 1808.
16. Edward Marks (1775–1822) was a neighbor at Coggin's Point; Ruffin maintained close relations with his family for years (Mrs. John Bennett Boddie, ed., *Historical Southern Families*, 19 [Baltimore, 1974]: 131).
17. "Yellow marl" and "blue marl" were terms Ruffin used in describing marl. They were distinguished not merely by color; yellow marl usually was found above blue marl, if the two were found together. Yellow marl predominated in the eastern Tidewater, blue marl in the western Tidewater. See Ruffin, *Calcareous Manures* (5th ed.), pp. 441–46. Marl Pit 7 was at the northwest edge of Finnie's Field, near the slope leading down to the river shore and Tar Bay. Marl Pit 9 was next to the eastern fork of Ruffin's Brook, between the farm road and Court House Field. It is one of the pits still visible.
18. Marl Pit 1 was near the center of Middle Field, across the farm road from Court House Field. Marl Pit 8 was in Ruffin's Valley, next to Ruffin's Brook.
19. [Ruffin's note]: See Exp. 10, p. 43 Essay on Cal. Man.
20. Finnie's Field and Court House Field formed the easternmost part of Coggin's Point Farm.
21. Brackets in original.
22. Brackets in original.
23. [Ruffin's note]: Exp. 11, p. 45.
24. [Ruffin's note]: Exp. 1 to 4, pp. 37 to 40.
25. Ruffin, "Former Poor and Exhausted Condition," pp. 112–16.

Appendix 4

1. [Ruffin's note]: Within the last few weeks, the reporter visited all the farms concerning which information of recent date will be given below, and submitted the queries to their several proprietors, and obtained and wrote down their answers; which answers were by them afterwards examined, corrected where deemed necessary, and finally approved. In each case, with the queries, a copy of the 'Essay on Calcareous Manures' was presented, for the purpose of enabling all to reply, with full understanding, on the subject of the 23d query; and the several answers to this last query were not taken at first, with the others, but only after time had been afforded for the deliberate reading and consideration of the pages referred to, and which are republished at a preceding page, (481,) [Editor's note: The page number refers to the original printing of the "Queries" in the *Farmers' Register*] for general reference. Such a mode of personal examination was by no means necessary; but it was resorted to in this case, both because published queries had been formerly tried in vain, and because, in the first beginning of this investigation, the explanations of the reporter might be needed, to make clear his own meaning, in queries which perhaps previously had been too obscurely stated; and which queries, after being thus tested by some trial, have been in part recast, and made more comprehensive, as well as more precise and clear,

than in their first form. The several answers were given, (and, as above stated, the purport written down as soon as expressed,) by each individual, without his knowing what any other had answered; except in one instance of joint operations in marling, and also in regard to the reporter's own answers, which were prepared after his being in possession of most of the others. Therefore, there was nothing of the opinions or facts of others furnished to serve either to guide or to test and correct any one's estimate or supposition of amounts and values. This, together with the circumstance that quantities and values are almost always stated upon mere supposition and by guess, and without any aid of previously written statements of precise measurements, will serve satisfactorily to account for much diversity in the estimates of products and values. But such diversity, under the circumstances stated, instead of impairing the value of the testimony, would strengthen it, in regard to the good faith of the witnesses, and their intention to furnish correct answers, in the mind of any judicious reader who might not know the other good and sufficient claims of these highly respectable individuals to entire confidence on that score.—ED.

2. Page numbers refer to Ruffin, *Calcareous Manures* (2d ed.).
3. James B. Cocke (d. 1865) was the nephew of Thomas Cocke and owner of Bonaccord, a farm in Prince George County near Aberdeen (Boddie, *Southside Virginia Families* 1:151). Only Cocke's response to Ruffin's first question is reprinted here, together with the note Ruffin wrote explaining the early experiment. Ruffin's own response, reprinted here in full, appeared as the last of eleven completed questionnaires.
4. James Cocke (d. 1783) of Bonaccord, Prince George County, was a member of his county's Committee of Safety in 1775. During the Revolution he commanded the cruiser *Raleigh* on its patrols of the James River. He and his wife, Elizabeth Poythress Cocke (d. 1800), had five children, of whom Thomas Cocke was the third (Smith, *Smith of Scotland Neck*, p. 197).
5. Ruffin wrote this paragraph about the old Bonaccord experiment in 1839, indicating that it took place about 1769; it was the earliest marling experiment Ruffin discovered. The page number refers to the second edition of the *Essay on Calcareous Manures* (1835), where Ruffin first published accounts of Bonaccord and about John Singleton's early experiments in Talbot County, Maryland (pp. 36, 89).
6. The page number refers to the second edition of the *Essay*.
7. Ruffin was not consistent in using the apostrophe in *Coggin's Point*. He also was inconsistent in recalling the month of his first application; in some accounts it was January, and in others, February.

Index

Aberdeen Farm, Prince George Co., Va., 184, 193, 261 n. 3
Acid soil, 171–72, 194–95
Addresses by ER:
  in Georgia, 126
  in Maryland, 123–24
  to Prince George farmers (1843), 68–69, 168–69, 177–78
  to Prince George society (1818), 28, 173, 198–201, 259 n. 12
  in South Carolina, 132–33
  to Virginia State Agricultural Society, 128
Agricultural Chemistry (Davy). *See* Davy, Humphry
Agricultural crisis, 26–27, 168–69, 193–94
Agricultural reform, 174–78
Agricultural societies. *See also* Agricultural Society of Prince George; Virginia State Agricultural Society
  of Edgecombe, N.C., 133
  in Georgia, 125–26, 134
  in Maryland, 123
  New York State Agricultural Society, 55
  Southern Central Agricultural Society, 125–26, 134
  United Agricultural Societies of Virginia, 28, 175, 247 n. 3
  United States (National) Agricultural Society, 130
  in Virginia, 123–24, 126–32
Agricultural Society of Prince George, 198, 259 n. 11
  ER's address to (1818), 28, 173, 198–201, 259 n. 12
  and tariff, 175

Amelia County, Va., 10, 20–21, 129
American Farmer, 28, 59, 88, 124
Arator (Taylor). *See* Taylor, John
Archimedes, 173
Association of Southern and Slaveholding States, 133
Aylett, P. H., 245 n. 191

Bacon, 111
Baltimore, Md., 19
Bank Reformer, 57, 63, 176
Banking theories of ER, 27, 49, 50, 52, 56–63
Banks, Joseph, 171, 194, 256 n. 9
Baptism, 152
Barbour, James, 237 n. 104
Beckwith, Agnes Ruffin (ER's daughter), 6, 150, 234 n. 77, 245 n. 193
Beckwith, Thomas Stanly (ER's son-in-law), 234 n. 77, 255 n. 1
Beechwood Farm, Prince George Co., Va. *See also* Coggin's Point Farm
  cottage, 50, 179, 233 n. 69, 258 n. 1
  house, 50, 142, 161–62, 233 n. 69, 258 n. 1
  Union occupation of, 10
Blake, Benjamin R., 245 n. 191
Bland, John T. (ER's son-in-law), 253 n. 44
Bland, Rebecca Ruffin (ER's daughter), 6
  death, 12, 242 n. 158
  marriage, 253 n. 44
  physician of, 255 n. 1
Bland, Theodorick, 235 n. 89

Bland Papers, 57, 236 n. 90
Board of Agriculture. *See* Virginia Board of Agriculture
Bolling, Robert B., 46, 231 n. 54
Bonaccord Farm, Prince George Co., Va., 212, 261 nn. 3–5
Booth, Edwin G., 248 n. 12
Botts, C. T., 237 n. 104
Boulware, William, 248 nn. 11–12
  biographer of ER, 2, 4, 125, 167
Brandon Church, Martin's Brandon Parish, Va., 153, 253 n. 6, 255 n. 24
Braxton, Carter, 74, 75, 77, 240 n. 129
  marl pits of, 84, 113
Braxton, Corbin, 76, 240 nn. 129, 132
Braxton, Mary Grymes Sayre, 240 n. 129
"Bring Flowers" (Hemans), 151, 155
Brown, John, 11
Buel, Jesse, 235 n. 79
Burials, 151–52, 180, 183, 185
Burke, Edmund, 176
Burwell, Nathaniel, 237 n. 104

Cabell, Nathaniel Francis, 130, 252 n. 32
Calcareous manure. *See* Marl; Marling
Campbell, Charles, 237 n. 96
"Carolan's Prophecy" (Hemans), 154, 155
Carter, Hill, 230 n. 39
Charleston, S.C.:
  and agricultural survey, 67
  Mercury, 69, 134
  visited by ER, 132–33, 234 n. 76
Children of ER. *See also* individual names
  allowances from ER's estate, 114
  daughters as housekeepers, 87, 116
  deaths, 12, 242 n. 158
  as dependents, 6, 134
  education, 47, 48–49, 86, 246 n. 196, 253 n. 49
  at fair of 1853, 129–30
  health, 25, 86
  marriages, 134, 253 n. 44

  survival of, 6, 12, 193
  trust funds, 246 n. 198
Clover:
  at Coggin's Point, 31
  at Marlbourne, 81, 84, 88, 92, 96, 97, 104–5, 175
Cocke, Benjamin, 258 n. 5
Cocke, Elizabeth Poythress (Thomas Cocke's mother), 261 n. 4
Cocke, Elizabeth Ruffin (ER's half sister), 222 n. 15, 233 n. 73
Cocke, James (Thomas Cocke's father), 212, 261 n. 4
Cocke, James (Thomas Cocke's son-in-law), 258 n. 4
Cocke, James B. (Thomas Cocke's nephew):
  and Bonaccord Farm, 212, 258 n. 6, 261 n. 3
  and suicide of Thomas Cocke, 183, 185
Cocke, Martha Cocke (Thomas Cocke's daughter), 181, 258 n. 4
Cocke, Nathaniel Colley (Thomas Cocke's son), 181, 184, 185, 258 n. 4
Cocke, Philip St. George, 128, 249 n. 15
Cocke, Sarah Colley (Thomas Cocke's wife), 181, 258 n. 4
Cocke, Thomas:
  Bonaccord experiment and, 261 n. 3
  burial, 180, 183, 185
  childhood and youth, 28–29, 180–81, 261 n. 4
  children of, 181
  criticizes *Essay on Calcareous Manures*, 29–30
  as guardian for ER, 4, 11, 28, 168, 193, 227 n. 7
  idea of death, 12, 183
  idea of soil sterility, 193
  marl experiments, 202, 203
  marriage, 181, 258 n. 4
  on politics, 183
  prepares for suicide, 184, 186–88
  reclusive disposition of, 180–81
  relations with ER, 21, 28–29, 180, 193

Cocke, Thomas: (*cont.*)
  slave (gardener) of, 212–13
  suicide of, 11, 179, 184–87
  visited by ER, 48, 179–80
Coggin's Point Farm, Prince
    George Co., Va. *See also*
    Beechwood Farm
  condition in 1813, 170
  Court House Field, 206
  draining of, 38–43
  erosion of, 23, 34, 192, 193
  graveyard, 153
  history of, by ER, 3
  houses, 230 n. 33, 233 n. 68
  inherited by ER, 5, 7–8, 190
  land value, 216
  marling of, 21, 26, 174, 197,
      204–6, 213–14
  purchased by Edmund Ruffin,
      Jr., 48, 50, 70, 234 n. 75
  reclaimed marsh, 25–26, 38, 39,
      43, 170
  vacated by ER, 23–24, 48
College of William and Mary, 5,
    223 n. 17, 232 n. 60
Columbia, S.C., 133
Commission merchant, 116
Compleat Body of Husbandry (Hale),
    190, 259 n. 1
Compromise of 1850, 133–34
Corn:
  and blacks' diet, 19
  crops at Coggin's Point, 17–19,
      22, 172, 174, 217–18
  crops at Marlbourne, 75–76, 81,
      84, 87, 90, 111, 112, 135,
      175
  culture at Coggin's Point, 32–33
  culture at Marlbourne, 106–7
  and erosion, 23, 34
  fodder, 85, 88
  markets, 18–19
  and marling, 112, 172, 217–18
  and peas, 101–4
  prices, 18, 19, 23
  storage, 18–19
  surpluses, 17–19, 26–27
  and vermin, 33
Cotton, 17, 20–23, 34, 217–18
Coultering, 241 n. 146
Crayfish, 39
Crop rotation:
  at Coggin's Point, 31–32, 34–35,
      203–4, 214–15
  at Marlbourne, 8, 89, 91, 96, 135
  and peas, 102–3
  at Shirley, 34
  at Westover, 34
Cultivator, 55, 235 n. 79
Curtis, Henry, 162, 255 n. 2
Custis, George Washington Parke,
    130, 251 n. 28

Dairy products, 31, 32
Davy, Humphry, 5, 171, 194–96,
    202
De Bow, James Dunwood Brown,
    125, 133, 248 n. 10
De Bow's Review, 2, 4, 125, 133, 167
Death, idea of:
  in ER's thought, 11, 12, 148–49,
      153–54, 163, 182, 186
  in Thomas Cocke's thought,
      182–83
Death wish:
  of ER, 117, 157
  of Thomas Cocke, 181
Debts. *See* Finances of ER
Democratic party, 61–62
Dew, Thomas R., 56, 235 n. 83
Diseases. *See also* Illnesses
  bilious fever, 25, 86, 228 n. 14
  at childbirth, 12
  heart disease, 12
  malaria, 25–26, 67, 86, 228 n. 14
  typhoid, 12, 161, 228 n. 14
Dorsey, Juliana Ruffin Coupland
    (ER's half sister), 222 n. 15,
    233 n. 73
Draining:
  at Coggin's Point, 38–43
  covered drains, 9, 38–39, 79–85,
      88–90, 98, 136
  cross-grips, 90, 243 n. 165
  ditches, designed by ER, 83,
      100 (illus.)
  English (stone) drains, 40
  grips, 83, 105, 241 n. 142
  main ditch, 9, 73, 81, 99–101,
      136, 240 n. 126
  at Marlbourne, 9, 72–73, 79–85,
      88–90, 97–101, 105, 136,
      240 n. 125
  open ditches, 80–81, 90, 97–101

Draining: (*cont.*)
  rain ditch, 243 n. 165
  theories of ER, 38–39, 43
  under-furrow, 83, 241 n. 144
  water-furrow, 83, 105, 243 n. 165
  wood pipes, 39–40
Drewry, Martin, 245 n. 191
Dupuy, Jane Ruffin (ER's daughter), 6, 147–48
  awareness of impending death, 143–46
  burial arrangements for, 151–52
  childhood and youth, 139–41
  death, 11–12, 139, 149–50, 161, 242 n. 158
  funeral, 152–53
  illness, 141–45
  marriage, 141, 253 nn. 1, 46
  medication and treatment of, 146, 149, 150
  provisions for infant of, 145
  selflessness of, 140, 142, 146, 148
  settles affairs, 144–45
  vacations at Springs, 91, 98
  visited by ER, 146–47
Dupuy, Jane Ruffin (ER's granddaughter), 139
  baptism, 152
  birth, 141
  death, 255 n. 27
  provisions for care of, 145
Dupuy, Jane S. Ruffin (ER's half sister), 222 n. 15, 253 n. 1, 254 n. 12
  and belief in heaven, 12
  marriage, 234 n. 73
Dupuy, John J. (ER's son-in-law):
  as attending physician, 144, 150–51, 255 n. 1
  and death of wife, 149
  marriage, 141, 253 nn. 1, 46
Dupuy, William J. (ER's brother-in-law), 253 n. 1

Edinburgh Encyclopedia, 202
Edmunds, John R., 251 n. 29, 252 n. 33
Elizabeth River, 147
Enclosing, 31–37, 191–93, 229 n. 30

Eppes, Charles, 228 n. 19
Eppes, Richard, 258 n. 5
Essay on Calcareous Manures, 1, 174
  editions, 93, 228 n. 24
  experiments recorded in, 207, 212
  main ideas in, 173–74
  publication of, 28–30, 173
  reactions to, 124, 174
  and soil theories of ER, 189, 196
  and Thomas Cocke, 29, 202
Essays and Notes on Husbandry (Bordley), 190
Estate of ER:
  distribution of, 114–16, 134
  growth of, 66–67, 114–15
  and reserved fund, 246 n. 199
Evergreen Farm, Prince George Co., Va., 4, 23, 222 n. 11

Fallowing, 33–35
Farm journals of ER:
  for Coggin's Point, 18–19, 20–21, 22–23, 205–7
  discontinued, 24, 218
  for Marlbourne, 82, 83, 88, 89, 90, 92, 94
Farmers' Register, 1, 46–48, 176
  apprentices for, 64
  and banking controversy, 59–60, 63
  as family enterprise, 9
  financial losses, 30–31, 47, 54, 56, 65–67
  founded, 30, 176
  printed at Shellbanks, 8, 9, 46–47, 231 n. 58
  printing office in Petersburg, 64, 234 n. 77, 238 n. 108
  removed to Petersburg, 8, 47–48
  sale of, 65
  subscriptions, 54–56, 65, 66, 116, 123, 126
  success of, 48
  withdrawal from, by ER, 63–64, 70
Ferruginous clay, 82, 241 n. 139
Finances of ER. *See also* Estate of ER; Investments of ER
  borrowing and lending, 50–53, 116

Finances of ER: (*cont.*)
  and interest rates, 20
  losses at *Farmers' Register*, 30–31, 47, 54, 56, 65–67
Fincastle, Va., 163
"First Views Which Led to Marling in Prince George County," 3, 4
Fisher, Elwood, 250 n. 16
Fontaine, William S., 245 n. 191
Food cycle, idea of, 12, 183
Fossil shells. *See* Marl
Franklin, Benjamin, 173
Funerals, 152–53, 180, 183

Garnett, James M., 237 n. 104
Garysville, Va., 68
Gee, Theron, 239 n. 121
Genesee region, N.Y., 107
Georgia, 125–26, 134
Gilmer, Thomas W., 235 n. 86, 237 n. 104
Governesses, 47
Grasses:
  Bermuda grass, 33, 230 n. 38
  bluegrass, 33, 230 n. 38
  broom-straw, 173
  greensward, 33
  hen's nest grass, 193
  poverty grass, 173
  wire-grass, 33, 97, 230 n. 38
Grazing, 21, 31–32, 109–10, 203–4
Greensand, 77, 240 n. 133
Gregg, D. H., 245 n. 191
Gwynn, Walter, 233 n. 66

Hammond, James Henry, 67–68, 239 n. 114
Hanover County, Va., 68, 70
Harrison, Sally, 228 n. 20
Harvie, Lewis E., 129, 248 n. 12, 250 n. 21
Haycocks, 8, 88
Heaven, idea of, 12, 149, 254 n. 10
Hemans, Felicia Dorothea Browne, 151, 154, 155, 255 n. 25
Hieron II (king of Syracuse), 173
Hoge, Moses D., 246 n. 196
Holsbrook, Mr. (tutor), 47, 232 n. 59
Hymns and songs, 150–55, 254 n. 10

Illnesses. *See also* Diseases
  apoplexy, 116, 181
  bronchitis, 116
  colds, 131
  dropsy, 162
Implements and tools. *See also* Machines; Plows
  coulters, 106
  handbarrows, 36
  harrows, 106
  hoes, 33, 72, 106
  spades, 99
"Incidents of my Life":
  composed by ER, 1–3
  and ER's diary, 10, 11
  intention in, 7, 118, 121
  and interpretation of career, 7, 11
  missing volume, 2–4
  and motives for suicide, 12–13
  sources for, 3, 4
  and theme of success, 5–6, 7, 10, 12
Inclosing. *See* Enclosing; Taylor, John, on enclosing
Investments by ER. *See also* Estate of ER; Finances of ER
  bonds and stocks, 8, 48, 115
  factories, 51, 54
  lending money, 20, 50–51, 53
  mines, 51
  railroads, 51–54, 66, 234 n. 76
  real estate, 54

James River, 153, 200
Johnson, Joseph, 237 n. 104, 257 n. 20

Kames, Henry Home, Lord, 198, 259 n. 10

Labor shortages, 28, 106–7, 108, 198
Land values:
  of Coggin's Point, 216
  of Marlbourne, 92–93
  and marling, 26
  in Virginia, 27, 177, 257 n. 20, 244 n. 175
Larry's (Larrey's) tract, Hanover Co., Va., 96, 244 n. 175

Leigh, Benjamin Watkins, 237 n. 100
Liberia, 57
Limited scale, idea of, 8, 20
Litter:
  at Coggin's Point, 35, 36, 37, 38
  at Marlbourne, 75, 107, 108
Livestock:
  cattle, at Coggin's Point, 31, 32
  cattle, at Marlbourne, 75, 82, 107, 109, 110
  hogs, 31, 32, 82, 89, 110
  horses, 32, 82, 107, 204
  mules, 32, 75, 82, 107
  oxen, at Coggin's Point, 31, 32
  oxen, at Marlbourne, 75, 107, 110
  sheep, at Coggin's Point, 32
  sheep, at Marlbourne, 75, 82, 95, 109, 110
Lyell, Charles, 239 n. 123

Machines, 8, 225 n. 36, 230 n. 37
Macon, Ga., 125
Madeira, 18
Manure. *See* Marl; Putrescent manure
Manuring, 36–38, 107–9, 199
Marks, Edward, 203, 260 n. 16
Marl, 78, 105, 135
  blue, 205, 260 n. 17
  composition of, 77–78, 172, 202, 214
  and crop production, 107, 112, 217–18
  defined, 201–2, 227 n. 6
  deposits at Coggin's Point, 195–97
  deposits at Marlbourne, 71, 74, 114, 135
  deposits in South Carolina, 68, 177
  deposits in Virginia, 172, 197, 200
  eocene, 71, 74, 114, 239 n. 123
  miocene, 74, 239 n. 123
  and putrescent manures, 208
  yellow, 205, 260 n. 17
Marl pits:
  Carter Braxton's, 75, 78, 113
  at Coggin's Point, 203, 205, 260 nn. 17–18
  John W. Tomlin's, 114
  at Marlbourne, 75
Marlbourne Farm, Hanover Co., Va., 75, 80, 82, 86, 115
  bought by ER, 8, 70
  condition in 1844, 71–75, 175
  crop production, 9, 75–76, 84–85, 111–12
  draining of, 9, 72–73, 79–85, 88–90, 97–101, 105, 136
  fences removed, 88, 89
  house, 82, 239 n. 124
  and land value, 92, 175
  Larry's (Larrey's) tract, 96, 136, 244 n. 175
  livestock, 82, 107–11
  main ditch, 81, 136, 240 n. 125
  marl deposits, 114, 135
  marling of, 8–9, 74–75, 78–79, 135–36, 174–75
  profits, 76, 92–93, 175
  and putrescent manures, 107–9
  Sulphur Cove, 80, 82, 99, 101, 114
  Talley's tract, 82, 97, 98, 100, 136, 241 n. 140
  wide beds, 105–6
Marling, 204
  and agricultural reform, 176
  and crop production, 26, 112, 172, 173, 209, 217–18
  and ER's doubts, 20–23
  early experiments by ER, 197, 213
  marl digging, 84
  in Maryland, 176
  methods prescribed by ER, 84, 204–5
  in North Carolina, 176
  and permanence of results, 173
  in Prince George County, 69, 203–4, 212–16
  and topsoil, 208
  in Virginia, 26, 69, 176, 203–4
Maryland, 123, 176, 261 n. 5
Maupin, Socrates, 130, 252 n. 31
Merchants Hope Church, Martin's Brandon Parish, Va., 255 n. 24
Meredith, John A., 240 n. 128

Index

Migration to the West, 169, 171, 194
Minge, Sarah Melville, 231 n. 54
Murdaugh, Edmund Christian, 144, 150, 253 n. 6
Mutton, 111

Nansemond River, 200
Nash, William, 239 n. 111
Nelson, Martha S., 163, 255 n. 5
Nelson, Robert B., 256 n. 5
New York, 55, 57, 107
Newcastle Farm, Hanover Co., Va., 74, 75
Newton, Willoughby, 92, 93, 129, 243 n. 167
Nichol, Andrew, 45–46, 231 n. 53
Nitrogen, 35
Norfolk, Va., 168, 253 n. 45, 253 n. 2
North Carolina, 102, 133, 176

Oats, 76, 81, 112, 217–18
Opium, 149
Overseers:
  at Coggin's Point, 44–45, 74–75, 213
  criticized by ER, 24, 45, 191
  at Marlbourne, 75
Overton, William G., 248 n. 12

Pamunkey River lands, 71, 85–86, 175
  compared to James River lands, 76
  condition in 1844, 77
Panic of 1837, 56, 57, 233 n. 66
Pasture:
  at Coggin's Point, 31–32
  at Marlbourne, 75, 96–97, 109–10, 136
Pate, John, 82, 241 n. 140, 244 n. 176
Patriarchy, idea of, 6–7
Pea fallow, 95
Peas, 89, 101–4, 111
  crops at Marlbourne, 91, 92, 94
  in South Carolina, 89, 101–2, 244 n. 179
Pens:
  for cattle, 36–37, 108, 110
  for hogs, 89
  and manure, 36

Pests and vermin, 19
  beetles, 109
  birds, 33
  grasshoppers, 21
  insects, 33, 216
  raccoons, 33, 34
  rats, 18, 33
  squirrels, 33
  weevils, 18
Petersburg, Va., 8, 19, 67
  and banking controversy, 60, 61–62
  ER's property in, 54, 64–66, 234 n. 77
  as residence of ER, 47, 70, 180
Philadelphia, Pa., 29, 30
Physicians:
  of Jane Ruffin Dupuy, 141, 150–51, 253 n. 1, 255 n. 1
  of Ella Ruffin, 162, 255 nn. 1–3, 5
  of Susan Travis Ruffin, 87
Pines, 172, 195, 201
Pleasants, Thomas S., 64–66, 231 n. 53, 238 n. 110
Plowing:
  balks, 84
  and corn tillage, 106
  coultering, 83
  methods at Coggin's Point, 33
  methods at Marlbourne, 74
  and weeds, 135
  in wide beds, 105–6
Plows. *See also* Implements and tools; Machines
  coulter, 83
  cultivators, 33, 106, 230 n. 37
  and draining, 43, 99–100
  four-horse, 84
  four-mule, 34, 79, 92, 99–100
  mould-board, 43, 84, 106
  one-horse, 84, 192–93
  shovel plow, 106
  three-horse, 208
  trowel plow, 33, 230 n. 37
  two-horse, 193
  two-mule, 34, 74, 84, 92
Political parties, 56, 61–62, 111, 113, 245 n. 191
Pollard, Edward C., 245 n. 191
Pork, 110

Price, Eliza, 163, 255 n. 4
Prince George County, Va.:
  address by ER (1818), 28, 173, 198–201, 259 n. 12
  address by ER (1843), 68, 168–69, 177–78
  agricultural society, 173, 175, 198, 259 n. 11
  birthplace of ER, 167
  career of ER in, 3–4
  marling in, 69, 203–4, 212–16
  reputation of ER in, 122
  residence of ER's children, 134
  and westward migration, 169
Publishing:
  in the North, 55
  in Virginia, 46
Putrescent manure. *See also* Marl
  beetles and, 109
  with calcareous manure, 31
  at Coggin's Point, 36, 38
  cornstalks, 35, 36, 37, 108
  defined, 229 n. 32
  dung, 35, 37, 104, 108–9
  failures of, 171
  leaves, 37, 75, 108–9
  at Marlbourne, 107–9
  and John Taylor's theories, 35–36
  weeds, 37
  wheat stubble, 35, 36, 37, 108

Raguet, Condy, 57, 235 n. 88
Railroads, 49, 51–54, 232 n. 64, 233 nn. 65, 66, 234 n. 76
Raleigh, N.C., 19
Rappahannock River lands, 37, 133
Red Sweet Springs, Va., 162
Redmoor Farm, Amelia Co., Va., 10
Richardson, William H., 128, 248 n. 12, 250 n. 18
Richmond, Va., 164
  and agricultural society, 126–30
  commission merchant, 116
  Enquirer, 69, 134, 243 n. 169
  fair, 128–30
  and *Farmers' Register*, 46
  and health of ER, 131
  Metropolitan Hall, 129
  mill for ER's wheat, 85
  Whig, 69

Ricketts, Robert, 231 n. 57, 234 n. 77
Rittenhouse, David, 173, 257 n. 11
Rives, William Cabell, 129, 223 n. 17, 251 n. 25
Roane, Thomas, 245 n. 191
Roane, William Henry, 240 n. 128
Rogers, William Barton, 77, 240 n. 134
Ruffin, Agnes (ER's daughter). *See* Beckwith, Agnes Ruffin
Ruffin, Charles L. (ER's son), 6
  career plans, 134
  and death of Jane Ruffin Dupuy, 149
  education, 246 n. 196, 253 n. 49
  relations with ER, 11
  resists religious conversion, 12, 149, 152, 254 n. 16
Ruffin, Charlotte Mead (ER's daughter-in-law), 150, 253 n. 44, 255 n. 18
Ruffin, Edmund I (ER's great-grandfather), 12, 222 n. 11
Ruffin, Edmund II (ER's grandfather), 4, 5, 7, 52, 234 n. 75
Ruffin, Edmund:
  birth, 4, 167
  childhood and youth, 4–5, 190
  and Civil War, 10
  and concern for reputation, 121–22, 123, 124, 126, 129–39
  considers migration to West, 171, 194
  and Davy's theories, 171, 199
  and death of Jane Dupuy, 149
  De Bow's Review portrait, 125
  deficiencies as businessman, 47, 52–53, 56, 116
  deficiencies as farmer, 43–44, 190
  deficiencies as slavemaster, 44
  depression of, 11, 23
  discovers acid soil, 172, 194–96
  editorial career, 1, 30–31, 46–48, 63–64, 123, 176
  education, 167
  farming career, 3, 7–8, 23–25, 31, 135, 169–75, 177
  fears senility, 52, 117, 132
  growth of family, 193

Ruffin, Edmund: (*cont.*)
  as guardian for siblings, 51, 116, 233 n. 73
  health, 25–26, 86–87, 98, 116–17, 167
  illnesses, 67, 131, 133, 246 n. 201
  inherits Coggin's Point, 5, 7–8, 168, 190
  marriage, 168
  militia duty, 5, 168
  moves to Shellbanks, 8, 23–25, 27–28, 224 n. 32, 228 nn. 19–20
  as official of agricultural society, 126–28, 131–32
  patrimony, 6, 22
  political views, 111, 113, 245 n. 191
  reading habits, 117
  as reformer, 3, 69–70, 93, 123–34
  relations with Thomas Cocke, 180–81, 193
  removes to Petersburg, 8, 24–25, 47, 232 n. 62
  resists religious conversion, 12, 149, 152, 254 n. 16
  as self-made man, 5–6, 22
  sells Coggin's Point, 70
  sells Shellbanks, 70
  settles at Marlbourne, 70–72, 175, 177
  siblings, 4, 222 n. 15
  slaveholdings, 8, 20, 223 n. 20, 225 n. 35
  state senator, 176
  student at William and Mary, 5, 167–68
  suicide of, 12–13, 226 n. 46
  and Taylor's theories, 170
  translates French works, 30
  and Virginia Board of Agriculture, 176
  withdraws from farming, 28, 48
Ruffin, Edmund, Jr. (ER's son):
  builds Beechwood cottage and house, 50
  and death of Jane Ruffin Dupuy, 142
  engineering career, 49
  farming career, 49–50
  marriage, 49, 258 n. 2
  occupies Coggin's Point, 6, 8, 48, 49–50, 102, 213
  reads "Incidents," 2, 3
  slaveholdings, 8, 49
  student at University of Virginia, 47, 49, 232 n. 60
  and suicide of Thomas Cocke, 187
Ruffin, Edmund Quintus (ER's grandson), 134–35, 253 n. 50
Ruffin, Elizabeth (ER's daughter). *See* Sayre, Elizabeth Ruffin
Ruffin, Elizabeth (ER's half sister). *See* Cocke, Elizabeth Ruffin
Ruffin, Ella (ER's daughter), 6
  death, 11–12, 161, 163, 242 n. 158, 253 n. 46
  education, 246 n. 196
  illness and treatment, 161–63
  selflessness of, 162
Ruffin, George (ER's father), 4, 5, 20, 168
Ruffin, George Henry (ER's half brother), 222 n. 15, 234 n. 73
Ruffin, Jane (ER's daughter). *See* Dupuy, Jane Ruffin
Ruffin, Jane Lucas (ER's mother), 4, 222 n. 13
Ruffin, Jane S. (ER's half sister). *See* Dupuy, Jane S. Ruffin
Ruffin, Jane Skipwith (ER's grandmother), 223 n. 16
Ruffin, Julian Calx (ER's son):
  completes S.C. survey, 67
  death, 10, 242 n. 158
  and death of Jane Ruffin Dupuy, 12, 149, 150
  helps Jem Sykes, 91
  marriage, 253 n. 44, 255 n. 18
  relationship with ER, 11
  settles at Ruthven, 6
  student at William and Mary, 232 n. 60
Ruffin, Juliana (ER's sister). *See* Dorsey, Juliana Ruffin Coupland
Ruffin, Mary Cooke Smith (ER's daughter-in-law), 49, 180, 233 n. 67

Ruffin, Mildred Campbell (ER's daughter). *See* Sayre, Mildred C. Ruffin
Ruffin, Rebecca (ER's daughter). *See* Bland, Rebecca Ruffin
Ruffin, Rebecca Cocke (ER's stepmother). *See* Woodlief, Rebecca Cocke Ruffin
Ruffin, Rebecca S. (ER's half sister), 222 n. 15
Ruffin, Susan Travis (ER's wife), 11, 242 n. 157
  death, 87, 114, 116
  health, 25–26
  marriage, 5
Ruffin, Thomas, 251 n. 25
Ruffin, Virginia (ER's granddaughter), 253 n. 50
Rust (in wheat), 20, 21, 22, 97
Ruthven Farm, Prince George Co., Va., 6

Sampson, Richard, 237 n. 104
Sands, Samuel, 244 n. 171
Sandy Point estate, Charles City Co., Va., 46, 231 n. 54
Sayre, Burwell (ER's son-in-law), 240 n. 129, 253 n. 46
Sayre, Elizabeth Ruffin (ER's daughter), 6, 147
  account of Jane Ruffin Dupuy's illness, 141–45, 149–51
  death, 242 n. 158
  marriage, 240 n. 129, 253 nn. 44–45
  notes by, 253 n. 2
Sayre, Mildred C. Ruffin (ER's daughter), 6, 91
  death, 242 n. 158
  marriage, 240 n. 129, 253 n. 46
  nurses Jane Ruffin Dupuy, 143–46, 150–51, 161
  opinion on Ella Ruffin's illness, 162
Sayre, William (ER's son-in-law), 240 n. 129, 253 nn. 44–45
Scott, Winfield, 129, 251 n. 23
Selden, John A., 230 n. 39
Self-reliance, idea of, 13
Seward, William H., 235 n. 86
Shellbanks Farm, Prince George Co., Va.:

and *Farmers' Register*, 8, 9, 46–47, 225 n. 40, 231 n. 58
marl deposits, 27
marling, 28, 207
settled by ER, 8, 23–24, 27–28, 224 n. 32, 228 nn. 19–20
sold by ER, 70, 239 n. 121
Shells. *See* Marl
Shelly, C., 245 n. 191
Shirley, Charles City Co., Va., 34, 230 n. 39
Singleton, John, 261 n. 5
Skinner, John Stuart, 59, 236 n. 94
Slavery and reform, 9
Slaves. *See also* Sykes, Jem; Sykes, John
  and Bonaccord experiment, 212–13
  children as herders, 89–90
  at Coggin's Point, 5
  and death of Jane Ruffin Dupuy, 143–44
  and draining of Marlbourne, 9, 72–74
  fugitives, 57
  health of, at Coggin's Point, 25–26
  health of, at Marlbourne, 86
  in "Incidents," 10
  and marling, 28, 74, 198, 204
  reluctance of ER to sell, 48, 115
  and suicide of Thomas Cocke, 184, 186, 187
  treatment of, by overseers, 24
Smith, Anne Dabney, 233 n. 67
Smith, Thomas Gregory, 233 n. 67
Soil testing, 171–72, 194–96, 202–3
Soil theories:
  of Humphry Davy, 171, 194, 196
  in Prince George County, 193
  of ER, 173–74, 189–90, 195–201
  of John Taylor, 171
Soils, 79, 194–95, 200
Sorrel, 172, 195, 201
South Carolina:
  agricultural survey of, 64, 67–68, 123, 176
  ER's illness in, 116, 133
  marl deposits in, 68, 177

South Carolina: (*cont.*)
  pea culture in, 89, 101–2, 244 n. 179
South Carolina Institute, 132, 133
Southern Magazine, 56, 57
Speeches. *See* Addresses by ER
Spratley, Richard, 240 n. 130
Spring Garden Farm, Hanover Co., Va., 74, 240 n. 128
Springs, medicinal (Va.), 91, 98, 113, 147, 162
"Statement of the closing scenes of the life of Thomas Cocke," 11
Steinbergen, Peter H., 237 n. 104
Stevenson, Andrew, 124, 248 nn. 5, 7
Suicide. *See also* Death, idea of
  idea of, in ER's thought, 182, 188
  of Philip St. George Cocke, 249 n. 15
  of Thomas Cocke, 11, 179–88
  of ER, 12–13
Surry County, Va., 20
Sykes, Jem, 9, 91, 98, 243 n. 166
Sykes, John, 243 n. 166

Talbot County, Md., 261 n. 5
Talley, Ezekiel S., 244 n. 176
Talley, N., 240 n. 130, 242 n. 153, 245 n. 191
Talley's tract, Hanover Co., Va., 96–97, 98
Tarbay Farm, Prince George Co., Va., 48, 180, 193, 258 n. 12
Tariffs, 175–76, 227 n. 1, 257 n. 16
Taylor, John:
  copy of *Arator* owned by ER, 259 n. 3
  on crop rotation, 34–35
  on enclosing, 31–37, 191–93, 229 n. 30
  and failures at Coggin's Point, 192
  on fallowing, 33–35
  influence on ER, 5, 35, 170, 191
  on manuring, 35–36
  on soils, 171
Threshing machines, 230 n. 37
Tobacco, 33
Todd, Charles S., 223 nn. 17–18

Tomlin, Bartholomew McCarty, 239 n. 124, 240 n. 129
Tomlin, John Walker, 114, 135, 245 n. 192
Tomlin, Mary Elizabeth Bolling Blakey, 239 n. 124
Totopotomoi Creek, 96, 99
Travis, Champion (ER's father-in-law), 223 n. 22, 242 n. 157
Travis, Elizabeth Boush (ER's mother-in-law), 242 n. 157
Travis, Susan (ER's wife). *See* Ruffin, Susan Travis
Tucker, Nathaniel Beverley, 56, 235 n. 82
Tutors, 47
Tyler, John, 129, 130, 251 n. 24

United States Census of 1850, 177
United States House of Representatives, Agriculture Committee, 175
United States Patent Office, 133
University of Virginia, 47, 49, 232 n. 60
Upshur, Abel P., 56, 57, 235 n. 81

Van Buren, Martin, 56
Vergil (Publius Vergilius Maro), 256 n. 4
Virginia Board of Agriculture:
  demise of, 123
  established, 63–64, 237 n. 104
  manuscript records, 247 n. 1
  ER as secretary, 176
Virginia Constitution of 1851, 245 n. 189
Virginia Convention of 1850–51, 111, 113, 245 n. 190
Virginia General Assembly:
  and agriculture, 123, 127
  and banking laws, 57, 60–61, 63, 236 nn. 90–91, 98
  neglects ER's address, 128
Virginia Military Institute, 253 n. 49
Virginia State Agricultural Society:
  criticized by ER, 131–32
  fair, 128–32
  founded, 123–24, 126–27, 247 n. 3, 248 nn. 5, 12, 249 n. 13

Virginia State Agricultural
  Society: (*cont.*)
  membership, 128–29
  spurned by ER, 123

Wallazz, Laurens, 64–66, 238 n. 109
War of 1812, 168, 256 n. 1
Warren, N.C., 19
Watts, Edward, 237 n. 104
Washington, D.C., 130
Weather:
  droughts, 18–19, 79, 81, 84–85, 92, 101, 111
  freezes, 75, 94–95, 103
  mildness of, in 1848, 91
  rainfall in 1846, 87, 88
Weeds:
  and clover, 104
  at Coggin's Point, 21, 31–32
  crabgrass, 102
  at Marlbourne, 135
  and trampling by livestock, 110
West Indies, British, 18
Westover, Charles City Co., Va., 34, 230 n. 39
Westward migration, 169, 171, 194
Wheat:
  crops at Coggin's Point, 19–23, 172, 174, 217–18
  crops at Marlbourne, 77, 84–85, 88, 91–92, 94, 97, 111–12, 135, 175
  culture of, at Coggin's Point, 33–35
  culture of, at Marlbourne, 107
  early purple straw, 94
  at Evergreen, 23
  and marling, 21, 112, 172, 217–18
  in New York, 107
  on Pamunkey River lands, 76–77
  prices, 19, 21, 94
Whig party, 61–62
White, Thomas W., 46, 231 n. 56
Wide beds, 83, 105–6, 241 n. 143
Withers, Thomas F., 162, 255n. 3
Woodlief, Peter, 233 n. 73
Woodlief, Rebecca Cocke Ruffin (ER's stepmother), 4, 23, 51, 227 n. 8, 233 n. 73
Works by ER:
  agricultural society communications, 128
  in *American Farmer*, 28, 88, 93, 102, 105, 124
  on banking, 57, 59
  Board of Agriculture reports, 64
  in Charleston *Mercury*, 134
  on clover, 88, 105
  on Compromise of 1850, 134
  on crop rotation, 102
  on draining, 43, 93
  on fodder, 88
  history of Marlbourne, 93
  on Liberia, 57
  on manure, 37, 104
  on marling, 84, 173, 207
  in Richmond *Enquirer*, 242 n. 169
  on soils, 28
  South Carolina survey, 67
  on southern rights, 133
  on wide beds, 105

York River, 200